Intertextuality and the 24-Hour News Cycle

RHETORIC & PUBLIC AFFAIRS SERIES

- *Eisenhower's War of Words: Rhetoric and Leadership,* Martin J. Medhurst, editor
- *The Nuclear Freeze Campaign: Rhetoric and Foreign Policy in the Telepolitical Age,* J. Michael Hogan
- *Mansfield and Vietnam: A Study in Rhetorical Adaptation,* Gregory A. Olson
- *Truman and the Hiroshima Cult,* Robert P. Newman
- *Post-Realism: The Rhetorical Turn in International Relations,* Francis A. Beer and Robert Hariman, editors
- *Rhetoric and Political Culture in Nineteenth-Century America,* Thomas W. Benson, editor
- *Frederick Douglass: Freedom's Voice, 1818–1845,* Gregory P. Lampe
- *Angelina Grimké: Rhetoric, Identity, and the Radical Imagination,* Stephen Howard Browne
- *Strategic Deception: Rhetoric, Science, and Politics in Missile Defense Advocacy,* Gordon R. Mitchell
- *Rostow, Kennedy, and the Rhetoric of Foreign Aid,* Kimber Charles Pearce
- *Visions of Poverty: Welfare Policy and Political Imagination,* Robert Asen
- *General Eisenhower: Ideology and Discourse,* Ira Chernus
- *The Reconstruction Desegregation Debate: The Politics of Equality and the Rhetoric of Place, 1870–1875,* Kirt H. Wilson
- *Shared Land/Conflicting Identity: Trajectories of Israeli and Palestinian Symbol Use,* Robert C. Rowland and David A. Frank
- *Darwinism, Design, and Public Education,* John Angus Campbell and Stephen C. Meyer, editors
- *Religious Expression and the American Constitution,* Franklyn S. Haiman
- *Christianity and the Mass Media in America: Toward a Democratic Accommodation,* Quentin J. Schultze
- *Bending Spines: The Propagandas of Nazi Germany and the German Democratic Republic,* Randall L. Bytwerk
- *Malcolm X: Inventing Radical Judgment,* Robert E. Terrill
- *Metaphorical World Politics,* Francis A. Beer and Christ'l De Landtsheer, editors
- *The Lyceum and Public Culture in the Nineteenth-Century United States,* Angela G. Ray
- *The Political Style of Conspiracy: Chase, Sumner, and Lincoln,* Michael William Pfau
- *The Character of Justice: Rhetoric, Law, and Politics in the Supreme Court Confirmation Process,* Trevor Parry-Giles
- *Rhetorical Vectors of Memory in National and International Holocaust Trials,* Marouf A. Hasian Jr.
- *Judging the Supreme Court: Constructions of Motives in* Bush *v.* Gore, Clarke Rountree
- *Everyday Subversion: From Joking to Revolting in the German Democratic Republic,* Kerry Kathleen Riley
- *In the Wake of Violence: Image and Social Reform,* Cheryl R. Jorgensen-Earp
- *Rhetoric and Democracy: Pedagogical and Political Practices,* Todd F. McDorman and David M. Timmerman, editors
- *Invoking the Invisible Hand: Social Security and the Privatization Debates,* Robert Asen
- *With Faith in the Works of Words: The Beginnings of Reconciliation in South Africa, 1985–1995,* Erik Doxtader
- *Public Address and Moral Judgment: Critical Studies in Ethical Tensions,* Shawn J. Parry-Giles and Trevor Parry-Giles, editors
- *Executing Democracy: Capital Punishment and the Making of America, 1683–1807,* Stephen John Hartnett
- *Enemyship: Democracy and Counter-Revolution in the Early Republic,* Jeremy Engels
- *Spirits of the Cold War: Contesting Worldviews in the Classical Age of American Security Strategy* Ned O'Gorman
- *Making the Case: Advocacy and Judgment in Public Argument,* Kathryn M. Olson, Michael William Pfau, Benjamin Ponder, and Kirt H. Wilson, editors
- *Executing Democracy: Capital Punishment and the Making of America, 1835–1843,* Stephen John Hartnett
- *William James and the Art of Popular Statement,* Paul Stob
- *On the Frontier of Science: An American Rhetoric of Exploration and Exploitation,* Leah Ceccarelli
- *The Good Neighbor: Franklin D. Roosevelt and the Rhetoric of American Power,* Mary E. Stuckey
- *Creating Conservatism: Postwar Words that Made an American Movement,* Michael J. Lee
- *Intertextuality and the 24-Hour News Cycle: A Day in the Rhetorical Life of Colin Powell's U.N. Address,* John Oddo

Intertextuality and the 24-Hour News Cycle

A Day in the Rhetorical Life of Colin Powell's U.N. Address

John Oddo

Michigan State University Press • East Lansing

♾ The paper used in this publication meets the minimum requirements of ANSI/NISO Z39.48-1992
(R 1997) (Permanence of Paper).

Michigan State University Press
East Lansing, Michigan 48823-5245

Printed and bound in the United States of America.

20 19 18 17 16 15 14 1 2 3 4 5 6 7 8 9 10

Library of Congress Control Number: 2014931993

ISBN: 978-1-61186-140-2 (pbk.)
ISBN: 978-1-60917-426-2 (ebook: PDF)

Book design by Charlie Sharp, Sharp Des!gns, Lansing, Michigan
Cover design by Erin Kirk New

Cover image of Secretary of State Colin Powell holding up a vial he said could contain anthrax as he presents evidence of Iraq's alleged weapons programs to the United Nations Security Council, 5 February 2003. (AP Photo/Elise Amendola, File.)

green press INITIATIVE Michigan State University Press is a member of the Green Press Initiative and is committed to developing and encouraging ecologically responsible publishing practices. For more information about the Green Press Initiative and the use of recycled paper in book publishing, please visit www.greenpressinitiative.org.

Contents

⌘

Tables

⌘

Acknowledgments

⌘

I could not have written this book without the feedback and support of many wonderful people. First, I would like to thank editor Martin Medhurst for backing this project and guiding me throughout the revision process. I am also deeply grateful to the three anonymous reviewers for their discerning remarks on earlier drafts of this work.

I am indebted, next, to my many professors, especially Christina Haas, Patricia Dunmire, Raymond Craig, and Paul Haridakis who served on my dissertation committee and offered me unwavering support. I would also like to thank my colleagues at Carnegie Mellon University—especially Barbara Johnstone, David Kaufer, and Andreea Ritivoi who reviewed earlier versions of this book and provided me with insightful feedback.

Many colleagues from other universities also supported me on this project. I am grateful to Stephen McKenna who generously offered me suggestions on a draft of chapter 2, and Dana Anderson who supported my ideas on intertextual ethos at the 2012 Rhetoric Society of America Conference. I am also honored by those who wrote the blurbs on the cover of this book: Thomas Huckin and David Zarefsky.

I wish to thank, too, the many people at Michigan State University Press who worked tirelessly to prepare my manuscript for publication. In particular, I thank Annette Tanner, Julie Loehr, Travis Kimbel, Dawn Martin, and Kristine Blakeslee. I also thank friends and colleagues who helped maximize the quality of the book images: Suguru Ishizaki, Jeffrey Hinkelman, Cory Tusar, and Les Bennett.

Some parts of this book were published previously, and I am grateful for permission to reuse this material. Much of chapter 3 was first published in an article in *Discourse & Communication* 7(1): 25–53 (2013), and is used by permission of Sage Publications. The *Time Magazine* cover on page 84 was used under license of Time Inc. Portions of the appendices on methodology first appeared in an article in *Written Communication* 30(3): 236–75 (2013), also used by permission of Sage Publications.

Of course, I am also grateful to many friends who offered me advice and encouragement along the way, including Rich Purcell, Chris Warren, Adam Hodges, Linda Flower, Christine Neuwirth, Danielle Zawodny Wetzel, Necia Werner, James Wynn, Jonathan Halsall, Christa Teston, Chad Wickman, and my fantastic students.

Finally, I wish to thank my entire family, especially my wife, Lindsay, and my children Amelia and Grace. I am so blessed to have your love and I dedicate this book to you.

Notational Scheme

⌘

After each excerpt from a given news report, you will note a parenthetical citation with the following information: journalistic institution, the date of the report, and the speaker or writer of the discourse. Thus, the following parenthetical—(NBC/2.5/AM)—refers to the NBC television news broadcast on February 5, 2003, and, more specifically, to Andrea Mitchell's report.[1] Importantly, there were two NBC broadcasts on February 5, 2003—one was the Special Report that aired live the morning of Powell's address and included pre- and post-speech commentary, and the other was the regular nightly newscast that aired later that evening. NBC SR/2.5 refers to the live special report; NBC/2.5 refers to the evening news broadcast. The table below lists the abbreviations for the names of all speakers and writers that appear in this study.

In my notational scheme, I refer to Colin Powell's presentation as "U.N." since it was delivered at the United Nations. Aside from this, references to Powell's address follow the same notational conventions. Thus, (UN/2.5/CP) refers to the transcript of Powell's February 5, 2003, U.N. address.

News Media	Abbreviation	Journalist/Speaker
NBC	AM	Andrea Mitchell
	AS	Amir al-Saadi
	BM	Barry McCaffrey
	CB	Campbell Brown
	CP	Colin Powell
	DF	Dianne Feinstein
	DK	David Kay
	DR	Donald Rumsfeld
	DV	Dominique de Villepin
	HB	Hans Blix
	JM	Jim Miklaszewski
	JS	Jack Straw
	JW	John Warner
	KA	Kofi Annan
	LH	Lee Hamilton
	RA	Ron Allen
	RB	Richard Butler
	SH	Saddam Hussein
	TB	Tom Brokaw
NYT	JPSW	Julia Preston and Steven R. Weisman
	SW	Steven R. Weisman
CNN.com	JKDE	John King and David Ensor
	NA	No Author Cited

INTRODUCTION

The Rhetorical Life of Colin Powell's U.N. Speech

⌘

Whether the orators of news have an art of inquiry and communication adequate to their mission is a question of large importance.
—Lloyd Bitzer, "Political Rhetoric," 1998

On the morning of 5 February 2003—a Wednesday—Secretary of State Colin Powell addressed the United Nations Security Council in New York City. In a nearly 90-minute PowerPoint presentation, Powell argued that Iraq was hiding weapons of mass destruction from inspectors in direct violation of U.N. Security Council Resolution 1441. These weapons posed a significant threat to world peace, Powell suggested, not only because Iraq had its own history of violent aggression, but also because Iraq had ties to the al-Qaeda terrorist network—a group that might use such weapons without compunction. Powell concluded that the Security Council had an urgent responsibility to disarm Saddam Hussein and the Iraqi leadership. As he put it:

> Given Saddam Hussein's history of aggression, given what we know of his grandiose plans, given what we know of his terrorist associations and given his determination to exact revenge on those who oppose him, should we take the risk that he will not someday use these weapons at a time and the place and in the manner of his choosing—at a time when the world is in a much weaker position to respond? The United States will not and cannot run that risk to the American people. Leaving Saddam Hussein in possession of weapons of mass destruction for a few more months or years is not an option, not in a post–September 11th world. . . . We must not shrink from whatever is ahead of us. We must not fail in our duty and our responsibility to the citizens of the countries that are represented by this body. (UN/2.5/CP)

After uttering these words, Powell thanked the Security Council president—and from a certain perspective, his speech had ended. However, from the perspective of this book, the rhetorical life of Colin Powell's speech had only just begun.

Within ten seconds of Powell's concluding remarks, his speech was being reanimated and re-represented by reporters and political pundits in a live "Special Report" on NBC News. Later that evening, NBC devoted nearly twenty more minutes of coverage to Colin Powell's address on the *Nightly News* program with Tom Brokaw. On NBC, one could not only *see* Powell's presentation—pictures of unmanned aerial vehicles, videos of Mirage jets—but could actually *hear* him, too, decrying the "sinister nexus" between Iraq and al-Qaeda. And, of course, NBC wasn't the only one. Within twenty-four hours of Powell's speech, the *New York Times* had published about a dozen articles—reports, analyses, and editorials—all devoted to "The Powell Indictment" (as the *Times* called it). A picture of Powell holding up a model vial of anthrax appeared above the fold on page A1. Meanwhile, on the Internet, CNN.com published additional stories about Powell's speech, summarizing his arguments, redisplaying still shots of his PowerPoint slides—and fitting everything into a running narrative theme: "Showdown: Iraq" (see figure). All along bits and pieces—and, indeed, large chunks—of Colin Powell's address were rearticulated and reassessed, stretched and condensed, analyzed and synthesized, twisted and distorted—but, above all, kept alive in journalistic discourse.

Figure 0.1. Banner displayed on CNN.com during the months preceding the Iraq War

No, the rhetorical life of Colin Powell's speech did not end when he stopped talking. Perhaps it changed colors, changed shapes, but there it was: recontextualized—and resuscitated—for the sake of an American public still deliberating about the prospect of war.

In fact, not only was Powell's speech *kept alive* by journalists, but, in a sense, it was *brought to life* by journalists. Like mad Dr. Frankenstein, the journalists tried to force Powell's speech into existence prematurely. For more than a week before the address—indeed, right up to the moment Powell opened his mouth—they discussed the speech, promoted it, previewed it, gave it form, even evaluated it in advance. For instance, the morning before Powell spoke, CNN.com *knew* that he would "detail travels in and out of Iraq by al-Qaeda operatives" (CNN/2.5/NA). Meanwhile, the *Times* foretold intercepted communications among Iraqi officials "indicating a pattern of hiding chemical, biological and nuclear weapons programs" (NYT/2.5/JPSW). And, mere moments before Powell uttered his first words, NBC analysts reported not only that Powell would present "a very compelling case" (NBC/2.5/DK), but that, afterward, the U.S. military would be postured to take down the Iraqis "in one smooth jerk" (NBC/2.5/BM). Yes, the journalists labored to bring this speech to life—and tried every tactic they could think of—predicting what Powell would say, how well he would say it, and whom he would say it to. But, like Dr. Frankenstein, what they ultimately created was a monstrosity—for what they ultimately helped to bring into existence was a war.

This book examines twenty-four hours in the rhetorical life of Powell's infamous U.N. speech. Specifically, I investigate the development and reproduction of this speech in mainstream news narratives—as it was first *precontextualized* in journalistic previews and later *recontextualized* in subsequent reports.[1] First, I study how Powell himself was characterized in news narratives, how his authority as a speaker was implicated by a mix of intertextual voices in the press. Next, I consider how reporters forecast Powell's rhetoric—how they represented Powell's address in advance and primed audiences to think about its substance and consequences. Finally, I analyze the transformation of Powell's speech in news media—how minute but important changes in language and visual material ultimately remade Powell's speech and resituated American audiences. In undertaking this study, I hope to reveal the decisive role that journalists played in shaping the American public's attitudes about Colin Powell, his U.N. presentation, and the desirability of war in Iraq. At the same time, I hope to confirm the theory that, in a media-saturated world, a public address cannot be reduced to a single communication between speaker and audience. As Powell's case illustrates, the public rarely confronts a neatly bounded political speech, and instead interfaces with mass-mediated fragments of discourse. This book carefully examines how such fragments are reassembled and modified by journalists—how political discourse is (re)constructed—and not merely recorded—by the press.

The Significance of Powell's U.N. Address— and the News That Covered It

I focus on Powell's U.N. speech because it represents a monumentally important rhetorical event, a "critical discourse moment" that burst into the media spotlight and propelled global discourse about war in Iraq (Chilton 1987, 12). Indeed, the historical significance of Powell's speech can hardly be overstated. For the first time ever, a sitting secretary of state would address the U.N. Security Council to present an argument for war. It would be unlike any other call-to-arms communication in American history: not merely a speech, but a multimedia presentation featuring satellite images and audio intercepts. Powell would address diverse and scattered audiences: esteemed members of the Security Council and unknown spectators in the packed visitor's gallery; American citizens tuning in at home and international viewers from China to Iraq. In fact, this is the only call-to-arms address in American history that was broadcast live around the world. And for good reason: people around the world were clamoring for evidence, solid evidence that the "threat" posed by Saddam Hussein justified military action. Certified by the CIA, Powell's address was supposed to provide this evidence. It was meant to be the definitive case against Iraq, a "trial-worthy prosecution" that would transform opinion—domestically and globally—about the propriety of war (DeYoung 2007, 441).

Of course, Powell's speech had enormous material implications. Most notably, his address would help determine if the United States and its allies would launch war in Iraq. Granted, the Bush administration appears to have been set on war regardless of whether or not Powell convinced the U.N. Security Council (O'Sullivan 2009, 160–69). Nevertheless, if Powell's presentation proved to be a total failure, the backlash could stop war in its tracks—despite Bush's intentions.[2] Thus, it is not an exaggeration to say that war and peace hung in the balance. Billions of dollars and hundreds of thousands of lives were at stake. This alone makes Powell's U.N. speech tremendously significant. But Powell's presentation had additional ideological implications, implications that went beyond the human and economic costs of battle and spoke directly to the credibility of global institutions and the legitimacy of the war itself.

Powell's Credibility and the Reputation of the CIA

First, the U.N. address would serve as a new measure of Powell's personal credibility. As discussed in chapter 2, at the time of his speech Powell was the most respected statesman in America, a man with a global reputation for honesty and integrity (O'Sullivan 2009, 6). The so-called dove in the administration was now staking his name on the need for war (Zarefsky 2007; Cheng 2012). Should he make a convincing case, his stellar reputation would only be enhanced. Should he fail in this endeavor, his perceived authority would be greatly diminished.

At the same time, Powell's address would function as an important test of the CIA's authority as America's premier intelligence organization. Unlike many public statements about Iraq by Bush administration officials,[3] *every sentence* of Powell's U.N. speech had been carefully vetted by CIA analysts—indeed by the CIA director himself, George Tenet. Now the CIA and its intelligence assessments would be fully on display. Was the agency's case on Iraq as devastating as the Bush team claimed, or did the United Nations actually have more accurate information about Baghdad and its alleged weapons? Powell's presentation would answer these questions, significantly impacting perceptions of the CIA's authority for years to come.

The Status of American Diplomacy

The status of American diplomacy was also implicated in Powell's speech. Following the terrorist attacks of September 11, 2001, the United States enjoyed a groundswell of support from foreign governments. But this support quickly evaporated as a neoconservative religious philosophy came to define American foreign policy during the Bush administration. As Domke (2004) explains, the administration adopted a communication strategy of "political fundamentalism," an approach that cloaked a deeply conservative religious worldview in ostensibly secular political rhetoric. Consistent with a conservative religious ideology, the administration regarded its own foreign policy initiatives as "unchallengeable steps in a God-ordained" progression (64). The Bush team believed that America had entered a "postdiplomatic age," an age in which foreign policy would not be negotiated, but proclaimed to the rest of the world (O'Sullivan 2009, 138).[4] But what the administration regarded as moral clarity, the rest of the world often regarded as bluster and intimidation (O'Sullivan 2009, 168).

As Bush began his dogmatic push for war in Iraq, America's foreign relations were seriously damaged—so much so that, by the time of Powell's speech, diplomatic relations with historical allies had started to fray. Just before Powell's U.N. appearance, foreign ministers from Germany and France publicly rejected any new war resolution, declaring that "nothing justifies cutting off inspections" and predicting that war would have "disastrous consequences" (quoted in DeYoung 2007, 433–34). In fact, among permanent members of the Security Council, only Britain favored military action. Meanwhile, France, Russia, and China strongly opposed war.

These governments had legitimate misgivings about military action, and they wanted to continue the inspections process before deciding on any new war resolution. Still, they were at least willing to consider Powell's evidence, since they deemed Powell to be different from the rest of the Bush administration: he represented not political fundamentalism, but "non-ideological" realism (DeYoung 2007, 437). In Europe especially, Powell was considered the most—and perhaps the only—trustworthy member of the Bush administration (O'Sullivan 2009, 142). If he presented an evidence-based case—without hyperbole and misleading allegations—he might restore confidence in the sincerity of American intentions about Iraq and recover a place for diplomacy and multilateralism in American foreign policy. If his case amounted to more inflammatory innuendo, America's standing in international politics would only further deteriorate.

The Authority of the United Nations

Powell's speech would also affect the perceived authority of the United Nations as a custodian of international security. In fact, Powell's entire case rested on the assertion that U.N. weapons inspectors were failing to uncover Iraq's WMDs—and failing to deter Iraq from producing additional munitions. Interestingly, Powell himself had lobbied to place U.N. inspectors in Iraq (Hoyle 2008, 292). Now, he would need to discredit the validity of their findings. For example, on January 27, 2003, Hans Blix, head of the U.N. weapons inspections commission, issued a report based on the work of about 250 inspectors who "had conducted some 300 visits to 230 sites in Iraq" (T. H. Anderson 2011, 120). Blix declared that, while it remained possible that Iraq had WMDs, at this point there was a "lack of evidence" (quoted in T. H. Anderson 2011, 121). Mohamed ElBaradei, director general of the International Atomic Energy Agency, was more unequivocal, reporting that he had seen "no evidence" of a reconstituted nuclear weapons program in Iraq, and further predicting that in just a few months he would be able to provide "credible assurance" that all such programs had been terminated (quoted in Hoyle 2008, 310). Two days later, Blix reemphasized that while Iraq was not fully cooperating with inspections, many of the Bush administration's allegations about Iraqi wrongdoing were baseless. He found no evidence that Iraq was moving and hiding illicit materials; no evidence that Iraq was withholding scientists or infiltrating the U.N. inspection agency; and no evidence that Iraq had ties to al-Qaeda. Like ElBaradei, Blix believed that disarmament could be achieved within a reasonable time "through the peaceful avenue of inspections" (quoted in Miller and Preston 2003).

If Powell was going to persuade members of the Security Council that war was now necessary, he would need to refute the studied assessments of these U.N. inspectors, providing unequivocal evidence that inspections were not neutralizing the threat posed by Iraq. Needless to say, this would destroy the integrity of the U.N. process and strengthen the claim—increasingly offered by the Bush administration—that the

Security Council must either accept war or consign itself to irrelevance.[5] In fact, even if Powell failed to convince the Security Council, his case could still be used to convince Americans that the U.N. was an ineffective institution, one incapable of enforcing compliance with its own resolutions.[6] Ultimately, this could provide the administration with a means to legitimize war, even if it were unauthorized by the U.N. After all, if Powell's case appeared rock-solid but the Security Council still opposed military action, then Bush could rationalize the choice to lead a "coalition of the willing" into battle.

Public Opinion Regarding the Legitimacy of War in Iraq

Finally, and most importantly for this study, Powell's speech would significantly impact how public audiences evaluated the justifiability of war in Iraq. Before Powell's address, domestic support for a military campaign in Iraq was mixed. Most Americans believed that Saddam Hussein was hiding weapons of mass destruction, and some suspected that weapons inspections would do little to diminish the threat he posed to the United States (Moore 2002). Nevertheless, by January 2003, most Americans were uneasy about the prospect of war. In one poll, 21 percent of the respondents indicated that war should not occur under any circumstances; 34 percent believed that war should only occur with U.N. sanction; and 33 percent supported unilateral action by the United States and its allies (Wardell 2003). This suggests that if Powell could win U.N. authorization, 67 percent of the American public would fully support the war. Without such authorization, however, a majority of Americans would oppose military intervention.

Internationally, public opinion was even more strongly against an invasion of Iraq, with most countries overwhelmingly opposed to violence (Goot 2004).[7] In fact, few world citizens believed the United States was interested in war merely because Saddam Hussein posed a serious danger (Goot 2004). In France, Germany, Russia, Turkey, Pakistan, Jordan, and Morocco, most people believed that "what really motivated the USA was a desire 'to control Mideast oil' with nearly half or more also saying the USA wanted 'to dominate the world'" (Goot 2004, 249). But, again, if the United States could secure the *imprimatur of the U.N.*, this dramatically boosted international public support for military action (Goot 2004, 242).[8]

Thus, Powell's address would be a key factor in determining the *perceived legitimacy* of the Iraq War—both at home and abroad. If he succeeded in gaining U.N. approval, the war would appear lawful—as would the Bush Doctrine of "preemptive" military force.[9] Without U.N. approval, however, the war might be regarded as a unilateral U.S. attack, an attack unsupported by key allies and unsanctioned by international law (O'Sullivan 2009, 169).[10]

The Mediation of Powell's Speech

With the prospect of war looming, the American public was intensely interested in Powell's address. According to a poll taken just before the speech (Moore 2003), nearly 90 percent of Americans reported that Powell's presentation would be important in determining their view about an attack on Iraq. More than half said that they might change their mind—one way or another—depending on the strength of Powell's case (Moore 2003). However, most Americans—57 percent—*did not see* Colin Powell deliver his address, and an additional 15 percent saw "only a few minutes" of his presentation on television (CNN/*USA Today*/ Gallup 2003, 51). A majority of U.S. citizens (62 percent) reported that they had only "heard or read about what Powell said" (CNN/*USA Today*/ Gallup 2003, 51). Thus, it is clear that most people did not hear Powell speak and, instead, formed their opinions based on *news coverage* of his discourse.

This is a remarkable combination of circumstances: a massively important public address that reached the public only indirectly through journalistic intermediaries. Of course, the mainstream news media are always influential in framing the discourse of political leaders and shaping public opinion (Bennett 2012; Entman 2004; McCombs 2004; Zaller 1992). But, in this case, they played an even more influential role than usual. Indeed, a key premise of this book is that in order to understand how Powell's speech addressed the American public, we need not look primarily at Powell's speech. After all, for most Americans, Powell's address was filtered through news narratives. To construct a coherent meaning of his presentation and its repercussions, these audiences had to connect fragments in the mainstream press, reengineering Powell's speech based on the semantic frames provided by the journalists. Indeed, journalists likely played a more pivotal role than Powell himself in shaping perceptions of the U.N. event—and its various material and ideological implications.

Situating Powell's Address in the Mainstream News

With this in mind, I address the following research questions: First, how was Powell's presentation transformed when it was precontextualized and recontextualized in multimodal news narratives? In other words, how was Powell's presentation transformed over time as aspects of it were (1) introduced and previewed in prior multimodal reports, and (2) relocated and redesigned in subsequent multimodal reports? Second, how did these transformations function to implicate, pre-position, and reposition audiences? That is, how did the transformations of Powell's address function to imply particular audience responses and actions?

To answer these questions, I examine news reports from NBC News, the *New York Times*, and CNN.com, focusing specifically on a highly influential set of "hard news" stories that appeared in the roughly twenty-four-hour period surrounding Powell's U.N. presentation. Needless to say, this was a critical time in the life of Powell's address—a time when many Americans, and many others around the world, were "tuned in," and thus capable of being persuaded. For each source, I located the "lead story" published before Powell's address, and the "lead story" published after. In addition, on NBC, I examined the live "Special Report" leading up to Powell's presentation, and the live coverage that came directly after he finished. In this way, I could account for how each of the three main news sources (television, newspaper, and Internet) precontextualized and recontextualized Powell's arguments.[11] (See appendix A for a complete list of the data sources.)

I have chosen to analyze these mainstream news stories, instead of stories from the alternative press, because as Bennett and colleagues (2007) emphasize, the mainstream news is the "news that matters the most and that still reaches the most people" (8).[12] Indeed, NBC, the *Times*, and CNN.com may all be considered elite news providers, ones with the ability to break original stories and set the tone for mainstream press coverage around the country. In fact, these three news providers play an important role in *intermedia agenda setting*, shaping the news content of other less powerful media outlets in the establishment press (Reese & Danielian 1989; Lopez-Escobar et al. 1998; Roberts & McCombs 1994).[13]

Beyond this, these three sources were chosen based on their reach, their reputation, and their lasting availability. First, NBC's *Nightly News* drew more viewers than any other news outlet during the Iraq War (Project for Excellence in Journalism 2004), making it likely that the NBC news reports about Powell's address were the most widely watched on television. In addition, polling data suggests that Tom Brokaw, anchor for NBC, was considered the "most trusted anchor" in America around the time of Powell's address ("Poll" 2003). Next, I have chosen to analyze the *New York Times* since it is generally considered the "newspaper of record" and because its articles circulate globally. In fact, the *Times* heavily influences others in the news industry, helping other outlets determine what to report and how to frame their reporting (Bennett, Lawrence, & Livingston 2007, 59; Golan 2006). Finally, I selected the news reports from CNN.com because it was (and remains) one of the most recognizable Internet news outlets.[14] In addition, the CNN.com stories archived in the *Wayback Machine* had fewer gaps in their content than stories from any other Internet news source.

These news narratives are dubbed "hard news" stories since they claimed to report about Powell's speech *without* editorializing. Granted, editorials about Powell's speech are worthy of consideration, especially given that editorial boards often serve as "opinion leaders" for the public (Powlick 1995; Schaefer 1997). But hard news stories are generally believed to suggest greater credibility due to the presumption of objectivity in the reporting (Bennett, Lawrence, & Livingston 2007, 125). Again, most Americans did not see Powell's speech, but they could always turn to these straight news reports to get an "unvarnished" account of what he said. Indeed, these hard news accounts may have carried even greater persuasive potential than the editorials, since the audiences who consumed them were arguably less aware of how news framing in the "objective" accounts was influencing their attitudes.[15]

Granted, some news contributors do offer opinions in the data under study—particularly in the television broadcasts. But these contributors represent a relatively small minority, and, importantly, their opinions are never identified as "editorial" content. Thus, even when opinion does emerge, it is not *labeled* as opinion, and is instead branded with a more "intellectual" title: analysis. Audiences of these hard news stories likely believed they were getting "factual" accounts of Powell's speech, occasionally coupled with "expert interpretations."

In examining these news reports, this book reveals how journalists both initiated the rhetorical life of Powell's speech and kept that life going in their multimodal reports. At the same time, it illuminates the discursive mechanisms by which reporters positioned audiences to accept Powell's justifications for war. I hope my project opens up new conversations for scholars in multiple disciplines, conversations about the run-up to war in Iraq, the intertextual trajectory of a rhetorical event, and the reframing of political discourse in the news.

Prewar Journalism in History, Rhetoric, and Media Studies

Researchers in history, rhetoric, and media studies have all produced rich analyses of the period before the Iraq War, drawing special attention to the discourse that convinced the public to endorse violence. Needless to say, understanding how Americans were persuaded by this discourse is an important goal, especially given that the Bush administration's original rationale for war crumbled after the invasion. In this section, I summarize what this research has to teach us about how the Iraq War was conceived within Bush's cabinet, and publicly justified in political and journalistic contexts. At the same time, I suggest how this research affords space for further inquiry into the hard news reports surrounding Powell's pivotal U.N. address.

Historians of the prewar period have tended to concentrate on the internal discourse between Bush administration members and various intelligence officials—providing "insider accounts" of the run-up to the Iraq conflict.[16] These chronicles of the prewar period typically summarize major public addresses by Bush administration officials,[17] quoting key excerpts that characterize the administration's prewar rhetoric. Historians sometimes expound upon Powell's U.N. presentation, since it arguably did more to build support for war than any other official pronouncement (O'Sullivan 2009, 194). In fact, some authors provide blow-by-blow accounts of the planning and delivery of Powell's address, while briefly acknowledging the responses of pundits and editorialists in the establishment press. They describe how Powell and his team huddled together and reviewed intelligence material to be included in the presentation, how dissenting opinions in the intelligence community were suppressed by the CIA, and how Powell ultimately built a tendentious case based mainly on unconfirmed allegations and ambiguous audiovisual evidence.[18] And they note the reception of Powell's speech in U.S. editorials that were "positive, if not unanimously uncritical" (Hoyle 2008, 334).[19]

This historical research is invaluable for our understanding of the neoconservative culture of the Bush administration, as well as the internal maneuvering of Powell and his team as they labored to convert secret intelligence into public arguments for war. This work also draws attention to the deferential stance taken by journalists on their opinion pages in the aftermath of Powell's presentation. Less apparent in this work, however, is a detailed analysis of the specific discursive techniques that moved public opinion. And though these histories informally discuss the role of the editorial press following Powell's speech, there remains much room to explore how the press preshaped and reshaped his address in hard news stories across multiple media.

For their part, rhetorical scholars interested in the prewar period have typically examined the political addresses that motivated public support for war.[20] Rhetoricians aim to both historicize these key public statements and explain thorough careful analysis the generic, argumentative, and stylistic features that made these statements persuasive. For instance, a fascinating special issue of the journal *Rhetoric & Public Affairs* published in 2007 contains seven articles meant to "scrutinize the rhetoric that brought America into [the Iraq] war" (Simons 2007, 177). While there is much to commend this outstanding collection of articles, there is also an important omission: a thorough examination of discourse in the *mainstream press*.[21] Indeed, only one article in the issue attempts to study how the press helped to promulgate the Bush administration's call-to-arms message (John et al. 2007). And, even in this study, the focus is not on the role that U.S. news coverage played in shaping perceptions of political discourse, but on how political actors "shaped U.S. news coverage" (197). In other words, the press is conceived of as a "conduit of the president's and the administration's outlook" (201)—and not as an agent responsible for pre- and redefining that outlook for the public.

Meanwhile, most other studies in the special issue tend to ignore the role of the press altogether.[22] Instead, these studies thoroughly analyze the call-to-arms arguments of one or a few members of the Bush administration. Jamieson (2007), for example, surveys statements by Bush administration figures and concludes that their claims about weapons of mass destruction were unwarranted based on the evidence, and, further, that "the public could have known . . . that the evidence did not satisfy a high standard" during the run-up to war (267). Similarly, Zarefsky (2007) investigates Colin Powell's U.N. address and finds that, while Powell's reasoning was legitimate given the circumstances, his evidence was tragically flawed. Like Jamieson, Zarefsky suggests that the public—among others—might have realized that Powell's case was unsound had his audience been "more committed to critical questioning of [the] evidence" (299).[23]

While Jamieson and Zarefsky are certainly right, their view may not take into account how press coverage can work against such critical questioning. During times of war, the public does not interface *solely* with the discourse of politicians. In fact, it is more likely that the public interfaces with journalistic recontextualizations of this discourse—that is, with press reports and analyses of political discourse. In a sense, the public is bombarded not just with the "talking points" of a given administration, but with mediated reinterpretations of these talking points. Thus, to fully appreciate how "public address" influenced people prior to the Iraq War, we must more carefully examine portrayals of political discourse in the news.

Of course, there is no shortage of research investigating American press coverage before the Iraq War—particularly in media studies, but also in rhetoric and discourse studies.[24] For example, Kuypers (2006) analyzes how journalists reported on five wartime speeches by George W. Bush delivered between 2001 and 2005. Analyzing both "hard news" stories and editorials, he finds that while reporters generally accepted the president's framing of events after the 9/11 attacks, they began presenting "oppositional frames" in the months that followed, ultimately distorting the president's justifications for war. For instance, Kuypers argues that the press failed to objectively report Bush's 2002 State of the Union Address, questioning or expressing "hostility toward the president's notion of an axis of evil" (72).[25]

Most other studies of American journalism in the prewar period, however, have found that the press essentially echoed and endorsed—rather than opposed—the administration's call-to-arms message.[26] For example, Entman (2004) argues that, but for a few weeks in summer 2002, the press largely cooperated with the Bush administration during its campaign for war in Iraq, noting that even purportedly liberal news outlets took a decidedly prowar stance on their editorial pages in the months before the invasion (107–14). In his study of post-9/11 discourse, Hodges (2011) further illustrates how key phrases from Bush's public statements, such as "weapons of mass destruction," were uncritically repeated by journalists during the run-up to war.[27] In a more extensive study of the period, Domke (2004) also finds that U.S. news stories and editorials "substantially echoed the public communications of the Bush administration" (162), and thereby functioned to disseminate, reinforce, and embed "the administration's fundamentalist worldview" in the public sphere (xi). Finally, Bennett and colleagues (2007) concur that the American press showed a "propensity for stenographic reporting" (30) during the prewar period, as they "echoed the Washington consensus" about alleged weapons of mass destruction in Iraq and the supposed connections between Saddam Hussein and al-Qaeda (39).

These scholars not only help characterize American journalism during the prewar period, but also provide explanations as to why the press so frequently recited—and so rarely questioned—the Bush administration's call-to-arms discourse. I elaborate on these arguments in chapter 1, but a brief summary is in order here. It is well known that the press carries out an important *agenda-setting* function, as news media selectively focus public attention on certain issues and thereby set limits on what the public is likely to think about and debate (McCombs 2004; McCombs & Shaw 1972). However, the press does not necessarily lead the way in setting the public agenda. Instead, journalists take their cues from *government* (Bennett & Manheim 1993; Hallin 1986; Herman & Chomsky 1988; Sigal 1973). As Bennett (1990) explains, the establishment press tends to *index* "the range of views expressed in mainstream government debate about a given topic" (106). In fact, journalists rely on prominent officials especially during periods of national crisis, so much so that Zaller and Chiu (1996) have described the wartime press as "government's little helper."[28] Importantly, when there is no government debate—or at least no debate among those the press views as "key players"—then there is no debate in the news (Bennett 2012; Bennett, Lawrence, & Livingston 2007; Mermin 1999). This seems to have been the case during the run-up to the Iraq War. When the leaders of the Democratic Party largely endorsed Bush's plans for an invasion, the press failed to offer a counternarrative that would challenge the administration's goals (Entman 2004; Domke 2004; Bennett, Lawrence, & Livingston 2007). Thus, the public received a rather one-sided story about the need to go to war, as the Bush administration's spin was widely echoed across the establishment news media.

The metaphor of the "echoing press" illuminates journalists' tendency to record and reiterate the statements of high-ranking government officials. Like any metaphor, however, it conceals other possible ways of understanding news discourse.[29] One limitation of the echoing metaphor is that it construes journalists as reactors to events, forensic rhetors who repeat past government claims.[30] But journalists can also report about government claims that have not yet been made. Indeed, they can precontextualize future rhetorical events, drawing them into the normative present and potentially constraining in advance how public audiences come to understand them. And even when journalists are focused on the past statements of government officials, they do more than faithfully record those statements. They characterize those government officials—positively or negatively—signaling whether or not they should be trusted. And they modify governmental discourse—incrementally enhancing, verifying, or qualifying the claims of the state, until those claims loosely resemble what they were when first uttered by the politicians. In short, journalists don't just echo official pronouncements. They *reconstitute* them, touching every aspect of a politician's speech—from the credibility of the speaker, to the rhetorical timing of the event, to the content of the assertions.

In this respect, the echo metaphor may be less appropriate than the metaphor of the *frame*.[31] Framing concerns the way news media choose to contextualize and evaluate selected events (Goffman 1974). More specifically, framing involves using words and images to define problems, diagnose their causes, convey moral judgments, and promote remedies (Entman 1993; 2004). Frames not only tell audiences what to think about, but more crucially tell them what to think (Bennett 2012, 23; McCombs 2004). That is, the frame metaphor draws attention to the *rhetorical* aspects of journalism, how reporters seek to influence their audiences' beliefs.[32] Unfortunately, as Entman (2004) suggests, there is no standard definition of framing, leaving the concept "vulnerable to criticism as an imprecise catchall that means slightly different things to each researcher employing it" (5). Frames are often conceptualized as broad, organizing themes that assign meaning to perceived reality (Bennett 2012, 42). Thus, one could think of frames (and counterframes) as global structures that are more or less developed in the news.[33] However, framing can also be analyzed microscopically, since even small variations in linguistic style can lead to very different audience responses (Entman 2004, 27).[34]

This book favors a *micro-discursive* approach to analyzing news frames, particularly the news frames that defined and evaluated Powell's address. Thus, rather than broadly analyzing several years of wartime press coverage (cf. Bennett, Lawrence, & Livingston 2007), I seek a deep, granular analysis of the news discourse surrounding one exceptionally important rhetorical event.[35] Admittedly, this tight focus limits the scope of my study, but it also permits an unusually detailed analysis of news texts. In fact, I employ a number of discourse analytic techniques designed to systematically examine the grammatical, syntactical, and lexical details of the news reports. As Weiss (2009) argues, such techniques allow us to get "inside" a news frame and see with greater clarity how journalists advance particular viewpoints (189).

My approach, however, is not solely focused on linguistic aspects of political and media discourse. It is fundamentally *multimodal*, since both Powell's speech and the news reports that covered it are comprised of multiple symbolic resources (Kress & Van Leeuwen 2001). As Entman (2004) has observed, "Research on framing and on news of foreign policy has paid scant attention to the visual dimension of media coverage, even though many scholars suspect it has substantial influence" (56). A unique feature of this book, then, is its careful study of both verbal *and* visual resources, including the ways these resources co-contextualize one another. Finally, my approach is *intertextual*, since news texts always draw upon and respond to prior rhetorical events—and anticipate future ones (Bakhtin 1981; 1986). Again, to fully understand Powell's discourse, we must examine how journalists pre- and reconfigured that discourse, how they modified Powell's words and visuals and shaped public attitudes about his speech.[36]

Ultimately, this book will contribute important new knowledge to historians, rhetorical critics, and media scholars alike. First, scholars across disciplines will better understand how and why the American public was moved to support the Iraq War at a critical moment in its genesis. I will show how journalists increased the persuasive potential of Powell's arguments, positioning the public to endorse violence. Through a variety of micro-discursive techniques, journalists (1) enhanced Powell's character and credibility; (2) predisposed audiences to regard his case as warranted even before it had been presented; and (3) recontextualized his arguments, after the fact, in ways that increased their certainty, salience and evidentiality. In light of these findings, I suggest that the micro-transformations that occur as journalists pre- and recontextualize a discursive event have a cumulative effect that may drastically alter what a political address comes to mean for audiences. In fact, in this case, Powell's speech was perhaps less relevant to public decision-making about war than its pre- and reincarnations in the press.

Next, for rhetorical scholars, this book will provide new insights into the persuasive functions of intertextual discourse—specifically, how political discourse is made more or less persuasive when intervened upon by journalists in the news media market. As noted, taking an intertextual perspective allows us to see how a politician's ethos and argument develop across a number of mass-mediated texts, as different voices in the news anticipate and re-represent that politician's discourse. This study reminds us that the meaning of Powell's U.N. presentation does not reside in his textual performance. The meaning of Powell's presentation is (re)constructed by its audiences—first by journalists and later by a public confronted with fragments of Powell's discourse in the news (Becker 1971; McGee 1990; McKerrow 1989).

Third, media scholars will gain a deeper awareness of the small-scale mechanisms by which journalists frame and reframe political rhetoric. As I illustrate throughout this book, the press often modifies political discourse in subtle ways, through minor and seemingly innocuous variations of verbal and visual material. Thus, I suggest that reporters do not merely *echo* the words of government officials (cf. Domke 2004). They cumulatively *transform* government discourse—pre- and redefining what political speech comes to mean for the public.

Finally, as a secondary aim, this book will highlight the utility of discourse analytic methods. I aim to introduce a systematic and micro-level approach to analyzing intertextual transformations across multimodal texts. The delicacy of this approach allows us to discern "hidden" mechanisms of persuasion, bringing to light subtle interconnections between fragments of verbal-visual discourse. Thus, the approach may be valuable to scholars across disciplines. However, I have placed most methodological material in appendices for the benefit of readers more interested in the substantive findings of this study. Appendices B and I, in particular, articulate the theories of discourse that inform this project and outline the constellation of analytic approaches employed in this book.

Overview of the Chapters to Follow

Chapter 1, "The Campaign for War in Iraq: Contextualizing Powell's Speech in Political and Media Discourse," provides a historical framework for my analysis. I illustrate how Powell's presentation was developed in the context of a long-term push for war in Iraq. I describe how the decision for war was made in 2002, and how the administration leveraged its power to politicize intelligence and market the war to the public. Ultimately, Powell's U.N. presentation would serve as "window dressing" (O'Sullivan 2009, 168). The event was staged so that the public might have a favorable impression of the administration's efforts at diplomacy, even though it had already settled on a policy of war. Next, I examine how and why Powell's call-to-arms rhetoric entered into a "patriotic" media climate. I explain how structural weaknesses in mainstream journalism helped ensure that the call to arms was both highlighted and endorsed.

Chapter 2, "The Chief Prosecutor and the Iraqi Regime: Intertextual Ethos and Transitive Chains of Authority," draws upon and complicates classical conceptions of rhetorical ethos—a term that encompasses character, credibility, and authority. I argue that, in a mass-media environment, ethos is constituted *intertextually* as competing voices struggle to characterize political figures (and their discourse) in the news. Drawing on the work of rhetorical scholars (e.g., Perelman & Olbrechts-Tyteca 1969) and linguists (Martin & White 2005), I investigate how news reports constituted the ethos of Colin Powell and Iraqi political leaders. Findings suggest that the reports evaluate Powell positively and Iraq negatively, and, thus, position audiences to regard Powell's voice as authoritative and Iraqi voices as untrustworthy. This ethos building and ethos destroying is accomplished not only by journalists, but also by the "sources" journalists incorporated into their stories. Thus, I introduce the notion of transitive chains of authority—discursive sequences by which rhetors attach their credibility to other "voices" in their texts, and implicitly endorse the attitudes expressed by those voices. Ultimately, a broad chorus of mass-mediated voices can define a person's character. Facing these powerful intertextual voices, I argue, political agents inevitably struggle to control their own ethos.

Chapter 3, "Undercutting Saddam's Denials: Precontextualization and Audience Alignment," is one of two chapters that "zooms in" on an NBC newscast. What interests me here is the way that an NBC broadcast selects certain verbal-visual representations of past events in order to enact a context for a future discursive moment: Powell's speech. Drawing on Martin and White's (2005) linguistic framework and scholarship on the rhetoric of futurity (Dunmire 2011; Grusin 2010), I show how journalists precontextualized Powell's address on the night before its delivery—and presented viewers with a supportive context for understanding Powell's argument. By representing Saddam Hussein as deceptive and even deserving of future violence, the journalists essentially prefigured and pre-confirmed arguments that Powell employed the next day. More importantly, because the news representations were presented as factual and universally agreed upon, they allowed viewers little space to consider alternative viewpoints—and little reason to question or resist the seemingly inexorable push for war.

Chapter 4, "America's Best Intelligence: Recontextualization and Rhetorical Transformation," focuses on the recontextualization of Powell's speech in the news. More specifically, the chapter concerns what I term rhetorical transformation—that is, the way elements of one rhetor's discourse are transformed as they are recontextualized in another rhetor's discourse. I identify the sometimes microscopic ways that Powell's presentation was transformed by journalists—and examine how these tiny transformations nevertheless functioned to reposition audiences. The chapter illustrates how, in reporting Powell's address, journalists inconspicuously deleted some of Powell's meanings, and added other meanings that were not originally apparent. In so doing, they enhanced Powell's overall argument, increasing the certainty of his utterances—and even adding new "evidence" to support his claims.

Chapter 5, "Political Discourse, the Press, and the Public Good," describes the implications of my study and identifies directions for future research. I discuss the value of my integrated analytic framework, and point out some of its limitations. In addition, I distill the book's major claims and suggest how these claims inform our understanding of the run-up to war in Iraq and complicate existing approaches to the study of rhetoric and news media. After recommending additional lines of research, I offer some final reflections on contemporary call-to-arms journalism. The main problem with prewar coverage in this study was not that the reporters failed to ask the "tough questions," but that they actually labored to make arguments for war more persuasive.

Chapter One

The Campaign for War in Iraq: Contextualizing Powell's Speech in Political and Media Discourse

⌘

After Secretary of State Colin L. Powell's presentation to the United Nations Security Council yesterday, it is hard to imagine how anyone could doubt that Iraq possesses weapons of mass destruction.
—"Irrefutable," *Washington Post*, February 6, 2003

On February 24, 2001, Colin Powell indicated to reporters that economic sanctions against Iraq had worked: Saddam Hussein posed no significant threat to the Gulf region, let alone to the United States. As Powell put it, "[Saddam Hussein] has not developed any significant capability with respect to weapons of mass destruction.

He is unable to project conventional power against his neighbors" (quoted in "Briefing" 2001). Roughly two years later at the United Nations, however, Powell had changed his tune considerably. Now Powell portrayed Saddam Hussein as a monumental threat, a leader who "hides weapons of mass destruction," "provides haven and active support for terrorists," and who is prepared to realize his "ambitions for regional domination" (UN/2.5/CP). How do we explain this apparent conversion? What motivated the rapid drive for war in Iraq?

Equally important, how might we explain the American news media's response to this drive for war? Why is it that U.S. reporters so readily accepted the administration's claim that Iraq posed a serious threat in 2002, when the same administration had reached the opposite conclusion in 2001? How is it that American journalists—like those quoted in the epigraph—found Powell's presentation so persuasive, when international journalists found it entirely unconvincing? In this chapter, I address these questions. I situate both Powell's speech and the news narratives that covered it in their proper social, historical, and intertextual context.

Warranting War: The Campaign for "Preemptive" Violence in Iraq

It is now well known that even before the terrorist attacks of September 11, 2001—and indeed before George W. Bush's inauguration—members of the Bush administration had considered "preemptive" military action against Iraq. As Hybel and Kaufman (2006) report, people like Dick Cheney and Paul Wolfowitz were advancing a policy of preventive violence in the early 1990s as a way to sustain the United States' superpower status in a post–Cold War world. By the late 1990s, the idea of preventive violence was specifically attached to Iraq. For instance, in January 1998, members of the Project for the New American Century urged President Clinton to remove Saddam Hussein from power before he could pose a threat to the United States. Of the 18 people who signed the recommendation, 11 would eventually serve under President Bush. In 2000, Condoleezza Rice—then an adviser to George W. Bush the presidential candidate—similarly wrote that Saddam Hussein must be deposed as a precautionary measure.

As Dunmire explains (2009), the events of 9/11 finally gave the administration a pretext for preventive war. To be clear, the Iraqi government had not suddenly become more dangerous. There was no new evidence indicating that Iraq had acquired weapons of mass destruction or better means of delivering them—nothing to refute Powell's February 2001 assessment that Iraq was even unable to threaten its neighbors. However, as Greg Thielmann, an aide to Colin Powell suggests, there was now a "faith-based" certainty among senior administration officials that Iraq needed to be dealt with (quoted in Leung 2009). Thus, days after the 2001 terrorist attacks, several members of Bush's team urged him to pursue military action against Baghdad (Hybel & Kaufman 2006). In particular, Dick Cheney and Donald Rumsfeld skillfully guided discussion toward the idea that Iraq presented a threat to the United States—and ultimately won Bush's support in the effort to depose Saddam Hussein (Warshaw 2009).

The public push to demonize Saddam Hussein began to intensify in late 2001—just months after the 9/11 attacks (Althaus & Largio 2004). During his State of the Union Address in January 2002, Bush strongly hinted at the prospect of violence, declaring that Iraq was continuing "to flaunt its hostility toward America and to support terror" (Bush 2002a). At this point, war was not a foregone conclusion; however, as early as July 2002, the administration had apparently settled on the use of force (T. H. Anderson 2011). Around this time, members of the Bush cabinet launched the White House Iraq Group (WHIG). The job of this group, according to Scott McClellan (2008), was to "coordinate the marketing of the war to the public," developing a "permanent campaign" strategy that would "set the agenda and influence the narrative" (142). WHIG not only manufactured talking points about Iraq, but also pressured the CIA to produce intelligence that could be exploited to sell an invasion (T. H. Anderson 2011, 104). In fact, a 2002 memo produced by British officials confirms that "intelligence and facts were being fixed around the policy" of war (quoted in Van Natta 2006).

By August 2002, Vice President Cheney was already drawing on this politicized intelligence, practically demanding that the nation take "preemptive" action against Iraq to facilitate "regime change."[1] At the time, Cheney suggested that a "return of inspectors [to Iraq] would provide no assurance whatsoever" that Saddam Hussein would comply with U.N. resolutions, and that it might even "provide false comfort that Saddam was somehow 'back in his box'" (Cheney 2002). Nonetheless, a month later, President Bush (convinced by Powell of the need for international legitimacy) addressed the United Nations General Assembly, and requested a new resolution that would place inspectors back in Iraq. He warned that if Iraq failed to comply with new resolutions, "action" would be "unavoidable" (Bush 2002b).

Bush reasoned that he could wage war under the banner of the U.N., but he had not yet convinced Americans that such war was necessary. Thus, the next month in Cincinnati, Ohio, he took his case directly to the public for the first time. Bush baldly asserted that Iraq had chemical and biological weapons and that it was reconstituting its nuclear weapons program. He discussed Iraq's supposed unmanned aerial vehicles (UAVs), alleging that Saddam Hussein was exploring how to attach deadly agents to these UAVs "for missions targeting the United States." And he described "high-level contacts" between Iraq and al-Qaeda, declaring that Iraq had provided weapons training to terrorists. While he expressed his "hope" that violence could be avoided, he cautioned that war would likely be necessary (Bush 2002c). Looking back, most of Bush's assertions were extremely dubious—based primarily on speculation and hearsay (Isikoff & Corn 2006, 146). In fact, by one account, Bush's Cincinnati address contained 11 misleading statements, the most by any of the administration officials in a single appearance (Waxman 2004, ii).

Whatever the merits of the speech, however, it helped generate support for war among U.S. lawmakers. In fact, Bush's Cincinnati address had been timed to coincide with congressional debate over a resolution that would authorize the president to use force in Iraq—essentially at his discretion. A few senators, like Robert Byrd and Edward Kennedy, objected to the proposed legislation, arguing that there was no clear evidence of an imminent attack from Iraq and claiming that the bill would give the president undue power to make war (Kelly 2010). However, the bill ultimately enjoyed substantial bipartisan support, as the vast majority of Democrats argued in favor of confronting Saddam Hussein. Bush had shrewdly brought the Iraq issue to the fore in the middle of a midterm election season, and few Democrats were willing to risk appearing "unpatriotic." Therefore, on October 10, 2002—three days after the president's Cincinnati speech—Congress authorized him to use force in Iraq in a nearly unanimous vote.

Meanwhile, Colin Powell was working diligently with members of the U.N. Security Council, trying to fashion a new resolution for Iraqi disarmament that would satisfy all parties. The matter was finally settled in November 2002. Finding that Iraq was in "material breach" of earlier resolutions, the U.N. adopted Resolution 1441, which gave the Iraqi leadership a final opportunity to disarm. Specifically, Resolution 1441 required that Iraq fully cooperate with "enhanced inspections," or else face "serious consequences." The phrase "serious consequences" was intentionally left undefined so that nations (e.g., France) that were unconvinced of the need for military action could safely vote for the resolution (Isikoff & Corn 2006, 158). Later, of course, the Bush administration would insist that "serious consequences" meant "war."

For two months U.N. weapons inspectors pored over Iraq, but by January 27, 2003, they had not found any significant evidence of WMDs or related programs. This was made very clear in two separate reports by Hans Blix and Mohamed ElBaradei. Blix did note, however, that Iraq was not always forthcoming with needed information. For instance, in December, Baghdad had issued a 12,000-page arms declaration that left many questions unanswered. Still, Blix reported that "Iraq has on the whole cooperated rather well so far," noting that Baghdad had provided inspectors prompt access to all sites. His overall conclusion was that the inspections were working, and that full disarmament could be achieved "within a reasonable time."

Despite the apparent lack of evidence, the administration continued to declare that Saddam Hussein had WMDs that the inspections were failing to uncover. In his State of the Union address on January 28, 2003, Bush again asserted that Iraq had huge stockpiles of chemical and biological weapons, including mobile biological weapons labs. He repeated allegations that aluminum tubes recently purchased by Iraq could enrich uranium for a nuclear weapon, adding that Iraq had recently sought large quantities of uranium in Africa (the State Department rejected both claims). Above all, he declared (contra Blix) that Iraq was deceiving inspectors and flouting the disarmament process. He announced that Powell would go to the U.N. Security Council soon to "present information and intelligence about Iraq's illegal weapons programs, its attempt to hide those weapons from inspectors, and its links to terrorist groups."

At this point, Bush was firmly committed to war.[2] In fact, according to a leaked memo, Bush privately told British prime minister Tony Blair on January 31 that regardless of the outcome at the U.N., a "coalition of the willing" would begin fighting sometime in early March (Isikoff &

Corn 2006, 180).[3] March had been selected in order to capitalize on what would presumably be favorable weather conditions—indeed, the president had originally hoped to launch the war even earlier (Woodward 2004, 319). Continued inspections would only delay this proposed start date. Moreover, if inspectors were allowed to finish their work but still found no WMDs, it would undermine the primary justification for violence. Thus, Bush could not consent to Blix's recommendation that inspectors be given more time. Indeed, as O'Sullivan (2009) notes, the administration felt that "the inspections had to be short-circuited, and the move toward an invasion had to begin before the inspections rendered an attack unwarranted" (175).

Powell's speech, then, was less about presenting intelligence to the U.N. than about terminating the U.N. inspections process. His overarching rhetorical goal was to show that inspections were not working and could never work. Certainly, Bush hoped that this argument would persuade members of the Security Council to cease inspections and adopt a new war resolution, but he was not optimistic—especially given the statements by Blix and ElBaradei.[4] Still, even if Powell failed to persuade the U.N., he could convince domestic audiences that diplomatic options had been tried and exhausted. And, as noted, Bush could always argue (to Americans anyway) that Resolution 1441 already sanctioned war, thereby claiming international legitimacy.[5]

Purportedly, Colin Powell had serious reservations about the campaign for war. He believed that Bush was giving up on the diplomatic process prematurely, and he worried that the president had not fully considered the long-term consequences of an invasion and occupation (Woodward 2004). Furthermore, in spite of his own confident public statements about Iraq's supposed weapons stockpiles, Powell secretly suspected that the intelligence on Iraq's WMDs was weak. In November 2002, he reportedly shared his doubts with his chief of staff, Lawrence Wilkerson: "I wonder what we'll do when we put half a million troops on the ground in Iraq and search it from one end to the other—and find nothing" (quoted in DeYoung 2007, 424). Ultimately, however, Powell's misgivings about the war had more to do with process than with substance. He did not want to avoid war in Iraq; rather, he wanted the war against Iraq in 2003 to resemble as much as possible the 1990–1991 campaign, a campaign carried out by an international coalition and with the approval of the U.N. (O'Sullivan 2009, 161–62).

As Powell began preparing his presentation in late January, perhaps he believed that he might still win U.N. support. But when he finally saw the intelligence on Iraq, he must have had his doubts. The White House had provided Powell with a 48-page draft, compiled largely by Scooter Libby and other members of WHIG. Powell instructed Wilkerson to vet the document at CIA headquarters, along with a small team including George Tenet and members of Vice President Cheney's office. Aware that his boss's reputation was on the line, Wilkerson scrutinized the draft, checking the original source material for every single assertion. After six hours of painful work, however, it became obvious that the draft was teeming with unsourced and misleading allegations. Wisely, Wilkerson and Tenet decided to pitch it and start over.

Now joined by Powell himself, the team began working from the National Intelligence Estimate (NIE), a 2002 document intended to express the coordinated judgments of the entire U.S. intelligence community.[6] But the NIE, too, was full of flawed data and politicized interpretations.[7] Reports of mobile biological weapons labs were not backed with hard evidence;[8] indications of chemical weapons were scant and dated;[9] intercepted communications about Iraq's alleged weapons were not definitive;[10] satellite images were grainy and indistinct;[11] allegations about Iraq's aluminum tubes and unmanned aerial vehicles were disputed within the intelligence community;[12] and details of Saddam's alleged links to terrorists were essentially baseless.[13] And this was the information that Powell *kept* in the presentation. As he later recalled, he and his team spent most of their time "trimming the garbage" (DeYoung 2007, 445). In fact, an early draft was so riddled with bogus intelligence that Powell lost his patience and declared the case "bullshit" (Isikoff & Corn 2006, 181). But the team continued working, and Powell eventually settled on a presentation that he believed was reasonably sound.[14]

In spite of this careful vetting of evidence, it is clear that Powell ignored advice to remove unsupported claims from his final presentation. Powell's own intelligence staff, the State Department's Bureau of Intelligence and Research (INR) sent Powell several memos, flagging for him about forty allegations that they considered weak. In response, Powell deleted many of these items, but knowingly left about a dozen unsubstantiated claims in the final draft of his speech (Isikoff & Corn 2006, 179).

Ultimately, the language of Powell's presentation echoed the language of other speeches by administration officials (Ivie 2005, 162). In fact, as shown in table 1.1, most of Powell's arguments had been rehearsed earlier by the president. Powell, of course, offered much more detail, including specifics about alleged weapons equipment and programs, and the names of suspected terrorists purportedly operating in Iraq. In addition, Powell offered previously classified data from satellite images and intercepted communications between Iraqi officials.[15] Nevertheless, the basic parameters of Powell's argument would seem quite familiar to audiences who had been listening to George W. Bush (see appendix C for details). As Zarefsky (2007) explains, the primary focus of the speech was on WMDs and the alleged efforts to obstruct the work of U.N. inspectors (282). Less important, but also included, was information on Iraq's past human rights violations and its supposed links to terrorists.

On the eve of his speech, Powell and British foreign minister Jack Straw reportedly met at the Waldorf Astoria in New York for a private

Table 1.1. Intertextual Links between Powell's Speech and Earlier Speeches by G. W. Bush

Argument/ Evidence	Bush (7 Oct. 2002)	Bush (28 Jan. 2003)	Powell (5 Feb. 2003)
There have been twelve years of Iraqi deception.	✓	✓	✓
Resolution 1441 is the final chance for Iraq.		✓	✓
Iraq has made no active effort to disarm.		✓	✓
Iraq is still producing weapons.	✓	✓	✓
Iraq is deceiving inspectors, concealing weapons.		✓	✓
Intercepted communication shows deception.			✓
Iraq removed prohibited weapons from palace.			✓

(*continued*)

Table 1.1. (*continued*)

Argument/ Evidence	Bush (7 Oct. 2002)	Bush (28 Jan. 2003)	Powell (5 Feb. 2003)
Iraq is hiding materials in homes and cars.			✓
Iraq is moving weapons to avoid inspection.			✓
Satellite photos show weapons being moved.			✓
Satellite photos show chemical weapons facilities.			✓
Iraq is blocking U2 surveillance.		✓	✓
Iraq is impersonating and coaching scientists.		✓	✓
Saddam ordered killing of cooperative scientists.		✓	✓
Iraq has mobile biological weapons labs.		✓	✓
Iraq has systems to deliver biological agents.			✓
Iraq has not accounted for anthrax.	✓	✓	✓
Iraq has not accounted for botulinum toxin.		✓	✓
Iraq has not accounted for other chemical weapons.	✓	✓	✓

(*continued*)

Table 1.1. (*continued*)

Argument/ Evidence	Bush (7 Oct. 2002)	Bush (28 Jan. 2003)	Powell (5 Feb. 2003)
Intercepted audio confirms nerve agents.			✓
Iraq has long-range ballistic missiles.	✓		✓
Iraq is developing new ballistic missiles programs.			✓
Iraq has UAVs to deploy biological or chemical weapons.	✓		✓
Iraq has historically lied about nuclear weapons.	✓		✓
Iraq has a stable of nuclear scientists.	✓		✓
Iraq has aluminum tubes to enrich uranium.	✓	✓	✓
Iraq is seeking magnets and balancing machines.			✓
Iraq has sponsored terrorists in the Middle East.	✓	✓	✓
Iraq has made contacts with al-Qaeda for decades.	✓		✓
Iraq assists a senior al-Qaeda leader, al-Zarqawi, who prepares chemical and biological attacks.	✓		✓

(*continued*)

Table 1.1. (*continued*)

Argument/ Evidence	Bush (7 Oct. 2002)	Bush (28 Jan. 2003)	Powell (5 Feb. 2003)
Iraq provided al-Qaeda with weapons training.	✓		✓
Saddam may supply WMDs to terrorists.	✓	✓	✓
Saddam's WMDs could allow regional domination.	✓	✓	✓
Iraq has tortured and killed its own citizens.	✓	✓	✓
If the U.N. fails to act, it will be irrelevant.	✓		✓
We should not wait for Saddam to grow stronger.	✓		✓
The United States cannot accept the threat.	✓	✓	✓

conversation. According to the British newspaper *The Guardian*, both men expressed "serious doubts about the reliability of intelligence on Iraq's banned weapons programme" (Plesch & Norton-Taylor 2003).[16] Perhaps this is why Powell demanded that during his address George Tenet sit right behind him, in full view of the cameras: he wanted the world to understand that he was the messenger and that responsibility for the case ultimately rested with the CIA (Unger 2007, 283). Whatever doubts Powell may have had about the evidence, he certainly kept them to himself at the U.N. Indeed, he projected confidence in the Security Council chambers, repeating the phrase "we know" thirty-two times. "My colleagues," he declared, "every statement I make today is backed up by sources, solid sources. These are not assertions. What we are giving you are facts and conclusions based on solid intelligence"

(UN/2 5/CP).[17] For the next hour, Powell presented his argument, supplementing his matter-of-fact delivery with giant diagrams of alleged weapons facilities and dramatic props like the model vial of anthrax.[18]

In the United States at least, the performance was very effective. Political leaders from both parties lauded Colin Powell and declared the need for war in Iraq.[19] Republican congressman Tom Delay, for example, epitomized the general views of his party. He remarked that the time had come to end Saddam Hussein's "tyrannical regime," and he rebuked the "appeasers" in the Democratic Party who, he said, were ignoring the overwhelming evidence against Iraq. Most leading Democrats, however, were hardly against an invasion (Huber 2003). In fact, Democrats seeking the 2004 presidency—John Kerry, Joseph Lieberman, Jon Edwards, Dick Gephardt—all praised Powell's speech and expressed their support for military action, without U.N. authorization. Joseph Biden, leading Democrat in the Senate Committee on Foreign Relations, declared that Powell's address was "powerful and irrefutable" (quoted in Hoyle 2008, 334). Others who had been on the fence about war now declared that Powell's evidence demanded the use of force. Democratic senator Dianne Feinstein, for example, said she was now convinced that inspections were useless and that alternatives to war were no longer viable.

Public reaction to Powell's address was also markedly positive. As noted in the introduction, even though most Americans didn't see Powell's presentation, they were nevertheless convinced by it. Approval for Powell's speech was very high, and support for an invasion of Iraq increased sharply after his performance (CNN/*USA Today*/Gallup 2003, 51).[20] In fact, according to one poll, nearly 60 percent of the country now felt that military action was the only way to deal with Saddam Hussein, and 10 percent of the country indicated that Powell's speech had directly caused them to change their minds and accept the need for an invasion (Barabak 2003). A Gallup poll found a sizable increase in the number of Americans who now believed that Iraq had weapons of mass destruction (CNN/*USA Today*/Gallup 2003, 59), and a *Los Angeles Times* poll showed a thirty-point boost in the number of Americans who believed that Saddam Hussein had connections to al-Qaeda (Gershkoff & Kushner 2005, 531). Crucially, the public now had little confidence in the efficacy of U.N. inspections. A week before Powell's speech, roughly 60 percent of Americans had "wanted U.N inspectors to be given at least 'several months' to continue their work" in Iraq. Now, 52 percent of the country said it wanted inspectors out in less than a month. In addition, 60 percent of Americans said they now would support war in Iraq, even if inspectors failed to uncover WMDs, as long as U.S. intelligence asserted that the banned weapons existed (Rennie 2003).

Powell's speech had certainly succeeded in the United States, but within the U.N. Security Council, it was a failure. Delegates were generally unimpressed with the slick editing and dramatic visual displays. In fact, some scoffed at the video screens and computers that had been installed specifically for Powell's presentation. Mexico's U.N. ambassador, Adolfo Aguilar Zinser, for example, saw all the special equipment as an indication that "this show wasn't for us. It was for an international audience, for the U.S. media" (quoted in DeYoung 2007, 448).

Aside from the theatrics, delegates were also unimpressed with the substance of Powell's argument. Among members of the Security Council, the United States and Great Britain remained the only two nations that supported an invasion. The other thirteen members of the Council were unconvinced—including the veto-bearing members, France, Russia, and China, who continued to voice grave doubts about war and to call for increased inspections. As French foreign minister Dominique de Villepin, argued, "The inspections regime . . . must be strengthened, since it has not been completely explored. The use of force can only be a final recourse. Why go to war if there still exists some unused space in [Resolution] 1441?" Tang Jiaxuan of China repeated this sentiment, saying, "We should respect the views of the [U.N. inspections agencies] and support the continuation of their work." Igor Ivanov of Russia added that Powell's case convincingly indicated only that "the activities of the international inspectors must be continued," since "they alone" can determine if Iraq is complying with the demands of the Security Council.[21] Ivanov and others wondered why, if the United States had such solid intelligence, it had not turned its information over to inspectors so they could do their jobs.

For their part, the Iraqi delegation seemed entirely unfazed, even rolling their eyes at Powell's allegations (Isikoff & Corn 2006, 187). Iraq's ambassador to the U.N., Mohammed Aldouri, was given only a few minutes to respond to Powell's lengthy presentation. Still, he managed to provide a critical—and looking back—accurate analysis of the evidence. "The pronouncements in Mr. Powell's statements on weapons of mass destruction are utterly unrelated to the truth," he said. "There are incorrect allegations, unnamed sources, unknown sources. There are assumptions and presumptions." Like Zinser, Aldouri suggested that Powell's presentation had not really been intended for the U.N. The goal, he said, was "to convince American public opinion first, and world public opinion in general, to launch a hostile war against Iraq" (quoted in "Iraq's Response" 2003). Meanwhile, U.N. inspectors were bitterly amused. According to Steve Allinson, who watched with about a dozen other inspectors in Iraq: "Various people would laugh at various times because the information [Powell] was presenting was just, you know, didn't mean anything—had no meaning." Reportedly, after watching the speech, inspectors turned to each other and said, "They [the Iraqis] have nothing" (quoted in "Ex-Aide" 2003).

The vast majority of opinion pages around the world also discredited Powell's presentation and rejected the proposed war in Iraq.[22] In North America, the *Toronto Star* found no sufficient reason to attack Iraq, commenting that the country "poses no more threat today than it did last week, last month or last year." And Mexico's *Jornada* strongly criticized Powell's evidence, even suggesting that some of it might have been fabricated. In Europe, opinion pages were more mixed, but still generally opposed to war. While the London *Times* discovered in Powell's speech clear proof of Iraq's illicit weapons, both the *Guardian* and the *Daily Mirror* found Powell's evidence unsatisfactory.[23] The French paper *Le Monde* also complained that, though the United States had promised a "day of proof," the public instead received a "day of repeated suspicions," and asked, "Will we go to war over suspicions?" Meanwhile, in Germany, the daily paper *Tagesspiegel* suggested that Powell's speech had not justified "the costs of war—including civilian deaths and the costs of years of occupation." And on the English website of the Russian newspaper *Pravda*, there was sharp criticism of Powell's evidence and this dry conclusion, "If people believe this report, they will believe that there are fairies at the end of the garden."[24]

In the days following Powell's presentation, the international public remained staunchly opposed to war, and, in mid-February, millions of people across the world protested a possible invasion (McFadden 2003). At the same time, Hans Blix addressed the U.N. Security Council for a final time. He rejected the bulk of Powell's allegations, and insisted that there was still no evidence of WMDs in Iraq. Blix believed the inspections were making progress and that any remaining questions about Iraq's WMDs would be answered by April 15 (DeYoung 2007,

455). But the Bush administration dismissed Blix and ignored world opinion. As planned, the United States and its allies attacked Iraq on March 19, 2003—without a new U.N. resolution.

Ultimately, of course, a year into the invasion, after many thousands of deaths, no weapons of mass destruction were found. The U.N. intelligence on Iraq had been accurate and the weapons inspections process had been vindicated. Still, the U.N. had shown itself to be powerless when it came to preventing an American-led invasion, and its legitimacy as a broker of international peace was called into question. Meanwhile, the CIA's reputation was devastated, American diplomacy was in shambles, and, perhaps for the first time, Powell faced substantial domestic criticism for his speech—a speech that was apparently based on flimsy evidence.

When *Washington Post* reporter Bob Woodward revealed in 2004 that Powell had had misgivings during the run-up to war, some wondered why Powell had not gone public. Perhaps out of loyalty to the president he had remained silent about his reservations, but his silence prevented the American public from fully evaluating the potential costs of an invasion (O'Sullivan 2009, 177).[25] By 2004, those costs were real. The fighting raged on, only now, more than ever before, "certain blood was being shed for uncertain reasons" (O'Brien 1990, 40).

The Patriotic Press: U.S. News Coverage

We can better understand why Americans initially approved of Powell's address, if we consider the status of post-9/11 American journalism. Several reporters describe how they felt pressure to avoid stories critical of the Bush administration after the terrorist attacks of September 11, 2001. For instance, CBS News anchor Dan Rather admitted in a 2002 interview with the BBC that he, and other journalists, felt compelled to avoid asking "tough questions" during the Afghanistan war because they did not want to appear "unpatriotic." As Rather explained:

> It starts with a feeling of patriotism within oneself. It carries through with a certain knowledge that the country as a whole—and for all the right reasons—felt and continues to feel this surge of patriotism within themselves. And one finds oneself saying: "I know the right question, but you

know what? This is not exactly the right time to ask it." (Quoted in Engel 2002)

A number of scholars[26] have suggested that this kind of reluctance to report stories "unfriendly" to the government is indicative of enduring structural problems in Western news media. As Kumar (2006) explains, "excessive reliance on government and corporate sources, professional journalism's deference to official sources, the lack of funding for investigative journalism, the marginalization of dissenting voices, and mechanisms that promote self-censorship" all affected U.S. news coverage during the run-up to the Iraq War (52).

In fact, it is easy to see why the Bush administration's prewar rhetoric succeeded, when we consider the "unwritten rules of Washington journalism" in conjunction with contextual factors operating in post-9/11 America (Bennett, Lawrence, & Livingston 2007, 14). First, the "profit orientation" of the corporate mass media virtually ensures that journalists will seek information from elite actors in government (Herman & Chomsky 1988, 2). Indeed, government sources make news gathering easier and cheaper: they create press releases, photo ops, congressional hearings, and other ready-for-news content. Elite institutions of journalism are compelled to rely on this information simply as a matter of economics (Colistra 2012).

As noted in the introduction, mainstream journalists hew so closely to Washington sources that their reporting tends to index the range of policy perspectives circulating in government (Bennett 1990; 1994; 1996; 2012; Gans 1979; Hallin 1994).[27] Often, different branches of government oppose one another in policy debates and press stories reflect these opposing branches, producing what we sometimes refer to as "balanced" coverage (Cook 1998; Mermin 1997; 1999). Indeed, the press thrives on stories of conflict, often framing its reports according to who's "winning" some policy contest, instead of focusing on the merits of the policy itself (Cappella & Jamieson 1997; Lawrence 2000; Patterson 1993). However, when journalists perceive a consensus among different branches of government, they are "generally unable to build and sustain" stories that counter the dominant narrative coming from Washington (Bennett, Lawrence, & Livingston 2007, 36).

Leading up to the Iraq War, the political landscape in Washington exhibited this kind of consensus, as congressional Democrats failed to produce unified opposition to the White House (Gershkoff & Kushner

2005). Even at the height of congressional debate, in fall 2002, a strong majority of Democrats supported Bush's policy of preventive war. And when Democrats officially authorized the president to use force at his discretion, the mainstream press titled its coverage decisively towards the consensus narrative in Washington, a narrative that saw the country heading for an invasion. Now the press took its cues from the administration leading the charge for battle, echoing Bush's discourse about the urgent threat from Iraq (Domke 2004; Entman 2004). Of course, certain legislators, like Russ Feingold and Dennis Kucinich, continued to oppose the president. But as far as the press was concerned, these politicians no longer had the power to influence outcomes (Sparrow 1999). Bush and the Republicans had "won" the political game, and so the press primarily derived its language from them.

Granted, there were many credible voices *outside* government that also challenged the Bush administration and might have supplied a legitimate counterframe. In the summer of 2002, for instance, former Republican leaders, like Brent Scowcroft and James Baker, declared their skepticism about war in Iraq. And many members of the public—from academics to average citizens—offered compelling antiwar arguments. However, because these figures were outside of government, they did not have the resources to sustain their counternarratives in the news. For example, they could not easily gain the media's attention by holding regular press conferences at the White House or by orchestrating a series of congressional investigations regarding the merits of the WMD threat. Thus, while these figures sometimes made a splash in the press, their criticisms quickly disappeared from the headlines (Entman 2004).

A somewhat different dynamic existed for credible international figures, like Hans Blix and Mohamed ElBaradei. They, too, contradicted the president's declarations about the existence of WMDs, and they had some power to create news through press conferences and the like. Even so, they could never hope to compete with the domestic propaganda machine of the Bush administration. And again, as Bennett and colleagues (2007) argue, the U.N. lacked, or was perceived to lack, the power to prevent the administration from invading Iraq (21). Thus, while U.N. and European voices were featured in news stories (Hayes & Guardino 2010), they were typically subordinated and deemphasized.[28] By the time of Powell's speech, the press regarded war in Iraq as an inevitability. Journalists focused overwhelmingly on the "insider pronouncements and politics of those determined to wage" war (Bennett,

Lawrence, & Livingston 2007, 37) and downplayed the discourse of those who wanted to stop it.

Perhaps if Powell had consistently publicized his reservations about the war, he would have provided the press with exactly the kind of counternarrative that can drive good critical reporting and stir public debate (Bennett, Lawrence, & Livingston 2007). Indeed, any member of Bush's cabinet or any high-ranking figure in the intelligence community might have been powerful enough to threaten the president's war plans and gain the lasting attention of the media. But the Bush administration was nothing if not unified.

In fact, Bush's team excelled at what Manheim (1991) terms "strategic political communication," the ability to craft effective discourse and control how it reaches the public through the press. After 9/11, the administration developed powerful messages, based on clear and emotionally compelling moral frames (Entman 2003). According to these frames, the world was divided into good and evil and people were obliged to choose between joining the administration (us) or effectively helping the terrorists (them) (Domke 2004; Ivie 2005). This kind of binary rhetoric was continued throughout the campaign for war in Iraq—and mechanisms were put in place to ensure that the message reached the public. In several nationally televised appearances, the president used his bully pulpit to circumvent congress and take the call-to-arms message directly to the people (Domke 2004, 158).[29] Meanwhile, the White House Iraq Group distributed talking points and carefully monitored public statements to ensure "message discipline." Whether in private conversations with reporters or public interviews on the Sunday talk shows, members of the Bush team consistently rehearsed the same script.

The administration also effectively managed a campaign for war by squelching dissent. Those who dared criticize Bush's policy were subject to a barrage of attacks from the likes of Karl Rove and Dick Cheney. (Joseph Wilson, Richard Clark, and Paul O'Neill would all attest to this.) Even external critics, be they Democrats or journalists, were roundly rebuked for "giving ammunition to America's enemies" (Bennett, Lawrence, & Livingston 2007; Domke 2004). Thus, through their effective messaging and strategies of intimidation, the administration controlled the landscape of post-9/11 discourse, dominating the airwaves with calls for war.

A final factor that inspired "prowar" media coverage was the American psyche itself, a psyche that, following 9/11, was characterized by both fear and love of country. It is no exaggeration to say that America was in "crisis mode" even months after September 11, 2001: still reeling from the terrorist attacks, perpetually reminded of new homeland security threats, and already absorbed in a "war on terror" in Afghanistan. To be sure, even during "normal" circumstances, commercial media are unlikely to challenge national leadership, since doing so might drive away corporate sponsors (Domke 2004, 167). But during times of crisis, when nationalism surges, the imperative to withhold criticism of government is even stronger (Domke 2004, 167). In this context, criticizing the government could lead to financial ruin (169). Moreover, we must not forget that individual journalists are influenced by the same cultural values as the rest of the population (Calabrese & Burke 1992; Gans 1979; Hallin 1987). In times of uncertainty, journalists—like the rest of us—often turn to political leaders for perspective, guidance, and leadership (Hallin, Manoff, & Weddle 1993; Hutcheson et al. 2004; Zaller & Chiu 1996). Particularly in the wake of a horrific attack that challenges the entire nation, journalists will often behave as Dan Rather recommended: by rallying around the commander-in-chief and giving the administration "the benefit of the doubt" (quoted in Blitzer & Kurtz 2001).

We see, then, that the American press was likely to echo and endorse the Bush administration's prewar rhetoric for a number of reasons—commercial imperatives to rely on government sources; a propensity for framing the news according to who's "winning" the political game; weak opposition from congressional Democrats; a very effective marketing campaign orchestrated by the executive branch; and deference to the administration in a national crisis that was shrewdly extended far beyond September 11 and its aftermath (Domke 2004, 156). Predictably, given this confluence of factors, mainstream news narratives before the Iraq invasion were dominated by prowar voices. For example, a study by Fairness and Accuracy in Reporting (FAIR) found that in a two-week period at the beginning of February 2003—the same period in which Powell delivered his address—the vast majority of U.S. guests on network news (NBC, ABC, CBS, PBS) programs were government or military officials who supported invading Iraq. In fact, "Just one of 267 U.S. sources was affiliated with anti-war activism—less than half a percent" (FAIR 2003).

Meanwhile, reporters skeptical of the war effort were sometimes silenced. As Jessica Yellin (2008), a correspondent who covered the White House for ABC News and MSNBC in 2002 and 2003, explained to Anderson Cooper, it wasn't just "self-censorship," but pressure from corporate executives that led journalists to produce positive stories about President Bush and his campaign for war:

> When the lead-up to the war began, the press corps was under enormous pressure from corporate executives, frankly, to make sure that this was a war that was presented in a way that was consistent with the patriotic fever in the nation and the president's high approval ratings. . . . The higher the president's approval ratings, the more pressure I had from news executives . . . to put on positive stories about the president. . . . They would edit my pieces. They would push me in different directions. They would turn down stories that were more critical. . . . That was my experience. (Yellin 2008)

In at least one instance, a political commentator was fired for espousing antiwar views. Specifically, Phil Donahue's show on MSNBC was canceled because, as a leaked internal memo reports, Donahue "seems to delight in presenting guests who are anti-war, anti-Bush and skeptical of the administration's motives" (quoted in Ellis 2003). The author of the memo goes on to complain that Donahue presented a "difficult public face for NBC in a time of war," and openly worries about voicing too much antiwar sentiment given that "our competitors are waving the flag at every opportunity" (Ellis 2003). (At the time of the cancellation, Donahue's show was the highest rated on MSNBC.)

But it wasn't just censorship. The media also intensified the call-to-arms message, snatching any "independent" sources that would verify the need for "regime change," while downplaying or ignoring facts that would damage the administration's argument for war (Kumar 2006, 60). In an internal review of its war coverage, the *New York Times* (2004) found that

> Editors at several levels who should have been challenging reporters and pressing for more skepticism were perhaps too intent on rushing scoops into the paper. . . . Articles based on dire claims about Iraq tended to get prominent display, while follow-up articles that called the original ones into question were sometimes buried. In some cases, there was no follow-up at all. ("The *Times*")

The *Times* cites as an example, the case of Iraq's attempt to purchase aluminum tubes allegedly intended for nuclear weapons manufacturing.

An initial article headlined, "U.S. Says Hussein Intensified Quest for A-Bomb Parts," was the featured front-page story on September 8, 2002. In the article, it is reported confidently that the aluminum tubes are "signs of a renewed Iraqi interest in acquiring nuclear arms." However, when the *Times* learned five days later that the use of the tubes was being debated in the intelligence community, "The misgivings appeared deep in an article on Page A13, under a headline that gave no inkling that [the paper was] revising [its] earlier view ('White House Lists Iraq Steps to Build Banned Weapons')" ("The *Times*").

Naturally, the Bush team took advantage of the reporters' willingness to suspend disbelief. In the case of the aluminum tubes mentioned above, an anonymous source first leaked the information about the tubes to the *New York Times*. That morning, on *Meet the Press*, Vice President Cheney cited the *Times* article as proof that Iraq was seeking to acquire nuclear weapons. Essentially, he was "citing an article that came from information leaked by his own administration" (Isikoff & Corn 2006, 36). According to Cheney, the evidence was "now public."[30]

It was in this friendly media climate that Colin Powell delivered his address. In sharp contrast to the international press, editorials around the United States raved. Over a hundred newspapers compared Powell's speech to Adlai Stevenson's U.N. appearance in 1962 (Unger 2007, 286). The *Washington Post* editors called the case irrefutable ("Irrefutable" 2003). The *New York Times* described it as "powerful" and "convincing" ("The Case" 2003). *USA Today* lauded Powell's "new and forceful evidence" ("Powell Lays Out" 2003). And the *Wall Street Journal* perhaps went furthest of all, declaring that Powell's evidence amounted not just to a "smoking gun," but to a "smoking fusillade of Saddam Hussein's efforts to resist and confound the U.N. order that he disarm" ("Powell's Smoking Gun" 2003).[31] It was a great victory for Colin Powell. Two years later, he would refer to it as a lasting blot on his record (Weisman 2005).

Conclusion

Not long after his U.N. presentation, Powell informed his chief of staff, Lawrence Wilkerson, that he wanted to give everyone who had worked on his speech an award: a signed plaque commemorating their efforts.

But Wilkerson told his boss he didn't want the prize (Isikoff & Corn 2006, 190). In fact, Wilkerson later recalled, he was feeling depressed. He regretted participating in what he referred to as a "hoax on the American people, the international community, and the United Nations Security Council" (Brancaccio & Wilkerson 2006).

Wilkerson had good reason to feel remorseful. There had been a calculated campaign by the administration to politicize intelligence, deceive the public, and lead the country to war. As O'Sullivan (2009) remarks, "The nation was subjected to an irrelevant debate about Iraqi culpability for 9/11 or possession of nonexistent WMD, when it should have been discussing what goals it had in Iraq, how they might be realistically achieved, and at what cost and consequences" (180). Sadly, Colin Powell had allowed himself to be a part of the "hoax." Instead of challenging the neoconservative thrust for war, he willingly served as its spokesman—providing crucial political cover for the administration as it pursued its misguided policies.[32]

Importantly, Powell's speech would not have succeeded in convincing the public had it not been for the assistance of the American press. For months before his presentation, mainstream news providers had actively helped promote the administration's falsehoods. They downplayed or ignored credible voices of dissent in Congress and the United Nations, while echoing and amplifying the administration's claims of an imminent threat from Iraq. And, at the crucial moment of Powell's speech, they failed to provide the American people with the kind of sober analysis that ought to obtain when considering questions of war and peace. In fact, instead of critically questioning Powell's evidence, they lionized him in their editorial pages.

These sycophantic editorials are disturbing, but they are only part of the journalistic discourse surrounding Powell's address. We must also consider the "objective" stories about his presentation. Indeed, for Americans who had not heard Powell's speech—the majority of Americans—these stories played a crucial role in shaping perceptions of Powell's arguments and evidence. In the remaining chapters, I analyze these stories in detail, showing how even the hard news strengthened Powell's credibility, predisposed audiences to respond favorably to his discourse, and subtly altered his claims to make them seem more certain and warranted.

CHAPTER TWO

The Chief Prosecutor and the Iraqi Regime: Intertextual Ethos and Transitive Chains of Authority

⌘

Ethos, like postmodern subjectivity, shifts and changes over time, across texts, and around competing spaces.

—Nedra Reynolds, "Ethos as Location," 1993

Several sources have suggested that George W. Bush deliberately chose Colin Powell to deliver the U.N. address because Powell, unlike other members of the Bush team, had a sterling public reputation. As Isikoff and Corn (2006) put it: "The idea—not a subtle one—was to attach Powell's credibility to the case for war" (174). Similarly, Unger (2007) argues that the lack of evidence in Powell's presentation was compensated for by the fact that "the presentation was being made by a man who had . . . become the most admired and respected person in America" (285). Unger reports that, at the time of his speech, 86 *percent* of the American public approved of Colin Powell.[1] Indeed, he writes, Powell came "before the U.N. as a voice of reason, as a man who appeared to have unassailable moral authority" (285). Finally, in his examination of Powell's presentation, rhetorical scholar David Zarefsky (2007) repeats this sentiment, claiming that Powell's "reputation as a skeptic on Iraq, if not an outright 'dove' within the administration, enhanced his credibility" (279). In the end, Zarefsky argues, "the credibility of the source" was able to "outweigh internal deficiencies in the evidence" (298).

These sources point to the importance of Powell's *ethos*—a term that encompasses character, credibility, and authority.[2] In the Aristotelian tradition, ethos is conceptualized as an *artistic creation*, a discursive display of character that rhetors construct for themselves. As Garver (1994) explains, "The chief way in which one displays character is by presenting an argument" (195). When rhetors choose appropriate lines of reasoning, they effectively exhibit "practical wisdom [*phronesis*], virtue [*arete*] and goodwill [*eunoia*]" (Aristotle 2007, 2.1.5). However, Aristotle also recognized the *non-artistic* ethos of the "moral virtues," the "accumulation of previous praxis" that results in the speaker's "ethical reputation" (Garver 1994, 193). This is sometimes called "prior ethos" (Amossy 2001) or "prediscursive ethos" (Maingueneau 1999). And it potentially determines whether a speech will carry any conviction with an audience. As Isocrates (1929) puts it: "The argument which is made by a man's life is of more weight than that which is furnished by words" (*Antidosis* 278).[3]

We tend to view both prior ethos and artistic ethos as manifestations of the *self*. Thus, we talk about how people "earn" their reputations, presumably as a consequence of their moral habits. And we think of artistic ethos as a persuasive strategy of "*self*-presentation" (Anderson 2007, 91, emphasis added), something we enact discursively for ourselves and by ourselves. However, traditionally speaking, ethos is composed socially, not individually. In fact, the Greek word *ethos* originally signified not just personal character, but a "habitual gathering place" (Halloran 1982) or communal "dwelling place" (Hyde 2004a).[4] As Reynolds (1993) argues, this latter definition of ethos calls to mind public congregations and suggests that ethos construction is negotiated between rhetor and community (328). In other words, one's ethos is co-constructed by many people within a social group. And, as Reynolds emphasizes, this "social group is not necessarily made up of like-minded individuals who gather in harmony" (329). Instead, it is characterized by "differences and conflict" (330), and one's ethos is always subject to "competing representations" (335).

Aristotle (2007) certainly recognized that ethos can be disputed in the public arena. As he remarks in the *Rhetoric*, we, as speakers, are "able to make both ourselves *and any other person* worthy of credence in regard to virtue" (1.9.1, emphasis added). Here, Aristotle confirms that we have the power to build a positive character for others in public rhetorical performances. However, Aristotle didn't just advise rhetors to make others "worthy of credence." He also suggested that rhetors should assign *blame* to others through insults and invective (1.10.41). In fact, as Kennedy (2007) points out, the ancient Greeks tended "to view life in competitive terms," and they considered it natural to discredit personal "enemies" (83). Thus, in Aristotle's contentious world, character was naturally a matter of debate for rival speakers in the agora.

In our technological culture, ethos is debated not in the public square, but in textual marketplaces (Reynolds 1993, 333). This is perhaps clearest in the context of academic writing, where a researcher's ethos is very much dependent on patterns of citation within and across texts (Hyland 2004; Gilbert 1977; Kaufer & Carley 1993; Latour 1987; MacRoberts & MacRoberts 1986; Swales 1990). Latour (1987), for example, shows that researchers invoke other texts not just to situate their work in an intellectual tradition, but to enhance their own credibility and weaken the credibility of their opponents. Indeed, writers consistently "deform" the work of the authors that they cite—rendering that work more or less authoritative. As Latour puts it, writers do "whatever [they] need to the former literature to render it as helpful as possible for the claims [they] are going to make" (37). They insert other articles into their papers, "distributing honour and shame, disabling some, strengthening others, borrowing without qualification from still more papers" (38). In this sense, scholarly credibility partly depends on how researchers cite prior literature, constructing or deconstructing the credibility of other writers referenced in their texts. However, as Latour points out, a researcher's credibility will also depend on *subsequent* literature, as other scholars refer to his or her work. If an article is praised by prominent figures in the field and widely cited in the discipline, then the author's credibility is enhanced. But if the article is criticized—or worse, ignored altogether—then the author's credibility is diminished.

What is true for academics is even truer for political figures. Scholars see their ethos co-constructed in relatively obscure journals and academic presses. But politicians must contend with a wider array of mass-media technologies, technologies that gather and publicly distribute many competing interpretations of their character and credibility. Indeed, in the context of mass-mediated journalism, notions of self-made ethos are simply problematic. Granted, politicians still attempt to project credibility in their often staged rhetorical performances. But they cannot entirely control how the press portrays their character or (re)constitutes their discourse—before, after, or even during a speech. Scholars of rhetoric and media have long recognized that journalists play a key role in shaping images of public figures (Bennett, Lawrence, & Livingston 2007; Edelman 1988; Entman 2004; Jamieson & Waldman 2003; Kaufer, Parry-Giles, & Beigman Kelbanov 2012; Parry-Giles 2000). According to Parry-Giles (2000), the media has the unique ability to "naturalize" a politician's image—to the point that this image comes to dominate our "evolving collective memory" (206). We can say with confidence, then, that the ethos of public figures doesn't fully belong to them or emanate exclusively from them. It is shaped and reshaped by a range of "alien" voices in the mainstream press (Bakhtin 1981, 276).

With this in mind, I introduce the term *intertextual ethos*—the notion that one's ethos is constituted within and across texts by a range of mass-media voices. As I explain below, these voices don't necessarily speak in unison. In fact, we may say that different voices battle over ethos, competing to ensure that their own version of a person's character prevails. Thus, when we look across media texts, we may find divergent characterizations of people, what Parry-Giles (2000) calls "varied and antithetical" images (206). However, mass-media voices can also converge in ways that solidify a person's credibility and constitute the trustworthiness of a rhetorical event. To illustrate these possibilities, I focus on a small (but influential) set of news reports surrounding Colin Powell's U.N. address, paying particular attention to the multimodal evaluative discourse therein. I find that the news narratives generally authorized Colin Powell as a rhetor, but discredited the Iraqi leadership. This ethos building and ethos destroying was partly accomplished by journalistic voices as they explicitly evaluated Powell and Iraq. But it was also accomplished indirectly through *transitive chains of authority* in which journalists lent their authorial credibility to other textual voices that shared their attitudes.

Locating Intertextual Ethos: The Act-Person Connection and Value-Based Discourse

Swearingen (1994) observes that the concept of *voice* is "intrinsic to ethos" (115). But in an intertextual world, ethotic voice cannot refer exclusively to the author's discursive persona. As Bakhtin (1981) emphasizes, texts are necessarily infused with a "diversity of voices" representing various "socio-ideological positions" (300).[5] This is particularly true in press reports, where the voice of the journalist alternates with voices attributed to other speakers (e.g., politicians). We must attempt to understand how these multiple and competing discursive voices interact with and interpenetrate one another to create various ethotic effects. In other words, we must account for intertextual ethos, the "polyphonic" development of character that emerges both within and across mass mediated texts (Bakhtin 1984, 6).

As noted, the concept of "intertextual ethos" has roots in Aristotelian rhetoric. Aristotle was perhaps the first to suggest that one's credibility is created dialogically by multiple rhetors in the public arena. However, I also draw the concept of intertextual ethos from the work of Chaim Perelman and Lucie Olbrechts-Tyteca (1969), who more clearly suggest how ethos is complicated by processes of recontextualization.[6] Perelman and Olbrechts-Tyteca explain that audiences generally presume an "act-person interaction," whereby a person's acts are considered to be revelatory of that person's stable character or ethos. For them, the presumed interaction between speaker and speech act is "perhaps the most characteristic part of argumentation" (317). The speaker is assumed to be "the best context for evaluating the meaning . . . of an assertion," while at the same time the assertion is thought to be indicative of the speaker's character (317).

Crucially, Perelman and Olbrechts-Tyteca argue that the act-person connection is complicated when a speaker repeats another person's words in a new context. In fact, they assert that "the words of other people, when repeated by a speaker, have changed their meaning," since in repeating those words, the speaker inevitably "adopts toward them a position that is in some way new" (317). Later, in words reminiscent of Bakhtin, they make this point emphatically: "The statement made is in fact not the same coming from one person as from another; its meaning does change. There is not just a simple transfer of values, but a reinterpretation in a new context, which is provided by what one knows of the presumed author" (318). As I see it, implicit in these passages is the concept of intertextual ethos. However, to uncover this concept, we must further develop Perelman and Olbrechts-Tyteca's reasoning about the speaker-speech connection.

The Belgian authors suggest that the meaning of an utterance changes when that utterance is repeated by a new speaker. The new speaker provides a new context for the speech and, thus, alters its meaning and significance. By saying this, Perelman and Olbrechts-Tyteca highlight what happens to the original meaning of an utterance, but they fail to point out what happens to the original *speaker* of that utterance. After all, if the interaction between speech and speaker is assumed, then any time we recontextualize someone else's utterance, we not only reframe that utterance, but also, indirectly, redefine the original utterance's *source*. By the same token, any time we evaluate (praise or blame) a *person*, we not only project that person's ethos, but also signal to our audience how they should interpret that person's *speech*.

Analytically, this means that to study intertextual ethos we should examine not only how rhetors characterize people, but also how they evaluate artistic performances. Thus, if we say that Colin Powell's speech is sloppy and unpersuasive, we also indicate something about Powell's rhetorical ethos. And, if we say Colin Powell is a notorious liar, we imply something about the veracity of his speech. In either case, the way we construct *our own* ethos will influence whether the audience will accept our judgments of other speakers and texts. To clarify matters, we might call the ethos a rhetor constructs for him- or herself *authorial ethos*, or the ethos of the authorial voice. Authorial ethos amounts to artistic self-presentation within a single text. Meanwhile, *intertextual ethos* is co-constructed: it emerges both within and across mass-mediated texts as different voices struggle to characterize a person and his or her discourse. Ultimately, any public figure's ethos will at least partly depend on other ethoses in the intertextual universe of the mass media. For example, a journalist with a good reputation and a credible authorial ethos can discredit a political figure with a stinging editorial criticism. The ethos of this political figure at least partly depends on the ethos of the journalist. (Of course, a journalist with a bad reputation and an untrustworthy authorial voice might discredit political figures by *praising* them.)

As noted, the chorus of voices that struggle over ethos can be discerned within a single text. An authorial voice regulates and refracts other textual voices, valorizing certain voices over others and guiding the audience on how to evaluate different characters (Bakhtin 1981, 292). In this regard, intertextual ethos hinges on two important points. First, following Fairclough (2003), we must consider which voices are represented in a given text and which are left out. This reveals something about intertextual ethos in that it reflects how the authorial voice implicitly sanctions voices actually represented in the text, while implicitly rejecting the authority of those voices excluded from the text.

Second, we must consider how the authorial voice "frames" other textual voices. As Fairclough notes, different voices can be represented in a positive or negative light, as different *values* are attached to different speakers and discourses. This is consistent with Aristotle's (2007) rhetorical theory, which posits that values can be "points of reference" for assigning blame and praise (1.9.1). By indicating their value positions, rhetors help enact their own ethos[7] as well as the ethos of any other textual speaker.[8] Such value signaling is evident in my earlier example, when I hypothetically referred to Powell as "a notorious liar." By choosing this representation of Powell, I referenced a value system that I believe my audience shares. Specifically, by suggesting that Powell violates shared social norms, I positioned my audience to be *opposed* to Powell—to find his character objectionable and contrary to *our* values.

To account for such value-based discourse, I draw on Martin and White's (2005) framework for attitude analysis. According to this scheme, there are three main "regions" of evaluative vocabulary: affect, judgment, and appreciation. *Affect* involves resources for construing emotional responses (happy/sad).[9] *Judgment* involves resources for evaluating human behavior according to shared community norms (right/wrong). *Appreciation* involves resources for assigning value to things—including natural phenomena and rhetorical performances (thorough/superficial). Typically, attitudes are *explicitly inscribed* in a text via core evaluative vocabulary (e.g., Powell's arguments were *logical*: positive appreciation). Other times, attitudes are *implicitly invoked* without such precise signals (e.g., Powell's conclusions followed from his premises: positive appreciation). (Readers who want more detail about linguistic and visual attitude analysis can consult appendix D.) Identifying verbal-visual attitudes allows us to trace how rhetors establish ethos for other speakers.[10] I shall often refer to attitudes when I analyze intertextual ethos in the news narratives that directly commented on Powell's U.N. address. But I begin my analysis with a more general discussion of Powell's pre-speech reputation.

Powell's Prior Reputation: An Intertextual Phenomenon

Even before Powell spoke at the U.N., his superb reputation had surely influenced American audiences. As pointed out in the beginning of this chapter, Powell was an enormously credible public figure with a compelling biography. The son of poor Jamaican immigrants, he overcame poverty and racism and rose to the highest echelons of military and civilian life. In 1989, he became the first African American (and the youngest person ever) to serve as chairman of the Joint Chiefs of Staff. Two years later, the four-star general orchestrated the Persian Gulf War, pushing Iraqi forces out of Kuwait and claiming victory in just forty-three days (Bumiller 2011). Feelings of nationalism surged,[11] and Powell's reputation soared. He was now introduced as a war hero, touted as a possible presidential candidate, honored on stamps and baseball cards, lionized in dozens of biographies, and even transformed into a GI Joe–like action figure by the toy maker Hasbro (Key 2000). His "success story" so resonated with Americans that his 1995 autobiography, *My American Journey*, became an instant best seller, and throughout the late 1990s audiences came in droves to listen to his lectures about life. By 2001, Powell was the public speaker that Americans most wanted to hear (Gillespie 2001), and when Americans were asked to name people they thought of as heroes, he was cited more frequently than any other living person (Taylor 2001).[12]

Powell was also regarded as one of the greatest American military generals of all time ("Greatest American" 2000), famous for his doctrine of using overwhelming force to defeat an enemy (Schmitt 1999). However, as Zarefsky (2007) indicates, when Powell became the first African American to serve as secretary of state, serving under George W. Bush, Americans likely considered him not a warrior, but a "dove."[13] It was well known that, before the Persian Gulf War, Powell had initially opposed military force in Iraq, favoring a strategy of deterrence and containment (Layne 1991). And it had also been widely reported that, in the new Bush administration, Powell alone was slowing the sprint to war.[14] Powell's apparent restraint earned him international recognition (Burkerman, MacAskill, & Henley 2002; Tibbetts 2002; Watson 2002)—and the confidence of the American public. One poll released just before Powell's address suggested that, when it came to U.S. policy toward Iraq, "Americans trusted Powell more than George W. Bush by a margin of 63 to 24 percent" (DeYoung 2007, 448).

Powell, then, had acquired a towering global reputation: as an accomplished African American who had defied the odds, a heroic general who had reestablished American military preeminence, and a man of principle who would only wage war as a last resort. But to understand *how* this reputation actually emerged, how it entered American consciousness, we must examine the mass-mediated discourse that characterized Powell, specifically the narratives that accumulated over many years in the mainstream press (Amossy 2001, 7). For example,[15] there is the 1989 ABC News profile in which Sam Donaldson extols Powell's "leadership, diplomacy, and intellect," and asserts that the general is the right man to lead the armed forces. There is the piece in *USA Today* that praises Powell's victory in the Persian Gulf and applauds his "direct, decisive, authoritative" leadership (Moss 1991). There are the scores of stories—starting in 1991 and peaking in 1995[16]—that cover Powell's potential run for the presidency: a flattering interview on *20/20* that describes Powell as a "devoted family man" and a "determined warrior" (Walters 1995); an article in *Newsweek* titled, "Can Colin Powell Save America?" (Klein 1994); a front-page *Wall Street Journal* piece titled "Moral Authority: Many Voters Believe Powell Could Bridge the Nation's Racial Divide" (Gaiter & Seib 1995).[17] There are the stories that reaffirm his status upon becoming secretary of state as "a black decorated war hero with universal appeal and impeccable credentials" (Pellegrini 2000). Finally, there are the stories that identify Powell as "a dove among hawks" in the Bush administration (e.g., Kibby 2001), and, in the weeks before his speech, as a "reluctant warrior" finally convinced of the need for battle (e.g., Schneider 2003).

With journalism like this it is easy to see why so many perceived Powell to be a credible speaker. His positive reputation had been reified again and again in the mainstream news. However, as we read these pre-speech news accounts, we also see that Powell's ethos is never entirely fixed. Within the sea of positive narratives about Powell's character, one discovers occasional waves of criticism. His status as a "war hero" is called into question as Powell is repeatedly criticized for failing to "go after" Saddam Hussein in the first Gulf War (e.g., Safire 1994). And his "unassailable" moral standards are also challenged. Some question his opposition to ending the ban on gays in the military (Trotta 1995); others point out that his doctrine of "overwhelming force" caused unnecessary civilian casualties in the Gulf War (McCarthy 1995).[18] Even more damning, some journalists accuse him of turning a blind eye to the My Lai massacre in Vietnam (Lane 1995), and covering up the Iran-Contra affair during the Reagan administration (Hitchens 2000). Even Powell's role as "dove" in the administration is at least qualified. As one speaker in a 2002 story asserts, Powell has "never fought the concept of war" in Iraq; he merely insists that the war be prosecuted with international support (Slavin 2002). These more critical representations of Powell's ethos were circulated far less frequently, but they are not negligible—and they may help to explain why at least some Americans disapproved of Powell in the days leading up to his speech.

Ultimately, Powell's pre-speech reputation was constituted *across texts*—by a host of intertextual voices. In this sense, Powell's reputation is not an object that "belongs" to him, but a vast array of intertextual representations that coalesce unevenly over many years in the mainstream press. His good name was likely "static" for most Americans, but not for all. And, in the twenty-four-hour period surrounding his address, Powell's credibility—strong as it was—could yet be altered. Of course, in his speech, Powell would work to reenact a positive ethos for himself.[19] But even this artistic ethos "belonged" to Powell only in a limited sense. Powell's discourse—and his display of ethos at the U.N.—would not reach American audiences unmediated. In the hours *before* he spoke, his U.N. presentation was already being evaluated in the press (see chapter 3). *During* his speech, journalists intervened again, supplying captions and re-representations of his talk on live TV.[20] And *after* his speech, his words were lifted from his presentation once more and reinterpreted in news narratives. Whatever ethos Powell himself projected was inevitably transformed by these processes.

Add to this the fact that Powell delivered his address on a Wednesday morning, while most American adults were busy at work, and we begin to see just how powerful the chorus of "outside" intertextual voices can be. Indeed, Americans may not have had an opportunity to listen to Powell, but they did have occasion to hear *other rhetors*—specifically journalists—reinforce Powell's credibility at length. I turn now to some of the most influential mainstream news narratives and closely examine how various voices competed and interacted to characterize both Powell and the Iraqi leadership.

Enacting One's Own Ethos: Self-Promotion

First, let's consider the ethos of the journalists who reported on Powell's speech. As noted, a journalist's credibility ultimately influences whether audiences accept the characterizations of other speakers and texts represented in that journalist's report. Most likely, the journalists in this study already enjoyed a strong prior reputation based on the status and popularity of their news organizations (see the introduction). Thus, I concentrate on how the journalists construed their own ethos artistically within the news texts. Specifically, I focus on journalists' attitudes about themselves and their colleagues. Following Perelman and Olbrechts-Tyteca (1969), I assume that attitudes expressed about the news narratives (acts) are also suggestive of attitudes about the journalists responsible for producing those narratives (person). Thus, this analysis also includes journalists' attitudes about their own work.

I focused on three main types of news providers: individual journalists, invited consultants, and the news institutions themselves. *Individual journalists* were responsible for reporting the hard news "objectively." These are the people we generally think of when we think of "journalists proper": anchors, field correspondents, and press writers. On NBC newscasts, journalists presented information alongside *invited consultants*, who presented "expert opinions" about current events. Since these invited consultants were anointed with journalistic titles (e.g., "NBC Analyst"), they were basically indistinguishable from other NBC reporters.[21] Finally, there were the *journalistic institutions* themselves: NBC, the *New York Times*, and CNN. Though more abstract than actual reporters and consultants, these wider institutions could nevertheless be characterized ethotically.

In table 2.1, I tally the negative and positive attitudes expressed about these three groups in each news narrative.

Table 2.1. Journalists' Attitudes about Themselves

Appraiser	Journalist/ Reporter		Invited Consultant		News Institution		**Total for Each News Story**
	Appraised						
	Neg.	Pos.	Neg.	Pos.	Neg.	Pos.	
NBC News (2.4)	0	1	0	0	0	3	**4+**
NBC News (2.5)	0	0	0	3	0	3	**6+**
NBC News (SR 2.5)	0	2	0	12	0	2	**16+**
NYT (2.5)	0	0			0	1*	**1+**
NYT (2.6)	0	0			0	1*	**1+**
CNN.com (2.5)	0	0			0	1	**1+**
CNN.com (2.6)	0	2			0	1	**3+**
Totals by Category	**0**	**5**	**0**	**15**	**0**	**12**	**32+**

*Attitude is expressed outside the body of the news narrative in the masthead of the newspaper.

Perhaps not surprisingly, the journalists in this study never evaluated themselves (or each other) negatively. They did, however, express positive attitudes about themselves and their reporting—if sparingly ($n = 32$). In other words, the journalists expended some rhetorical labor not just to report the news, but to indicate to their audiences that they were *qualified* as news reporters.

This ethotic move is not always explicit—and often entails invoked positive judgments of the journalists themselves. For instance, the byline of one CNN.com article reads: "CNN **Senior** White House Correspondent John King and National Security Correspondent David Ensor contributed to this report" (CNN/2.6/JKDE). In this example, I have bolded the only inscribed positive attitude—the word "Senior," which is a positive judgment of *capacity*. In other words, this word indicates that John King has experience that makes him an especially capable White House correspondent.[22] However, I also coded "National Security Correspondent"—the description of David Ensor—as an invoked token of positive judgment. Even though there is no explicitly positive lexical resource in this title, it nevertheless suggests that Ensor has a special capacity—a unique credential—that qualifies him as a reporter.

Similarly, on the NBC newscasts, Tom Brokaw typically offered some positive remark about a given reporter's ethos as he introduced that reporter to the public. For instance, in introducing Andrea Mitchell just after Powell's speech, Brokaw said, "We're going to go to NBC's Andrea Mitchell now, who is our **Chief** Foreign Affairs Correspondent *who has been tracking this minute by minute, and hour by hour, day in and day out*" (NBC SR/2.5/TB). Here, Mitchell's authority as a journalist is constituted with an inscribed judgment of positive capacity ("Chief"), but also with an invoked judgment of positive tenacity (underlined text). In other words, Mitchell's ethos is constructed in ways that suggest that she is both experienced and tireless in her journalistic efforts. In fact, Brokaw expressed positive judgments about reporters like Mitchell, but also about news-affiliated consultants. For example, General Barry McCaffrey is described not only as an "NBC News Consultant," but also as a "one of the **key** American military commanders during Operation Desert Storm" (NBC SR/2.5/TB). Likewise, other consultants were praised. For instance, former congressman Lee Hamilton is described as "**one of the most highly regarded** members of the Washington community" (NBC SR/2.5/TB). Indeed, on NBC, *anyone* explicitly brought on to report or analyze the news was judged positively. In a sense, people were not allowed to speak to the television audience until Brokaw had made clear *why* their speech was authoritative or trustworthy.

The *New York Times* was the only news outlet that did not explicitly express a positive attitude about its journalists. However, in a slogan on the masthead at the top of the paper the *Times* includes the following famous motto: "All the News That's Fit to Print." I included this as an asterisked token of positive attitude since the phrase appears on the same page as the news stories about Powell—but is not included in the body of the actual news narratives. Nevertheless, the motto signals that the *Times* is a credible news institution. Here, by expressing a positive appreciation of the news stories in its pages (fit to print)—the *Times* suggests something about its own authority to assess the newsworthiness of certain stories. In other words, the *Times* is saying that the reader can trust its judgment when it comes to deciding what is and is not news.

Interestingly, news organizations also employed visual resources to constitute themselves as authoritative news providers. One good example of this occurs on NBC's *Nightly News*, when Tom Brokaw unveils a segment called "Iraq Watch." In this segment, as Brokaw verbally describes how Powell's speech is being received by the international community, a virtual radar screen appears above his left shoulder—and a virtual radar vector spins clockwise, presumably to "pick up" Iraq-related news stories all over the gridded globe (see excerpt 2.1).

This visual clearly suggests something positive about NBC's ethos as a news provider—one with the commitment and (technological) capacity to locate stories around the world and present them to the public.[23]

Enacting Others' Ethos: Characterizing the Disputants

By evaluating themselves positively, the journalists positioned audiences to accept them as authoritative and credible. Having constituted themselves as such, they also positioned audiences to accept *their judgments of other characters* in the news as equally credible. Thus, we now move from individual ethos development (in which rhetors characterize themselves) to intertextual ethos development (in which rhetors labor to characterize other agents). In this case, powerful rhetors—journalists—enact others' ethos by evaluating voices and texts brought into their news accounts "from the outside." Here, I am particularly interested in the ways journalists characterized Colin Powell and Iraqis—the two principal disputants in the conflict. By constituting a positive or negative ethos for either disputant, the journalistic texts potentially positioned the audience to align

Excerpt 2.1. (NBC/2.5/TB)

Frame	Soundtrack
	How's it playing?

Table 2.2. Journalists' Attitudes about Powell and Iraq

	Appraised			
Appraiser	Powell/Powell's Presentation		Iraq/Saddam/Iraqi Rebuttals	
	Neg.	Pos.	Neg.	Pos.
NBC	0	48	32	2
NYT	2	15	3	0
CNN.com	0	8	3	0
Total for News Voices	**2**	**71**	**38**	**2**

itself on either side of the debate over future war. Table 2.2 presents results in this category. (For additional details, consult appendix E.)

The various journalistic institutions differ in terms of how frequently they expressed attitudes about Powell and Iraq. The reporters on NBC offered numerous evaluations (82); the NYT journalists employed evaluations less frequently (20); and the CNN.com reporters expressed attitudes relatively sparingly (11). Nevertheless, across all three news sources, there is a very clear discrepancy in how journalists evaluated Colin Powell and his speech as opposed to the Iraqis and their response. In fact, the journalists expressed attitudes about Powell and his performance that were overwhelmingly positive (71/73); meanwhile, they expressed attitudes about Iraqis and their speech acts that were overwhelmingly negative (38/40). In addition, they expressed attitudes about Powell *more frequently* than they did attitudes about Iraq (75:40). Thus, they endowed Powell's positive ethos with a special rhetorical presence in their texts (Perelman & Olbrechts-Tyteca 1969). I examine a few illustrations of this trend below.

Perhaps the most interesting phenomenon is that the journalists in this study—who frequently credit themselves with objectivity—practically fawned over Colin Powell and his speech. For instance, following Powell's address, the *Times* reported:

> Overall, the picture that emerged today in the Council—and also on television screens across the nation and around the world—was that an administration that for many weeks had tried and failed to persuade skeptics of the urgency of the Iraq problem was now getting a chance to **lay out**

> **its indictment** of Iraqi conduct. It came in the form of a **nearly encyclopedic catalog** that **reached further than many had expected**. (NYT/2.6/SW)

Here, I have bolded only those attitudes that can reasonably be categorized as evaluations of *Powell's speech* (there are other attitudes expressed in the passage, as well). First, note how the verbal process and wording chosen to represent the administration's speech act—*to lay out its indictment*—subtly endorses the content of that speech act. The *Times* not only refers to Powell's speech as an indictment (a nominalization suggesting that Powell is some kind of prosecutor),[24] but it also suggests that this indictment was *laid out*. This choice of lexical resources indicates that Powell organized his argument in a compelling way.[25] If this doesn't seem immediately apparent, just imagine the other verbal processes that might have been chosen but were not: *to make an argument* about Iraqi misconduct, *to make a claim* about Iraqi misconduct, *to charge* Iraq with misconduct, and so on.[26]

In addition to this endorsement of Powell's speech act, the *Times* also includes explicitly positive appreciations of Powell's presentation both in terms of its composition (*encyclopedic*) and its impact (*reached further than many had expected*). In addition, the *Times* referred to Powell's presentation as an "**extraordinary** public revelation of the C.I.A.'s tools" (NYT/2.6/SW)—and thereby positively evaluated both the impact and the quality of the evidence in Powell's case. Finally, the *Times* offered that "part of the impact of his materials was that they seemed in some ways to **evoke the U-2 photographs presented by Adlai E. Stevenson** in this same chamber in 1962" (NYT/2.6/SW). In this case, the *Times* invokes a positive attitude about Powell's case by enacting what Van Leeuwen (2007) calls a "moralized comparison" (99)—essentially painting Powell's speech as positive by comparing it favorably to a different speech in which an American diplomat famously presented compelling (and true) evidence of hidden weapons.

Similar positive appreciations of Powell's case were rare, but evident on CNN, which referred to Powell's allegation of Iraq's links to terrorism as "the **most detailed** explanation yet" offered by the Bush administration (CNN/2.6/JKDE). Meanwhile, positive assessments of Powell's case proliferated on NBC, which commented on the impact of Powell's speech (e.g. *critical*, NBC/2.4/TB; *important*, NBC/2.5/TB), the composition of Powell's speech (*detailed*, NBC/2.5/JM; *comprehensive*, NBC SR/2.5/DF), and the value of Powell's evidence (*compelling*,

NBC SR/2.5/DF; *powerful*, NBC SR/2.5/DK; *a bill of particulars*, NBC SR/2.5/TB; etc). Needless to say, these positive evaluations of Powell's presentation positioned the viewer to regard his case as convincing and to regard Powell himself as credible and authoritative.

However, the journalists did not stop at expressing positive attitudes about Powell's case; they also expressed positive attitudes about Powell, the person. For instance, in NBC's "Special Report," NBC analyst David Kay remarks—before Powell has even delivered his speech—that "the most compelling piece of evidence is actually going to be **the integrity of Colin Powell**" (NBC SR/2.5/DK). Then, literally seconds after Powell's address, Brokaw calls Powell the "**chief prosecutor** for the Bush administration" (NBC SR/2.5/TB). A bit later, Lee Hamilton—an invited analyst—describes Powell as follows: "the administration's **most persuasive** advocate who has the **greatest credibility in the world**, the **dove in the administration**" (NBC SR/2.5/LH). In each of these instances, there is at least one positive judgment about Powell's character—including positive attitudes about his capacity as a speaker and arguer (*chief prosecutor*, *most persuasive*), his trustworthiness (*credibility*), and even his ethics (*integrity*, *dove*). Once again, assuming act-person interaction, these positive representations of Powell's personal *ethos* position audiences to regard Powell's *case* as convincing, accurate, and, perhaps, even morally righteous. More importantly, it is obvious that Powell is not the only person responsible for enacting his ethos. Instead, journalists labored to create Powell's "sterling reputation," both before and after his speech.

In contrast, journalists *negatively* evaluated Saddam Hussein, Iraq, and the Iraqi response to Powell's allegations. In some cases, journalists expressed explicitly negative attitudes about Iraq by using unflattering epithets. For instance, CNN referred to the "**Iraqi regime**" (CNN/2.5/NA), a term that invokes a negative judgment of Iraq's propriety since the word is almost always used to describe states that are especially oppressive.[27] Such negative epithets were used only rarely to describe Iraq, but they were *never* used to describe the United States. Indeed, it is hard to imagine a U.S. journalist referring to the "American regime."

The journalists' negative judgments about Iraq more usually referred to that country's alleged weapons of mass destruction (WMDs). In fact, the news narratives often *assumed* that Iraq was hiding WMDs or posing some threat, and thus invoked negative judgments about Iraq's ethos. For instance, NBC analyst Richard Butler comments before Powell's speech that the case against Iraq is already "substantially proven" because, as he baldly asserts, the Iraqis "**have weapons of mass destruction**" (NBC SR/2.5/RB). Given that this is precisely what Iraq was denying at the time, Butler's assertion positions the audience to view Iraq as both threatening and deceptive. Even Tom Brokaw assumes that Iraq presents a threat to the United States. He says before Powell's address: "The administration recognizes that it must still persuade the American people war is not only likely, but now the best means of dealing with **the dangers that Iraq poses**" (NBC SR/2.5/TB). Here, the notion that Iraq poses dangers is presupposed—what is at issue is whether or not war is the best means of dealing with those dangers.[28]

Interestingly, the journalists rarely offered explicit evaluations of Iraqi speech acts, such as the rebuttals offered by Saddam Hussein, Tariq Aziz, Amir al-Saadi, and Mohammed Aldouri. In some of the news narratives in this study, these rebuttals were not mentioned—and thus could not be evaluated. And, for those news texts that did report them, they typically avoided assessing whether the retorts were good or bad. Thus, while Powell's argument was represented as a *compelling, powerful, persuasive case*, the Iraqis' rebuttal was represented simply as a response. Of course, when journalists did advance attitudes about the Iraqi response to Powell's charges, those attitudes were negative. For example, Brokaw refers to Iraq's rebuttal as "**mocking** of the United States" (NBC/2.5/TB)—a representation that likely positioned his American audience to regard the Iraqi response as offensive. Once again, Iraq's reputation is not exclusively created by the Iraqis themselves; nor does it come ready-made before the journalists speak. Instead, journalists actively work to define a negative Iraqi ethos for their American audience.

In the televised newscasts, the visual data tended to reinforce a sense of moral "polarization" between Powell's positive character, and the negative character of the Iraqis (Van Dijk 1998). Take the frames from the lead-in to NBC's nightly newscast that aired in the evening after Powell's address (excerpt 2.2). The commas in the spoken text represent pauses; *italicized* text represents extra vocal emphasis.

In the first frame, Brokaw offers a kind of headline for the entire news segment: "Text, Lies & Videotape." There are two things worth noting about this headline: (1) its play on "sex, lies and videotape" positions the viewer to regard this news story as salacious, juicy, and entertaining, and (2) the word

Excerpt 2.2. (NBC/2.5/TB)

Frame	**Soundtrack**
	**Brokaw:** Text, lies, and videotape
	*Sec*retary of State Powell tells the U.N.
	Saddam *hides weapons*, de*ceives* inspectors,
	and supports *ter*rorists.

Note: To save space I have removed some of the frames.

"Lies" suggests a negative judgment of Iraq's veracity, positioning the viewer to regard Iraq as deceptive. Interestingly, it is the visual data in this frame that directs the reader to associate the word "lies" with Iraq. Specifically, the word "Lies" is colored green, creating an eye-rhyme and thus a semantic link with the green color of the Iraqi flag that waves in the background. In addition, the image of Saddam Hussein—raising his arm in a Hitler-esque salute—is co-deployed with the text. Indeed, he is the only human figure on the screen, and thus the only person who may be interpreted as the "liar."

A moment later, in frame 2, Powell appears on the screen holding up, and apparently speaking about, a model vial of "anthrax." (If the viewer was not aware that this was Powell, Brokaw makes it clear by uttering Powell's name as his image appears on screen.) The nameplate reading "United States" in the shot with Powell guides the viewer in understanding that Powell is not *of Iraq*, but is an American talking *about*

Iraq. More importantly, Powell's reported allegation—specifically that Saddam *deceives* inspectors—is semantically linked to the word "lies" in NBC's headline. Indeed, *lies* and *deceives* are synonymous.

Thus, Brokaw suggests a "SADDAM LIES" thematic formation[29] through a verbal-visual link between the word "lies" and an image of Saddam Hussein. Then, moments later Brokaw reports Colin Powell's synonymous allegation that Saddam deceives. In this way, Brokaw not only denigrates Saddam Hussein's character; he also represents Colin Powell as an agent who tells the truth. After all, if the viewer accepts as true Brokaw's verbal-visual implication that Saddam/Iraq lies, then the viewer should also accept as true Powell's synonymous assertion that Saddam deceives. I'll have more to say about this in the discussion of transitive chains of authority below.

Non-Authorial Voices: Representing the Intertextual Struggle for Ethos

The above example illustrates that the authorial voices of journalists are not the only ones that appear in news narratives. In fact, news narratives almost always feature attributed voices—what I shall refer to as *non-authorial voices*. While authorial voices "narrate" the story and speak directly to the audience, non-authorial voices do not address audiences in the same fashion. In fact, non-authorial voices appear to have originated in some other context, and are merely *cited* by the author in the present discursive interaction. For example, whenever I quote Aristotle in this book, you immediately recognize his voice as non-authorial. That is, you recognize that his words originate elsewhere and that his voice is separate from my authorial voice. Similarly, in the context of journalism, non-authorial voices emerge from "sources" whose words have been recontextualized and re-represented by reporters.

As indicated in table 2.3,[30] signaling a non-authorial voice often involves representing a sayer, a verbal process, and speech that is (usually) either quoted or reported.

In the table a number of attitudes are being expressed—all negative judgments about Iraq—but, in each case, the judgment is attributed to a non-authorial speaker, Powell. Now, we begin to see that it is not just journalists who work to establish others' ethos. Instead, *multiple voices*

Table 2.3. Example of Reported Speech

Sayer	Verbal Process	Receiver	Reported Speech
Secretary of State Powell	tells	the U.N	Iraq *hides weapons*[t –JUDGMENT: veracity], *deceives inspectors* [t –JUDGMENT: veracity] and *supports terrorists* [t –JUDGMENT: propriety]

struggle to constitute the ethos of a given social actor. Since journalists incorporate these non-authorial voices into their texts, they can't help but reveal traces of this struggle over ethos. However, journalists, as the architects of news content, manage how this struggle over ethos is represented. In Bakhtin's (1981) terms, they orchestrate the polyphony of voices—controlling whether and to what degree the full spectrum of ethotic opinions finds expression.

I identified four categories of non-authorial voices: U.S. voices (which include Powell's voice), U.N. voices, Iraqi voices, and international voices. Table 2.4 indicates the kinds of attitudes that each of these groups reportedly expressed about Colin Powell and Iraq. (For additional details, consult appendix E.)

Overall, the results indicate that non-authorial speakers produced slightly more positive attitudes about Colin Powell and his speech (29) than negative ones (21). Most positive evaluations of Powell were attributed to U.S. voices—typically U.S. politicians. Meanwhile, *almost all* of the negative evaluations of Colin Powell were attributed to Iraqi voices—and roughly half of them were attributed to Iraqi voices in a single news narrative (NBC/2.5). Not surprisingly, then, there is an evident polarization between Iraqi voices and U.S. voices when it comes to attitudes about Powell's presentation. This polarization is equally clear when it comes to attitudes about Iraq and the Iraqi rebuttal. Almost all of the negative evaluations of Iraq were attributed to U.S. voices, while nearly all positive evaluations of Iraq were attributed to Iraqi voices. However, overall, there are *far more* negative evaluations of Iraq than there are positive ones (141:12). This is because the news narratives were dominated by U.S. voices—especially Powell's—while Iraqi voices were far less present. Consequently, audiences were exposed to negative evaluations of Iraq more than they were exposed to any other kind of attitude.

Table 2.4. Attitudes of Non-Authorial Voices in News Narratives

Appraiser	Powell/Powell's Presentation		Iraq/Saddam/Iraqi Rebuttals	
	Neg.	Pos.	Neg.	Pos.
U.S. Voices*	2	22	130	0
U.N. Voices	1	6	9	2
Iraqi Voices	17	0	0	10
International Voices	1	1	2	0
Total for Non-Authorial Voices	**21**	**29**	**141**	**12**

(Column group heading: Appraised)

*Powell's voice is included among U.S. voices.

It is easy to see the variable status of Powell's ethos, when we examine Iraqi voices and their attitudes about Powell's presentation. Indeed, Powell's good reputation is potentially threatened by these voices as they labor to characterize Powell in decidedly negative terms. Of course, since these voices came from Iraqi sources—sources that were consistently discredited in the news stories—they had little hope of changing American attitudes about Powell. Still, their existence is not negligible. They indicate that the nature of Powell's ethos was fought over discursively in a rather polemic intertextual battle. Were it not for other intertextual voices—including those that already enacted Powell's positive ethos in prior mass-mediated texts, as well as those that worked to reenact his ethos in the present discursive moment—these Iraqi voices might have carried the day in defining Powell's character and rhetorical performance.

The most stunning anti-Powell assertions appear in the NBC evening news broadcast following Powell's address, when a number of negative appreciations of Powell's presentation are attributed to General Amir al-Saadi. For instance, al-Saadi is reported to have called Powell's speech "**nonsense**" (NBC/2.5/RA) and is reported to have said that "any **third-rate intelligence agency** could have produced such **fabrications**" as were evident in Powell's address (NBC/2.5/RA). In addition, al-Saadi is also represented on video saying that "this was a **typical American show complete with stunts and special effects**" (NBC/2.5/AS). In both instances, al-Saadi suggests something negative not only about the evidence in Powell's case (*nonsense, fabrications, show*), but also about the character of the people who produced that evidence (*third-rate*).

This NBC news broadcast was unique in that it attributed to Iraqis so many negative evaluations of Powell and his address. Most of the other news narratives featured non-authorial speakers who expressed more positive evaluations of Powell than negative ones. Sometimes, the positive attitudes about Powell were attributed to U.N. delegates. For instance, the *Times* reports the following: "Diplomats said the most **compelling** information **seemed to prove** that Iraq had cleaned up and removed incriminating information at countless sites, in many cases just before inspectors went there" (NYT/2.6/SW). Here an explicit positive valuation of Powell's information (*compelling*) is complimented by a positive, if "toned down," endorsement of Powell's evidence (*seemed to prove*). Among U.N. voices, there were more positive evaluations of Powell and his speech than negative ones (6:1). Meanwhile, among international voices there were only two attitudes expressed about Powell—one positive and one negative. Overall, then, the news narratives represented a world of voices—outside Iraq and the United States—expressing mostly favorable attitudes about Powell and his address.

Most of the positive evaluations of Powell were attributed to U.S. voices. Interestingly, many U.S. voices expressed positive attitudes about Powell and his presentation even *before* Powell spoke at the U.N. For example, before Powell's speech, CNN attributed several positive assessments of Powell and his case to unnamed U.S. officials. I present two examples in the bullets below:

- *Officials said* Powell's **highly technical** and **elaborate** presentation will include about 30 slides, several audiotape intercepts and satellite photographs. (CNN/2.5/NA).
- Powell has been **intimately involved** in reviewing U.S. intelligence on Iraq's alleged weapons of mass destruction program and links to terrorist groups, *officials said*. (CNN/2.5/NA).

In the first bullet above, CNN attributes a positive appreciation of Powell's case to "officials." More specifically, the officials comment positively on the *complexity* of Powell's presentation. Then, in the second bullet, CNN attributes a token of positive judgment about Powell (suggesting his *tenacity* in preparing for the presentation).

Following Powell's address, other American voices were represented in the news narratives, again lauding Powell and his presentation. For example, NBC reported that "almost all Republicans and Democrats" were "**praising the strength** of Powell's case" (NBC/2.5/CB). Moments later, they featured Republican senator John Warner saying that Powell had "**laid out the facts**" (NBC/2.5/JW) and Democratic senator Dianne Feinstein saying that Powell had presented a "**very impressive** chain of evidence" (NBC/2.5/DF).

Meanwhile, non-authorial voices very rarely expressed positive attitudes about Iraq. And, almost always, these positive evaluations of Iraq came from Iraqis themselves. For instance, the *Times* attributed the following quotation to Saddam Hussein: "There is **only one truth, and therefore I tell you** [t + judgment: veracity] as I have said on many occasions before, that **Iraq has no weapons of mass destruction** [t + judgment: propriety]" (NYT/2.5/JPSW). In this instance, Saddam Hussein presents himself as *honest*, and presents the Iraqi government as *behaving properly* according to the expectations of the international community (expressed in the first U.N. resolution). Elsewhere in the news narratives, other Iraqi voices expressed similar sentiments: presenting themselves as truthful, and their behaviors as morally respectable.

However, these positive attitudes about Iraq were, in a sense, "drowned out" by the overwhelming number of negative attitudes that were attributed to non-authorial U.S. voices in these news narratives. Most notably, Powell himself was represented in the news, expressing all sorts of negative judgments about the Iraqi leadership.[31] The instance I referred to in excerpt 2.2 is representative of this phenomenon. But, even if we put Powell's voice aside, the news narratives contained *other* U.S. voices that also condemned Iraq.[32]

For instance, even before Powell's speech, the *Times* attributed the following quotation to Deputy Secretary of State Richard L. Armitage: "Our **fear** has been, as we've tried to explain, the nexus of [Saddam Hussein's] **weapons**, his **bloody-mindedness** and **terrorist groups**" (NYT/2.5/JPSW). Here, Armitage is represented as expressing negative attitudes that are both affectual (*fear*) and judgmental (*weapons*, *bloody-mindedness*, *terrorist groups*) with regard to Iraq. Similarly negative attitudes are found elsewhere in the pre-speech coverage in the *Times*: "'There is a clear, concerted effort by Iraq to **hide component parts, weapons sites and witnesses from the inspectors**,' another official said" (NYT/2.5/JPSW). In this case an invoked negative judgment (indicating Iraq's dishonesty) is attributed to an unnamed U.S. official.

Post-speech coverage also included U.S. voices, other than Powell's, that expressed negative attitudes about Iraq. For instance, CNN gave a great deal of attention to the comments of Condoleezza Rice. Below I include an annotated excerpt from this news narrative:

> U.S. national security adviser Condoleezza Rice said **Saddam had to know what Zarqawi was doing** [t – judgment: veracity] and she accused the Iraqi leader of being **responsible for "a network that is spreading poisons throughout Europe"** [t – judgment: propriety]. "The **potential marriage of weapons of mass destruction with terrorism** [t – judgment: propriety] is everyone's **nightmare**," [t – affect: insecurity, disquiet] said Rice. She suggested that the cost of not taking action against Iraq could be **another September 11–type attack** [t – affect: insecurity, disquiet], but this time with **weapons of mass destruction that could kill tens of thousands** [t – affect: insecurity, disquiet]. . . . Saddam had one final opportunity to "come completely clean" with weapons inspectors, but **he wasted it by deceiving** them [t – judgment: veracity], she said. (CNN/2.6/JKDE)

This example includes both negative judgments suggesting the improper and immoral behavior of Saddam Hussein as well as invoked negative emotions (i.e., fear and disquiet) that could result from Iraq's immoral behavior. In other words, Rice is represented expressing attitudes that present Iraq as unethical now (*spreading poisons throughout Europe*, *deceiving*) and potentially very threatening in the future (*another September 11–type attack . . . could kill tens of thousands*).

One might ask *why* the news narratives chose to include so many non-authorial voices that condemned the Iraqi government. Likely, the press was merely indexing the bipartisan consensus in Washington about the "Iraqi threat" (Bennett 1990). In any case, such negative evaluations of Iraq were endowed with more *rhetorical presence* than any other kind of evaluation in these journalistic texts (Perelman & Olbrechts-Tyteca 1969). Thus, while the news narratives reveal traces of an intertextual struggle over ethos, they also manage that struggle in rather lopsided ways. The journalists exhibit Iraqi voices laboring to weaken Powell's ethos, but—as if to compensate—they show "rival" U.N. and U.S. voices who reenact a positive ethos for Powell. Meanwhile, the journalists present a proliferation of voices condemning Iraqi leaders, but only a few "voices in the wilderness" who vie to restore Iraqi integrity.

Ethos by Indirection: Transitive Chains of Authority

As noted, journalists can explicitly *endorse* a non-authorial speaker's words by choosing a verbal process that indicates that those words are warrantable.[33] However, it was more typical in this study for the journalists to represent attributed speech with relatively neutral verbal processes (e.g., *says*, *asserts*, *tells*), or distancing verbal processes (e.g., *claims*).[34] For example, returning once more to excerpt 2.2, a relatively neutral verbal process is used to construe Powell's speech act: "Secretary of State Powell *tells* the U.N. Iraq hides weapons, deceives inspectors, and supports terrorists."

When speech is attributed in this way it positions the audience to view the proposition being advanced as just one among a number of alternatives, as Martin and White (2005) explain:

> To the degree that the reader interprets the writer in such instances as having nothing invested in the position being advanced in the reported material . . . such acknowledgments [of other voices] allow the writer to remain aloof from any relationships of either alignment or disalignment. They present the writer as some sort of "informational fair trader" who simply conveys the views of others and who is therefore unimplicated in any relationship of solidarity which the reader may enter into with the quoted source whose viewpoint is being reported. (115)

However, Martin and White are careful to point out that even when statements are attributed to sources in more or less neutral ways, there are still myriad ways that an author can *indirectly* indicate his or her support for (or opposition to) an attributed value position. The above example is a case in point. Brokaw does not directly endorse Powell's negative evaluation of Iraq. But he does deploy visual and verbal resources which produce a negative thematic formation (IRAQ LIES) that is synonymous with the one attributed to Powell moments later (IRAQ HIDES/DECEIVES).

This is certainly an indirect endorsement of Powell—which

simultaneously positions audiences to view Powell as credible and to view Iraq as untrustworthy. This indirect ethos building (and, indeed, ethos destroying) works by what I call a *transitive chain of authority*, whereby an authorial voice lends credibility to a non-authorial voice by implication. In other words, transitive chains of authority position audiences to *infer* that certain non-authorial speakers have the endorsement of the authorial voice.[35]

Transitive chains of authority can initially be classified under two main headings: corroboration and vouching. *Corroboration* occurs when an attitude expressed by the authorial voice is elsewhere rearticulated and thus corroborated by a non-authorial voice. In other words, an evaluation advanced by the authorial voice is semantically similar to an evaluation advanced by a speaker brought in from the outside. Consequently, the audience is able to infer that the authorial voice and the non-authorial voice are "on the same side," and, thus, whatever credibility the authorial voice may have is indirectly bestowed upon the non-authorial voice that shares the author's view. The example from the NBC newscast that I've been discussing is a good illustration of corroboration. First, the authorial voice of Tom Brokaw expresses a negative judgment about Iraq, and moments later the non-authorial voice of Colin Powell is represented expressing virtually the same negative judgment. Because both speakers are essentially saying the same thing, the audience is positioned to infer that Brokaw's viewpoint is being *corroborated* by Powell. Put another way, the audience is being positioned to regard Powell's assertion as valid since it corresponds to the "facts" being reported by Brokaw (see table 2.5).

Importantly, a given authorial attitude can be corroborated by more than one non-authorial speaker, or at more than one moment in a text. Thus, if later in the newscast, the "IRAQ LIES" attitude were again attributed to Powell, it would still implicitly carry Brokaw's authorial

Table 2.5. Corroboration

Transitive Chain of Attitudes
1. Brokaw produces the attitudinal meaning "IRAQ LIES."
2. "IRAQ LIES" is also an attitudinal meaning produced by Powell.
3. Brokaw and Powell are related in their attitudinal assessment of Iraq, i.e., part of the same shared community of attitude.

credibility. And, if the "IRAQ LIES" attitude were to emerge again in the newscast—this time attributed to Donald Rumsfeld—Rumsfeld would be viewed as corroborating a position advanced by both Brokaw and Powell. And, Rumsfeld, too, would enjoy Brokaw's authorial credibility. In either case, the negative judgment of Iraq would gain added rhetorical presence.

Closely related to corroboration is vouching. *Vouching* occurs when the authorial voice of the journalist explicitly endorses a non-authorial voice, which later explicitly evaluates some other person or text. In other words, if a journalist deems one rhetor's speech as authoritative, then that rhetor's evaluations of others become more authoritative. In a sense, the journalist "vouches" for a speaker, positioning the audience to regard that speaker's evaluations *of others* as credible.

When the *Times* referred to Powell's case as a "nearly encyclopedic catalog," called Powell's revelations "extraordinary," and compared Powell's presentation to the presentation by Adlai Stevenson, it *vouched* for Colin Powell. Thus, any words attributed to Powell elsewhere in the article—and most of the words in the article *were* attributed to Powell—were implicitly "marked" by the authorial voice as credible. For instance, the *Times* reported the following elsewhere in the article: "[Powell] said various records and intelligence showed that Mr. Hussein was **making nuclear weapons** and **developing rockets and aircraft to deliver all his weapons**" (NYT/2.6/SW). By itself, this reported assertion appears to belong only to Colin Powell; the *Times* is not explicitly endorsing it. However, the explicitly positive evaluations of Powell's case cited above prepared the reader to regard this assertion as credible—as part of the "encyclopedic catalog" that was Powell's case. Ultimately, the audience is positioned to regard *Powell's* negative evaluations of Iraq as authoritative (see table 2.6).

It is worth pointing out that corroboration and vouching have their opposites: contradiction and discrediting. Thus, an attitude expressed

Table 2.6. Vouching

Transitive Chain of Attitudes
1. NYT vouches for Powell: "encyclopedic catalog."
2. Powell discredits Iraq: "making nuclear weapons."
3. NYT implicitly sanctions Powell's negative judgment of Iraq.

by a journalist may be *contradicted* by the attitude expressed by some non-authorial speaker. For instance, when General al-Saadi of the Iraqi government says during the NBC 2.5 broadcast, "We have nothing to hide," this positive judgment of Iraqi behavior stands in direct contradiction to Brokaw's verbal-visual attitude: "IRAQ LIES." The viewer, because he or she has already been positioned to trust Tom Brokaw, is "set up" to distrust the Iraqi official.

Meanwhile, instead of being vouched for, a non-authorial speaker may be *discredited* by a journalist. For instance, when Brokaw calls the Iraqi response to Powell's speech "mocking of the United States," he essentially discredits the nature of this response. Thus, moments later, when it is reported that, in issuing the Iraqi response, al-Saadi called Powell's presentation "nonsense," the viewer is positioned to disregard this negative assessment of Powell's case as something that is merely "mocking" and not substantive.

Transitive chains of authority reveal how the non-authorial voices brought into a text may be "re-perspectivized" by a text's authorial voice (Linell 1998, 151). Certainly, I cannot trace every transitive chain of authority in this corpus. However, there is really no need to. One need only compare the results in table 2.2—which indicates journalists' attitudes about Powell and Iraq—with the results in table 2.4—which indicates non-authorial attitudes about Powell and Iraq.

The pattern is clear enough: the journalists overwhelmingly evaluate Powell and his speech positively, and evaluate Iraq and its response negatively. These evaluations—even if there are only a few of them in a given report—serve as important signposts that articulate authorial attitudes and suggest to audiences how they ought to respond to the other attributed voices that appear in a news narrative. From the start, in this study, authorial voices positioned audiences to be aligned with Powell and his arguments, and opposed to Iraq and its arguments. Thus, journalists implicitly *vouched for* Colin Powell. Or indeed, they *implicitly corroborated* Powell's negative portrayals of Iraq by producing similar negative portrayals of their own. Meanwhile, journalists implicitly *discredited* the Iraqi speakers. Or indeed, their positive portrayals of Powell *contradicted* the negative portrayals attributed to Iraqi speakers. In short, insofar as audiences trusted the credibility of the journalists reporting and interpreting the news, they were positioned to regard Colin Powell and his case as credible, and the Iraqis and their response as untrustworthy.

Conclusion

This chapter directs attention to the social and historical competition over ethos building, introducing the notion of *intertextual ethos.* This term refers to the diversity of voices that struggle to establish a person's character within and across news texts. According to this view, any attempt to create ethos for oneself must be placed alongside others' attempts to create that person's ethos in mass-mediated journalism. "Ethos" does not autonomously emerge from a lifetime of actions; nor is it a matter of artistic self-presentation in a given speech. Instead, ethos is continually (re)enacted by a chorus of voices—over time and across many mass-mediated contexts. Since there is a diversity of opinions about a person at any given moment, no one's ethos is ever fully unified. Since opinions continually evolve—and since different audience members are familiar with different subsets of what others have said—one's ethos is constantly in flux. In fact, the intertextual struggle over a person's ethos can even rage on after that person has died.[36] Nonetheless, a strong majority of voices—or a small concentration of very powerful media voices—can converge to create a unified ethos for a person. In such cases, one's reputation may at least partially "stabilize."

This chapter has shown how key American news outlets labored to characterize both Colin Powell and Iraqi politicians in the twenty-four-hour period surrounding Powell's U.N. address. The different voices included in these news narratives competed with one another. Some sought to denigrate Powell; others sought to lionize him. Some sought to condemn the Iraqi government; others sought to grant it some legitimacy. Taken as a whole, however, the voices generally authorized Colin Powell as a rhetor and discredited the Iraqi leadership. Thus, the news narratives ultimately worked to reify Powell's positive reputation—stabilizing his "good name" and endorsing his U.N. performance.

This study confirms that supposedly neutral news narratives are rife with evaluations of agents and events—even *overt* evaluations (Entman 2007). As noted, NBC distinguished itself in this regard—offering an extraordinary number of evaluations of Colin Powell and the Iraqi leadership. The *Times* and CNN.com offered many fewer evaluations, but this does not mean their reporting was more impartial. Impartiality is determined by the strategic weight and placement of evaluations and not just raw counts. In fact, a crucial implication of this chapter is that journalists may use evaluative discourse sparingly but *strategically* to build and destroy ethos. In other words, even a few journalistic evaluations signal to audiences how to "read" the ethos of other voices in a given text.

In a sense, the rhetorical impact of an explicit evaluation is not localized to the specific textual moment in which it appears. Instead, like a dye injected into the human body, the substance of a given evaluation seeps out of its original location to color other aspects of a text. Thus, for example, a journalist's negative evaluation of Iraq at the beginning of a report eventually serves to discredit discourse *attributed* to Iraqi voices later in the unfolding text. By the same token, a journalist may choose to offer only a restrained negative evaluation of a group (e.g., the *Iraqi regime*), but also recruit other voices into a text that can make the same negative evaluation far more transparent (e.g., the *brutally repressive dictatorship of Iraq*.) Indeed, non-authorial voices that corroborate a journalistic attitude are resources for journalists—"hired guns" who can freely and repeatedly express those ethotic opinions that journalists—because of their professed commitment to objectivity—may only hint at on occasion.

Intertextual ethos, then, is a complicated matter involving a whole array of voices in a given text and the various attitudes that these voices espouse about real people and artistic performances. I have introduced the concept of *transitive chains of authority* as a way of tracing how the authorial voice in a text "links up" with, or dissociates itself from, other voices—ultimately in ways that align audiences with certain characters and oppose them to others. In this study, the authorial voices of journalists endorsed, whether explicitly or indirectly, other "like-minded" voices from the U.S. political arena. Taken together, these voices created an evaluative chorus so powerful that it drowned out and subverted other voices in the text—namely, Iraqi voices. Meanwhile, Powell's ethos was enhanced as both his character and his presentation were represented by journalists—and their intertextual allies—as unassailable.

It is clear that *many* voices are at work in the construction of ethos. Scholars of rhetoric and media discourse must consider the relationship among these voices—and begin to understand how they interact within and across texts to characterize certain actors and performances. This is particularly important when analyzing mainstream news stories, since establishment journalists have the capacity to signal to enormous audiences how various people and events ought to be evaluated. Indeed, members of the public may never meet Colin Powell—or even hear him speak—but they will still form an opinion of him based on how he is characterized by a mix of voices in the news. The same can be said for other public figures—from General David Petraeus to Kim Jong Un. Their ethos does not merely reside within them—it is at least partially created by the mainstream press.

Of course, during the run-up to war, how a given person's ethos is constructed by journalistic texts can literally have life-and-death consequences. After all, evaluative discourse not only positions audiences to align themselves with certain people—but also disposes them to *act against* certain others. In the present study, any journalist who signaled that Powell was good enough to trust simultaneously, if indirectly, suggested that Saddam Hussein was bad enough to kill.[37]

Chapter Three

Undercutting Saddam's Denials: Precontextualization and Audience Alignment

> There are those who despise us [journalists] for writing the news before it happens. They fear us not because we are journalists but because we can predict the future; you should see how amazed they are when things turn out exactly as we've written them. And quite a few things do happen only because we've written them up first. This is what modern journalism is all about.
>
> —Orhan Pamuk, *Snow*, 2004

Recontextualization involves extracting elements from one context and relocating them in another (Bauman & Briggs 1990; Linell 1998). Thus, a journalist reporting Colin Powell's speech necessarily recontextualizes that speech—extracting Powell's words from his address and relocating them in a given news narrative. Importantly, this kind of reporting is oriented towards the past. However, as Bakhtin (1981) notes, discourse is not only "oriented toward the 'already uttered'" (279), but also toward subsequent utterances: every utterance anticipates an answer, a future response (280). In this chapter, I examine such "prospective intertextuality" (Lemke 1991, 35), the ways texts link to and anticipate subsequent texts (Fairclough 2004, 114). Specifically, I investigate a semiotic process in which journalists anticipate, preview, and evaluate future rhetorical events, a process I refer to as *precontextualization*.

Precontextualization occurs any time a text introduces and predicts elements of a symbolic event that is yet to unfold. However, precontextualization not only entails describing or predicting future discourse. It also entails *providing a context* for that discourse, and requires that speakers embed an upcoming rhetorical event within and among representations of events from the present and past. As people situate a projected discursive event among other representations of reality, they inevitably remark on its legitimacy. Depending on how they precontextualize future discourse, it—and its material consequences—may appear (un)reasonable, (un)desirable, or (un)necessary. Thus, precontextualization is, like recontextualization, deeply implicated in "the construction and exercise of power" (Bauman & Briggs 1990, 77). Those who precontextualize future discourse help control what that discourse *means*—predefining sociopolitical reality and setting the course for future action in the world.

I begin this chapter by situating the notion of precontextualization within existing work on the rhetoric of futurity (e.g., Dunmire 2011; Jaworski, Fitzgerald, & Morris 2003; Jaworski & Fitzgerald 2008).[1] Arguing that studies of futurity must begin to contend with the impact of multimodality, I offer an analytic framework that integrates multimodal text analysis with other forms of discourse analysis. I then investigate how journalists on NBC precontextualized Powell's address the evening before he delivered it, occasionally comparing the NBC report to similar reports in the *New York Times* and CNN.com.

I reveal that the journalists enacted a supportive context for Powell's near-at-hand address. They prepared viewers to imagine Powell's speech and its sociopolitical impact as already present and "real." Furthermore, they positioned audiences (1) to align themselves with Powell and against Iraq, and (2) to regard war with Iraq as legitimate and inevitable. The journalists not only precontextualized Powell's speech, a *semiotic event*, but also projected a future war in Iraq, a *material event*. Thus, I argue that precontextualizing rhetorical events can play a key role in legitimizing and enabling future material events. Insofar as elite actors legitimize future discourse, they help set the stage for the material consequences of that discourse.

Precontextualization in Mainstream Journalism: Foundations and Conventions

Richard Grusin (2010) argues that in post-9/11 America the practice of *premediating* future events before they happen has supplanted the practice of reporting events from the present and recent past. Grusin asserts that this "logic of premediation" (41) has intensified in U.S. media—particularly news media—because of the widespread desire to avoid the shock experienced on 9/11. As Grusin puts it, "The desire of demand among US media has been to make sure that when the future comes it will already have been premediated, to prepare the public to be ready for the future not as it emerges immediately into the present, but before it ever happens" (12). According to Grusin, premediation is not necessarily concerned with getting the future right. Instead, it is concerned with propagating many competing future scenarios, so that any future that eventually emerges cannot come as a surprise. This culture of premediation, Grusin asserts, was particularly evident in U.S. news media coverage during the run-up to the Iraq War. In fact, he argues that leading up to the war journalists premediated so many future military scenarios that "the war in Iraq came to be seen as an inevitable event, indeed seemed . . . to have *already been* a televisually mediated news event" (43, emphasis added).[2]

Grusin's concept, premediation, describes the media *culture*. He refers to a new "logic of premediation"—which he sees as "characterizing the media regime of post-9/11 America" (47). *Precontextualization* refers to a particular semiotic process enacted *within* the media regime that Grusin describes. It is a micro-level phenomenon that flourishes in a culture anxious to premediate reality. Specifically, precontextualization describes those processes by which journalists introduce and contextualize future rhetorical events. It entails describing and evaluating future discourse—and (indirectly) evaluating the material consequences of that discourse. Here, I assume a mutual inference between future discourse and the material events described therein. Thus, when journalists legitimize future speech, they also effectively legitimize the material events promoted in that speech (and vice versa). Precontextualization, then, focuses attention on the rhetorical strategies whereby journalists evaluate future discourse—and, potentially, set the course for future material action.

Journalists precontextualize political discourse partly because politicians are adept at managing the news. Indeed, precontextualization in mainstream media generally coincides with the political imperative to circulate messages ahead of time—to set the news agenda and "forge favorable public opinions" (M. J. Kumar 2007, 7). Before major speaking events, politicians often provide the press with excerpts or complete versions of their texts, increasing the likelihood that their talking points will be publicized (Boorstin 1961; Herman & Chomsky 1988; Jamieson 1988). And even when such "advance copies" are not released to the media, "official sources" connected with a political team usually "leak" key details about the speech before its delivery (Erickson 1989). By leaking details about a speech beforehand, politicians ensure that their soon-to-be-uttered claims will be reified in the press. At the same time, they also control the "rhetorical timing" of news stories about the upcoming speech, and help ensure that their future discourse will capture public attention (Erickson 1989, 207).

However, it would be a mistake to assume that journalists report about anticipated political discourse merely because politicians are strategic communicators (Manheim 1991). Journalists, too, have great incentive to deliver "the scoop" on upcoming political oratory. The "profit orientation" of the mass media virtually ensures that journalists will seek information from political elites and publish that information as early as possible (Herman & Chomsky 1988, 2). "Advance copies" and strategic leaks are "ready for news," and journalists can access and publish them without having to do costly research or analysis (Bennett 2012; Herman & Chomsky 1988, 19; Klaehn 2002). Moreover, since journalists maximize profits by breaking stories before their competitors, it is only natural that they will aim to report about a major speech as early as possible—even before that speech has been delivered.

Interestingly, Jaworski and colleagues (2003) have shown that uncertainty about the future actually has greater "news value" than certainty (47). In other words, the more uncertain journalists are about an upcoming event, the more likely they are to report about it. This suggests that politicians may actually maximize news coverage for an upcoming address by providing *fewer* details about it. By the same token, journalists need not rely exclusively upon "advance copies" and strategic leaks. They may independently predict or conjecture about what a politician will say and thereby increase the newsworthiness of their reporting. As a journalistic practice, then, precontextualization takes a number of conventional forms—from quotation of an advance copy to pure speculation about future discourse (see appendix F).

Examining Precontextualization: The Multimodal Rhetoric of Futurity

Precontextualization of any kind concerns *the rhetoric of futurity*—the semiotic processes by which rhetors position audiences to imagine and evaluate the future. Long ago, Aristotle (2007) reasoned that "we judge future things by predicting them from past ones" (1.9.40). However, as Dunmire (1997; 2005; 2008; 2011) contends, the shift from past to future is not the only, or most important, rhetorical inference. Rather than seeing the future as the "terminus of deliberation" (2008, 85), Dunmire argues that the future can function as a "starting point" of argumentation. That is, representations of the distal future (relatively distant in time from the speech moment) may function to legitimize action in the proximal future (relatively close in time to the moment of speaking).[3] More specifically, speakers may shift from representations of what *will happen* at some distant future moment to exhortations of what *must happen* now (Dunmire 2008, 83).[4]

In her work, Dunmire (1997; 2005; 2008) has focused on the linguistic means by which rhetors represent the future—and privilege certain futures over others. For instance, Dunmire shows how nominalization and modality may be employed by speakers to represent the future for rhetorical ends. *Nominalization* involves naming processes, and, in essence, transforming verbs into nouns, objects, and entities (e.g., the verb *invade* is transformed into the noun *invasion*). Dunmire (1997) illustrates that nominalizations can transform possible future events into objectified future "facts." For instance, a representation of a possible future (e.g., *Iraq may invade Saudi Arabia*) might be transformed into a nominalized future reality that demands a response (*an Iraqi invasion of Saudi Arabia must be stopped*). As Dunmire (2005) puts it: "Such representations construe future events as assumed rather than contingent," transforming "potential future actions that could or might be taken . . . into an objectified and atemporal reality that exists in and of itself in the present" (493).

Modality refers to those resources by which rhetors qualify the certainty or the social desirability of their propositions. More specifically, *epistemic* modality tends to qualify the certainty of given utterances. Meanwhile, *deontic* modality concerns social obligation, and, in the future, comments on the desirability of a proposed course of action. As indicated before, Dunmire (1997; 2005; 2008) has shown how epistemically modalized distal futures may serve as the grounds for enacting more proximal deontically modalized futures: e.g., Iraq will *definitely* invade (distal/epistemic); therefore, we *must* confront Iraq (proximal/deontic). Table 3.1 illustrates two broad types of rhetorical movements in time: (1) the Aristotelian (2007) movement from past to future, and (2) Dunmire's (2008) movement from distal future to immediate future (or present).

While Dunmire and Aristotle focus on linguistic projections of the future, I am concerned with *multimodal* projections of the future. After all, verbal *and* visual representations are critical in positioning

Table 3.1. Rhetorical Movements in Time

Rhetorical Movement	Description	Example
Past/Present ⇒ Future	A past or current event suggests that it is necessary, warranted, or legitimate to carry out some future course of action.	We now have the international community on our side, so we should attack.
Distal Future ⇒ Immediate Future/ Present	A distal future event suggests that it is necessary, warranted, or legitimate to take some course of action now, or in the more immediate future.	Iraq will pose a great danger in the future; so the U.N. should pass a war resolution now.

audiences to regard certain futures as more likely or more desirable. Take, for example, the image in figure 3.1, which was taken from the cover of a 2010 issue of *Time* magazine. Here a "visual collocation" indicates the social role of the depicted girl.[5] More specifically, the girl is marked as a Muslim "Other" both by her hijab and by her skin color. Meanwhile, resources of *distance*, *gaze*, and *expression* enact a close interpersonal relationship between the depicted girl and the viewer (see Baldry & Thibault 2005). That is, the "close shot," direct eye contact, and slight frown all work to establish a relationship of intimacy and sympathy. However, it is the physical mutilation—the girl's missing nose—that complicates the interpersonal dynamics of this image. In fact, the depicted mutilation is naturally endowed with rhetorical *presence* (Perelman & Olbrechts-Tyteca 1969), and is capable of eliciting powerful emotions of disgust and alarm in the viewer.[6] By itself, the image indicates the recontextualization of some past event: the brutal disfigurement of a young girl.[7] However, the image should be interpreted in conjunction with the written headline—"What Happens If We Leave Afghanistan"—and, in its multimodal context, it is not a recontextualization of the past, but a projection of the future. In other words, it is being proposed through a conditional (if/then) statement that the mutilation of the girl *will happen*—if "we" leave Afghanistan.[8] Thus, the future mutilation of young Afghani girls is dependent on our actions; presumably it can only be prevented if we continue the Afghanistan war.

This kind of multimodal argument is very similar, then, to the linguistic arguments described by Dunmire (2008) in which epistemically modalized representations of the future serve as grounds for more immediate (deontically modalized) courses of action. In this instance, the argument would go something like the following:

- Young girls will be mutilated in the future, if we leave Afghanistan (*distal future*).
- We can prevent the mutilation of young girls, if we stay in Afghanistan.
- Therefore, we should stay and fight in Afghanistan. (*immediate future*).

Obviously, this enthymematic linguistic transcription is by no means equivalent to the multimodal argument.[9] In fact, linguistic representations

Figure 3.1. Cover of *Time*, August 2010. © 2010 Time Inc. Used under license. Photograph by Jodi Bieber.

of the future—even nominalized representations—could never match the rhetorical presence of futures objectified in images.

In this chapter, I examine how rhetorical events are precontextualized in multimodal news stories. I ask:

- Is future discourse legitimized or implicitly "argued for" in mainstream news reports? If so, *how* is future discourse situated in multimodal narrative contexts such that it seems warranted or desirable?
- How are audiences positioned with regard to representations of the discursive and material future? That is, to what degree are audiences allowed "space" to intervene in or challenge the projected course of future events?

A major concern in this chapter is the degree to which journalists use *engagement* resources (Martin & White 2005) to open up or close down "space" for alternative viewpoints. On the one hand, engagement concerns how rhetors position themselves within the *intertextual field of voices* represented in a text—that is, whether rhetors present themselves as standing in solidarity with, standing against, or standing neutrally in relation to other speakers and their value positions (93). On the other hand, engagement accounts for how rhetors position themselves with regard to their *putative audiences*—that is, the signals rhetors use to reflect how they expect audiences to respond to them and their representations of others.

Martin and White (2005) suggest that rhetors manage their relationship with putative audiences by signaling their "tolerance for alternative viewpoints" (96). While monoglossic utterances signal "zero tolerance" for alternative viewpoints, heteroglossic utterances acknowledge alternative perspectives. These heteroglossic utterances may be *dialogically contractive*, as speakers seek to suppress, fend off, or challenge the expression of divergent viewpoints.[10] Or they may be *dialogically expansive*, allowing for and even inviting different points of view. In appendix G, I summarize Martin and White's (2005) overall engagement scheme and outline some other methodological premises for this chapter.[11]

Overview: The NBC Report

I focus my analysis on the NBC nightly newscast that aired on February 4, 2003, the night before Powell's address.[12] However, I sometimes compare NBC's preview to similar previews in the *Times* and on CNN.com in order to reveal important similarities and differences across the intertextual field of news narratives.

Near the end of the NBC telecast, Tom Brokaw introduced a report featuring correspondent, Andrea Mitchell. This news segment was devoted to contextualizing and previewing Powell's upcoming speech. Indeed, NBC had been reporting on Powell's speech for more than a week.[13] This particular segment, then, was one of many that precontextualized Powell's address and prepositioned audiences to understand it. The analysis will focus on two major phases of the NBC narrative: (1) *Brokaw's introduction*—a preview of the news story, and (2) *Mitchell's report*—the "meat" of the story.

It does not appear that NBC (or any other news outlet) was given advance copies or even excerpts of Powell's text.[14] In fact, the textual details of Powell's speech were "kept under tight wraps" by the Bush administration ("Powell Takes Iraq Case" 2003). Thus, Brokaw and Mitchell do not "pre-quote" Powell. Instead, they generally attribute to "official sources" information about the nature and "quality" of Powell's evidence. As I show below, the NBC journalists precontextualize Powell's future speech in ways that strengthen him—priming audiences to interpret Powell's speech as warrantable and to regard Iraq as dangerous and deserving of violence. Indeed, NBC not only legitimized Powell's future arguments, but also helped to naturalize a future war in Iraq, construing violence as an "unchangeable, inevitable, and natural" outcome (Hall 1982, 76).

Setting the Stage for a Showdown: Brokaw's Introduction

In excerpt 3.1, I have transcribed the first twelve seconds of Brokaw's introduction to the segment. Time (in seconds) is indicated in column 1, a snapshot of each corresponding visual frame is provided in column 2, and the audio soundtrack—in this case Brokaw's voice—is transcribed in column 3.

Visually, in frame 1, the newscast opens with a medium close shot of Brokaw standing in front of a rather large screen. As the camera zooms in on Brokaw, he speaks directly to the television audience; his gaze is directed at the viewer. Thus, the viewer is entered into a close interpersonal relationship with the anchor (Kress & Van Leeuwen 1996, 89)—in fact the viewer is positioned rather like an interactant in a dialogue with Brokaw. At the same time, the words "IN DEPTH" are repeated in horizontal rows on either side of the screen. The salience of these words is enhanced since Brokaw also utters them aloud (NBC news *in depth* tonight). In this way, viewers are not only positioned to regard Brokaw as socially close, but they are also positioned to regard this journalistic report positively—as an "in-depth" look at a future event.[15] Here, then, is one more example of a news institution constructing its own ethos.

In the visual track, aside from Brokaw, there are two main *actors* depicted on screen: first, Saddam Hussein in frames 2–6, and, later, Colin Powell in frames 7–11. Both men are displayed on the screen behind Brokaw—each is framed in an oval shape, each is seated at a table, and each is speaking to someone out of shot (not to the viewer). Visually, then, Saddam Hussein and Colin Powell are depicted as figures who are similar to one another (i.e., framed the same way; performing the same action) and important for the viewer to contemplate and observe. Still, they are not interactants in a dialogue with the viewer. Indeed, even though they are depicted in separate shots, they almost seem to be interacting *with each other* based on the way their bodies are turned. Arguably, this heightens the sense of the "showdown" that Brokaw reports. In any case, both men are represented as significant thematically—in fact, both are also talked about in Brokaw's spoken report.

Meanwhile, in the soundtrack, I've italicized those portions of Brokaw's speech in which he placed added stress on a given stressed syllable. Brokaw stresses certain key words: *show*down, *count*down, *Pow*ell, *could*, *war*, and *dam*age control. The forceful articulation of these words renders them more present for the viewer—more salient and more pertinent than the others (Perelman & Olbrechts-Tyteca 1969). Some of these stressed words represent nominalized *events* (showdown, countdown, war,[16] damage control); one of them represents an *actor* (Powell), and one of them is a *modal auxiliary*—in this case an epistemic modal (could) that qualifies the likelihood of a future event (i.e., war).

Excerpt 3.1. (NBC/2.4/TB)

Time	Frame	Soundtrack
1.		NBC news
2.		in depth tonight.
3.		The *show*down with Iraq.
4.		And the *count*down
5.		to a speech
6.		by Secretary of State
7.		Colin P*ow*ell

(continued)

Excerpt 3.1. *(continued)*

Time	Frame	Soundtrack
8.		at the U.N. tomorrow
9.		that *could* move
10.		the world closer to *war*.
11.		Saddam Hussein is already
12.		trying to do *dam*age control.

In terms of temporality, there are no references to past events, but three of the events that Brokaw emphasizes—the *showdown*, the *countdown*, and the *damage control*—appear to be happening *now* in the present. Interestingly, Brokaw selects rather dramatic words to represent these events. In Martin and White's (2005) terms, he chooses words that "up-scale" the force, or intensity, of his attitudes. First, the conflict with Iraq is represented as a "showdown"—a maximally intense word[17] that calls to mind both Western gunfights and advertisements for sporting events (e.g., "Showdown in St. Louis! The Rams take on the Broncos"). Arguably, given the way this word is used in movie trailers and sports promotions, it positions the viewer to regard a potential military conflict as an entertaining spectacle. Moreover, the word "showdown" is strongly future-oriented. Even if the showdown is happening now, we understand that a decisive conclusion is near at hand. The word points forward to the end of the conflict in which the "hero" will triumph and the "villain" will fall. It is noteworthy, then, that "showdown" is co-deployed with the video image of Saddam Hussein, presumably the "villain" in the current melodrama.

Meanwhile, the word "countdown" is used to represent the run-up to Powell's speech. Once again, this maximally intense word[18] calls to mind promotional advertising. It is common, for instance, to see a "countdown clock" running on your television screen before an idealized event like the Super Bowl. Indeed, we "countdown" to the things we *look forward to*: weddings, holidays, retirement. So when Brokaw refers to the "countdown" to Powell's speech, he implies that the speech itself is exciting and important—an idealized future event that the viewer should not miss. Since the noun ("countdown") is preceded by a definite article ("the"), its uniqueness and familiarity are presupposed. Also, since "countdown" is nominalized, its status as a real object is assumed. In a sense, though no person is represented counting down, all are aware of *the countdown*—and can do nothing to stop it. The "clock" is ticking down inexorably to a predetermined rhetorical event, an event we "eagerly await." Thus, metaphor is used as a mechanism of precontextualization, a mechanism that construes future discourse as proximal enough to impact the present moment (Cap 2006), to garner public interest and excitement in the here-and-now.

As Brokaw discusses the countdown, the words "IN DEPTH" fade from the screen—and two new words appear just below Saddam Hussein's image. First, the word "TARGET" appears along with a colon. Crucially, the proximity of this word to Saddam's image creates a meaningful relationship of equivalency. The viewer is to understand that the target *is* Saddam Hussein. Of course, the word "target" also has an anticipatory bent. It is something to be aimed at—or, in a military context, to be *shot at*—in the future. And, if we follow the gunslinger metaphor suggested by the word "showdown," the viewer is positioned to regard Saddam Hussein as the "villain" in the ongoing production—the one who *will be* targeted, and presumably gunned down by the "hero" in the "final scene."[19]

The "target" is expanded a moment later in frame 6. Now, the wording reads, TARGET: IRAQ. Of course, Saddam Hussein is a part of Iraq[20] - arguably, he is the "face of Iraq." So, the target may be considered both Saddam Hussein and Iraq. In any case, it is worth asking *who* is targeting this pair. Who is aiming at Saddam Hussein and his country? While there is more than one possible answer to this question, it seems likely that "we" are aiming the metaphorical gun. After all, the words "Target: Iraq" are presented to the *viewer*. So, it's reasonable to assume that the viewer is to regard Saddam Hussein + Iraq as an enemy, as a legitimate target for aggression. In this way, NBC not only predicts future violence, it practically demands it.

Aside from the *showdown* and the *countdown*, there is one other event that is represented as happening now: namely, the damage control. With the video image of Colin Powell now playing on the screen, Brokaw reports that "Saddam Hussein is already trying to do damage control," in anticipation of Powell's U.N. speech. It's worth noting that "doing damage control" generally has a negative connotation. The term has come to be associated with political spin, the "plain lies or baseless denials" that politicians articulate in order to avoid the "consequences of . . . deceptions that are now being discovered" (Lewis 2001, 78). Needless to say, "spinning" a story in order to avoid public criticism is hardly a noble endeavor.

So Saddam Hussein is again represented negatively—*discredited* (see chapter 2)—as someone who is trying to manage the press in the face of Powell's impending "leak." He is not "defending his reputation" or "denying accusations"; he is doing "damage control." And this damage control is represented as anticipatory. Importantly, Saddam Hussein might have been represented as responding to *past* allegations of wrongdoing. After all, the Bush administration had been accusing Iraq of transgressions for many months. But here Saddam Hussein is represented as responding directly to *Powell* and his *future* address. This not only enhances the sense of a personalized conflict—a showdown as it were—between Saddam Hussein and Colin Powell.[21] It also enhances the sense that Saddam Hussein's response is somehow remarkable. Indeed, by choosing the word "already," Brokaw projects onto his audience a feeling of counterexpectancy (Martin & White 2005, 120–21). In other words, while Brokaw and the audience *would have expected* the Iraqi leader to wait until after Powell's speech to issue a response, he has surprised us all and issued a *preemptive* response instead. This subtly positions the viewer to regard Powell's speech—which hasn't yet occurred—as already damaging to Saddam Hussein and Iraq, already impinging on the normative present. Thus, even before Powell has delivered his address, NBC subtly *vouches* for him, positioning viewers to regard his argument as devastating in the here and now.

Brokaw's report also includes more direct references to the future. He explicitly refers to Powell as an actor who will give a speech at the U.N. *tomorrow*—in the proximate future. Meanwhile, war is a material event that *could* happen in the more distal future—at some point after Powell's speech, and, in part, as a *result* of Powell's speech. After all, Powell's speech is represented as a potential vehicle to war—indeed something that can "move the world closer to war." Of course, the comparative "closer" presupposes that the citizens of the world—including the individuals watching this newscast—are *already* close to war. So, perhaps, it's not quite right to say that the war depends on Powell's speech. Instead, the war seems to be near at hand *regardless* of Powell's speech. In fact, the speech could merely make the war a bit more proximate than it already is. Interestingly, we find a similar representation of the future in the *New York Times*: "The impact of Mr. Powell's presentation will determine how soon the United States will go to war to disarm Iraq" (NYT/2.5/JPSW). Here, too, the notion that the United States will go to war in Iraq is presupposed and Powell's speech is construed as something that could merely make the war happen sooner. Across the news narratives, then, future war is represented as nearly inevitable.

Importantly, most of Brokaw's utterances are monogloss assertions that provide no space for alternative viewpoints. Specifically, Brokaw positions the viewer to regard it as self-evidently true that they are in the midst of a showdown and a countdown, and that the world is already close to war. The only thing that Brokaw leaves open to debate (through the modal auxiliary *could*) is whether or not Powell's speech will move the world clos*er* to war.

Insofar as Powell moves the world closer to war with Iraq, he helps to fulfill what has already been represented as the viewer's goal: eliminating the Saddam-Iraq target. We may observe, then, an implicit rhetorical movement from distal future to proximal future: the distal war is desirable; thus, Powell's more immediate speech aimed at war is desirable. Table 3.2 represents the implicit argument in a series of linked rhetorical syllogisms.

Intermedia Similarity: The Showdown on CNN.com

Interestingly, CNN.com also employed the metaphor of the "showdown" in its preview of Powell's address. In fact, a banner reading "Showdown: Iraq" was displayed on CNN's website just above the headline about Powell's speech (see the introduction, figure 0.1). As in the case of NBC, then, CNN.com sought to promote the conflict with Iraq as an interesting melodrama. In fact, the "Showdown" banner at the top of the screen was supplemented with another "showdown" image that sat right next to the verbal story about Powell's upcoming speech (see figure 3.2).

Here the showdown theme is even larger and more salient. What's more, CNN adds the subtitle "Weapons Hunt." The maximally intense noun "hunt" again heightens the drama, suggesting a passionate pursuit for weapons, and perhaps implying that the weapons actually exist. After all, we typically don't hunt for things, unless we think those things are present somewhere.[22]

Interestingly, when visitors click on either "Showdown" image, they are delivered to the same page: a "special report" that provides additional

Table 3.2. Linked Syllogisms

Syllogism A: Present to Future	
Premise	Targets are meant to be eliminated.
Premise	The target is Saddam Hussein and Iraq (present).
Conclusion	Thus, Saddam Hussein and Iraq should be eliminated (distal future).
Syllogism B: Distal Future to Immediate Future	
Premise	Saddam Hussein and Iraq should be eliminated (distal future).
Premise	The war we are close to will eliminate Saddam Hussein and Iraq (distal future).
Premise	Powell's speech tomorrow (proximal future) could bring us closer to this future war.
Conclusion	Thus, Powell's speech is legitimate and desirable since it potentiates the elimination of the Saddam-Iraq target.

Figure 3.2. Content box expressing negative judgment of Iraq (CNN/2.5)

information about the conflict with Iraq and supplies context for Powell's upcoming speech (see figure 3.3).[23]

An exhaustive study of this page is beyond the scope of this book; however, even a cursory look at the headlines and narrative themes reveals that CNN.com represents Saddam Hussein as the "villain" of the melodrama, and projects future war with Iraq as desirable and inevitable. Note, for example, the lead paragraph at the top right of the screen:

> More than 10 years after the Persian Gulf War, the world is locked in another showdown with Iraqi President Saddam Hussein. Iraq has accepted a new U.N. resolution demanding that U.N. inspectors be given unhindered access to any suspected Iraqi weapons site or face "serious consequences." But President George W. Bush has warned that the United States will have "zero tolerance" for any Iraqi interference with inspections and made it clear that it will launch military strikes against Iraq if it deems it necessary.

This paragraph serves to link the current "showdown" with the original Gulf War, suggesting a kind of continuation of an ongoing conflict between Saddam Hussein and the entire world. The fact that the world is "locked in" the showdown with Saddam suggests that there is no way out of the conflict. Indeed, Saddam Hussein is presented as a threat to world peace that *needs* to be dealt with—for a second time. Meanwhile, President Bush is identified as the ultimate authority figure, one who is able to issue warnings

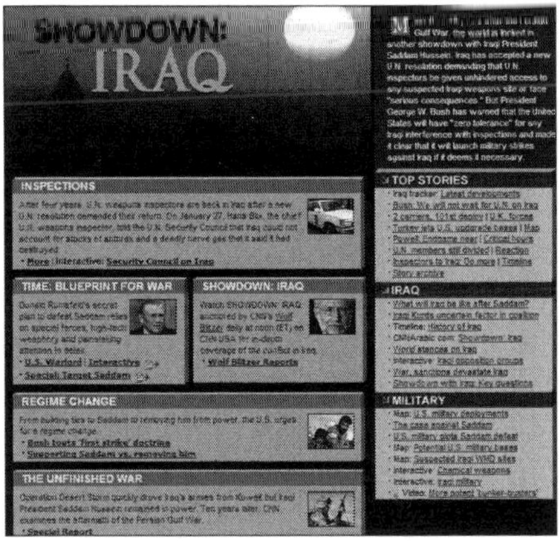

Figure 3.3. "Showdown Iraq" special report (CNN/2.5)

to Iraq and declare a "zero tolerance" policy. Moreover, he is empowered to take the country to war, when "it" deems necessary. In short, just as on NBC, we have the makings of a personalized melodrama that pits a "repeat offender" against an authority figure who has "had enough."

Meanwhile, beneath the main image on the page, one finds additional headlines that both anticipate and legitimate future war in Iraq. Under the "Blueprint for War" headline, for instance, we find discussion of "Donald Rumsfeld's secret plan to defeat Saddam Hussein." Consistent with Grusin's (2010) findings, readers are tantalized with premeditations of the war—indeed "secret" revelations of how the war might play out. Meanwhile, a "Target: Iraq" headline in the same content box suggests that violence against Baghdad is imminent—just as on NBC. Below this, one finds a story devoted to "Regime Change" and the president's "first-strike doctrine." Again, the reader is invited to imagine future war time scenarios—a preemptive strike and overthrow of Saddam Hussein. Finally, at the bottom of the page, one discovers a story about Operation Desert Storm called "The Unfinished War." The obvious implication here is that the "unfinished" 1991 Gulf War needs to be completed now, ten years later.

Beneath the lead paragraph, there are three additional content boxes in a vertical column, each of which contains several bulleted links to related stories. Once again, the top stories in each box envisage and, at times, promote future war. For example, there is a link to a map of "U.S. military deployments," showing where troops are stationed in the Persian Gulf and where they might be headed. Another headline includes this provocative question: "What will Iraq be like after Saddam?" Interestingly, this headline presupposes that the war will take place and that Saddam Hussein will eventually be removed from power. The subject of the article concerns whether democracy will be able to flourish in Baghdad once the inevitable war is over.

Of course, this "special report" page is only indirectly connected to the news narrative specifically about Powell's upcoming speech. Nevertheless, the fact that CNN provided multiple links to this page suggests that it wanted its readers to explore it in greater detail. A visitor clicking on these links the day before Powell's speech would encounter representations of the past, present, and future that, taken together, establish a legitimizing context for Powell's address. After all, if Powell were to succeed in attaining his argumentative goal—a new war resolution—it would allow the country to "complete" its unfinished military campaign and potentially secure a future of democracy in Iraq.

Introducing Colin Powell: The Covert Protagonist

Let's return now to the NBC broadcast. Following his brief introduction of the news segment, Brokaw presents Andrea Mitchell, "NBC's chief foreign affairs correspondent," for the "in-depth" report (NBC/2.4/TB). However, in the next shot, instead of seeing and hearing Andrea Mitchell, the viewer sees Colin Powell. Powell is outside walking away from the camera and toward a car—but looking back, presumably to answer a question that the viewer can hear being posed to him by an unseen reporter: "Mr. Secretary, are you confident you will make your case, sir?" (NBC/2.4/AM). To this, Powell smiles and remarks, "You'll see" (see excerpt 3.2).

This brief exchange between Powell and the unseen reporter once again establishes Powell as the covert "protagonist" of the news story (Fairclough 2003).[24] Brokaw first enacted this "protagonist" theme by presenting Powell in a showdown with his moral counterpoint and antagonist, Saddam Hussein. Now Powell is singled out as the "main character"—the one who is literally followed by the camera (not to mention the reporters), the one who smiles self-assuredly at the viewer, and, with this expression, projects confidence that he will "make his case."

Interestingly, the theme "Powell Is Confident" is also evident in

Excerpt 3.2. (NBC/2.4/CP)

Time	Frame	Soundtrack
24.		You'll see

the CNN.com report. Observe figure 3.4, which was displayed saliently, just to the right of CNN's verbal report about Powell's upcoming address.

As you can see, this is actually a link to a video about Powell's speech, a link that is unfortunately no longer working. For our purposes, let's focus on the multimodal elements of the content box itself. The caption in this box reads: "U.S. Secretary of State Colin Powell is expected to present detailed proof of Iraqi deception to the U.N. Security Council. CNN's John King reports. (February 5)." Thus, Powell's speech is precontextualized in the most positive light possible, as "detailed proof of Iraqi deception." Specifically, the adjective "detailed" represents a positive evaluation of the complexity of Powell's upcoming address, suggesting that it will be a comprehensive presentation. Meanwhile, the noun "proof" indicates conclusive evidence of Iraqi wrongdoing, evidence that cannot be refuted. Significantly, the caption employs a passive verb (*is expected*) that fails to identify the person or people who expect that Powell will submit this proof.[25] In fact, the passive construction seems to imply a *universal* agent (Robinson 2000). In other words, the expectation that Powell will present detailed proof seems to be widespread. Crucially, this positive language inscribes the accompanying image with meaning. Powell is displayed next to the caption, gazing directly at the viewer with a slight grin on his face. Given that Powell is construed verbally as someone who is expected to supply "detailed proof," his smiling expression takes on an air of confidence. As in the NBC broadcast, the viewer is positioned to regard Powell as self-assured, and is further positioned to regard Powell's future case as conclusive.

Returning to NBC, Powell remains the central focus of the camera. As he circles around his car, Andrea Mitchell's voiceover begins (excerpt 3.3).

In excerpt 3.3 Powell is simultaneously represented as the actor in the visual frame and in the verbal report. The viewer is told by Mitchell

Figure 3.4. Video link to story about Powell's address (CNN/2.5)

that Powell is an agent who performed an action (i.e., he *came to practice his speech*), in a specific location (*in New York*), and at a particular time (*the day before his make-or-break appearance*). From this verbal report, the viewer infers that New York is also the location of the *visual* shot. In addition, Powell's confident smiling is further contextualized temporally—he is feeling self-assured *after* practicing his "make-or-break" address. In any case, Powell's role as the lead actor of the news story is, by this point, firmly established.

A moment later, Mitchell continues her report, saying that Powell "also tried to *soften up* Security Council skeptics like China—one of five members who can *block* U.N. support for war with Iraq" (NBC/2.4/AM). This verbal report is co-deployed with a new visual shot: Powell is displayed sitting at a table—again staring at the camera with a smirk on his face—and as the camera pans to the other side of the table, the viewer sees several Asian men and women seated across from Powell. What interests me here is the way that both Powell's speech and a future war with Iraq are subtly precontextualized in Mitchell's discourse. First, Powell's represented action—"softening up" the Chinese delegates—is a preparatory one. In other words, Powell is construed as having taken actions to "prepare the way" for, and reduce resistance

Excerpt 3.3. (NBC/2.4/AM)

Time	Frame	Soundtrack
25.		The day before
26.		his make—or—break U.N.
27.		appearance Colin Powell
28.		came to New York
29.		to practice his speech.

to, his future rhetorical endeavor. Thus, Powell's future speech act is implicitly invoked.

However, it is the *possible* response to Powell's speech—not Powell's speech itself—that is the focus of Mitchell's report. Specifically, Mitchell construes an epistemically modalized future in which any Security Council (SC) member *can* block U.N. support for war with Iraq. First, this assertion implies that the *purpose* of Powell's speech is to garner U.N. support for war with Iraq. So the audience is once again prepositioned to regard war as the ultimate goal of Powell's address. I shall note, in passing, that during his speech, Powell never explicitly called for war. In fact, he reportedly told French delegates after the speech, "I wasn't talking about war, but about strengthening inspections" (CNN/2.6/JKDE).[26] But, as in Brokaw's introduction, Mitchell does not entertain the possibility that Powell's speech might be about strengthening inspections—it is presupposed to be a call-to-arms address. Again, what is at issue is not the purpose of the speech (war), but how the UNSC will react. In this regard, the modal qualifier *can* allows the audience space to imagine a couple of future scenarios:

- The SC members can block U.N. support for war.
- Or they can permit U.N. support for war.

The latter scenario is presumably the one that Powell desires; the former is presumably the one he does not want. But, it's important to note that in *either* scenario, a more distal future of war with Iraq is still "on the table." The SC members can block or permit U.N. *support* for war; they cannot necessarily block the war itself. Once again, it seems that war is a potentiality (perhaps even a probability) regardless of Powell's rhetorical success or failure at the U.N.

Defining Saddam's Discourse: A Preemptive Response with Five Minutes to Midnight

Following this assertion, Mitchell's narrative takes a turn away from Powell and toward the other central actor in the showdown: Saddam Hussein. In a new visual shot, the Iraqi leader appears puffing on a cigar while seated at a table. Just before he erupts in audible laughter, Mitchell provides the report shown in excerpt 3.4.

With this, Mitchell reiterates Brokaw's earlier representation of Saddam Hussein as someone preemptively responding to Colin Powell's future address (rather than reactively responding to past accusations). And, once again, Mitchell construes Saddam's "preemptive response" as countering the viewer's expectation through her use of the coordinating conjunction *but*. As before, the viewer is pre-positioned to regard Powell's speech as "demanding a response" even before it has been delivered. The viewer is positioned, then, to interpret Saddam's jolly laughter not as "quiet confidence," but as "false bravado." After all, if he was truly confident, he wouldn't be doing "damage control."

Excerpt 3.4. (NBC/2.4/AM)

Time	Frame	Soundtrack
42.		But, in *Bagh*dad, Saddam Hussein was *not wai*ting for Powell's speech.

Note: For simplicity, I have included only one representative visual frame—even though the spoken report in the soundtrack column spanned many similar frames.

A moment later, the shot changes to show Saddam Hussein seated at a different table, across from three reporters (see excerpt 3.5). Mitchell continues her report as shown in excerpt 3.5.

In this case, Saddam Hussein is represented as a "sayer" in a verbal process. Because Mitchell uses the relatively neutral verb *told* to represent Saddam's speech act, the viewer is positioned to regard Saddam's denials (*no links to al-Qaeda*; *no weapons*) as dialogically "open." In other words, Mitchell does not "take sides" with regard to Saddam's reported speech—and the viewer is relatively free to interpret his speech act as one of many in a range of dialogic options. Of course, this apparent "openness" to Saddam's assertions is complicated by the earlier suggestions throughout this news narrative that Saddam Hussein is an enemy of the viewer (a "target") who is trying to preempt Powell's speech because (1) it will be (or perhaps already is) damaging and (2) it will bring the world closer to what has been projected as the viewer's desired goal: a war to eliminate Saddam Hussein. In other words, Saddam Hussein has already been *discredited* earlier in the text, and this inevitably colors how viewers later regard his represented speech.

In any case, in excerpt 3.6, Saddam Hussein is given a chance to "speak" and defend himself. I put "speak" in quotation marks because the viewer actually hears the voice of a translator "speaking over" Saddam's natural voice (which is audible, but not salient in the soundtrack).

Here Saddam Hussein is represented expressing a forceful denial: that Iraq has *no* weapons of mass destruction *whatsoever*. Of course, this denial presupposes the opposite positive assertion—that Iraq *has* weapons of mass destruction—and it is thus a partially dialogic utterance. However, Saddam distances himself from those who *claim* that Iraq has weapons, and goes so far as to challenge such claimants to "bring

Excerpt 3.5. (NBC/2.4/AM)

Time	Frame	Soundtrack
44.		In his first interview in *twelve* years, airing tonight on British TV, he told an *anti*war British politician he has *no* links to al-Qaeda and *no* illegal weapons.

Note: The spoken report spanned many frames similar to the one shown.

forward" evidence and prove their charge. In this way, Saddam Hussein is represented doing all he can to suggest that the accusations against him are not credible and unsubstantiated. And despite the fact that he has already been tagged as the "antagonist" in this newscast, his assertions are endowed with *rhetorical presence*. After all, his vocal emphases tend to enhance the strength of his denials (no weapons whats*oever*, we challenge *any*one), and the fact that he is allowed to speak (almost) directly to the camera heightens the salience of his assertions.

However, Saddam's emphatic denials are immediately followed by a shot of Hans Blix, the chief weapons inspector in Iraq, seated at a press conference at the United Nations. Blix is relatively distant from the camera, seated with his legs crossed in front of several reporters. Mitchell reports, "Today Hans *Blix* said Iraq *must* do more to cooperate" (NBC/2.4/AM). Here Blix is introduced both visually and verbally as a new actor in the news report. Importantly, unlike Saddam Hussein, Blix has not previously been represented by journalists as a "target" of any kind. Instead, Blix's authority is *enhanced* on screen by a visual caption that appears beneath his image in bold white letters: "Dr. Hans Blix/ Chief U.N. Weapons Inspector." In a sense, the journalists *vouch for* Blix, and the viewer is positioned to trust him much more than Saddam Hussein. More specifically, the viewer is positioned to accept Blix's deontically modalized assertion that it is Saddam Hussein who *must* do more to cooperate in order to prevent a war. In other words, Saddam Hussein is represented as the agent who is most responsible for determining whether or not war will happen. In this way, future war is presented as contingent on the behaviors of only one actor, who happens to be the "antagonist" in the news narrative. The viewer is not to understand the projected war as contingent on the behaviors of the United States—arguably the principal aggressor in the conflict.[27] While

Excerpt 3.6. (NBC/2.4/SH)

Time	Frame	Soundtrack
58.		Iraq has no weapons of mass destruction what-*soever*. We challenge *any*one who claims that we have [weapons] to *bring forward* any evidence and present it to public opinion.

Note: The spoken report spanned many frames similar to the one shown.

Saddam Hussein must do more to cooperate, the United States need not do anything at all.

In any case, as a new close shot of Mr. Blix appears on screen, Mitchell continues her report, introducing a "juicy" sound byte, as shown in excerpt 3.7.

Here war is once again invoked as a nearly inevitable future. In fact, Blix's use of a metaphor (*five minutes to midnight*) endows this future with special presence: it is mere minutes away. Moreover, however "ominous" it may be, the war is "naturalized" in Blix's metaphor—it is represented as "just as impossible to stop as the rhythm of day and night" (Van Leeuwen 2007, 99). Of course, NBC might have chosen to highlight any number of quotations from Blix that called the inevitability of war into question. Indeed, Blix was working diligently to prevent the war and still held out hope that the inspections process could be continued. NBC chose to ignore such declarations—as well as Blix's recent rejections of U.S. allegations about WMDs in Iraq. This is just one way that it succeeded in promoting a prowar narrative, while downplaying voices of dissent.

Undercutting Saddam's Denials: Enacting the Saddam Lies *Thematic*

Blix's grim political assessment is followed by what may be the most crucial representation in Mitchell's report (see excerpt 3.8).

In a very distant shot, three U.N. weapons inspectors descend a staircase[28]—presumably somewhere in Iraq. Meanwhile on the soundtrack, Mitchell reports that these inspectors "found *anot*her empty

Excerpt 3.7. (NBC/2.4/AM.HB)

Time	Frame	Soundtrack
73.		**Mitchell:** and [Blix] said ominously **Blix:** Isn't there five minutes to mid*night* in your political assessment?

Note: The spoken report spanned many frames similar to the one shown.

chemical weapons warhead, *un*dercutting Saddam's den*i*als." This is a crucial representation of a past event—one that implicitly diminishes Saddam's credibility. First, this is a monogloss assertion—an unchallengeable "fact"—that leaves no space for alternative viewpoints. In fact, this representation positions the viewer to reassess Saddam's earlier denials (*no weapons, no links to al-Qaeda*) in the light of this newly unveiled information. Now, in retrospect, Saddam's earlier speech act is no longer to be regarded as one of many in a range of possible dialogic options. Instead, it is to be regarded as a falsehood—a story that has been "undercut"—*contradicted*—not by someone else's assertions, but by the "facts." In a sense, reality itself is construed as the arbiter of truth—and, in this case, reality seems to have judged that Saddam Hussein is an untrustworthy scoundrel.

However, there is a good reason to question Mitchell's monogloss assertion. For one thing, the chemical weapons warhead was "empty"—and, one would think, rather unremarkable. It is questionable whether one (or more) *empty* warheads "undercut" Saddam's claims that he has no weapons of mass destruction. In fact, it could be argued that an empty warhead is not a weapon of mass destruction

Excerpt 3.8. (NBC/2.4/AM)

Time	Frame	Soundtrack
76.		As weapons inspectors found *ano*ther empty chemical weapons warhead, *un*dercutting Saddam's den*i*als.

Note: The spoken report spanned many frames similar to the one shown.

at all, but a useless scrap of metal. Indeed, Mitchell's choice to report that this warhead self-evidently undercut Saddam's denials is provocative, if not manipulative. In fact, in other news accounts, the meaning of these empty warheads is not at all clear. Take the following excerpt from the *New York Times*:

> In Baghdad today, the weapons inspection team said it had discovered another empty Sakr-18 chemical warhead, at the Al Taji ammunition depot north of Baghdad. The warhead was similar to one found at another depot on Jan. 16. Mr. Blix said it was still unclear whether the empty munitions were "the tip of the iceberg" of chemical warheads Iraq has not accounted for, *or the "debris" of their destruction*. (NYT/2.5/JPSW, emphasis added)

In the *Times* report, one can see how resources of engagement might have been used by NBC to open up the space for alternative viewpoints. First of all, the proposition that empty warheads were found in Iraq is not taken for granted in the *Times*. In fact, this assertion is attributed to "the weapons inspection team," making it possible for dialogic alternatives. Second, the empty chemical warhead is not just described vaguely as "another"—making it possible for the viewer to imagine that a fleet of such warheads had been located—but as a warhead that is "similar to" (not identical to) *one* found elsewhere in Iraq. Finally, and most importantly, the *meaning* of the empty munitions is not presented as self-evident. Instead, a *possible* interpretation of the empty warheads is *attributed* to Mr. Blix. In fact, in a highly modalized assertion, Blix is represented as saying that the weapons *could* be "debris" left over from the destruction of a chemical weapons program. If true, this would *confirm* Saddam's denials, not undercut them.

But Mitchell's "in-depth" report simply does not allow for this dialogic possibility. The empty warheads undercut Saddam's denials, and that's that. Importantly, Mitchell's report not only positions the viewer to retroactively reinterpret Saddam's earlier assertions, but also primes the viewer to interpret *subsequent assertions* made by other voices in the news narrative. In fact, a moment after Mitchell reports that the warheads undercut Saddam's denials, Donald Rumsfeld appears on screen making assertions that *corroborate* Mitchell's negative assessment of Saddam Hussein's credibility. Rumsfeld, who is not introduced by Mitchell, simply emerges on the screen already talking. In fact, the viewer first hears Rumsfeld speak while the shot of the weapons inspectors is still on the screen. Thus, the *presence* of this new—and as of yet unidentified voice—captures viewers' attention as they are forced for a moment to imagine who is speaking. When Rumsfeld's image appears a moment later, he is speaking from behind a podium at the Pentagon and gesturing emphatically (see excerpt 3.9).

Obviously, Rumsfeld's discourse is full of negative judgments—both explicit (*local liar*) and inscribed (*he never . . . rarely tells the truth*) that characterize Saddam Hussein as habitually untruthful. Interestingly, Rumsfeld never mentions Saddam's name. He refers only to "the local liar." In fact, it is left to the viewer to infer that this liar is Saddam Hussein, and the viewer is able to make this inference only because of what came before: namely, Mitchell's reporting about Saddam's untrustworthy denials. Thus, a thematic-semantic link is formed between Mitchell's report and Rumsfeld's accusation. In particular, the thematic formation "SADDAM LIES" that was implicit in Mitchell's report is, here, made explicit in Rumsfeld's diatribe. Ironically, the notion that "Saddam lies" is repeated and endowed with presence in the news narrative—even as Rumsfeld identifies this theme as something that people are "forgetting to say."

Providing Support for a Precontextualized Claim: Strengthening Powell's Speech

Notably, it is at this point in the news segment, on the heels of Rumsfeld's disparaging remarks, that Mitchell turns to Powell's upcoming

Excerpt 3.9. (NBC/2.4/DR)

Time	Frame	Soundtrack
86.		This is a case of the local *liar* coming up again and people repeating what he said and forgetting to say that he never . . . almost never . . . *rarely* tells the *truth*.

Note: The spoken report spanned many frames similar to the one shown.

Excerpt 3.10. (NBC/2.4/AM)

Time	Frame	Soundtrack
93.		Powell will try to make that point tomorrow.

Note: The spoken report spanned many frames similar to the one shown.

speech. In fact, her report precontextualizes Powell's speech by linking it explicitly to Rumsfeld's "local liar" comments.

In excerpt 3.10, "that point" refers anaphorically to Rumsfeld's earlier assertion: "This is a case of the local *liar* coming up again and people repeating what he said and forgetting to say that he never . . . almost never . . . *rarely* tells the *truth*." Thus, the "SADDAM LIES" thematic is enacted *again*, and further endowed with presence. However, this time, the thematic is represented as a point that *Powell* "will try to make" in his upcoming address at the (now empty) U.N. Security Council pictured in the shot. Mitchell's precontextualization of Powell's discourse leaves very little space for alternative viewpoints. That Powell will try to make the "Saddam lies" point appears to be inevitable.[29]

In fact, there is a clear rhetorical movement from a representation of a past material event (*weapons inspectors found another warhead*) to a precontextualization of a proximal discursive event (*Powell will try to make the "local liar" point*)—a movement that represents Powell's future claim as warranted based on past "facts." This is clear in the simplified Toulmin (1958) diagram shown in figure 3.5.

In short, NBC prepositions audiences to interpret Powell's future claim as reasonable based on the unchallengeable "evidence" found by weapons inspectors. Interestingly, Powell *did* go on to enact the "SADDAM LIES" thematic formation at several moments in his address the next day. For example, at one point, he remarks that "Iraqi denials of supporting terrorism take their place alongside the other Iraqi denials of weapons of mass destruction. It is all a web of lies." At another point, he asserts that "Saddam Hussein . . . has not told the truth," and goes on to suggest that his "lies [have been] graphically and indisputably demonstrated by intelligence" (UN/2.5/CP). Thus, Powell reiterates the overarching thematic formations evident in Mitchell's report: Saddam lies—and *we*

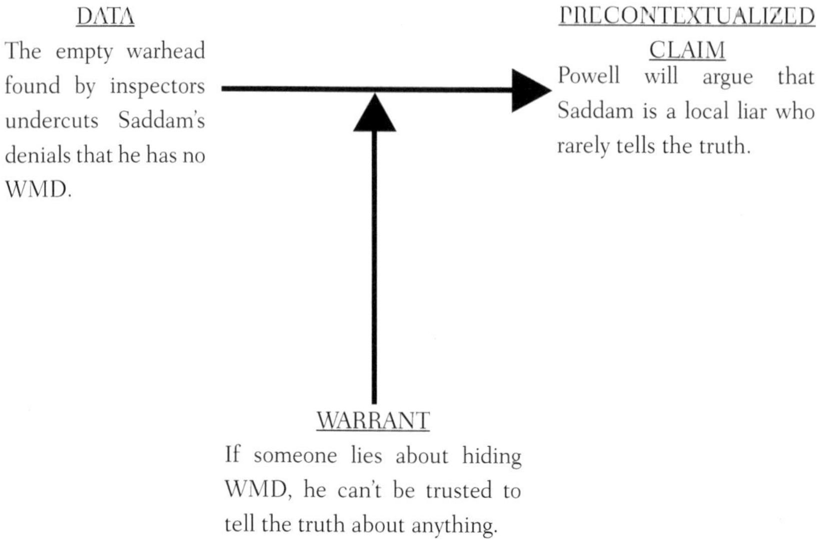

Figure 3.5. Toulmin diagram of precontextualization on NBC

know he lies because his denials are *contradicted* by the evidence. The NBC report on February 4, then, not only precontextualizes Powell's address, but also prefigures and pre*corroborates* one of Powell's central arguments. At the same time, NBC reinforces the "POWELL VERSUS SADDAM" thematic formation first suggested by Brokaw in his introduction to the segment. If Saddam Hussein is "the local liar," then Colin Powell is—or, rather, *will be*—the "bringer of truth."

Seeing the Future: Displaying Powell's Evidence

In excerpt 3.11, Mitchell goes on to report that Powell will try to make the "Saddam lies" point, "using eq*uip*ment brought into the Security Council today" (NBC/2.4/AM).

What interests me here is the way that Mitchell prepares audiences to "look for" certain evidence (*satellite pictures* and *intercepted communications between Iraqi officials*) that presumably will help Powell make the "Saddam lies" argument. Again, even before Powell has delivered his address, NBC endows some of his evidence with presence. In particular, satellite pictures are made salient to the viewer. Mitchell not only identifies satellite pictures in her spoken report, but she also presents an actual satellite image in the visual track. Importantly, the camera zooms in and focuses on this satellite photograph, giving viewers the sense that they are descending from outer space—getting closer and closer to some important object on the ground. As the virtual space between

Excerpt 3.11. (NBC/2.4/AM)

Time	Frame	Soundtrack
98.	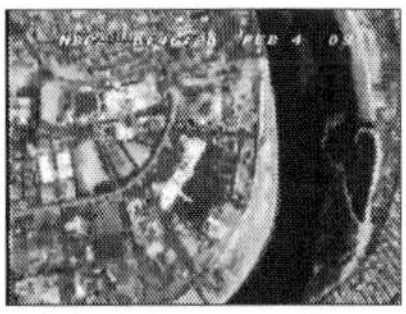	so he can show
99.		satellite pictures
100.		and play *audio*
101.		of intercepted
102.		communic*ations*
103.		between I*raqi* officials.

the depicted world and the viewer is reduced, the viewer can't help but wonder what is being depicted on the ground. But this information—as well as where this image actually came from—is difficult to determine.[30] All the viewer knows, at present, is that images like this will be used to prove Powell's point: that "Saddam lies." Viewers can "tune in" for details when Powell actually presents his case.

In fact, all three of the news outlets examined in this study prime[31] audiences to look for satellite photographs and intercepted communications in Powell's presentation. But the *New York Times* and CNN.com provide even more details about Powell's case—and sometimes suggest that Powell's as-of-yet unveiled evidence *already* proves Iraqi wrongdoing. Take the following excerpt from the *Times*:

> [1] Secretary of State Colin L. Powell will show the United Nations evidence on Wednesday that Iraq has worked to conceal illegal arms from international inspectors, American officials said today. . . . [2] Mr. Powell's presentation, which is to take up to 90 minutes, will include recently intercepted communications within Iraq indicating a pattern of hiding chemical, biological and nuclear weapons programs from United Nations inspectors. . . . [3] Among the evidence the administration was considering declassifying were satellite photographs showing activity at inspection target sites shortly before inspections teams arrived, an administration official said. [4] The photographs clearly show soldiers digging holes, moving equipment or burying things, the official said. (NYT/2.5/JPSW)

In the opening sentence of the *Times* report, the reader is told that Powell "will show" evidence "that Iraq has worked to conceal illegal arms from inspectors." Here the auxiliary verb indicates certainty about what Powell will do. That is, the *Times* isn't reporting that Powell *may* show evidence, but is asserting that he *will* show evidence. More importantly, the *Times* suggests that Powell's future claim (*Iraq has worked to conceal illegal arms from inspectors*) will be substantiated by data. Notice that the *Times* uses a "noun of proof"—*evidence*—as opposed to a "noun of projection"—for example, *claim*, *argument*, or *contention* (Halliday & Matthiessen 2004, 467–82). In other words, rather than saying that Powell *will present his claim* that Iraq has worked to conceal weapons, the *Times* asserts that Powell *will show evidence* that Iraq has worked to conceal weapons. The former would suggest a mere assertion, but the latter suggests an assertion backed by support.

Of course, the *Times* attributes the entire locution to "American officials," helping readers understand that other viewpoints are possible. But the reporting clause (*American officials said*) appears at the very end of the sentence. As Fahnestock (2011) argues, when reporters use such "trailing attributions," the content of the paraphrased utterance (i.e., *Powell will show evidence that Iraq has worked to conceal arms*) "assumes greater fact status," since readers are initially positioned to absorb the information as "true" (312). Much the same can be said about sentences 3 and 4. In both cases, the reader is presented with precontextualizations of Powell's speech that make his evidence appear fact-like (*satellite photos show activity at inspection target sites*; the *photographs clearly show soldiers digging holes, moving equipment, or burying things*) before ultimately learning that these "facts" are really paraphrased statements leaked by administration officials.

However, sentence 2 includes no attribution at all. It is asserted that Powell's speech "will include recently intercepted communications within Iraq indicating a pattern of hiding chemical, biological, and nuclear weapons programs from United Nations inspectors." Here the *Times* not only previews the intercepted communications that would appear in Powell's presentation, but also suggests that these intercepts are already "indicating a pattern of hiding" weapons from inspectors. In linguistic terms, the participle "indicating" has no tense, and thus the intercepts seem to be indicating Iraqi wrongdoing always and already. In fact, this sentence is rather interesting for its cross-temporal dimensions. Communications that *were* intercepted in the recent past *eternally* indicate a pattern of Iraq hiding WMDs. And all of this *will be* included in Powell's presentation tomorrow.

A similar phenomenon is evident in this excerpt from CNN.com:

> [1] Among the evidence, U.S. officials said, Powell will play audiotapes of intercepted conversations in which Iraqis talk about concealing evidence from inspectors and coaching scientists on how to answer questions. [2] They said Powell also will present satellite photographs of material being moved from sites in Iraq just before visits by U.N. inspectors and intelligence detailing Iraqi imports of banned weapons materials. (CNN/2.5/NA)

Once again, we find precontextualizations of Powell's presentation that are attributed to unnamed U.S. officials. Unlike the *Times*, however, CNN foregrounds the source of the assertions so that readers more readily recognize them as "official" viewpoints, rather than universally agreed-upon facts. Even so, the official reports suggest that Powell's evidence transparently indicates Iraqi wrongdoing in the normative present. In sentence 1, the main clause attributed to U.S. officials is easily recognized as a projection of a future rhetorical event: "Powell *will play* audiotapes of intercepted communications." But the additional subordinate clause is set in the present tense (*in which Iraqis talk about concealing evidence from inspectors and coaching scientists on how to answer questions*). There is a subtle temporal shift here from the future to the present, one that effectively brings Powell's evidence into the here and now. Moreover, the fact that the present-tense clause is unmodalized positions readers to regard it as less open to doubt. In this construction, the Iraqis don't *seem to* be talking about concealing evidence; they talk about concealing evidence. Thus, yet-to-be-heard audiotapes are represented as self-evidently and presently indicative of an Iraqi effort to hide things.

A similar observation can be made about sentence 2. Here, there are two main clauses attributed to U.S. officials, each of which projects a future happening (**bolded**):

A. **Powell also will present satellite photos** of material being moved from sites in Iraq just before visits by U.N. inspectors.
B. **[Powell will present] intelligence** detailing Iraqi imports of banned weapons materials

In each case, however, elements tacked on to the main clauses suggest that Powell's evidence is presently unambiguous. At the end of clause A, for instance, we find a prepositional phrase: "satellite photos *of material being moved from sites in Iraq just before visits by U.N. inspectors*." Here, the prepositional phrase indicates an atemporal relation between the photograph and what it depicts. In other words, the photographs are represented as *eternally* and *unequivocally* showing material being moved in Iraq. Indeed, it's not that the photographs *might* show material being moved; they are simply photographs *of* material being moved—always and already. Similarly, in clause B, the word "intelligence" is modified by a participial phrase: "intelligence *detailing Iraqi imports of banned weapons materials*." Here, the word "detailing" connotes thoroughness and completeness. The implication is that Powell will not merely mention Iraqi imports of banned weapons, but will present a robust account of them. Also, "detailing" is another participle that is unmarked for tense. Thus, once again, evidence that has not yet been revealed is assumed to specify Iraqi wrongdoing always and already. At one level, then, these precontextualizations of Powell's address are dialogically open: sourced to speakers whose positions may not be universally shared. At another level, though, the precontextualizations tend to close debate about Powell's evidence, presenting it as clearly indicative of Iraqi deception and misconduct in the normative present. In any case, the fact that all three news outlets previewed the same content—satellite photographs and audio intercepts—suggests just how well the Bush administration managed the news. Obviously, these items were strategically leaked—and faithfully reported.

Looking beyond Powell's Speech: Identifying the Hardest Sell and Envisioning the Path to War

Let's return now to the NBC broadcast. After reporting that French prime minister Jacques Chirac is still doubtful of "the war option" (NBC/2.4/AM), Mitchell appears on screen for the first time—standing at a distance from the viewer, behind the horseshoe-shaped table that is the centerpiece of the U.N. Security Council chambers (see excerpt 3.12). As she walks around the perimeter of the table, a new camera tracks her in a more intimate medium-close shot (see frame 122 in excerpt 3.12).

In this excerpt, Mitchell precontextualizes both proximal future discourse (Powell's address) and more distal future discourse (other nations' reactions to Powell's address). In particular, the visual information works to preview what it will be like in the actual Security Council chambers *during* Powell's proximal address. The horseshoe-shaped table, the chairs where delegates will actually sit, and the placards (reading Germany, Mexico, Pakistan, Russian Federation) make present for the viewer both the location and the prospective audience of Powell's speech.

The viewer is initially positioned as a distant observer of the scene, as Mitchell (who is presumably standing behind the seat where the French delegate will sit) reports that "France will be the hardest sell." Interestingly, here, the viewer is prepositioned to view France *from*

Excerpt 3.12. (NBC/2.4/AM)

Time	Frame	Soundtrack
119.		Here in the Security Council
120.		tomorrow, *France* will be
121.		the hardest *sell*.
122.		But U.S. officials believe
123.		if Colin Powell's
124.		evidence is *strong*
125.		enough to win

(continued)

Excerpt 3.12. *(continued)*

Time	Frame	Soundtrack
126.		over *France*,
127.		the other critics,
128.		even *Russia*,
129.		may follow.

the perspective of Colin Powell and the administration. For one thing, France is singled out as an *important* audience member of the future address, an audience member whose reaction to Powell's address will, one assumes, be more significant than the reactions of other "less important" nations (Mexico, for example). In fact, France is represented as an audience member who will present special difficulties, that is, who will be "the hardest sell." Notably, the *New York Times* offers a similar portrayal, suggesting that France will be "the major holdout" against a new war resolution (NYT/2.5/JPSW). Such descriptions position the audience to regard France as President Bush might: as an *obstacle* to be overcome, a client to be "sold" on Powell's argument. Other possible future roles for France (e.g., "France will be the greatest advocate for peace") are not made available to the viewer. Indeed, rather than representing France as a future agent capable of communicating its own discourse, NBC projects France as a passive listener who may be influenced by Powell's discourse. Observe, too, that the focus of the story is on the game of power politics: whether the administration can maneuver around roadblocks (e.g., France) in order to "win" support for war. Such "game faming" is typical of press reports (Patterson 1993; Cappella & Jamieson 1997). In fact, as Bennett and colleagues (2007) argue, game framing was particularly evident in news coverage before the Iraq War. Stories overwhelmingly emphasized how and whether the administration could solicit votes for war, and "not the truth or propriety of the effort" (19).

Moments later on NBC, in the tighter camera shot, Mitchell's spoken discourse enacts a slightly more distal future—beyond the immediate reactions to Powell's address and on to subsequent reactions. This more distal future is construed as highly contingent. For one thing, it is attributed to U.S. officials, a general and ambiguous category of speakers.[32] As such, this future scenario is represented as one dialogic option among many. For another thing, the future is represented in a conditional (if/then) statement, where the epistemically modalized proposition in the "then" clause—*other critics, even Russia, may follow*—is construed as dependent for its realization on the proposition in the "if" clause—*if Colin Powell's evidence is strong enough to win over France*.[33] We see here an instance of precontextualization drawn from an "official" source, a source that merely speculates about a hypothetical scenario.

But it is important to note that, even if this future scenario is speculative, it is endowed with *rhetorical presence* (Perelman & Olbrechts-Tyteca 1969). Specifically, Mitchell presents—and leads the audience to imagine—a future that would be very desirable for Powell and the administration: a future in which France may be won over by Powell's "strong evidence," and in which other nations may subsequently fall in line like dominoes. Of course, based on the same leak, Mitchell could have offered a different precontextualization of Powell's address and its potential impact: "If Colin Powell's evidence is not strong enough to persuade France, other critics may also reject Powell's arguments." In Mitchell's original construction, this possibility is rendered "anti-present" (Gross & Dearin 2003, 138). The future that the viewer is positioned to be interested in is the one that leads to war. Again, what is desirable for the Bush administration is made most available to the viewer.

Evaluating Future Rhetoric: How Good Will the Evidence Be?

A moment later, Mitchell asks the following question: "How good will the evidence *be*?" (NBC/2.4/AM). The question is interesting for a number of reasons. First, the answer to this question is directly relevant to whether or not, according to Mitchell's precontextualization of the future, France and other nations will be won over by Powell's evidence. Depending on how the question is answered, the viewer will be positioned to imagine a future in which other nations support or reject a new war resolution.

Second, even though the question remains unanswered at this point, it nevertheless *presupposes* that Powell's evidence will be at least somewhat *good*. Just imagine if Mitchell had asked, "How *bad* will the evidence be?" The viewer would have been positioned to presuppose that Powell's evidence will be *to some degree* "bad." By asking the opposite question, Mitchell precludes the possibility of "badness," and positions the viewer to presuppose that Powell's evidence will be at least *somewhat* "good" (in the worst possible case) and perhaps even exceptionally "good." In Martin and White's (2005) terms, Mitchell presumes a positive valuation of Powell's future evidence (good), leaving only the *force* of this valuation as an open question (how good?). Again, Powell's argument is presumed to be at least somewhat strong, even before he has spoken a word of it.

Finally, what's interesting about this question is that it also presupposes an *answer*. Indeed, Mitchell is not asking an open question about Powell's future evidence. She is not asking her audience *to wonder* about how good Powell's evidence will be with the expectation that we'll all find out tomorrow when he actually delivers his address. She is posing this question because she intends to answer it—*now*—almost a full day before Powell's speech is scheduled to take place.

So, how good will the evidence be? In excerpt 3.13, Mitchell answers this question.

Mitchell answers the question regarding how good Powell's evidence will be not by referring to any specific pieces of evidence in Powell's case, but by modalizing to various degrees what arguments Colin Powell will be able to "prove." At work in this excerpt, then, is a particular kind of epistemic modality known as *potentiality*. As Iedema, Feez, and

Excerpt 3.13. (NBC/2.4/AM)

Time	Frame	Soundtrack
132.		Today Powell
133.		was still reviewing whether
134.		they can prove sig*nifi*cant
135.		links between Saddam
136.		and al-*Qaed*a.
137.		But officials say
138.		Powell is con*vinc*ed

(continued)

Excerpt 3.13. *(continued)*

Time	Frame	Soundtrack
139.		he can still [sounds of marchers, chanting, begins and continues through remaining frames]
140.		establish a pattern that will
141.		be an in*dict*ment
142.		of Saddam Hussein.

White (1994) suggest, potentiality concerns "the capacity of an individual to perform some function":

> When we address the capacity of an individual to perform some function we are not saying that they will, or necessarily do perform that function. Rather, we are making a statement about the likelihood of the action based on our assessment of the participant's capabilities. (10)

Mitchell's report addresses Powell's potential to accomplish two related rhetorical goals: (1) prove significant links between Saddam and al-Qaeda, and (2) establish a pattern that will be an indictment of Saddam Hussein.

Before moving on to an analysis of how these future potentialities are modalized, it is worth pointing out that by identifying these two rhetorical goals, Mitchell directs her viewer to "be on the lookout" for them in

Powell's address. In fact, as in the case of the "SADDAM LIES" thematic formation, both the "TERROR TIES" formation, and the "INCRIMINATING PATTERN OF BEHAVIOR" formation do appear in Powell's actual address. In table 3.3, I have italicized instantiations of each of these thematic formations, as they were construed in both the NBC news narrative on February 4 and in Powell's presentation. For the sake of simplicity, I have left out the visual data that accompanied the spoken utterances.

Here the NBC precontextualizations do not necessarily corroborate the arguments that would be made by Powell in his speech. In fact, as I suggest below, NBC modalizes whether these arguments will, in fact, be made. However, by focusing on these particular thematic formations, NBC does endow them with presence, and, in a sense, prepares

Table 3.3. Precontextualizing Thematic Formations that Appear in Powell's Address

Thematic Formation	NBC, February 4	Powell's Address
Terror Ties	Today Powell was still reviewing whether they can prove *significant links between Saddam and al-Qaeda*.(NBC/2.4/AM)	What I want to bring to your attention today is the potentially much more *sinister nexus between Iraq and the al-Qaeda terrorist network*, a nexus that combines classic terrorist organizations and modern methods of murder. (UN/2.5/CP)
Incriminating Pattern of Behavior	But officials say Powell is convinced he can still establish *a pattern that will be an indictment of Saddam Hussein*. (NBC/2.4/AM)	What you will see is an accumulation of facts and *disturbing patterns of behavior* [that] *demonstrate that Saddam Hussein and his regime have made no effort—no effort—to disarm as required by the international community.* (UN/2.5/CP)

the audience to attend to them if— and, indeed, when —they appear in Powell's address.

With this in mind, let's return to a consideration of *potentiality* as it is expressed in the NBC broadcast. First, the likelihood that Powell will prove significant links between Saddam and al-Qaeda is construed as dependent upon his current review of the evidence. Since no information is given about what the ongoing review will find, the viewer is positioned to believe that Powell's argument is pending. He may find that he has the evidence to prove significant links, or he may not. This doesn't really tell the viewer much about "how good Powell's evidence will be." In fact, it suggests that we still don't know.

However, even as Mitchell's spoken report leaves unanswered the question of whether *Powell* will prove links between Saddam and al-Qaeda, the visual information that is co-deployed with this report helps to endow such links with rhetorical presence in the here and now. Specifically, just as Mitchell utters the words "links between Saddam," an image of Saddam Hussein appears on the screen (frame 135). The shot of Saddam is on screen only for a moment, but the viewer can nevertheless identify him[34]—the most salient figure on the left side of the picture—as he walks toward a point in space just to the right of the camera. Meanwhile, several Iraqi soldiers are also discernible as they stand and salute. Literally a second later, just as Mitchell utters the name "al-Qaeda," a new shot appears on the screen, in which several men dressed in black hoods pull themselves across a horizontal ladder (frame 136). Of course, Mitchell's spoken discourse and the visual image position the viewer to understand that these men are members of al-Qaeda—they are terrorists in training. Interestingly, within this scene one of these al-Qaeda terrorists, who, like Saddam in the shot before, is the most salient figure on the left side of the screen—also moves toward a point in space just to the right of the camera. The succession of images from Saddam to al-Qaeda implies a mutual relation between these two entities. In fact, the sheer proximity of these two images in the visual track gives this mutual link a visual presence that arguably compensates for and counteracts Mitchell's assertion that Powell is still reviewing whether such a link can be proven.

With regard to the next represented argumentative goal, Mitchell positions the viewer to be somewhat more confident about Powell's ability to "establish a pattern that will be an indictment of Saddam Hussein." First, Mitchell's use of the conjunction *but* serves to suggest that Powell's ability to prove the second argumentative goal is not jeopardized by his potential inability to prove the first. Specifically, *but* enacts a counterexpectancy whereby the viewer's presumed expectation (that Powell won't be able to indict Saddam Hussein because he may not be able to prove significant links between Saddam and al-Qaeda) is countered and supplanted by the proposition that Powell (according to U.S. officials) is confident he can still indict Saddam. We may consider this a *concede + counter* pairing (Martin & White 2005, 125–26). NBC *concedes* that Powell may not be able to prove the existence of "terror ties," but *counters* that he can still prove an "incriminating pattern of behavior."

Importantly, the counterproposition is *attributed*, opening dialogic space for alternative viewpoints. However, this dialogic expansion is mitigated by the fact that the assertion is attributed, once again, to a general and ambiguous category of speakers—"U.S. officials." As Edelman (1977) observes, journalists often attribute speech to such "mythical groups"—groups that cannot be monitored and whose titles are self-legitimizing. Thus, even though Mitchell attributes the assertion about Powell's ability to indict Saddam, she attributes it to a group that is essentially invisible and, thus, unchallengeable. Moreover, the lexical term chosen to represent these invisible speakers, *officials*, overtly suggests that the assertion itself is "official." Thus, the "good news" about Powell's ability to indict Saddam is represented as "insider knowledge" from credible sources, rather than "political spin" passed on by administration propagandists.

One might argue that Mitchell's report is nevertheless dialogically expansive since the assertion attributed to U.S. officials is additionally "sourced" to Powell, who apparently expressed to those officials his conviction about his ability to indict Saddam before those officials reported this "news" to NBC. That this is obvious to the viewer is true enough. However, one must keep in mind that Powell himself has already been implicitly authorized as a credible speaker—*vouched for*—elsewhere in the news report (e.g., as the one who will expose Saddam Hussein's lies). Given this characterization, the viewer is positioned to regard Powell's conviction as an indication that his case will be solid. Moreover, the notion that Powell is "convinced" that he can indict Saddam Hussein further establishes a thematic formation that has been in the works since the beginning of the report: "POWELL IS CONFIDENT." Indeed, Powell's confidence was made *present* in the very beginning of Mitchell's report (see analysis of excerpt 3.2) where Powell was displayed smiling self-assuredly. Now, he is "convinced"—a word that Mitchell endows with presence through added vocal emphasis—that he will prove his case. In short, Mitchell's attributions ultimately position the audience to believe that Powell is *quite capable* of establishing an incriminating pattern of behavior to indict Saddam Hussein.

So far, this analysis has not even touched the interesting visual data that is co-deployed with Mitchell's report in frames 137–42. Previous visuals in this news narrative typically enacted a clear semantic relationship with the verbal text. For instance, the visual image of hooded men on a horizontal ladder stands in a meronymous relationship with the co-deployed spoken words "al-Qaeda." In other words, the viewer is positioned to understand that these hooded men are *part of* al-Qaeda. In frames 137–42, however, such semantic ties are not easily observed. Instead, as Mitchell's report focuses on Powell and his conviction, the visual track does not include images of Powell, but displays various shots of what is apparently a military rally in Iraq. Importantly, these visuals index the material context in which Powell's future discourse is situated. Ultimately, the verbal and visual modes work together to enact a kind of cross-temporality, whereby the future is juxtaposed with the present. Specifically, the value of Powell's future evidence (represented in Mitchell's spoken discourse) is positioned against the backdrop of a "militarized" Iraq (represented visually).

In frames 137–38, as Mitchell utters the words "But officials say Powell is convinced," the viewer sees, in a very long shot, many hundreds of people standing under a large portrait of Saddam Hussein and holding up signs that reveal the colors of the Iraqi flag. The portrait of Saddam and the Iraqi flag colors collocate to suggest that this is some kind of rally. On the surface, this image has nothing to do with Powell being "convinced." However, it does serve to characterize the country of Iraq, which has been mentioned several times throughout the news narrative—and which has already been characterized as a "target" in this news narrative. Specifically, this visual narrative indexes a celebration both of Iraq and of the Iraqi leader, Saddam Hussein, that is, "the local liar."

In frames 139–40, the verbal-visual interplay begins to get interesting. The shot changes from the distant picture of hundreds of rallying Iraqis to a close shot of one Iraqi leading a march toward the camera—and toward the viewer. The person leading the march is dressed in a white hood that completely covers his face, but for the eyeholes. He holds a rifle on his left shoulder and appears to have other weapons attached to his white uniform. Also discernible in the image are several rows of soldiers dressed in military fatigues, who march in unison behind the hooded man and who also carry rifles. As Mitchell reports that Powell "can still establish a pattern," one can hear chanting and shouting—ambient sounds of the depicted world.

Crucially, in this visual narrative, the viewer is positioned to regard Iraq as *threatening*, particularly in light of the "TARGET: IRAQ" thematic that appeared earlier in this newscast. First, it is significant that the "virtual proximity" between the viewer and the Iraqi soldier in the hooded white uniform is maximal. Here I am measuring "virtual proximity" as a product of camera angle and distance, as well as the body position and visual salience of the depicted participant. This Iraqi soldier is pictured at a direct camera angle and in a close shot. He appears "large on screen"—indeed larger than any other depicted figure in this newscast (including Tom Brokaw)—as he walks toward, and almost into, the viewer.

This unusual proximity endows this hooded soldier with presence. However, this proximity is regarded as threatening to the viewer, not only because the solider is "invading the viewer's space," but because he is carrying weapons and hiding his face behind a white hood. In fact, the white hood that covers this man's face is intratextually linked to the *black hoods* worn by the al-Qaeda terrorists in frame 136. This visual similarity positions the viewer to regard this man not just as a soldier, but as some kind of Iraqi *terrorist*.[35] Once again, the "TERROR TIES" thematic formation is enacted visually and intratextually *by* NBC, moments after NBC has reported that Powell may not be able to prove that this link exists. Thus, apparent visual evidence of Iraqi terrorists *in the normative present* confirms one of Powell's *future* (precontextualized) claims. Moreover, Powell's proximal discourse seems desirable insofar as it "wards off" a more distal danger: namely, a violent attack potentially invoked by this threatening image.

In the final two frames (141–42), the image changes once again to a more distant shot of this march. Now several soldiers dressed in traditional military fatigues and berets are displayed marching. These soldiers carry Iraqi flags, a poster inscribed with the Iraqi insignia (what appears to be an eagle), and a portrait of a mustachioed man who appears to be Saddam Hussein. The rhythmic chant of these marchers is heard in the background, as Mitchell utters the words "an in*dic*tment of Saddam Hussein." This time, verbal-visual synonymy is established as Mitchell's utterance of "Saddam Hussein" seems to refer to the mustachioed man in the poster. As a result, Mitchell's spoken report about the possible future "indictment of Saddam Hussein" is related to the military rally being depicted in the visual track. In a sense, it appears that Saddam Hussein will be indicted *because* of what's going on in the visual track—because he is the leader of a country that harbors terrorist-soldiers, because he oversees a military that threatens the viewer, and, by extension, the United States.

Conclusion

There are several important implications of this chapter. First, from a methodological standpoint, this study makes clear that scholars interested in rhetoric and media should not neglect the role of multimodality in their analyses. Put another way, this analysis makes clear that studies which focus only on print-linguistic aspects of texts are destined to give an incomplete picture of those texts' rhetorical features. If, for instance, I had only focused my analysis on the linguistic aspects of this NBC news text, I would have missed crucial visual data (e.g., the "Target Iraq" headline; the virtual proximity to the terrorist-soldier) that surely impacted how audiences were positioned to interpret both the proximal future (e.g., Powell's speech) and distal future (e.g., war with Iraq). Scholars who overlook or dismiss such visual data may ultimately diminish the credibility of their research.

Next this chapter advances our understanding of precontextualization, a form of prospective intertextuality that draws future discourse into the normative present. More specifically, precontextualization should be viewed as a rhetorical strategy whereby journalists anticipate and evaluate future discourse—and potentiate certain material futures. In fact, the precontextualization of future political texts is *typical* in corporate media discourse and takes many forms. When mainstream journalists rely on advance copies and "leaked" information, they give political actors power to shape the news. Still, the press has incredible freedom to characterize future political discourse. Even when journalists report "leaks" from political insiders, they are still free to reinterpret these leaks, to saturate them with their own meanings and embed them in their own narrative frames. Moreover, journalists are free to precontextualize future discourse *without consulting* political sources. They can speculate about what will be said—or even predict it with apparent certainty.

Of course, the future is necessarily contingent and unknowable, and, consequently, representations of the future are necessarily "fictitious." But journalists position audiences to regard their predictions of the future as "based on real events"—that is, as plausible reports of what may well—and should—happen. Indeed, because journalists frequently construe *past events* as "factual" and universally agreed upon, they often offer viewers a seemingly self-evident context for understanding future discursive and material happenings. For instance, the NBC journalists represented the finding of empty chemical weapons munitions as naturally indicative of Saddam Hussein's untrustworthiness. This "fact" provided an unchallengeable (and ultimately supportive) contextual lens through which audiences could view Colin Powell's future accusations of Iraqi deceit and Saddam Hussein's past refutations of hiding WMDs. Even before Powell spoke, the "evidence" supplied by NBC already seemed to warrant his case; and even as Saddam Hussein claimed to have no weapons, the same evidence "undercut" his denials.

Similarly, journalists may also construe *present events* in ways that position audiences to view some future material actions as desirable. In this study, representations of the present were often characterized by ideological polarization, predisposing audiences to adopt a violent posture toward Iraq (Van Dijk 1998). For instance, NBC journalists tended to construe an adversarial conflict—indeed a "showdown"—between America and Iraq, which was personified in the dispute between the covert protagonist, Colin Powell, and the covert antagonist, Saddam Hussein. Audiences were not only positioned to "take sides" in this conflict, but also to view one side—Iraq—as a legitimate "target" for aggression.

Crucially, at the same time, audiences were positioned to regard the conflict itself as an entertaining melodrama—a spectacle that one can sit back and enjoy. In fact, as the current "showdown" was represented as leading almost inevitably to war, audiences were positioned as passive spectators—"watchers" of the future, rather than agents who might give the future a shape. Ultimately, the journalists constrained the realm of future possibilities. They framed the news exclusively from the perspective of the Bush administration—envisaging "favorable" scenarios in which Powell might win over opponents at the U.N. and secure a resolution for military action. In a sense, the administration's "path to war" was illuminated by reporters, while possible avenues to peace were concealed or ignored.

CHAPTER FOUR

America's Best Intelligence: Recontextualization and Rhetorical Transformation

⌘

> The result of the politics of recontextualization is to favorably position one representation of an issue over another—that is, to instill a given representation with cultural value so that it becomes shared or "common sense" knowledge. Therefore, the way in which the politics of recontextualization plays out impacts broader social understandings of the world.
>
> —Adam Hodges, "The Politics of Recontextualization," 2008

Chapter 3 focused on how journalists projected a future rhetorical event and pre-positioned audiences to adopt certain attitudes toward Powell and his rhetoric. I termed this type of anticipatory intertextuality "precontextualization." In a sense, journalists pre-formed Colin Powell's address—construing it as a "real thing" even before it took place. The present chapter shifts focus to how journalists *re*-represent a rhetorical event that has already occurred. This type of past-oriented intertextuality is known as recontextualization. In essence, recontextualization involves extracting elements from one communicative event and relocating those elements in a new discursive context (Bauman & Briggs 1990). However, as Linell (1998) suggests, recontextualization is never the simple movement of a fixed meaning from one text to another (145). Meanings are not simply reiterated; they are *transformed*. Indeed, according to Bakhtin (1981), recontextualization is "*always* subject to certain semantic changes" (340, my emphasis), as prior discourse is re-represented "with varying degrees of precision and impartiality (or more precisely partiality)" (339). A rhetor may choose to endorse, oppose, or "re-perspectivize" elements of a prior text, refashioning those elements as demanded by a new situation (Linell 1998, 151). Recontextualization, then, is best thought of as a rhetorical "tool for re-conceptualiz[ing] and re-accenting" prior discourse (Bakhtin 1981, 339). With this in mind, this chapter concerns what I term *rhetorical transformation*—that is, the way elements of a political speech are transformed as they are recontextualized in multimodal news discourse. Specifically, I examine how journalists transformed Powell's presentation—and repositioned audiences to interpret Powell's argument.

I show that the news reports recontextualized Powell's address both implicitly and explicitly. In fact, even when the reports did not directly cite Powell's assertions, they nevertheless rearticulated "talking points" discernible in his U.N. performance. Even when journalists were not talking about Powell, then, they still managed to echo some of his central arguments. Meanwhile, when journalists explicitly sourced assertions to Powell, they typically rendered those assertions more certain, more substantiated, more salient, and more legitimate. Indeed, they overwhelmingly represented Powell as authoritative, and re-represented his case in ways that maximized its warrantability. Crucially, though the journalists usually transformed Powell's individual assertions in microscopic ways, the cumulative effect of these transformations was to enhance the persuasive potential of his entire address. Thus, this chapter shows how minor and seemingly innocuous alterations can accumulate to induce a globally different perception of a public address.

Different Types of Recontextualization across Multimodal Texts: An Inventory

For the purposes of analysis, scholars often distinguish between several different forms of recontextualization (Bazerman 2004; Fairclough 2003; Halliday & Matthiessen 2004; Thibault 1991). Perhaps the two most familiar kinds are quotation and reported speech. Briefly, *quotation* attempts to re-represent prior speech verbatim and is marked by a paratactic dependency structure[1]—and, in written texts, by quotation marks (e.g., Jack said, "I ate the sandwich"). Meanwhile, *reported speech* attempts to rearticulate the meaning or "gist" (not the wording) of an earlier assertion, and is marked by a hypotactic dependency structure (e.g., Jack said that he ate lunch). Of course, reporting speech allows a person more freedom to reinterpret or "spin" recontextualized discourse for persuasive ends. As Bazerman (2004) explains, reporting "filters the meaning" of the original text such that it may be "thoroughly infused" with the reporter's attitudes and purpose (88).[2]

Aside from quotations and reports, *recordings* of prior speech are also used frequently in television news broadcasts. In a recording, speech filmed in its original context is replayed in a new context. In fact, recording, not quotation, is the closest one can come to reproducing an original speech event since it retains aspects of the original context (ambient sounds, visuals of setting, original vocal inflection, etc.).[3] Still, even recorded speech is transformed as it is recontextualized. For instance, if a recorded speaker's name and "credentials" are flashed on the screen as she or he speaks, this speaker may be considered more authoritative than a recorded speaker who remains anonymous and who is given no institutional title. In any case, recordings, quotations, and reports all involve some kind of clear attribution to a prior speaker—either through language (*X said*, *according to* X, etc.) or visual data (a figure on the visual screen appears to be speaking "for himself"). Thus, these may be considered *explicit* forms of recontextualization that overtly source meanings to their "original context."

In addition to these explicit forms of intertextuality, there are also more implicit types: namely, thematic formations and assumptions. In fact, one can recontextualize a (verbal-visual) thematic formation, without ever citing, or even knowing, the antecedent source from which it was drawn (Thibault 1991, 125). For instance, if I say, "In America, all of us are equal," I may not intend it, but I am rearticulating and recontextualizing a thematic formation "originally" expressed in the Declaration of Independence. But intertextuality can be even more implicit (and unintentional) than this. For instance, a meaning may be present only in the form of an *unstated assumption* or presupposition[4]—and these unstated assumptions may be considered recontextualizations of what were originally *stated* propositions in prior texts (Fairclough 2003, 17). So, for example, when journalists in this study refer to "Iraq's weapons," they presuppose that these weapons exist. Of course, the implicit thematic formation—"IRAQ HAS WEAPONS"—may be found, stated explicitly, in antecedent texts (e.g., speeches by George W. Bush).

Thus, we can imagine a cline of intertextuality, ranging from explicit and typically intentional forms (like quotation) to implicit, often unintentional forms (as when rhetors draw upon the same thematic formations in different texts). I have charted this cline of recontextualization in table 4.1.[5]

Most studies of intertextuality have focused on the recontextualization of verbal data—speech and writing.[6] However, it is clear that recontextualization involves multimodal discourse—including language, sounds, gestures, images, and so on. This means that when elements of one text are recontextualized in another, these elements are themselves

Table 4.1. Types of Recontextualization

Cline	Type	Description	Example
Explicit ↑	Recording	Original speech or event is replayed in a new context.	[Video clip of Powell speaking at U.N. in NBC 2.5 broadcast.]
	Quotation	Textual voice specifies an original speaker and restates verbatim what was said.	"You're going to have to use your mind as well as your eyes and ears to take in the complete picture," a White House official said. (NYT/2.5/JPSW)
	Report	Textual voice specifies the original source and (purportedly) attempts to reproduce the "gist" of the original speech.	Powell claimed that Zarqawi and his lieutenants helped establish this terrorist training camp in northern Iraq. (NBC/2.5/JM)

(*continued*)

Table 4.1. *(continued)*

Cline	Type	Description	Example
↓	Thematic Formation	One text is linked to another text on the basis of a shared meaning relation (synonymy, hyponymy, argument pattern, visual transitivity, visual repetition, etc.). Shared thematic formations are implicit recontextualizations when there is no attribution to the original speaker who first issued the theme.	*Thematic*: U.N. FACES IRRELEVANCY IF IT DOES NOT CONFRONT IRAQ a. Colin Powell: This body places itself in danger of irrelevance if it allows Iraq to continue to defy its will without responding effectively and immediately. (UN/2.5/CP) b. Richard Butler: The Security Council must now address this in the most serious way or . . . face consigning itself to irrelevancy. (NBC/2.5/RB)
Implicit	Assumption	One text is linked to another text on the basis of an unstated and taken-for-granted assumption. Either an implicit presupposition in one text is stated outright in another text, or both texts share the same assumptions.	*Assumption:* IRAQ POSSESSES ILLEGAL WEAPONS a. NYT: Mr. Powell also planned a furious round of diplomatic pressure on Security Council nations to accept . . . a second resolution authorizing force . . . if Iraq does not quickly cooperate in revealing *its illegal weapons*. (NYT/2.5/SWJP) b. Colin Powell: My second purpose today is . . . to share with you what the United States knows about *Iraq's weapons of mass destruction*. (UN/2.5/CP)

Note: For the sake of simplicity, I have not included visual data or vocal emphases in the examples.

multisemiotic—and are transformed in multisemiotic ways. Drawing on recent scholarship in intertextuality and social semiotics,[7] I developed a systematic methodology for examining how an "original" multimodal text is transformed in small ways as it is recontextualized (Oddo 2013). Briefly, I constructed a table in which recontextualizations of Powell's speech were placed alongside Powell's original discourse (see excerpt in table 4.2). I then charted the specific transformations that occurred as verbal-visual elements of Powell's text were recontextualized in the multimodal news narratives.

This comparison was rigorous and micro-analytic. I systematically identified changes on the basis of small, but clearly identifiable, discursive categories.[8] Based on this analysis, I assessed how audiences were *repositioned* as a consequence of journalistic recontextualizations. In other words, I determined how, in transforming elements of Powell's presentation, journalists prompted audiences to interpret Powell's original claims in new ways.[9] Using this method allowed me to discern micro-transformations across texts—micro-transformations that I would have otherwise missed. As I illustrate below, these small verbal-visual changes have enormous rhetorical and material implications, as they may combine to alter the *overall* meaning of a given political argument.

Rhetorical Transformation and Audience Repositioning: NBC, the Times, and CNN.com

When journalists explicitly recontextualized Powell's address, they transformed it in at least one of four ways: they deleted meanings, added new meanings, relexicalized[10] meanings, and reordered meanings (see table 4.3).

What was the rhetorical significance of these transformations? Typically, they served to enhance and legitimate Powell's argument. *Enhancement* occurred most frequently (n = 89) in the data corpus, as journalists repeatedly positioned audiences to regard Powell's claims as more salient, more certain, or more warranted than they otherwise would have. Meanwhile, *legitimation* was the next most common phenomenon (n = 45), as journalists commonly added verbal-visual "commentary" that rendered both Powell and his argument more authoritative or reasonable (see chapter 2). It is worth repeating that since recontextualization always involves transformation, journalists were never completely "faithful" to Powell's claims. However, there were several instances when the journalistic changes were so inconsequential that Powell's discourse could be said to have been *"impartially" re-represented* (n = 37). Of course, even when journalists "objectively"

Table 4.2. Charting Recontextualization, Transformation, and Audience Repositioning

Original Source Material: Powell's Presentation		Recontextualization: NBC News		Rhetorical Transformation	Audience Repositioning
Verbal	Visual	Verbal	Visual	type : token	type : token
Iraq had a program to modify aerial fuel tanks for Mirage jets. This *video* of an Iraqi test flight obtained by UNSCOM some years ago shows an Iraqi F-1 *Mirage jet* aircraft. Note the *spray* coming from beneath the *Mirage*; that is 2,000 liters of *simulated anthrax* that a *jet is spraying*.		Powell played *tape* of a *Mirage jet* retrofitted to *spray simulated anthrax*		• Deletion: past tense possessive clause: "Iraq had . . ." • Deletion: process-actor-circumstance: "obtained by UNSCOM some years ago" • Deletion: present-tense relational clause: "that is 2,000 liters . . ." • Addition: actor-process: "Powell played" • *No attribution*	Enhancement: enhanced presence; dialogic contraction

Note: To save space, I have deleted several details from the original analysis.

re-represented Powell's utterances, they still endowed these utterances with greater rhetorical presence, effectively echoing and reinforcing his argument for war (Domke 2004). Finally, journalists did sometimes *qualify* Powell's argument ($n = 24$), positioning audiences to view his claims as less certain or less substantive than they would have if they had viewed the original speech. However, these qualifications generally had little "force," since they often co-occurred with enhancements and legitimations that muted their effects. In any case, the journalists did more than repeat Powell's claims. Indeed, they typically *remade* Powell's claims, repositioning audiences to regard his presentation as stronger than they otherwise would have. (See appendix H for details about categories of audience repositioning and frequencies for each news provider in the corpus.)

In fact, the journalists not only explicitly enhanced Powell's arguments, but they also included other sources who, without ever mentioning Powell, essentially reiterated the gist of his claims. In other words, thematic formations from Powell's address were *implicitly* recontextualized in the news narratives as journalists and other speakers reproduced Powell's "talking points"—without ever attributing them to Powell. As shown in table 4.4, the different news outlets tended to include speakers who *rearticulated* Powell's thematic formations, but generally featured only a few speakers who offered an implied *rebuttal* to Powell's claims.[11]

In order to more clearly illustrate what became of Powell's speech in the news, I have elected to analyze two segments of the NBC broadcast on February 5 in greater detail. In the first portion of the analysis,

Table 4.3. Transformation Types

Category	Definition
Deletion	Meanings articulated in the original speech are deleted or omitted in the recontextualized version.
Addition	Meanings that were not present in the original speech are added in the recontextualized version.
Relexicalization	A meaning from the original speech is re-represented in the journalistic text using different but near-synonymous lexical forms.
Reordering	Elements from the original speech are reordered—resequenced or juxtaposed in new ways.

I study Andrea Mitchell's report in which she recontextualizes Powell's arguments about Iraq's alleged weapons of mass destruction and efforts to deceive U.N. inspectors. Then, in the second portion of the analysis, I examine Jim Miklaszewski's report in which he recontextualizes Powell's arguments regarding Iraq's supposed ties to the al-Qaeda terrorist network. I will occasionally compare these NBC reports to similar reports in the *New York Times* and on CNN.com, accounting for some of the interplay between different media narratives.

Brokaw's Introduction: Extolling a Masterful Performance

Andrea Mitchell's NBC report followed a brief introduction by Tom Brokaw (see excerpt 4.1). In this introduction, Brokaw stands next to a recontextualized video image of Colin Powell speaking at the U.N. Security Council. Behind Powell's image, two large digital flags—one American and one Iraqi—wave in the background; and beneath Powell's image is the caption: "Making the Case."

Here Brokaw introduces several recontextualizations of Powell's presentation. In fact, we might call these *macro-recontextualizations*,

Table 4.4. Implicit Recontextualization of Powell's Arguments

Category (#)	Example
Rearticulation NBC: 14 CNN: 11 NYT: 1 Total: 26	*Repeated thematic*: IRAQ POSSESSES/SEEKS WMDs a. Powell: We have amassed much intelligence indicating that Iraq is continuing to make these weapons. (UN/2.5/CP) b. NBC: [Iraq is] continuing to make new weapons of mass destruction while this process is going on. (NBC/2.5/RB)
Rebuttal NBC: 4 CNN: 2 NYT:3 Total: 7	*Rebutted thematic:* SADDAM HUSSEIN SUPPORTS TERRORISM a. Powell: Saddam was a supporter of terrorism long before these terrorist networks had a name. And this support continues. (UN/2.5/CP) b. NBC: U.S. officials stress there is no evidence that links Saddam Hussein to 9/11 here in the U.S. or any other terrorist attacks. (NBC/2.5/JM)

since they attempt to summarize Powell's entire presentation. Specifically, Powell's entire speech is condensed into the following nominal phrases: "the case" (printed on the screen), "the administration's case against Saddam Hussein," and "a masterful performance." Moreover, Powell's presentation is *enhanced* with a kind of Us-Them thematic (Van Dijk 1998), supplied by the American and Iraqi flags waving in contradistinction to one another. Keep in mind that earlier in this newscast, Iraq had already been associated with a negative value: deception. In fact, as noted in chapter 2 (see excerpt 2.2), at the very beginning of this broadcast, Brokaw presented the lead "headline"—*text, lies, and videotape*—as an image of the Iraqi flag waved on screen (NBC/2.5/TB). Thus, when the Iraqi flag reappears on screen in the frames above, it does not merely represent "one of the nations involved in a conflict." It represents a negatively moralized "Them."

Meanwhile, Powell, the American, is *legitimated* in Brokaw's spoken discourse. First, the verbal process used to represent Powell's speech (*spelled out*) suggests a subtle endorsement of Powell's case (Martin & White 2005). Powell did not merely *present* the administration's case, but he *spelled it out*—presumably with clarity and aplomb. Furthermore, in a circumstance of manner (Halliday & Matthiessen 2004, 267), Powell is construed as having spelled out his case "with a prosecutor's rhetoric." This implicit comparison to a prosecutor is evaluative, suggesting both Powell's skill as a rhetor and the lawfulness of his case.[12] Finally, in an exceedingly positive appreciation, Powell's artistic performance is described as "masterful." Indeed, like the previous clauses, this bare, monogloss assertion (*it was a masterful performance*) leaves no space for dialogic alternatives. The audience is to take for granted that Powell skillfully "spelled out" the American case for war. In fact, this

Excerpt 4.1. (NBC/2.5/TB)

Time	Frame	Soundtrack
19.		He spelled out with *vi*sual aids and a prosecutor's *rhe*toric the administration's case against Saddam Hussein. It was a *mas*terful performance but was it en*ough*?

Note: The spoken report spanned many frames similar to the one shown.

positive depiction of Powell's ethos is *qualified* only by a degree of uncertainty as to whether Powell persuaded his audience: was his masterful performance *enough*? Mitchell's report presumably answers this vague question.

Legitimizing the Case: America's Best Intelligence

Standing outside, and gazing directly into the camera in a close shot, Mitchell begins her report as follows: "Armed with America's *best* intelligence, Colin Powell tried to persuade the world that Saddam Hussein will *never let* U.N. inspectors *find* his hidden weapons" (NBC/2.5/AM). Here, is another macro-recontextualization in which Powell's entire presentation is converted into a compact summary. Like Brokaw, Mitchell also *qualifies* Powell's performance by adding an element of "teleological uncertainty," that is, uncertainty as to whether Powell accomplished his argumentative goals. Specifically, Mitchell adds the conative verb phrase (*tried to*), creating doubt as to whether Powell succeeded in "persuading the world." Elsewhere, however, Mitchell transforms Powell's presentation in ways that position audiences to believe that it *ought* to have been persuasive—even if it didn't necessarily succeed with the international community. Most importantly, Mitchell *legitimates* the argument attributed to Powell by adding a strongly positive modifier: "armed with America's best intelligence." The judgment that Powell is "armed" metaphorically suggests that he is well prepared for rhetorical combat. Of course, the metaphor enacts an Us-Them logic (one does not take up arms unless there is an enemy), and likely positions the audience to regard Powell's address as one that could lead to actual war.[13] Meanwhile, the added circumstantial element (another circumstance of manner)—"with America's best intelligence"—clearly suggests that the evidence that Powell presented was superlative. After all, if *America's best evidence* didn't persuade the world, then nothing can. Moreover, since the intelligence is construed as belonging to the entire country (*America's*), the assertion practically demands a nationalistic response. In this way, Mitchell continues *vouching* for Colin Powell, and reaffirms the Us-Them dyad first suggested by Brokaw. While They are associated with deception, We are associated with outstanding evidence that can expose their lies.

In addition, as Mitchell relexicalizes Powell's thesis, she transforms one of Powell's allegations into a taken-for-granted assumption. Specifically, "hidden weapons" alleged to exist by Powell and the Bush administration are *assumed* to exist empirically in Mitchell's report. Put another way, according to Mitchell, Powell did not try to persuade people that Saddam Hussein *has* hidden weapons, but that Saddam Hussein will never let inspectors *find* these weapons. Thus, from the beginning of Mitchell's report, one can observe "dialogic contraction" by which one of Powell's key claims—that Iraq is hiding weapons—is transformed into a presupposed fact. As I describe below, the NBC journalists were fond of this type of *enhancement*.

Cataloging Powell's Evidence: A Chilling Example

A moment later, Mitchell disappears from the visual track of the news narrative and a new video image emerges on screen: Colin Powell and then-CIA director George Tenet talking with delegates at the U.N. Security Council. In a voiceover, Mitchell explains that "Powell came pre*par*ed," after working together with Mr. Tenet for several days "to *build* a case of Iraq's de*cep*tion and de*ni*al" (NBC/2.5/AM). Here, once again, Powell's presentation is *legitimated* with a positive judgment (*prepared*), and transformed into a nominal phrase that rearticulates the prosecutor metaphor first issued by Tom Brokaw (*a case of Iraq's denial and deception*).[14] Then, as a distant, high-angle shot of the Security Council appears on screen, Mitchell reports that Powell and Tenet "showed *sat*ellite photos, quoted defectors, and played *au*diotapes of intercepted conversations" (NBC/2.5/AM). All of the clauses in this clause complex may be considered macro-recontextualizations, since they condense entire phases of Powell's presentation into relatively brief assertions. The clauses are also essentially "*impartial*"; there are no overt enhancements, legitimations, or qualifications. However, the juxtaposition of the three clauses in a single clause complex essentially reorders Powell's case—bringing together in close proximity elements of Powell's argument that were originally relatively dispersed. Arguably, as the sentence is expanded clause by clause, the viewer gets the impression that Powell's "evidence" is proliferating with each piece piling on top of the last.

A moment later, in excerpt 4.2, Mitchell introduces a recording from Powell's address in which Powell translates an intercepted conversation—in Mitchell's words, a "chilling example" of Powell's evidence.

NBC *enhances* this recording of Powell's address in two important ways. First, as the transcript of the voice intercept emerges on screen, and Powell's voice is heard in the soundtrack, NBC once again adds digital images of waving Iraqi and American flags. To be sure, the flags are not nearly as salient as the transcript in the foreground; however, their presence suggests a now recurring "nationalist" thematic that pits Americans against the Iraqis.

Next, and more obviously, Mitchell's introductory evaluation (*chilling*) signals to viewers what affectual response they should adopt toward Powell's evidence—categorically declaring that the voice intercept is scary and alarming.[15] However, there is nothing inherently scary about the voice intercept. Mitchell, like Powell, assumes that the officers in the recording are working to remove notes about "nerve agents" in an effort to hide weapons from inspectors. But this is not the only possible interpretation of the intercepted communication. In fact, according to *The Iraqi Perspective Report*, a study published by the United States Joint Forces Command, the intercept was actually evidence of "an attempt by the [Iraqi] regime to ensure that it was in *compliance with U.N. resolutions*" (Woods et al. 2006, 93, my emphasis). As it turns out, the officers were trying to "prevent suspicion" of wrongdoing by removing "lingering traces of weapons fielded in the past" (93). I don't mean to suggest that Mitchell (or Powell for that matter) could have known this at the time. However, Mitchell did not have to assume that Powell's interpretation of the intercept was the only one. And, certainly, she did not need to *enhance* Powell's suggestion of Iraqi wrongdoing by positioning viewers to regard as "chilling" Powell's translation and interpretation of this innocuous conversation.

Interestingly, NBC was not the only news outlet to increase the persuasive potential of Powell's audiotapes. For example, CNN.com describes "an intercept of Iraq military officers discussing how to hide evidence of banned weapons programs."[16] Here, CNN assumes that the intercept includes the voices "of Iraqi military officers," excluding the possibility that the intercept might have captured the voices of some other speakers. Bear in mind that the leadership in Baghdad

Excerpt 4.2. (NBC/2.5/AM CP)

Time	Frame	Soundtrack
64.	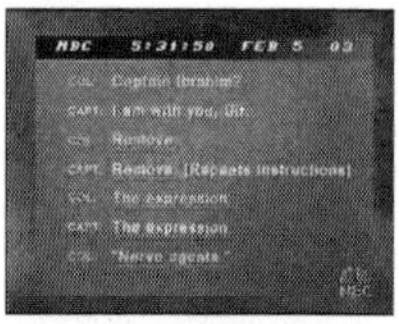	**Mitchell:** One *chill*ing example:
65.	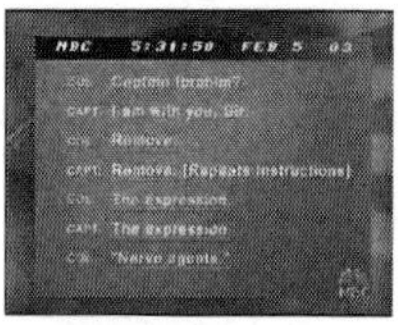	[arabic male voice] **Powell:** Re*move*. Remove. The ex*press*ion. The ex*press*ion. I got it. Nerve agents
71.	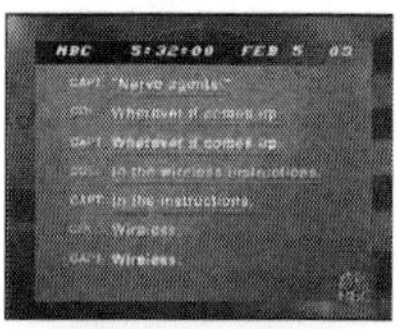	Nerve agents. Wher*ev*er it *comes up*.
76.		The senior officer is con*cer*ned that somebody might be *list*ening. Well *some*body *was*.

Note: The spoken report spanned many frames similar to the ones shown.

specifically denied the authenticity of these audiotapes, charging that they were fabrications. Thus, CNN had good reason to acknowledge *who said* the intercept was "of Iraqi military officers," specifically by attributing this allegation to Powell. More importantly, CNN categorically asserts that the speakers on the tape are discussing how to hide banned weapons, leaving no space for audiences to consider alternative viewpoints about what the intercept reveals. Like NBC, CNN construes Powell's interpretation of the audio as the only interpretation possible.[17]

Meanwhile, the reporting in the *New York Times* was even more problematic:

> Among the evidence presented at the United Nations Security Council were recordings of Iraqis referring to "nerve agents," and to apparent efforts to remove incriminating material before the arrival of United Nations inspectors. Scratchy-sounding voices in Arabic saying, "We evacuated everything," "Remove," and "Forbidden ammo," echoed eerily in a chamber clearly tense over the possibility of war. (NYT/2.6/SW)

Like CNN, the *Times* takes for granted that the recordings are "of Iraqis," instead of acknowledging that Powell had *claimed* that Iraqi speakers were featured on the tapes. Moreover, the *Times* subtly alters what the Iraqis actually discuss in the recordings. According to the *Times*, the Iraqis refer to "nerve agents," but as shown in excerpt 4.2, the speakers actually refer to *the expression* "nerve agents" as it appears in "wireless instructions." In other words, the Iraqis talk about the words "nerve agents," not actual nerve agents. This is potentially a very important distinction, but the *Times* fails to draw attention to it, leaving audiences to imagine that the tapes clearly reveal Iraqis talking about existing WMDs. Next, the *Times* suggests that the tapes also include "apparent efforts to remove incriminating material." On the one hand, the evidential descriptor "apparent" qualifies whether or not the tapes definitively show efforts to remove incriminating material. After all, what is apparently true is not necessarily true. On the other hand, the word "apparent" may also suggest that the efforts to remove incriminating material are *easily* recognized—not just by Powell, but by anyone listening to the tapes.

Interestingly, the *Times* reporters do not elect to review Powell's audiotape evidence in any detail. Instead, they extract a few words from three different recordings in Powell's presentation, and rearrange these words in a series of "scare quotes" so that they seem to be part of single thread: "'We evacuated everything,' 'Remove,' and 'Forbidden ammo.'" In fact, in re-representing these quotations, the *Times* excluded a number of crucial details, details that would tend to mitigate the sense that the recordings showed Iraqi misconduct. For example, the word "remove" comes from the recording discussed above in which one speaker instructs another to remove *the expression* "nerve agents"—not actual nerve agents. Meanwhile, the clause "we evacuated everything" was extracted from a different recording of two speakers alleged to be Iraqi officers. In Powell's translation, a speaker said to be an Iraqi colonel says, "We have this modified vehicle.

What do we say if one of [the inspectors] sees it?" Another speaker identified as a general answers, "I'll come to see you in the morning. I'm worried you all have something left." The colonel then says, "We evacuated everything. We don't have anything left." From this translation, it's difficult to know exactly what the colonel has "evacuated." But by framing this discussion as "an apparent effort to hide incriminating material," the *Times* positions readers to believe that "we evacuated everything" means "we hid banned weapons." Finally, the phrase "forbidden ammo" comes from yet another recording allegedly involving Iraqi officers. In this case, one speaker announces to another that officials are coming to inspect "for the possibility [that] there is by chance forbidden ammo." This speaker does not suggest that he or his listener actually have "forbidden ammo"; he merely says that officials are coming for this "possibility." The speaker then goes on to remind his listener "to inspect the scrap areas and the abandoned areas." Again, there is no language explicitly about hiding or removing weapons here, and the recording may even reflect efforts to comply with the U.N. mandate.[18]

Through a kind of "manipulative silence" about the full content of the audiotapes, the *Times* effectively conceals relevant information from its readers (Huckin 2002). Indeed, by stringing together only a few "scary words" from the recordings, the *Times* may have led audiences to believe that the Iraqis had explicitly discussed evacuating and removing prohibited weapons. And, like Mitchell on NBC, the *Times* reporters imply that the voices on the tapes naturally provoke an emotional response of fear and disquiet. Specifically, they report that the voices "echoed eerily" in the Security Council chamber, suggesting that the words themselves were cause for alarm—and perhaps insinuating that Powell's evidence was strong enough to increase "the possibility of war."

Enhancing the Danger: Possible Concerns Become Menacing Threats

Let's return now to the NBC broadcast. In the next portion of her report (excerpt 4.3), Mitchell recontextualizes visual-verbal elements of Powell's argument about Iraq's alleged chemical and biological weapons capabilities.

First, as Mitchell reports that "Powell played tape of a Mirage *jet ret*rofitted to spray *sim*ulated anthrax," a grainy, black-and-white reconnaissance video appears in the visual track. In the video, an aircraft (presumably the Mirage jet from Mitchell's spoken discourse) zips through the air emitting a fog-like spray (presumably the simulated anthrax). In his presentation, Powell did indeed play (a slightly longer version of) this "Mirage jet" video. However, Mitchell's recontextualization of this video *enhances* Powell's argument in very significant ways.

Originally, when Powell played the video, he said:

> Iraq had a program to modify aerial fuel tanks for Mirage jets. This video of an Iraqi test flight obtained by UNSCOM some years ago shows an Iraqi F-1 Mirage jet aircraft. Note the spray coming from beneath the Mirage; that is 2,000 liters of simulated anthrax that a jet is spraying. (UN/2.5/CP)

Powell says that Iraq *had* a program to modify Mirage jets—not that Iraq currently *has* a program. In her report, however, Mitchell makes no indication that the program presumably no longer exists. Also, Powell asserts that the video of the Mirage jet was "obtained by UNSCOM [the United Nations Special Commission] *some years ago.*" As it turns out, "according to U.N. inspectors' reports, the video *predated the 1991*

Excerpt 4.3. (NBC/2.5/AM)

Time	Frame	Soundtrack
82.		Powell played tape of a Mirage *jet ret*rofitted to spray *sim*ulated anthrax.
84.	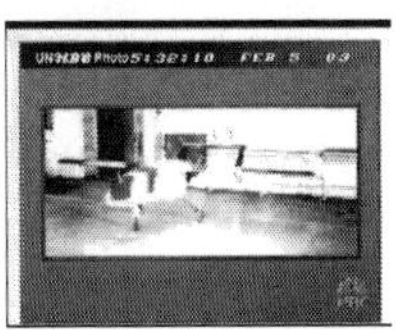	And a *mod*el of Iraq's *un*manned drones capable of spraying *chem*ical or germ weapons within a radius of at least *five*-hundred-*fifty* miles.

Note: The spoken report spanned many frames similar to the ones shown.

Persian Gulf war, when the Mirage was said to have been *destroyed*" (Hanley 2003, my emphasis). But Mitchell deletes both the source of the video and, crucially, the temporal circumstance indicating that the video was obtained *in the past*. In doing so, she effectively detemporalizes Powell's video "evidence," *enhancing* Powell's argument by repositioning viewers to regard a past (and presumably defunct) "threat" as a proximal (and presumably dangerous) one.

But Mitchell's deletion of the temporal circumstance from Powell's address is just the first significant transformation of the "Mirage jet" argument. Equally important, Mitchell does not attribute the assertion that the Mirage jet in the video has been "retrofitted to spray simulated anthrax" to anyone. In other words, instead of attributing the assertion to Powell (and positioning the viewer to consider Powell's assertion as just one dialogic option among many), Mitchell makes an unattributed and unmodalized assertion that positions the viewer to disregard alternative viewpoints.[19] Indeed, this is another a clear instance of dialogic contraction in which one of Powell's debatable claims has been converted into a self-evident and incontrovertible fact.

Just after replaying the Mirage jet video, Mitchell recontextualizes a different PowerPoint slide from Powell's presentation: a still photograph of an unmanned aerial vehicle (UAV). Mitchell reports that this is "a *mod*el of Iraq's *un*manned drones capable of spraying *chem*ical or germ weapons within a radius of at least *five*-hundred-*fif*ty miles." Here is yet another instance of dialogic contraction. Once again, instead of attributing to Powell the *claim* that Iraqi UAVs are capable of spraying chemical and biological weapons, Mitchell positions her audience to regard this information as categorically true.

In fact, Mitchell not only fails to attribute the UAV allegation to Powell, but she also skews what Powell actually said about the drones. For one thing, Powell did not say that the UAVs were "capable of spraying chemical or germ weapons." In fact, while Powell said that UAVs are generally "well suited for dispensing chemical and biological weapons,"[20] he left some room for doubt as to whether *Iraq* had actually equipped *their* UAVs for this purpose. As Powell put it: "There is ample evidence that Iraq has dedicated much effort to developing and testing spray devices that could be adapted for UAVs" (UN/2.5/CP). Here, Powell says that Iraqis have *dedicated much effort to* developing and testing spray devices. He does not say that they have *succeeded* in their efforts to develop functional spray devices. Furthermore, he modalizes the probability that the spray devices (which may or may not have been successfully developed) will be used in UAVs. Specifically, he says that they *could* be adapted for UAVs—not that the spray devices *will be* adapted for UAVs, and certainly not that the spray devices *have already been* adapted for UAVs. But Mitchell deletes Powell's modalizations—essentially increasing the certainty of his assertions and positioning viewers to regard Iraq's UAVs as already equipped to spray WMDs. What is a *potential* threat in Powell's presentation becomes a *current capability* in Andrea Mitchell's report.[21]

Moreover, Powell never said that the drones were "capable of spraying weapons within a radius of at least 550 miles." Specifically, the spatial circumstance, *within a radius of at least 550 miles*, simply does not appear in Powell's address. This makes Mitchell's report somewhat baffling. She positioned viewers to believe not only that Iraq had UAVs equipped with functioning spray tanks (something Powell represented as uncertain), but that these UAVs were already capable of delivering weapons within a well-defined radius (something Powell never even said). In so doing, Mitchell *enhanced* Powell's argument almost beyond recognition, even adding new evidence to strengthen his claims.

Enhancing Certainty: Transforming Interpretations into Facts

A bit later in the newscast (see excerpt 4.4), Mitchell reported another intercepted communication in Powell's presentation. In the first shot of the visual track, NBC displays a video of several U.N. inspectors walking (presumably in Iraq). As the camera follows these inspectors, Mitchell reports that Powell played another voice intercept "as evidence Iraq was *cheat*ing the inspectors all *along*." Thus, through a kind of verbal-visual intersemiosis, the inspectors referred to in Mitchell's verbal report are synonymous with the inspectors pictured in the visual track. The viewer is to understand that Powell played a tape as evidence that Iraq was cheating these (or similar) inspectors. Importantly, when introducing the tape in his presentation, Powell never describes it "as evidence that Iraq was cheating the inspectors all along." He certainly implied this argument, but he never stated it directly. Thus, by assigning a circumstantial role to the recorded conversation, Mitchell makes explicit an argument that was only implicit in Powell's presentation—and, thus, helps Powell to transform an ambiguous recording into "evidence" of cheating.

More importantly, in the next shot, Mitchell positions the viewer to interpret the taped conversation as self-evidently revelatory of Iraqi wrongdoing. She reports in an unmodalized, unattributed assertion: "Two top officers are overheard plotting to de*ceive* chief nuclear inspector Mohamed ElBaradei."[22] This is yet another instance of *enhancement* by dialogic contraction. Instead of attributing to Powell the *claim* that officers are plotting to deceive ElBaradei, Mitchell represents this allegation as an undisputed and obvious fact.[23] To illustrate this point, it is instructive to compare Mitchell's report to a corresponding report on CNN.com:

> One intercept, *Powell said*, was between a colonel and brigadier general of Iraq's elite Republican Guard discussing hiding a vehicle before U.N. inspectors arrived to search a site. *Powell said* it indicated the Iraqi officials knew inspectors were coming and what they would be looking for. (CNN/2.6/JKDE, emphasis added)

The CNN reporters "*impartially*" *re-represent* Powell's claims. They consistently identify Powell as the source behind the allegations about the audio intercept, positioning readers to understand that alternative viewpoints are possible. The CNN reporters may "echo" Powell's charges (Domke 2004), but, unlike Mitchell, they do not position audiences to believe that the evidence autonomously reveals a "plot to deceive."

In fact, Mitchell's suggestion that anyone can "overhear" an Iraqi conspiracy is puzzling since, as far as I can tell, there is nothing in the tape that overtly signals deception. In Powell's translation of the intercept—which is notably a recontextualization in its own right—an officer reports having a "modified vehicle" (whatever that is) and asks his superior what he should say if one of the inspectors sees this vehicle (see frames 152 and 155).[24] Nowhere in the conversation do the Iraqis say that the "modified vehicle" is a weapon; nor do they say that they will hide it from ElBaradei. As noted earlier, one speaker eventually declares, "We evacuated everything." But this is rather ambiguous. In fact, the interpretation that this tape is a "plot to deceive" is a real leap.[25] But Mitchell not only accepts this interpretation—she makes this interpretation the *only one available to the viewer*, effectively dissuading her audience from considering dialogic alternatives.

Excerpt 4.4. (NBC/2.5/AM.CP)

Time	Frame	Soundtrack
138.		**Mitchell:** As evidence Iraq was *cheat*ing the inspectors all a*long*, Powell played a conversation taped the day be*fore* they returned to Iraq last No*vem*ber.
145.		Two top officers are overheard plotting to de*ceive* chief nuclear inspector Mohamed ElBaradei.
152.	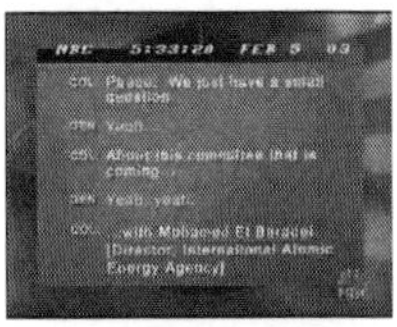	[Arabic voices; grainy] **Powell:** But they're *wor*ried. We have this modified vehicle.
155.	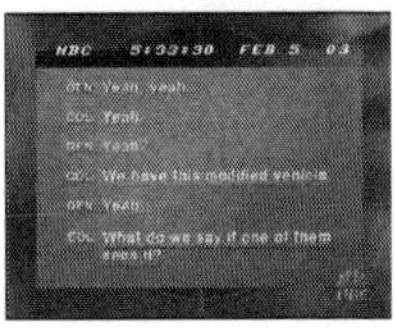	*What* do we *say* if one of them *sees* it?

Note: The spoken report spanned many frames similar to the ones shown.

Re-representing the International Response: They Didn't Budge?

After presenting Powell's apparently "incriminating evidence," Mitchell finally describes the international response to Powell's speech (see excerpt 4.5).

Here de Villepin's assertion that there is "room for enhancing the inspections' regime" is an *implicit rebuttal* of a claim made in Powell's address: namely, that further inspections cannot succeed because Iraq will only continue to obstruct the inspectors' progress. The presence of de Villepin's rebuttal in the newscast provides viewers with a dialogic alternative to Powell's argument. Moreover, the assertion that Powell's "opponents . . . did not budge," as Mitchell puts it, creates additional teleological uncertainty. That is, it positions viewers to regard Powell as potentially unable to reach his rhetorical goal of persuading an international audience.

However, what really interests me in this instance is the coordinating conjunction "but," which Mitchell utters as a kind of transition from her report about Powell's address to her report about international reactions to Powell's address. Here, "but" functions as a token of *counterexpectancy* (Martin & White 2005). In this case, Mitchell indicates that both she and the viewer *would have expected* Powell's opponents to "budge," and counters this expectation with the (surprising) news that they did not. Of course, given some of the overtly positive evaluations of Powell's presentation that came before in the newscast (*masterful performance, armed with America's best intelligence*), perhaps it would seem surprising that Powell did not win over his critics. In any event, it is interesting that even as Mitchell portrays speakers who essentially rebut Powell's arguments, she adds a subtle *enhancement* that positions the audience to regard these speakers as almost stubborn "opponents" who "don't budge" in the face of evidence that "we" all know to be compelling.[26]

Excerpt 4.5 (NBC/2.5/AM.DV)

Time	Frame	Soundtrack
174.		**Mitchell:** But op*pon*ents like the French foreign minister did not budge.
178.		**de Villepin:** There is *room* for *enhancing* the inspections' regime.

Note: The spoken report spanned many frames similar to the ones shown.

Introducing Uncertainty: Is There an al-Qaeda Link?

Following Andrea Mitchell's report, Tom Brokaw introduces a segment by correspondent Jim Miklaszewski (see excerpt 4.6). In this introduction, Brokaw stands and speaks next to a cluster of images: a video of Saddam Hussein speaking at a press conference, a digital illustration of the Iraqi flag, and a large caption reading, "Al Qaeda Link?"

This introduction may be considered a macro-recontextualization of Powell's case—which condenses and relexicalizes the phase of Powell's argument in which he seeks to establish a "connection between Saddam Hussein and al-Qaeda." At this point, Brokaw positions the viewer to regard the strength of this argument as somewhat open to question. He says that the administration (here a meronym for Colin Powell) provided details of the alleged connection. Of course, in an argumentative context, the provision of details is generally a positive thing, so Brokaw positions viewers to regard Powell's case as thorough (as opposed to simplistic). However, the caption in the visual track literally includes a big question mark that renders the "al-Qaeda link" uncertain. Moreover, Brokaw himself casts some doubt on whether the allegations of an Iraq–al-Qaeda connection are compelling by openly asking, "How strong is that case?" Notably, in framing the question this way, Brokaw presupposes that Powell's case is to some extent strong (somewhat strong, moderately strong, quite strong, very strong, etc.). More importantly, however, he suggests that Miklaszewski's report will answer his question. In other words, Brokaw positions the viewer to regard Miklaszewski's report as an authoritative assessment of Powell's "al-Qaeda link" allegations.

Qualifying Powell's Argument: Possible Links and Thin Ice

Just as Brokaw completes the introduction, Miklaszewski is shown gazing directly into the camera as he stands outside the Pentagon. He says the following: "Tom, there was plenty of *new*, *det*ailed information about Iraq's alleged ties to terrorists. But a Pentagon official says when Powell got to possible links between Baghdad and al-*Qae*da he was s*kat*ing on thin ice" (NBC/2.5/JM).

Excerpt 4.6. (NBC/2.5/TB)

Time	Frame	Soundtrack
214.		And today for the *first* time the administration provided details for what it has *al*ways insisted was a con*nec*tion between Saddam Hussein and al-*Qae*da. How strong is *that* case?
215.		Here's NBC's Jim Miklaszewski at the Pentagon.

Note: The spoken report spanned many frames similar to the ones shown.

Here, Miklaszewski begins his segment with some *legitimizing* evaluations of Powell's argument. Specifically, he calls Powell's information both *new* and *detailed*. However, Miklaszewski also qualifies Powell's argument, using a hearsay evidential (*alleged*) that positions viewers to understand that someone has *claimed* that Iraq has ties to terrorists, and that this claim is open to question. Furthermore, in the report attributed to a Pentagon official, one of Powell's argumentative thrusts is essentially delegitimized. Not only is the Pentagon official reported to have used a modal qualifier (*possible*) that in itself reduces the certainty of Powell's argument; but the Pentagon official is also represented as saying that Powell was "skating on thin ice" as he described "links between Baghdad and al-Qaeda." The fact that this assertion came from an American—what's more a Pentagon official—makes it both difficult to challenge and especially damaging to Powell. After all, the viewer is being positioned by Miklaszewski to regard this Pentagon official as a kind of "expert" who is credible to assess the strength of Powell's argument. Thus, though Miklaszewski opens his report with some legitimizing evaluations of Powell, he generally positions viewers to regard as questionable Powell's allegations of an Iraq–al-Qaeda connection.

This was a rare *rebuttal* of Powell's case. Indeed, NBC was the only news provider in this study to cite U.S. officials who explicitly challenged Powell's argument about Iraqi support for al-Qaeda. Meanwhile, the *New York Times* and CNN.com included no credible rebuttals to

Powell's argument—indeed, they openly legitimated Powell's suggestion of "terrorist links." CNN, for example, positively evaluates Powell's case, reporting that he provided "the *most detailed* explanation yet" of Iraq's alleged ties to al-Qaeda. Meanwhile the *New York Times* reported that an "intelligence *breakthrough*" linking al-Qaeda and Iraq had allowed Powell to present "a more *detailed* and *well-documented bill of particulars* than many had expected" (Tyler 2003). In fact, NBC was the most critical news organization when it came to Powell's allegations of Iraqi support for al-Qaeda. But, as we will see, even the NBC report ultimately served to enhance and legitimate Powell's claims.

Visualizing the Saddam-Osama Connection: The Threat Continues

After his introduction, Miklaszewski disappears from the screen and an image of Osama bin Laden, smiling and looking directly into the camera, emerges in his place (see excerpt 4.7). Bin Laden appears to be speaking, but only Miklaszewski's voice is audible in the soundtrack.

In this recontextualization, Miklaszewski reports that "Powell claimed the *ties* between Osama bin Laden go back nearly ten years." Powell, in fact, did make a roughly synonymous assertion in his presentation. However, Miklaszewski *qualifies* Powell's assertion by using a distancing reporting verb (Powell *claimed*) that positions the viewer to regard Powell's utterance as open to debate. Meanwhile, in the visual track, the image of bin Laden is immediately followed with video image of Saddam Hussein sitting at a table and presiding over a meeting with Iraqi military commanders. Thus, even as Miklaszewski's spoken report positions viewers to regard the ties between bin Laden and Saddam Hussein as debatable, the visual information that is co-deployed with this report helps to endow these ties with rhetorical presence. In fact, in terms of presence, the rapid transition—from images of bin Laden to images of Saddam Hussein—perhaps created more of an impact on viewers than Miklaszewski's distancing reporting verb.

Also, when Miklaszewski says, "And the threat continues today," he is somewhat ambiguous as to whether this proposition is being attributed to Powell. Did Powell *claim* that the threat continues today? Or is the continuation of "the threat" simply a reality?[27] After this ambiguous attribution, Miklaszewski plays a brief clip of Colin Powell speaking at the U.N. Security Council. In the clip, Powell suggests that the "nexus" between Iraq and al-Qaeda "combines *class*ic terror organizations and modern methods of murder." This clip represents a relatively *"impartial" re-representation* of Powell's argument. That is, the replay doesn't "distort" Powell's colorful remarks in any significant way, but it does endow these remarks with a great deal of rhetorical presence. Indeed, by choosing to replay a clip of Powell's performance, NBC allows Powell to speak "directly" to the news audience—granting him an exclusive platform from which he can offer his intensely negative judgments of Iraqi behavior (*terror*, *murder*).

Excerpt 4.7. (NBC/2.5/JM.CP)

Time	Frame	Soundtrack
240.		**Miklaszewski:** In making his case, Powell claimed the *ties* between Osama bin Laden and
244.		Saddam Hussein go back nearly *ten* years.
247.		And the threat continues today.
250.		**Powell:** A nexus that combines *class*ic terror organizations and modern methods of murder.*

A New Spin on Powell's Visual: Re-representing a Bin Laden Collaborator

Next, in excerpt 4.8, Miklaszewski reports alleged links between Iraq and terrorism.

In frames 254–57 of excerpt 4.8, Miklaszewski asserts that "the strongest terrorist link made today was not with bin Laden," as a distant shot of the U.N. Security Council appears on the screen. In this case, the visual track of the newscast is not all that remarkable. The shot of the U.N. Security Council serves merely to anchor Powell's rhetorical event in its physical context. The viewer is positioned to interpret this scene merely as a space where Powell made his assertions.

More interesting is Miklaszewski's spoken discourse in these frames. Once again, the coordinating conjunction *but* plays an important role in establishing a shared sense of *counterexpectancy* between Miklaszewski and the viewer. Specifically, Miklaszewski implies that based on Powell's assertion of ties between Osama bin Laden and Saddam Hussein, both he and the viewer *would have expected* Powell's strongest evidence to link Iraq directly "with bin Laden." However, Miklaszewski suggests that Powell's case actually defied this shared expectation. That is, instead of linking Iraq directly "with bin Laden"—the very face of al-Qaeda—Powell (merely) linked Iraq with a bin Laden colloaborator, Abu Musab al-Zarqawi.[28] This *qualification* would tend to suggest to the viewer that Powell's assertions of Iraq's terrorist ties were perhaps not as compelling as they *might* have been.

Nonetheless, one cannot overlook Miklaszewski's explicitly positive appraisal of Powell's assertions about Zarqawi. Indeed, Miklaszewski refers to the "link" between Iraq and Zarqawi as "the *strongest* terrorist link made today." This use of the superlative "strongest"—a word that Miklaszewski emphasizes with additional vocal stress—clearly suggests an intensified positive valuation of Powell's case. In fact, it implies that there were other "strong" terrorist links in Powell's presentation. Importantly, the viewer is positioned to accept this positive *legitimation* as an undisputed feature of the report.

Also noteworthy is the nominalized phrase "terrorist link" itself. Recall that nominalization is a grammatical transformation whereby verbs, which describe processes and actions, are converted into nouns, which describe objects and entities.[29] In this case, the verb "to link" has been reclassified as a noun: "the link." To uncover the implications

Excerpt 4.8. (NBC/2.5/JM)

Time	Frame	Soundtrack
254.		But the *strongest*
255.		terrorist link
256.		made today was
257.		*not* with bin Laden
258.		but with
259.	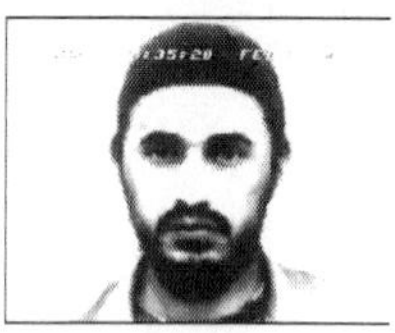	*this* man
260.	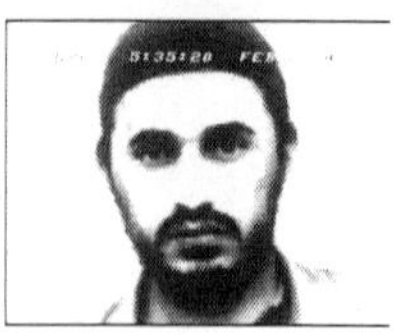	Abu Musab

(continued)

Excerpt 4.8. *(continued)*

Time	Frame	Soundtrack
261.		al-Zarqawi, who
262.		Powell described
263.		as a *bin Laden* colla*b*orator.

of this transformation, we can perform a parallel analysis (Thompson 2004), comparing Miklaszewski's assertion with a "congruent" but "denominalized" version (see table 4.5).[30] The most important effect of this nominalization is that what was in reality a *rhetorical act* performed by Powell (i.e. *Powell most strongly linked Iraq to this man*) is reclassified as a material entity with its own autonomous existence (*the strongest terrorist link made today*). In other words, the "terrorist link" seems to be a real, solid thing—and not an arguable proposition that was put forth by a rhetor.

In fact, Miklaszewski positions the viewer to ignore Powell's role in linking al-Zarqawi to Iraq. Notice the passive voice in the embedded clause (italicized): "the strongest terrorist link [*that was*] *made* today was with this man." Here, the agent who made the terrorist link is omitted. Granted, viewers could surmise that this agent was Colin Powell, but the fact that Powell is not foregrounded as the responsible agent helps keep the viewers' attention on "the link" itself and not the person responsible for constructing it. The word "made" is also important. Typically, the verb "made" suggests a completed material process, that is, the completed construction of a *physical* object (e.g., "She made the dresser"). Miklaszewski might have said that the link had been "asserted" or "claimed" by Powell, thereby specifying it as one person's debatable allegation. Instead, by choosing to represent the link as something *made*, he further establishes it as a reified object, something concretely real and, thus, incapable of being argued against.[31]

Perhaps an even more compelling feature of this excerpt concerns the recontextualization and transformation of a visual element from Powell's presentation—specifically the image of Abu Musab al-Zarqawi that emerges clearly in frame 259. Originally, this image of Zarqawi appeared in the fortieth slide of Powell's PowerPoint presentation—a slide titled "Al-Zarqawi's Iraq-Linked Terrorist Network" (see figure 4.1). The image of Zarqawi's face was one of many faces displayed in Powell's chart.

The chart in figure 4.1 represents what Kress and Van Leeuwen (1996) refer to as classificational diagram in which a superordinate figure—in this case al-Zarqawi—is related to other interordinate and subordinate figures—in this case, the other "terrorists" in the diagram (81–88). The viewer looking at this slide is positioned to observe that al-Zarqawi is an important figure in the diagram, but is also positioned to observe all the other relationships between the various participants in the chart. In short, the viewer is positioned to discern how various people are connected to each other and to (linguistically represented) locations in Europe.

However, in frame 259 of Miklaszewski's report, Zarqawi's image is presented by itself—completely extracted from the chart and its other photographs, and magnified. This extraction and enlargement brings

Table 4.5. Parallel Analysis of "Terrorist Link"

<table>
<tr><td rowspan="3">Miklaszewski's Report</td><td>The strongest terrorist link</td><td colspan="2">made</td><td>today</td><td>was</td><td>with this man</td></tr>
<tr><td colspan="4">Carrier</td><td>Pr: Relational</td><td>Attribute</td></tr>
<tr><td>Goal</td><td colspan="2">Pr: Material</td><td>Circ: Temporal</td><td colspan="2"></td></tr>
<tr><td rowspan="2">Congruent Version</td><td colspan="2">Powell</td><td colspan="2">most strongly linked</td><td>Iraq</td><td>with this man/ terrorist</td></tr>
<tr><td colspan="2">Attributor</td><td colspan="2">Pr: Relational</td><td>Carrier</td><td>Attribute</td></tr>
</table>

Zarqawi's image closer to the viewer. Consequently, the viewer gets to engage with Zarqawi's face in ways that were perhaps not possible during Powell's address. Zarqawi's gaze—directed into the camera—enacts a kind of personal relationship with the viewer. And, arguably, his blank expression—unsmiling and stern—suggests that this relationship with the viewer is not a friendly one. Meanwhile, the absence of color in the photograph suggests that Zarqawi is not a part of the viewer's world.[32] Indeed, the photo has all the features of a "mug shot"—marking Zarqawi as a criminal Other. All of this is communicated instantly as Miklaszewski brings "*this* man" into the viewer's living room in frame 259.

The extraction of this image from Powell's chart and its magnification in the newscast are noteworthy transformations. However, NBC further enhanced the "eeriness" of this image by animating it on screen. Indeed, in frames 260–63, the image "comes to life." What was originally a static shot of an alleged terrorist is here a dynamic image that literally

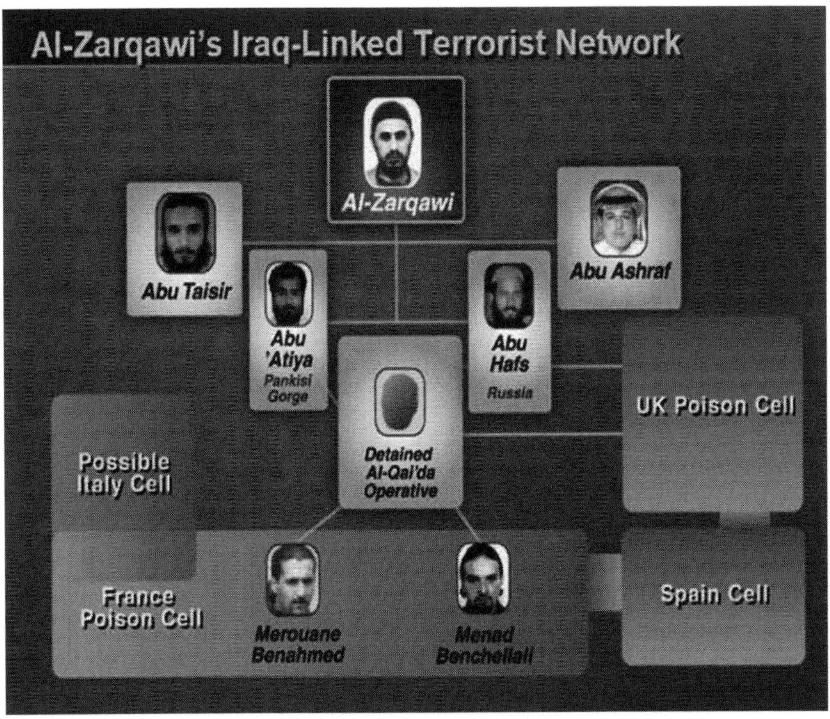

Figure 4.1. Slide 40 of Powell's presentation

approaches the viewer as it rotates on the screen. Needless to say, in terms of pathos, this movement positions the viewer to feel a sense of disquiet and alarm. Zarqawi seems to be "coming at" the viewer—and threatening to invade the viewer's world. This animation clearly represents an instance of a visual evaluation—a negative judgment of al-Zarqawi that simultaneously elicits a negative affectual response from the audience: fear.

Miklaszewski's report of Powell's speech in the soundtrack is, thus, complicated by this emotionally arresting image. Arguably, the rhetorical presence of this image prevents the viewer from assessing Powell's evidence of Iraq's links to terrorism. Certainly, the salience of the image demands the viewer's attention. And perhaps this *enhancement* requires that the viewer focus on the "scariness" of this "bin Laden collaborator"—and not on the quality of Powell's case.

Interestingly, we find a very similar recontextualization on CNN.com. Figure 4.2 reproduces the headline, lead paragraph, and image that appeared in the CNN story detailing Powell's discussion of Iraq and terrorism.

As on NBC, the image of Zarqawi's face has been removed from Powell's slide 40 and significantly enlarged so that viewers can more closely interact with it. Interestingly, despite the salience of Zarqawi's image, Zarqawi's *name* never appears in the headline or lead paragraph. In fact, the lead paragraph only refers vaguely to a "shadowy figure" in northeast Iraq. This epithet, "shadowy figure," was chosen not only because it portrays Zarqawi as a dark and nefarious character, but also because readers can quickly associate it with the image displayed on the screen. Readers can discern a semantic association between the gray hues in the photograph and the word "shadowy," which connotes darkness and the absence of color. Furthermore, readers can guess that Zarqawi is the "shadowy figure" because they readily expect such a figure to be pictured in a "mug shot" like the one displayed here. Importantly, Powell never referred to Zarqawi as a "shadowy figure." Thus, CNN's epithet serves another important function: it enhances Powell's argument, heightening the sense of alarm about a terrorist suspect allegedly operating in Iraq.

The headline of CNN's article is also important. As Van Dijk (1988) suggests, headlines and lead paragraphs serve as crucial macro-propositions in news articles, providing readers with memorable summaries of an article's content. CNN's headline is particularly

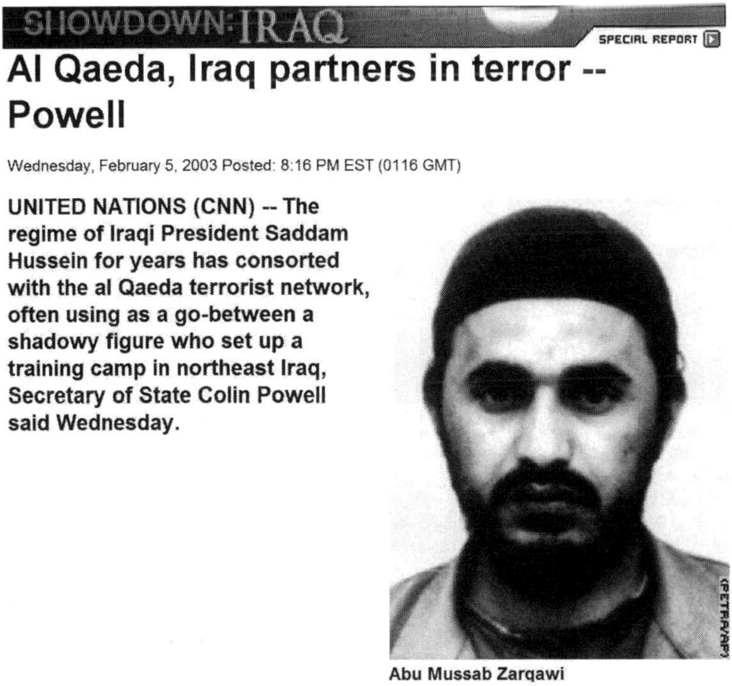

SHOWDOWN: IRAQ SPECIAL REPORT

Al Qaeda, Iraq partners in terror -- Powell

Wednesday, February 5, 2003 Posted: 8:16 PM EST (0116 GMT)

UNITED NATIONS (CNN) -- The regime of Iraqi President Saddam Hussein for years has consorted with the al Qaeda terrorist network, often using as a go-between a shadowy figure who set up a training camp in northeast Iraq, Secretary of State Colin Powell said Wednesday.

Abu Mussab Zarqawi

Figure 4.2. Headline, lead, and image from CNN.com article

provocative: "Al Qaeda, Iraq partners in terror—Powell." Again, Powell never actually called Iraq and al-Qaeda "partners in terror." In fact, while Powell often charged that members of the Iraqi government had met with members of al-Qaeda, he was careful to avoid saying that a formal alliance existed between the two groups. But CNN foregrounds the notion of a *partnership*, effectively enhancing Powell's claim and perhaps positioning readers to imagine that Iraq and al-Qaeda collaborate in terrorist operations.

A similar distortion is found in the lead paragraph, where CNN attributes to Powell the idea that Zarqawi often served as a "go-between" for Saddam Hussein's government and al-Qaeda.[33] Again, Powell never referred to Zarqawi as a mediator between al-Qaeda and the Iraqi leadership. In fact, Powell never referred to *any* direct communication between Zarqawi and the Iraqi government. Powell asserted that Zarqawi had set up a terrorist training camp "in northern Kurdish areas *outside Saddam Hussein's controlled Iraq*" (emphasis added). Powell claimed that, although Zarqawi's camp was located in an area outside of Saddam's jurisdiction, Saddam had managed to place an agent in the radical group that governed the area—Ansar al-Islam. In 2000 (notably, a year before Zarqawi's arrival in Iraq), this unnamed agent of Saddam's government had given al-Qaeda "safe haven" to operate in the northern part of the country. Of course, Powell's argument begs the question: If Saddam Hussein did not *control* the northern part of the country, then how could he authorize someone to give terrorists "safe haven" there?[34] But even if we accept Powell's tenuous reasoning, it in no way implies that Zarqawi was "often" used by Saddam Hussein as a "go-between." Again, in Powell's presentation, Zarqawi never even interacts with the Iraqi government.[35] But in CNN's lead paragraph Zarqawi appears to be a crucial point man for Baghdad. As indicated above, this kind of enhancement was typical in the NBC broadcast as well.

The Image Speaks for Itself: Converting Another Claim into a Fact

Powell's slide 40 does eventually appear on screen in the NBC broadcast (see excerpt 4.9), as Miklaszewski reports Powell's claims on the training of terrorists.

Here, once again, Miklaszewski uses the reporting verb "claimed" to distance himself from Powell's assertion and open up space for his audience to consider dialogic alternatives. However, in the same breath, he also *enhances* the certainty of several of Powell's claims. First, Miklaszewski refers to "this terrorist training camp in northern Iraq" and displays a satellite photograph from Powell's presentation. The deictic—*this*—clearly establishes a relationship of co-referentiality between the "terrorist training camp" mentioned in Miklaszewski's spoken report and the photograph displayed in the visual track. Crucially, it is represented as self-evident that this satellite photograph *actually depicts* a terrorist training camp. Miklaszewski does not say "this *alleged* terrorist training camp"; he simply says "this terrorist training camp." Likewise, the assertion that the camp is "producing ricin and other deadly poisons" is not attributed to Powell. Once again, through a kind of dialogic contraction, Powell's claims are converted into incontrovertible facts.

This is particularly significant because, even at the time of Miklaszewski's report, there were serious questions about the credibility of this specific argument. In fact, the *New York Times* reported that Kurds in northern Iraq were confused by Powell's suggestion of a terrorist training camp there. According to the *Times*, these Kurds were "unaware of a terrorist training camp" in the area, and had "questioned whether Powell was mistaken or had mislabeled the photograph" (Chivers 2003). But Miklaszewski fails to represent any sort of dispute about Powell's allegations. Indeed, he transforms these allegations into certainties.[36]

Miklaszewski also fails to mention an important qualification noted by Colin Powell: Saddam Hussein had *no control* over northern Iraq where this camp was allegedly located. Indeed, as shown above, Powell had used some specious reasoning to connect Zarqawi's camp with Baghdad. But Miklaszewski fails to represent this reasoning, positioning audiences—who presumably didn't know much about Iraqi politics and governance—to assume that Saddam himself was "allowing" a terrorist camp in his country.[37]

Excerpt 4.9. (NBC/2.5/JM)

Time	Frame	Soundtrack
265.	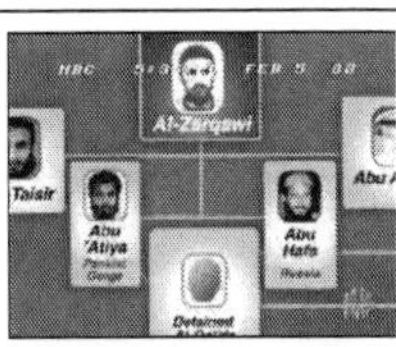	Powell claimed that Zar*qaw*i and his lieutenants helped establish *this*
269.		terrorist training camp in northern I*raq* that is producing the *dead*ly toxin *ri*cin and other poisons.

Note: The spoken report spanned many frames similar to the ones shown.

Another Terrorist Link: Praising and Objectifying Powell's Discourse

A few moments later in the newscast, as another shot of Osama bin Laden appears on the screen, Miklaszewski reports on an additional "link" between Iraq and the al-Qaeda leader (see excerpt 4.10).

In this recontextualization, a few clauses from Powell's presentation are relexicalized and condensed into a brief nominal phrase: "the most direct terrorist link between Iraq and bin Laden." Here is another superlative positive evaluation (*most direct*)—signaling not only that the current link between Iraq and bin Laden is relatively straightforward, but also that Powell's presentation included other (less) direct links between Iraq and al-Qaeda. In addition, we find another nominalization (*terrorist link*) that seems to have its own concrete reality. In other words, Powell is not portrayed as an agent *alleging* a relationship between Iraq and bin Laden. Instead, the most direct link between Iraq and bin Laden is construed as a real, solid thing. Thus, Miklaszewski again selects discourse that *vouches for* Powell—*legitimizing* his evidence.

Of course, Miklaszewski attributes the "most direct link" to an outside source, saying that the terrorist link "apparently comes from a . . . detainee now in custody." Here the evidential (*apparently*) *qualifies* the certainty that this evidence actually originated with this unnamed al-Qaeda source,[38] signaling to the audience the contingency of the attribution and freeing viewers to consider other dialogic alternatives. However, Miklaszewski chooses an attributional verb phrase (*comes from*) that tends to signal that the terrorist link has "material reality." Normally, *comes from* is a material process that encodes the movement

Excerpt 4.10. (NBC/2.5/JM)

Time	Frame	Soundtrack
298.		The most dir*ect* terrorist link between Iraq and bin Laden apparently comes from a *sen*ior al-Qaeda leader now in custody.

Note: The spoken report spanned many frames similar to the one shown.

of objects in the physical world (e.g., the plate comes from France), not a verbal process that construes the production of human speech. By choosing this phrase, then, Miklaszewski represents the "terrorist link" rather like a stable object that "moves" from some location, as opposed to an arguable assertion that is verbalized by a person.[39] Thus, as before, viewers are positioned to imagine that the "terrorist link" in Powell's presentation has the "solid" quality of a physical object, and not the more contingent quality of an argumentative claim.

Deleting Details and Adding Visual Evidence: Disambiguating and Substantiating Claims

A moment later, in excerpt 4.11, Miklaszewski elaborates on the nature of this "most direct terrorist link," recontextualizing one of Powell's more specific assertions.

Before analyzing Miklaszewski's report, I reproduce a transcript of the prior assertion from which this report was drawn. Originally, Powell said the following:

> [The detainee] says bin Laden and his top deputy, deceased al-Qaeda leader Mohammed Atef, did not believe that al-Qaeda labs in Afghanistan were capable enough to manufacture these chemical or biological agents. They needed to go somewhere else. They had to look outside of Afghanistan for help. Where did they go? Where did they look? They went to Iraq. The support this detainee describes included Iraq offering chemical or biological weapons training for two al-Qaeda associates beginning in December 2000. He says that a militant known as Abu Abdula al-Iraqi had been sent to Iraq several times between 1997 and 2000 for help in acquiring poisons and gases. Abdula al-Iraqi characterized the relationship he forged with Iraqi officials as successful. (UN/2.5/CP)

Comparing Miklaszewski's recontextualization to Powell's original assertion, one can find some very significant deletions and relexicalizations. First, in Powell's address, bin Laden *and his top deputy* are represented as the actors who looked to Iraq for help in weapons training. However, in Miklaszewski's report, bin Laden is represented as the sole actor. Second, in Powell's speech, bin Laden and his top deputy seek help in

Excerpt 4.11. (NBC/2.5/JM)

Time	Frame	Soundtrack
305.	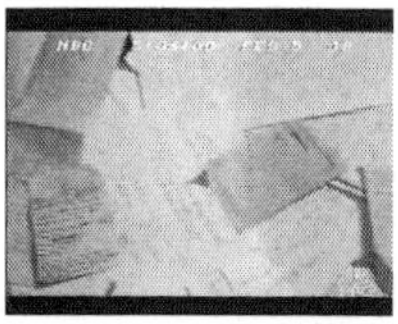	According to Powell
306.		the detainee says
307.		in December 2000
308.		bin Laden turned
309.		to Iraq
310.		for *help* in
311.		developing chemical

(*continued*)

Excerpt 4.11. *(continued)*

Time	Frame	Soundtrack
312.	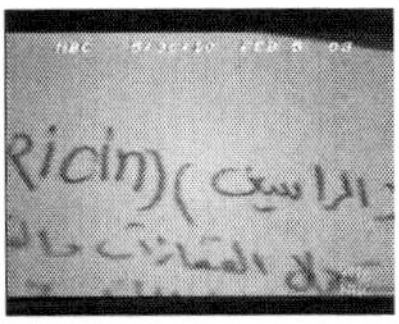	and *biolo*gical
313.	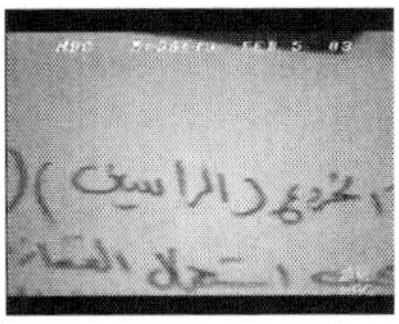	weapons . . . and *got* it.

manufacturing chemical "or" biological agents. But, in Miklaszewski's report, bin Laden is represented as seeking help in developing chemical "and" biological weapons—a slightly more frightening prospect. Third, in Powell's assertion, bin Laden and his top deputy "went to Iraq" for help. In Miklaszewski's recontextualization, though, this material process is relexicalized such that bin Laden "*turned to* Iraq for help." These are not synonymous constructions. Going to a place and looking for help is not the same as *turning to* a place for help. One goes and looks for help as a stranger; but one *turns to* someone for help when a relationship of trust has already been established. Thus, by relexicalizing the material process in Powell's assertion, Miklaszewski essentially *enhances* the sense that there is a "direct link" between bin Laden and Iraq.

Furthermore, in looking at Miklaszewski's report, one might get the impression that, in December 2000, bin Laden traveled to Iraq *himself* to acquire help in developing weapons of mass destruction. To be fair, Powell does say at one point that "they [i.e., bin Laden and his top deputy] went to Iraq." However, upon close inspection of Powell's argument, it is apparent that, *in December 2000*, bin Laden never personally went to Iraq or interacted with any Iraqis. Instead, Powell attributes to the detainee the assertion that "Iraq"—a rather generic and impersonal social actor (Van Leeuwen 2008, 23–54)—offered "chemical or biological weapons training for two *al-Qaeda associates* beginning in December 2000." These unnamed "al-Qaeda associates" represent a rather ambiguous pair of social actors. Indeed, one might question the exact nature of their affiliation with the al-Qaeda terrorist network. (After all, is an al-Qaeda "associate" the same thing as an al-Qaeda "member"?) Yet Miklaszewski fails to even represent these al-Qaeda "associates" in his report. Instead, he represents bin Laden—whose affiliation with the al-Qaeda terrorist network is beyond doubt—as the sole actor who sought help from Iraq.[40]

Most importantly, contrary to Miklaszewski's report, Powell does not necessarily say that bin Laden "got" the help he was looking for. For instance, Powell never says if, according to the detainee, the two al-Qaeda associates actually *accepted* Iraq's alleged offer of help in chemical "or" biological weapons training. In fact, Powell's only suggestion that al-Qaeda received help from Iraq comes from an *additional* source. It's worth noting here that Miklaszewski is representing (or, rather, failing to represent) *three* layers of reporting: (1) Powell reports what (2) an unnamed detainee reportedly said (3) about what a "militant" named Abu Abdula al-Iraqi reportedly said. (That Miklaszewski earlier positioned his audience to regard this chain of hearsay as the "most direct terrorist link" in Powell's presentation is laughable—and infuriating.)

In any case, according to Powell, the detainee said that al-Iraqi was sent to Iraq "for help in acquiring poisons and gases," and that al-Iraqi "characterized the relationship he forged with Iraqi officials as successful." In table 4.6, I compare, at a fine level of detail, Powell's original representation with Miklaszewki's recontextualization.

In Powell's address, a sayer (*al-Iraqi*) uses a positive, but indistinct attribute (*successful*) to characterize his relationship with unnamed "Iraqi officials." Powell doesn't say if *bin Laden* sent al-Iraqi to Iraq, or even if this "militant" is associated with al-Qaeda. Perhaps more importantly, Powell doesn't say *what it means* that al-Iraqi reportedly characterized his relationship as "successful." (Did he actually acquire the alleged poisons and gases?) In short, there is a lot of ambiguity in Powell's assertion. In addition, the attribution to al-Iraqi (via the detainee, and via Powell) is dialogically expansive, leaving plenty of space for audiences to consider alternative viewpoints. But in Miklaszewski's discourse the attribution is omitted and the ambiguity is essentially cleared up. The sayer (*al-Iraqi*) is deleted, and the indistinct attribute (*successful*) is transformed into a completed material process "starring" Osama bin Laden as the lead actor. In a sense, *Al Iraqi says he forged a successful relationship* becomes *bin Laden got help in developing chemical and biological weapons*.

Even more important than these linguistic *enhancements*,

Table 4.6. Transitivity Analysis of Powell's Original Assertion and Miklaszewski's Recontextualization

Powell's Assertion	al-Iraqi	characterized	the relationship he forged with Iraqi officials	as	successful
	Sayer	Pr: Verbal	Verbiage		
			Carrier [implied]	Pr: Relational [implied]	Attribute [implied]
Miklaszewski's Report	[bin Laden]	got	it [help in developing chemical and biological weapons]		
	Actor	Pr: Material	Goal		

however, are the visual enhancements—not originally present in Powell's presentation—that NBC co-deploys with Miklaszewski's spoken relexicalization of Powell's argument. First, in frames 305–9, a high-angle shot of a flat surface appears in the visual track. As Miklaszewski reports that "according to Powell, the detainee says in December 2000 bin Laden turned to Iraq," the camera pans across the surface to show a number of hand-written documents, which have apparently been strewn about haphazardly. At this point, though viewers are unable to read these documents, they are nevertheless positioned to regard them as somehow related to Miklaszewski's spoken discourse. That is, the viewer is to understand that these documents have something to do with bin Laden turning to Iraq.

In frame 310, just as Miklaszewski begins to finish his verbal report, asserting that bin Laden turned to Iraq for help "and got it," a new, close-up shot of a single document appears on screen. One handwritten word, in particular, stands out: "ricin." Ricin is, of course, a biological weapon. In fact, earlier in his report, Miklaszewski identified ricin as the "deadly toxin" being produced at Zarqawi's terrorist training camp. So this handwritten word "ricin" has been defined for the viewer, who can relate "ricin" (via hyponymy) to Miklaszewski's spoken nominal, "biological weapon." In other words, the viewer is positioned to understand that ricin is a kind of biological weapon, and, thus, exactly the kind of thing Osama bin Laden was allegedly interested in obtaining from Iraq. Importantly, in the document displayed on screen "ricin" is the only recognizable English word. In fact, all other words in the document appear to be written in Arabic.

Thus, the viewer is left to interpret why the word "ricin" would appear in Arabic documents, and is further left to make the connection between these documents and Miklaszewski's spoken report. Given Miklaszewski's co-text, the most plausible explanation for the documents available to the viewer is that they are "evidence" of al-Qaeda's alleged effort to secure help from Iraq in developing chemical and biological weapons. Perhaps these documents were written by members of al-Qaeda based on information they received from Iraqi officials. Or maybe they were written by Iraqi weapons specialists and shared with al-Qaeda operatives. Viewers may not be able to piece together all the details, but they understand well enough that these documents (1) were obtained by authorities, and (2) have something to do with the help bin Laden reportedly got from Iraq. Indeed, following Toulmin (1958), one could say that NBC positions the viewer to regard these documents as real, tangible data in support of Powell's recontextualized claim.

The argument laid out in figure 4.3 is certainly not bulletproof, but it doesn't have to be. It is enough that in Miklaszewski's report there is a quasi-logical relationship (Perelman & Olbrechts-Tyteca 1969, 193) between the "evidence" in the visual track and Powell's recontextualized claims in the soundtrack. Indeed, the viewer has already been primed to believe in "strong terrorist links" between Iraq and al-Qaeda. In the context of the spoken report, then, the "ricin" document stands as proof of impropriety, and—whatever questions the viewer may have about it—it seems to confirm that such terrorist links exist.[41]

Conclusion

An important contribution of this chapter is the methodological framework offered for analyzing intertextual transformations and the concomitant repositioning of rhetorical audiences. It is my contention that only a highly exacting and meticulous analytic framework, such as the one outlined in this chapter, would be capable of tracing the transformations that occur during the process of recontextualization. In fact, this methodology not only allows for a close examination of the minute lexicogrammatical changes that occur as one person's speech is

NBC-Supplied Visual DATA

Powell's Recontextualized CLAIM

The detainee says, in December 2000, bin Laden turned to Iraq for help in developing chemical and biological weapons—and got it.

WARRANT

Documents written in Arabic that contain the word "ricin" can be taken as evidence of a biological weapons plot by a terrorist from bin Laden's network or an Iraqi official.

BACKING

1. Both Iraqis and members of al Qaeda are of Arabic descent and write in Arabic script.
2. Members of al Qaeda have been shown by authorities to be developing ricin in Northern Iraq (according to Miklaszewski's report).

Figure 4.3. Toulmin diagram showing NBC's provision of evidence for Powell's claim

reported in a new context, but also for an investigation of small changes in the "visual grammar" of texts. Furthermore, this methodology provides a principled way of accounting for the rhetorical impact of these transformations. More specifically, it allows one to draw on theories of rhetoric, argumentation, and systemic-functional grammar in order to address how rhetorical audiences are *repositioned* as elements of one text are re-represented and transformed in another.

Ultimately, such a precise methodology is necessary because, as this analysis has shown, the transformations that accompany recontextualization are often quite microscopic. In fact, this is a central finding of this chapter: transformations in intertextual meaning relations are frequently tiny, but observable through careful analysis. Of course, just because the transformations are often small does not mean that they are insignificant. A powerful implication of this study is that these micro-transformations ultimately have a *cumulative effect*. When numerous arguments from an original speech event are adjusted and modified as they are re-represented in a new context, what eventually emerges is a *globally* different re-presentation of the original speech. In other words, an audience that interacts only with the recontextualized version of a speech may get an entirely different picture of what was actually said and displayed. In the present study this is particularly critical, since, as I have suggested elsewhere, most Americans did not view Powell's speech. Instead, they were confronted with an accumulation of micro-transformations in the press that likely positioned them to regard Powell's speech as more persuasive than it actually was.

Clearly, it is a myth that journalists can "accurately" and "literally" report prior discourse. They cannot help but transform multimodal discourse as they recontextualize it in their news narratives. Still, we may question whose interests journalists serve as they report about call-to-arms rhetoric. It doesn't take a genius to understand that when journalists describe a political actor's call-to-arms speech as "masterful" and "compelling," it serves the interests of that political actor. Likewise, it's obvious that, when journalists re-purpose an image of an alleged terrorist so that it whirls toward the viewer, this positions audiences to be afraid of this character. I don't expect journalists to be impartial. I don't even think it's possible to be impartial. But, at the very least, mainstream journalists could refrain from making overtly evaluative comments, and could avoid using camera tricks typical of tabloid programs like *TMZ* or *A Current Affair*.

What's more troubling, however, are the more microscopic transformations that occur when journalists recontextualize others' discourse—the deletion of a temporal circumstance or modal auxiliary; the addition of a token of counterexpectancy; the slight paraphrase that, nevertheless, significantly alters meanings. Again, these transformations are so minute that they are almost imperceptible—and yet, in aggregate, they reposition audiences in profound ways.

In this study, I was fortunate. I had the resources and the time to examine the potential rhetorical impact of these tiny transformations. But most consumers of the news aren't so fortunate. Most consumers of the news cannot "check" the journalists to see how they have recontextualized others' discourse. In fact, there is often no record of the original text, and, thus, no way of checking the journalists in the first place. So, on the one hand, the public cannot trust journalists (or anyone else) to be "faithful" in their recontextualizations of others' speech. On the other hand, for logistical reasons, viewers and readers cannot check for themselves what "original" speakers may have said.

If we accept that "micro-rhetorical shifts" inevitably occur during recontextualization (Stewart 2008, 267), then we also give up the illusion of "accurate reporting." This makes good theoretical sense, but it brings little comfort to those of us who would still like to believe that an informed citizenry is indispensable to a democratic society. If there is no such thing as "accurate reporting," then how can any of us truly be informed?

Perhaps we can't be—at least not in any total sense. But, if this study is any indication, we may rest assured that when war is proposed by political leaders, journalistic "information" will serve the interests of the state.

Chapter Five

Political Discourse, the Press, and the Public Good

⌘

> It is hard to imagine how intertextual chains could avoid involving discrimination (in a general sense); not everything said can be carried along or should survive in the flow of communication ending up on record. An important issue, however, is when and how such discrimination amounts to misuse (and misuse from whose viewpoint?).
>
> —Per Linell, "Discourse across Boundaries," 1998

This book has examined twenty-four hours in the extended rhetorical life of Colin Powell's U.N. address. Specifically, I have investigated how Powell's multimodal presentation was transformed as it was pre- and recontextualized in various mainstream news narratives. At the same time, I have studied how, as a consequence of these journalistic transformations, public audiences were pre- and repositioned to respond to Powell's argument. In this concluding chapter, I will discuss the contributions of this study, identify directions for future research, and consider the implications of my project both for scholars and for the general public.

I begin by reviewing the multi-methodological approach I adopted in this book. I discuss the value of my integrated analytic framework, and point out some of its limitations. Second, I review the major claims made in previous chapters, and suggest how these claims contribute to existing knowledge about the run-up to the Iraq War and the rhetorical functions of mainstream media journalism. Third, I recommend additional lines of research, which might expand upon and amend the present study. Finally, I offer some overtly political reflections on contemporary call-to-arms journalism.

Methodological Advantages and Limitations

An underlying claim of this study has been that scholars of rhetoric and media studies can benefit from adopting a micro-discursive, intertextual, and multimodal analytic framework:

- *Micro-discursive* because textual semantics—including rhetorical semantics—are realized in and through more microscopic features of the functional grammar
- *Intertextual* because, in forming their own discourse, rhetors necessarily draw upon and transform other discourse for persuasive ends
- *Multimodal* because texts are never comprised of exclusively print-linguistic resources, and, thus, rhetoric is a multisemiotic phenomenon

With these assumptions in mind, I have attempted to integrate a number of methodological procedures in order to systematically answer research questions of importance to rhetorical study. In chapter 2, I coupled a close analysis of multimodal evaluative discourse with an analysis of various "voices" operating in texts in order to investigate how ethos is constituted intertextually. In chapter 3, I explored how interactive linguistic resources (e.g., evaluation, modality, attribution, etc.) were co-deployed with visual representations of reality to predict and legitimate a future rhetorical event. Finally, in chapter 4, I combined systemic-functional and multimodal text analyses, and generated new procedures for intertextual comparison, in order to chart rhetorical transformations—and the concurrent repositioning of audiences—across discursive events. As the previous chapters suggest, I believe that we can expand the scope of rhetoric and media inquiry if we embrace a constellation of fine-grained analytic methods from linguistics and social semiotics (see appendix I for a summary of the analytic approach). In fact, we cannot fully understand how journalists frame and reframe political rhetoric unless we adopt methods that allow us to closely examine verbal-visual discourse across media (inter)texts.

That said, I have no illusions that these methodological procedures are without limitations. First, and most glaringly, this kind of analysis is confined to texts. I do not examine the practices of textual production (i.e., the material, technical, and social processes by which real actors create texts in real situations); nor do I examine reception and consumption (i.e., the divergent ways that texts are interpreted and used by heterogeneous audiences). In a sense, a textual analysis examines the residue of textual production and the prelude to audience response. It can reveal something about the choices that rhetors make when assembling texts, and the ways audiences are positioned and constrained by texts. Nonetheless, to obtain a more comprehensive view of the motivations for and influence of texts, one would need to combine textual analysis with qualitative research exploring the social practices by which texts are produced and interpreted.[1]

Second, although the multifaceted approach to (inter)textual analysis outlined in this book is sophisticated, it is by no means completely fixed or comprehensive. Importantly, several of the methodological procedures introduced in this study are still being developed. For example, Martin and White's (2005) scheme for analyzing evaluative discourse has stabilized over the years; however, they acknowledge that there is still "a need to develop social semiotic principles for classifying lexis"—possibly through corpus studies (58). Likewise, Baldry and Thibault (2005) suggest that approaches to multimodal text analysis also need to be further elaborated, particularly approaches to coding intersemiotic relations within texts (248). Obviously, the same can be said for the tentative coding schemes I have produced to analyze visual evaluations, intertextual transformations, and rhetorical repositioning. While I believe the various coding categories I have generated represent important methodological starting points, additional research is needed to further develop and modify my schemes.

The principal advantage of my methodology is that its detail-oriented focus reveals how minute verbal-visual meaning relations "add up" within and across media texts to significantly (re)position audiences. Indeed, the methods help us conceptualize the experience of audiences in a fragmented, intertextual, and multimodal world. The main disadvantage of my approach is that the analysis is so exacting and complicated that it is impractical to apply it to a large body of texts, and, thus, to make general claims based on a larger corpus of data.[2] In short, micro-analytic approaches make it difficult to formulate macro-level claims. Nevertheless, the systematic procedures I have used in this study allow me to "ground statements about textual meaning in a principled and replicable way" (Baldry & Thibault 2005, xvi). Furthermore, some claims about media rhetoric and the Iraq War *are* made possible through close textual analyses. I enumerate the key claims of this study in the following section.

Major Claims

U.S. public support for the Iraq War was solidified by the news media that covered Colin Powell's U.N. speech.

More than a decade after the start of the Iraq War, Powell's February 5, 2003, speech is still regularly cited as the most critical rhetorical event in the run-up to the invasion of Baghdad. Historian Christopher O'Sullivan (2009) remarks that Powell's presentation "did more to build support for war than the actions of other U.S. officials" (194). Karen DeYoung (2007) echoes this sentiment, calling Powell's speech "crucial" because it "convinced many skeptical Americans that the threat posed by Iraqi dictator Saddam Hussein was real" (4). A 2010 issue of *Newsweek* goes even further, declaring that Powell's address was not only one of the most important moments in the prewar period, but one of the most important moments in the opening decade of the century. Hans Blix, who wrote the *Newsweek* article, had this to say, "Sadly, but as calculated, Powell's presentation helped to build U.S. support for launching a war that should not have taken place—and that has had terrible consequences. . . . The presentation did not become an indictment of Iraq but an example of unscrupulous and manipulative use of intelligence."

Colin Powell appears irritated that his speech is so often singled out as the most crucial rhetorical event before the war. "It's annoying to me," he told authors Michael Isikoff and David Corn (2006), that "everybody focuses on my presentation" when "the same goddamn case" had been presented earlier to Congress and the president in the form of the 2002 National Intelligence Estimate (NIE) (190). Powell also objects to charges that he manipulated intelligence. He insists that he, like everyone else, was simply deceived by the NIE. He didn't realize he was presenting false information at the U.N., he says, adding that he is "mad at [himself] for not having smelled the problem[s]" in the CIA's intelligence file (2012, 223).

Powell's insistence that he was unwittingly deceived by the CIA is difficult to accept. Both Bob Woodward (2004) and Powell's former chief of staff, Lawrence Wilkerson (Friedman 2013a), have revealed that Powell had serious doubts about the CIA's evidence, even wondering aloud whether any WMDs would ultimately be found in Iraq.[3] Moreover, Powell included in his presentation many allegations that his own State Department had warned him were weak and indefensible. And as Woodward (2004) illustrates, Powell even fabricated evidence during his presentation, embellishing his translations of intercepted communications in order to cast them "in the most negative light" (310). The fact is that Powell doubted the veracity of the administration's case for war, yet presented it anyway, even helping to exaggerate the evidence. His U.N. speech was tendentious and deeply misleading—and he is ultimately responsible for it.

We must also question Powell's attempt to downplay the significance of his speech and elevate the significance of the National Intelligence Estimate. Granted, the NIE is an extremely important document that did much to solidify congressional support for war.[4] And, of course, Powell drew mainly from the NIE in assembling his U.N. presentation. But it is simply untrue that Powell presented "the same case" as the NIE. For one thing, Powell transformed the intelligence data from the NIE as he recontextualized it in his U.N. address. Moreover, Powell included in his speech crucial information that never appeared in the NIE—information about Iraq's alleged attempts to deceive inspectors and prevent them from uncovering banned weapons. For many Americans, this information about the "failure" of the U.N. was ultimately what justified an American-led war. Finally, Powell overlooks a key difference between the NIE and his speech. The NIE was a classified document—indeed, most of it remains classified to this day.[5] By contrast, Powell's U.N. presentation was a public performance, one specifically designed to inform Americans about Iraq's alleged WMDs and to change attitudes about the necessity of an invasion. The American public may never read the NIE, but Americans will not soon forget Powell's U.N. exhibition.

On the other hand, Powell may be correct that his speech has received undue attention. After all, there were other texts and speeches that helped generate support for war. The "rhetoric of evil" that characterized Bush's discourse about Saddam Hussein had "helped to close the circle of deliberation" about the need for war in Iraq well before Powell's speech (Ivie 2005, 161). Moreover, as Goodnight (2006) observes, public addresses by Bush and Cheney had already inflated the "imminence" of the Iraqi threat and had already succeeded in pressuring Saddam Hussein to prove a negative, that is, to prove that he did not have WMDs. These addresses effectively "lowered the rhetorical bar" for Powell's address, setting "lax proof standards" for justifying the use of preventive force (Keller & Mitchell 2006b, 19). In fact, as shown in chapter 1, the overarching arguments of Powell's presentation had already been uttered by the president in nationally televised orations. Powell was not offering a brand-new case to the public; he was rearticulating an existing case at greater length.

How then do we account for the perceived importance of Powell's address? What made it such a decisive event in the public campaign for war? Perhaps the answer lies not in the speech itself, but in the mainstream news that mediated and distributed the speech, elevating its import and legitimacy. Indeed, Americans might not have regarded Powell's address as crucial if the news media had not promoted it as such. One might even say that Powell's U.N. performance was a pseudo-event (Boorstin 1961): a production of "synthetic novelty" that had been arranged entirely for media consumption (9). After all, the Bush administration had already presented a public case for war—and had already *decided* on the policy of war. In fact, Bush held out very little hope of persuading members of the U.N. Security Council to accept a new war resolution. With plans for an invasion already set, the overarching goal was to construct a "political spectacle" (Edelman 1988), one dazzling enough to garner additional attention and boost public support for violence. American news media would help provide this spectacle, "co-manufacturing" Powell's presentation (Boorstin 1961, 23) and establishing it as *the* case for war in Iraq.

But the American press didn't just enhance the value of Powell's address; it also shaped the substance of Powell's rhetoric, defining for large segments of the public what Powell would say and, later, what he actually said. It bears repeating that most Americans did not see or hear Powell's presentation. Instead, they learned the "facts" of Powell's case from journalists. The historians and pundits are somewhat off the mark, then, when they declare that Powell's speech is what convinced the American public to accept war in Iraq. A major claim of this book is that Powell's presentation was not as crucial as the press reports that covered it. Indeed, without the help of journalists, Powell's speech might never have succeeded in changing American minds.

Journalists not only echo but also (re)constitute political discourse.

Journalists clearly played a pivotal role in shaping American attitudes about Powell's speech—and, by extension, attitudes about war in Iraq. With this in mind, we must scrutinize the mechanisms by which journalists report political discourse. Media scholars who have studied the prewar period have consistently charged the press with echoing the claims of the Bush administration (Bennett, Lawrence, & Livingston 2007; Domke 2004; John et al. 2007). These charges are certainly warranted. In fact, the present study confirms that American journalists covering Powell's address disproportionately emphasized administration sources and overwhelmingly reproduced key claims from Powell's presentation (e.g., the inadequacy of U.N. inspections). As shown in chapter 1, there are several reasons why journalists consistently gave voice to Powell and the administration's perspective:

- The journalistic tendency to index the range of views coming from elite actors in Washington (Bennett 1990) and the tendency to frame the news in terms of who's "winning" the political game (Cappella & Jamieson 1997).

- Heightened uncertainty and patriotism that prevented critical coverage of the Bush administration following the 9/11 attacks (Domke 2004).
- Widespread support for war among leading congressional Democrats, and the absence of a consistent "antiwar" message within the circles of Washington power (Huber 2003).
- The perceived impotence of the U.N. and other foreign leaders with regard to halting a war in Iraq (Bennett, Lawrence, & Livingston 2007).
- The strategic communication of the Bush administration; its ability to manage the news through "message discipline" and intimidation (Bennett, Lawrence, & Livingston 2007; Domke 2004; John et al. 2007).

In the end, both journalistic routines and sociopolitical circumstances ensured that the press would echo the tenor and substance of Powell's address. And, as Bennett and colleagues (2007) argue, there is reason to believe that the press would again echo the claims of the state if similar circumstances obtained in the future.

A key implication of this work, then, is that mainstream reporters must significantly alter norms of news production—especially during campaigns for war. Most importantly, mainstream journalists must do more to seek out and consistently report credible voices from outside of government. This does not mean that they should incorporate an "alternative view" just for the sake of creating a sense of balance in their reports. Sometimes there is a legitimate consensus on an issue and there is no need to muddle the picture by including dubious counterclaims from alternative sources (as has been done in the global warming controversy).[6] When it comes to matters of war and peace, however, journalists need to be highly suspicious of bipartisan consensus. For one thing, it is well known that call-to-arms rhetoric has historically been laced with oversimplifications, misrepresentations, and outright deceptions (Campbell & Jamieson 2008; Ivie 2005). Moreover, this deceptive call-to-arms discourse has not been confined to a single political party: Democrats and Republicans have historically agreed on key matters of national security, including the necessity of continual military intervention in response to attacks on the homeland and new emerging "threats" (Bacevich 2010). Given American history, journalists should both expect and question the Washington consensus that is likely to emerge before a war.

And they should regularly present voices—from grassroots organizations and international institutions—that contradict the U.S. government when it is seemingly unified in its desire for violence. It should hardly matter whether these alternative voices are "winning" the political game in Washington, or whether they are perceived to have enough power to halt the United States' war plans. What should matter is whether they are in a position to speak credibly about a proposed intervention and its justifications. Crucially, opposing voices were available to journalists at the time of Powell's presentation. Skepticism about his speech was offered by U.N. inspectors, international leaders, private citizens around the world, and domestic progressive organizations like the Institute for Public Accuracy. But these voices were either ignored or downplayed in mainstream press reports. Powell's claims were repeated without substantial challenge from legitimate countersources, and the public was deprived of a robust and evenhanded debate.

The problem of the echoing press is extremely important; however, this book shows that "echoing" is not the only problem. Journalists are important rhetorical agents in their own right and their rhetorical work extends far beyond repeating the claims of the state. In fact, journalists both preconfigure and reconfigure political discourse, subtly *modifying* the claims of government officials and significantly altering public perceptions of political rhetoric. Of course, it is well known that journalists (re)frame political speech (e.g., Entman 2004). My goal has been to detail the often subtle rhetorical mechanisms by which such framing is accomplished, probing the intricacies of voice, semantics, stance, and multimodal argument. As I suggest below, such work helps us better understand several key ways that journalists influence a speech's persuasive potential:

- How they manage the play of (inter)textual voices in their reports, ultimately shaping perceptions of each political speaker's ethos.
- How they precontextualize political arguments, priming audiences to respond positively or negatively to future rhetorical events and their material consequences.
- How they recontextualize prior political discourse, transforming the meaning of a rhetorical event through a succession of minor verbal and visual alterations.

Arguably, these small-scale journalistic practices are even more important than the general tendency to echo government claims. After all, if journalists' only fault was that they faithfully *recorded* political arguments, the public might still have a legitimate chance to weigh those arguments on their own merits, evaluating the evidence offered by politicians as that evidence was made available in the press. But, as media scholars understand well, a press report about a political speech is more like a fictional narrative than an unedited transcription. Journalists tell audiences which characters are likeable and legitimate, which utterances are significant and noteworthy. They constrain expectations about what different characters will say, and reshape the content of what characters have already said. Surely, the public would benefit from hearing alternative viewpoints from outside of government, but this may not be enough if journalists still confer greater credibility to government voices, and pre- and reshape government claims in ways that enhance their certainty and evidentiality.

Certainly, journalists need to be more aware of the small-scale and often unconscious ways that they (re)construct political discourse. But analysts of news media need to give these small-scale interventions greater attention as well. In fact, we obtain only a partial understanding of the functions of American journalism when we perform content analyses that focus on shared overarching themes between political addresses and subsequent press reports. As the findings of this study indicate, we must also focus on the micro-rhetorical aspects of news framing and "the subtle management of audience interpretation" both before and after a political speech (Entman 2004; Weiss 2009; Fairclough 1995, 83). After all, when an important political speech, like Powell's, reaches the public primarily through journalistic intermediaries, the small and seemingly innocuous ways that journalists pre- and recontextualize that speech may be more important than any general "patterns of co-occurrence" between the speech and ensuing press reports (Hart 1987, 215). In sum, scholars of media and rhetoric should complement large-scale thematic analyses with detailed investigations of the verbal *and* visual resources that journalists employ as they effectively pre- and redefine major political communications.

A public figure's ethos is primarily constructed within and across media texts.

Often, we think of ethos as the character one creates for oneself in a rhetorical performance—through reasoning and strategies of self-presentation. However, a major contention in chapter 2 is that a public figure's ethos is an *intertextual phenomenon*—that is, one person's ethos is constituted within and across media texts by a variety of competing voices. A politician may seek to build an image of him- or herself in a given public address. But that image is always complicated by the web of media intertexts that both precede and follow that politician's performance. First, as rhetorical scholars know well, media narratives are crucial in forming a politician's pre-speech ethos. Often, long before the politician has announced a public address, journalists and others have already managed to co-construct that politician's reputation. Thus, long before Colin Powell spoke at the U.N., he had already been characterized in the news for months (if not years) as man of integrity and a "dove" in the administration.

But journalists don't stop at forming a public figure's "general reputation," shaping conventional wisdom about a politician's stable character traits and beliefs. They also control that politician's ethos as it relates to a *particular rhetorical occasion*. In fact, as soon as journalists pre- and recontextualize a political address, they immediately suggest whether the political speaker can be trusted for that specific rhetorical performance. This kind of speech-specific ethos is constructed by a number of intertextual voices in the media. First, and most explicitly, journalistic voices may directly evaluate a politician's character and performance. In other words, journalists explicitly inscribe texts with their own attitudes—commenting either positively or negatively on political speakers and their speech, and thereby enacting for those speakers a kind of ethos.

But journalistic voices are not the only ones present in the news. Other voices are also drawn into press reports, and these voices, too, express attitudes about different speakers and texts. For example, news reports in this study featured (among others) (1) reporters' voices and their attitudes about Colin Powell's U.N. speech, (2) Powell's voice and his attitudes about Saddam Hussein and the Iraqi leadership, and (3) Iraqi voices and their attitudes about the Bush administration and its argument for war. News reports, then, are an important site of intertextual struggle, a place where different and sometimes opposing voices compete with each other to characterize political agents and their speech. However, journalists manage this intertextual struggle in two important ways: first, by choosing whose voices will be "heard" in their news accounts, and, second, by framing chosen voices so that some appear more legitimate than others.

In fact, the attitudes that journalists make explicit in their news narratives act as "signposts" by which audiences can retroactively and prospectively interpret the ethos of other textual voices. Indeed, a journalist need only express an attitude about a person once to set off a transitive chain of authority that colors an entire text. For instance, a journalist's expression of a single positive attitude about Colin Powell's speech (1) implicitly authorizes (and legitimates) Powell's negative characterizations of Iraq, and (2) implicitly discredits Iraqis' negative characterizations of Powell. In this study, journalists often overpopulated texts with the voices of those who were ideologically "on their side," and, in a sense, used these "surrogate" voices to repeatedly express attitudes that they were likely precluded from expressing on their own (since they must appear "impartial"). Ultimately, the complex interaction of various evaluations sprinkled throughout an intertextual set of texts by different competing voices may be more significant in constructing a person's character than that person's own interventions to create ethos for him- or herself.

An important implication of chapter 2, then, is that we need to weaken the presumed link between ethos and "self-presentation," and explore more fully the chorus of opposing mediated voices that struggle to shape perceptions of one's character. Such a reevaluation of ethos may appear contrary to tradition, which has tended to regard ethos as a projection of the rhetorical self.[7] But contemporary scholars have increasingly argued for a "readjustment of some of our settled teachings" about ethos (Benson 2004, ix). And, in fact, most analysts already take for granted that ethos need not involve self-presentation.[8] Even Aristotle recognized that one's ethos could be constructed by others. Thus, the notion of intertextual ethos is not a break from tradition, but a recognition of the conditions of life in a media-saturated world. When public figures speak, their words are reprinted, retweeted, *recontextualized* by others—and whatever ethos they attempted to project in their speech is necessarily remade in the process. Indeed, the images that political leaders construct of themselves are relocated in news narratives alongside conflicting images produced by other mediated speakers. Scholars of media rhetoric and public address should conduct their analyses with an eye toward this complexity, investigating the ways that ethos is splintered and reassembled in the intertextual field. We must accept that, if ethos is a "dwelling place" (Hyde 2004), it is a dwelling place for multiple and competing voices.

Precontextualization is a noteworthy journalistic practice.

In chapter 3, I pointed out that intertextuality is not just past-oriented, but future-oriented. With this in mind, I defined *precontextualization* as a rhetorical strategy whereby journalists anticipate and contextualize future discourse in ways that position audiences to regard it as (il) legitimate. Consistent with much media scholarship, I found that journalists whose primary rhetorical objective is presumably forensic—that is, to claim *what happened*—are equally as likely to deal in deliberative affairs—that is, to claim *what ought to happen*. In fact, these journalists not only speculated about future discourse, but also employed a variety of multimodal resources to represent future discourse as desirable, inevitable, or, indeed, "already here." For instance, Powell's speech was represented as *presently* "powerful" enough to instigate a preemptive response from Saddam Hussein. Furthermore, Powell's future speech was legitimated not only through positive evaluations, but also through implicit intertextual arguments. Indeed, in Toulmin's (1958) terms, the journalists themselves supplied "factual" premises that served to warrant Powell's future claims.

I understand that in using the term *precontextualization*, I am perhaps evoking the thorny issue of context. Following Van Dijk (2009), we can informally define context as the relevant aspects of a situation that influence text and talk (vii).[9] Given this definition, readers may wonder whether we need a specialized term like "precontextualization" at all. Indeed, a journalistic preview might be better understood as simply another part of the rhetorical situation, no different than other situational elements that influence a given political address (e.g., audience, speaker intentions, the kind of communicative and political act, historical events, etc.). If this is the case, why invent a new term?

I want to clarify that I don't see precontextualization exclusively as a "prior" element of the rhetorical situation that influences some "later" discourse. It may be true, for instance, that the NBC report affected Powell's speech, but I am not particularly interested in how the journalists influenced *Powell* (or his U.N. performance). Instead, I am interested in the ways journalists influenced enormous public audiences, by preconfiguring Powell's speech in mass mediated discourse. In other words, rather than see precontextualization only as a property of the pre-speech situation, we should also see it as a willful rhetorical action undertaken in mainstream journalism, a form of prospective intertextuality that draws future discourse into the normative present.

In using this term, then, I am not suggesting that we divide context into the different temporal domains surrounding some speech (e.g., "pre-context," "context," "post-context"). But I am proposing that we recognize intertextuality on a temporal continuum, especially in journalistic discourse where precontextualization and recontextualization are relevant counterpoints. Just as journalists recontextualize and redefine political discourse, they may also precontextualize and predefine the same discourse. As I hope to have shown, the timing of these journalistic interventions matters. When journalists precontextualize political discourse, they *prime* audiences to see this discourse (and its consequences) through a particular ideological prism. And they potentially constrain what audiences come to believe about a future speech—whether it is justified by current or past events, rooted in solid evidence, or poised to achieve desirable ends.

In the end, journalists have remarkable freedom to precontextualize future speech events in ways that comport with their own rhetorical objectives. Granted, journalists tend to draw news content primarily from the circles of government power (Bennett 1990), making it likely that they their precontextualizations of future discourse will largely echo the "leaks" they receive from Washington insiders. However, as Jaworski and colleagues (2003) suggest, journalists also have great incentive to speculate about future discourse independently. In many ways, they are free to imagine and project those future scenarios that they find most advantageous or interesting. This only underscores the importance of analyzing precontextualization in rhetoric, discourse, and media studies. Too often analyses focus exclusively on the editorial commentary that follows a public address. But the news reports that precede political communication are equally, if not more, important. These reports subtly regulate interpretations of future discourse. Indeed, they may determine in advance whether or not audiences find a speech persuasive.

Intertextual micro-transformations have a cumulative rhetorical impact.

In chapter 4, I examined the rhetoric of recontextualization in mainstream journalism. Employing a delicate analytic method, I charted the rhetorical transformations that occurred as Colin Powell's presentation was recontextualized in multimodal news narratives. My analysis revealed that, as they recontextualized fragments of Powell's speech, the journalists transformed his meanings in myriad ways, deleting words and phrases, reordering arguments, adding commentary, and rewording (or repicturing) prior utterances. In general, these transformations repositioned audiences to regard Powell's claims as more certain, more salient, and more warrantable. Indeed, the journalists strengthened Powell's arguments—legitimizing Powell and his case with positive evaluative discourse, and enhancing Powell's claims with supportive "evidence" not originally present in his address.

Very often, the journalists transformed Powell's discourse in relatively microscopic ways—deleting an auxiliary verb, or adding a coordinating conjunction. Such small changes may appear inconsequential; however, these changes can have a major cumulative impact. Indeed, when claim after claim is "tweaked" as it is recontextualized, audiences eventually get a globally different picture of an original speech event. And, given that rhetorical audiences often do not interface with original speech events, these micro-transformations in the press are enormously influential in creating "shared or 'common sense' knowledge" about what a politician actually said (Hodges 2008a, 501).

The study of micro-transformations may contribute to our understanding of news bias, particularly bias in the reporting of political speech. For some scholars, bias amounts to partisan reporting. Indeed, some have charged that the press perpetuates a liberal bias that "actively harms conservatives" (Kuypers 2002, 236).[10] The news reports examined in this book show little evidence of such liberal bias. If anything, this study indicates that, when there is an overall consensus for war in Washington, press reports tend to become more *hawkish*—not necessarily more Democratic or Republican (Bennett, Lawrence, &, Livingston 2007; Mermin 1999; Zaller & Chiu 1996).

In fact, most scholars reject the notion of consistent partisan bias in the press (D'Alessio & Allen 2000; Dennis 1997; Niven 2002), and suggest instead that the most significant biases are those related to routines of narrative framing (Entman 2007). Thus, news stories will generally give preference to whatever political group seems most powerful, triumphant, or united (Cappella & Jamieson 1997; Lawrence 2000). And they will consistently frame their reports in ways that promote fear, melodrama, and personalized conflict (Altheide 2002; Bennett 2012; Gans 1979; Gitlin 1980; Graber 1989). Certainly, we see these kinds of framing biases in this study: a preference for the "winning" prowar side of the debate, personalized narratives pitting Colin Powell against Saddam Hussein, melodramatic headlines, and a predilection for fear-inducing language and visuals.

Probably, any analysis would discern these glaring "slants" in news coverage. But this study shows that press bias can be even more subtle. Indeed, even if we put aside the flashy headlines and dramatic visuals, even if we deleted the overtly evaluative language, even if we created more "balanced," two-sided reports, we would still find microscopic alterations of prior discourse, alterations that ultimately enhanced the persuasiveness of Colin Powell's entire address. It is difficult to know why journalists made these small alterations. Why, for example, did journalists enhance Powell's rather dubious claims that Iraq actively assisted al-Qaeda? Were they conforming to norms of news production—trying to emphasize the "danger" implied by Powell's assertions? Or were they simply responding to space limitations and time pressures, relaying the "gist" of Powell's arguments without carefully attending to important details and caveats? In either case, the journalists were probably not even aware of how they were changing Powell's discourse. And that is precisely what makes this kind of press bias so disturbing. Reporters may not even know when they are modifying individual claims, and editors are unlikely to catch their small alterations. It is left, then, to scholars—particulars scholars of public address and media discourse—to expose and explain these subtle and potentially more pernicious press biases. The quality of our democracy may depend on it.

Audiences construct the meaning of political speeches by assembling mass-media fragments.

A final implication of this study concerns the question of whether rhetors or audiences construct texts. It is still tempting to imagine that public orators control their own discourse, that they directly impact audiences as they deliver self contained and unified speeches. However, as Becker (1971) observed long ago,[11] communication in a mass-mediated society is much more fragmentary and diffuse: political speeches are carved up into bits and circulated through space and time across chains of media discourse. To understand a political address, then, we must understand its intertextual trajectory—the way "the message to which the receiver is exposed is scattered" over various media channels (31). Ultimately, it is not the rhetor who is most responsible for textual construction, but audiences—audiences who are bombarded with discursive fragments and left with the hermeneutic challenge of putting the pieces together again (McGee 1990, 288).

Certainly, in a complex intertextual universe, different audience members will come to construct political speeches differently. As Barthes (1977) points out, individuals have different knowledge sets and different textual experiences that ultimately bear upon their readings of a given political utterance. However, audiences also have "common textual knowledges" that enable them to construct meanings in similar ways (Ott & Walter 2000, 432). Paradoxically, mainstream news outlets play a pivotal role in both the fragmentation of political discourse and the generation of shared public knowledge about that discourse. On the one hand, mainstream news media function to decenter political speech, breaking it into morsels and reengineering it through processes of pre- and recontextualization. In this sense, journalists produce unstable and heterogeneous constructions of a public address, weaving together decontextualized fragments of the address along with other voices and texts. In a sense, the "original" speech ceases to exist as it is variously disintegrated and reframed. Words and images are deleted or modified; evaluative inflections are added; and new voices are brought to bear. As different media outlets circulate new iterations of the speech, they create a plurality of fragmentary sources from which public audiences must construct meaning.

Even so, despite the fact that they are faced with diverse mediated fragments, individuals may nevertheless come to see a speech in relatively uniform ways. In fact, mainstream news media may also act as important "centering institutions" (Blommaert 2005, 75) that homogenize the meaning of political discourse for the public.[12] In other words, mainstream journalists often ensure a kind of shared cultural experience. Granted, public audiences may encounter a host of mass-mediated news fragments about any political address. But because mainstream news media operate according to the same conventions and economic imperatives, their constructions of a political speech are typically analogous (Bennett 2012). Thus, in this study, all three news outlets—the *New York Times*, CNN.com, and NBC—produce strikingly similar stories about Colin Powell's speech. Varied as they are, they all broadly reinforce Powell's credibility, promote his performance in advance, and enhance the persuasiveness of his evidence.

Importantly, the *Times*, CNN.com, and NBC play a major role in setting the *intermedia agenda*, shaping the news content of other less powerful media outlets (Reese & Danielian 1989). We can speculate, then, that other news providers also increased the persuasive potential of Powell's address. And insofar as Americans interfaced with mediated news fragments of Powell's speech, they were likely to piece together a positive picture of his performance—indeed, an enhanced version of his performance. In the end, Powell had little control over his discourse, when compared to his audiences. But this may have worked in his favor. After all, the mainstream journalists who pre- and reconstructed his speech gave it an important boost—besieging the public with "improved" fragments of his presentation and inducing audiences to construct a favorable perception of his argument for war.

An important corollary of this discussion is that we can better account for the rhetorical life of a political speech if we adopt methods that scrutinize the subtle verbal-visual interventions that journalists make when they report about that speech. In other words, we should increasingly focus on the intertextual chains that political speeches enter into, and the small transformations that speeches undergo as they move along these media chains (Fairclough 1995, 198). It is not unusual in public address scholarship to focus almost exclusively on a major political speech and its internal argumentation patterns. Meanwhile, media discourse is often treated as "surrounding context," subsidiary discourse that helps us understand the impact of a major address. Certainly, it is important to examine political speeches in their own right, and one can always learn something by carefully studying a single rhetorical performance (Selzer 2004). But we cannot fully understand how a political speech influences the public unless we study how it is adapted for the public in mediated texts. In fact, the rhetorical impact of any political argument ultimately depends upon both the precontextualizing discourse that anticipates it and the recontextualizing discourse that subsequently gives it shape.

Directions for Future Research

This book studied how Powell's presentation was pre- and recontextualized in a few mainstream, American journalistic texts—texts that often "improved the lie"[13] of the Bush administration's argument for war. However, as Hodges (2008b) suggests, recontextualization need not be a method for enhancing the claims of the state. It may also be a site for parody, subversion, and resistance. If this study is any indication, oppositional re-representations of prewar rhetoric are unlikely to be found in mainstream sources—but they may be accessible through other media. Future research might explore how call-to-arms rhetoric is recontextualized in alternative news outlets—magazines, blogs, and other online news sources. Or research could examine how American prowar speeches are covered by the international press—*Al Jazeera*, the BBC, *Le Monde*, *The Guardian*, and so on. Or, indeed, researchers could investigate how such speeches are pre- and recontextualized by "fake news" sources—*The Onion*, *The Daily Show with Jon Stewart*, and so on. Ultimately, the data explored in this project represents a drop in the ocean of press coverage surrounding an important call-to-arms address. Additional research should attempt to account for the full scope of media interventions.

Future research might also consider how *anti*war rhetoric is pre- and recontextualized in the press. Powell's speech, of course, drew enormous attention—both before and after it was delivered. The justification for this coverage seems to be that Powell's was a speech that "could move the world closer to war" (NBC/2.5/TB). It occurs to me that there was also a good deal of rhetoric that could move the world *away* from war. As noted, there was a massive worldwide protest days after Powell's address. And, in early March—before the war was launched—a British agent exposed the NSA's efforts to spy on U.N. Security Council members, presumably to blackmail them into a favorable vote (Mitchell & Mitchell 2008). Either one of these would seem to be newsworthy. And it is worth investigating how—and, indeed, if—the press (re)represented these events in news narratives.

Finally, future research should investigate the historical relationship between journalistic discourse and call-to-arms discourse. As Carvalho (2008) has suggested, diachronic studies of media discourse are currently lacking:

> Most studies of media discourse are like snapshots examining some news items in detail but covering a short time span (often only a day or a few days). While this may be relevant for some events, most public issues have a significantly long "life," which is tied to representations in the media. Understanding the evolution of matters such as war, terrorism or climate change, and the ways they are interdependent in relation to the media, is one of the most important contributions to be made by social researchers. (164)

The present study has sought to examine a day in the rhetorical life of Colin Powell's address. However, there were other days in the journalistic life of Powell's speech. Indeed, a year after Powell's address—when there were clearly no weapons of mass destruction in extra-linguistic reality—the press re-represented Powell's discourse *again*, but not so glowingly. It would be interesting to examine how Powell's speech has been re-purposed in the press in the years since it was first delivered.

Moreover, it is clear that Powell's address was just one "critical discourse moment" (Chilton 1987, 12) in the intertextual history of "war on terror" rhetoric. It would also be productive to compare journalistic reports of Powell's speech with journalistic reports of other post-9/11 call-to-arms speeches in order to locate continuities and transformations in the discourse across time. Beyond this, additional research is needed to examine how call-to-arms rhetoric has been pre- and recontextualized over longer swaths of history. How, for example, was FDR's call-to-arms rhetoric represented in the press, and how might this compare to contemporary representations of call-to-arms discourse? Such questions are important to answer as we continue to grapple with the mediation of public address in American history.

Contemporary Call-to-Arms Journalism and the Public

As you might expect, in the aftermath of the Iraq War, a number of journalists reassessed their pre-invasion coverage. I already discussed in the introduction a *mea culpa* of sorts presented by the *New York Times* editors ("The *Times*"). The *Times* (2004) never apologizes for its coverage (that would be asking too much), and often qualifies its role in misinforming the public (the editors were "*perhaps* too intent on rushing scoops into the paper"; critical stories buried on page A10 "*might well have* belonged on

Page A1"). Still, at least the *Times* voluntarily offered an acknowledgment that its prewar coverage was "not as rigorous as it should have been."

Other news institutions were far more reluctant to admit any wrongdoing. In this regard, NBC News deserves special criticism. NBC journalists were by far the worst offenders, in my study, when it came to legitimating and enhancing Colin Powell's claims. Other, more longitudinal studies of NBC's prewar coverage confirm that NBC tended to promote the war and represent it as inevitable (e.g., Lule 2004). It is also worth noting that, unlike the *Times*, which was delivered to roughly 700,000 homes in 2003 (New York Times Company 2011), NBC *Nightly News* reached, on average, 10.9 million viewers each newscast (McClintock 2003). Arguably, then, NBC played a huge role in advancing and enhancing erroneous government claims. However, it wasn't until former White House press secretary Scott McClellan (2008) charged the media with being "complicit enablers" during the run-up to war that NBC reflected on its coverage (125).[14]

NBC anchor Brian Williams interviewed former anchor Tom Brokaw:

> **Williams:** Are you confident, taking the coverage in toto—that the right questions were asked, the right tone was employed—and should it be viewed in the context to that time?
>
> **Brokaw:** It needs to be viewed in the context of that time. . . . This president was determined to go to war. It was more theology than it was anything else. That's pretty hard to deal with. Look, I think all of us would like to go back and ask questions with the benefit of hindsight, but a lot of what was going on then was unknowable. The CIA insisted that he had weapons of mass destruction. (Quoted in Mitchell 2008)

Brokaw is surely correct that Bush was unwavering in his crusade for war. Still, Brokaw's response reflects some of the deep, systemic problems with contemporary journalism. Here, Brokaw assumes that "official" sources, such as the CIA, need to be consulted and trusted in the absence of evidence, and he assumes that nothing can be done when a president is determined to go to war.

But what troubles me even more—in both Williams's question and Brokaw's response—is the assumption that the main problem with prewar coverage was that the "right questions" were not asked. This assumption is shared by many academics. Keller and Mitchell (2006c), for instance, argue that the press would have served the public better by more frequently posing "timely and carefully worded" critical questions (255). Domke (2004) agrees, asserting that "the chief failure of the press was that they too rarely questioned the administration's discourses" (184). As I see it, though, the lack of critical questions was not the most important failure of the press. The problem was not even that journalists served as "stenographers," essentially taking dictation for the Bush administration. Again, they didn't just repeat administration claims. The problem was that journalists, in re-representing claims, labored to make those claims *more persuasive*. They transformed bad arguments for war into better ones.

Personally, I'm not interested in whether NBC asked the right questions. But I would like to know why the network's journalists treated a public address by a government official as if it were a movie premiere. I want to know why they explicitly endorsed an argument for war as "compelling," "masterful," and "powerful." I want to know why the words "Target: Iraq" were displayed on screen. I want to know why NBC believed that they could assess Powell's evidence before his speech. I want to know why NBC believed it could offer a judicious analysis of Powell's evidence ten seconds after he stopped talking. I want to know why hedges and qualifications from Powell's argument were omitted in the NBC reports. I want to know why seeming visual evidence of Iraqi wrongdoing was *added* by NBC journalists. The occasional "tough question" would have been nice, too. But it would not have remedied these catastrophic failures of journalism.

If this sounds harsh, consider NBC's reporting in light of the following principles excerpted from the Society of Professional Journalists' (1996) own "Code of Ethics":

- Make certain that headlines, news teases and promotional material, photos, video, audio, graphics, sound bites and quotations do not misrepresent. They should not oversimplify or highlight incidents out of context.
- Never distort the content of news photos or video.
- Give voice to the voiceless; official and unofficial sources of information can be equally valid.
- Distinguish between advocacy and news reporting. Analysis and commentary should be labeled and not misrepresent fact or context.
- Admit mistakes and correct them promptly.

NBC's breach of the principle in the last bullet is perhaps most troubling. For Brokaw's response suggests that he believes that nothing, aside from a few more questions, could have been done differently by his journalistic institution during the run-up to the Iraq War. This makes it rather likely that the next time an administration tries to take the country to war, NBC will provide similar coverage. After all, as Brokaw underscores, prewar news coverage inevitably responds to the prewar context, and "there's always a drumbeat at that time."

This leaves the public in a rather difficult position—faced frequently with specious political arguments for war and journalists who function to make these arguments seem more attractive. What can be done? Countless scholars argue that citizens need to develop *critical media literacy* (Bagdikian 2004; Bennett 2012; Fairclough 1995; Kellner 2001; Kellner & Share 2005; Luke 1994; 1997). I certainly concur with this recommendation. In particular, this research suggests that citizens need to be critically aware of what Hodges (2008a) refers to as the "politics of recontextualization" (501)—the ways that journalists recontextualize and transform other discourse for political ends. Beyond this, members of the public should examine the content and structure of news narratives and investigate the practices by which such narratives are constructed. Likewise, they should scrutinize corporate ownership of news media, and actively seek out alternative news sources that are less beholden to profit-making. Finally, citizens would also benefit from a *critical historical literacy*—particularly one that examines why wars are fought and how they are marketed to the public via journalists. As Tom Brokaw said in his interview with Williams, "All wars are based on propaganda." What he didn't say—and doesn't seem to recognize—is that the propaganda comes from political leaders *and* the press.

Ultimately, the public needs to ask why it is necessary in the first place that readers and viewers should have to "watch out" not only for illegitimate call-to-arms rhetoric produced by politicians, but also for illegitimate call-to-arms rhetoric produced by journalists. It's truly an unfair burden. And while I'd love to see citizens critically examine the government and the media, they must eventually demand a *better* government and a *better* media. This is the real project that must begin if unnecessary wars are to be prevented.

Appendix A

Data Corpus

⌘

Table A.1. Main News Reports Analyzed

Author	Title of Program/Article	Date
Steve Capus (executive producer)	*NBC Nightly News with Tom Brokaw*	February 4, 2003, 6:30 PM
Steve Capus (executive producer)	*NBC News Special Report: The Case against Iraq*	February 5, 2003, 9:24 AM-11AM
Steve Capus (executive producer)	*NBC Nightly News with Tom Brokaw*	February 5, 2003, 6:30 PM
Julia Preston & Steven Weisman	"Powell to Charge Iraq Is Shifting Its Illegal Arms to Foil Inspectors," *New York Times*	February 5, 2003, (morning)

(continued)

Table A.1. *(continued)*

Author	Title of Program/Article	Date
Steven Weisman	"Powell, in U.N. Speech, Presents Case to Show Iraq Has Not Disarmed," *New York Times*	February 6, 2003, (morning)
Anonymous	"Powell to Make Case against Iraq: Secretary of State to Give Crucial Address to Security Council," *CNN.com*	February 5, 2003, (morning)
John King & David Ensor	"Powell: Iraq Hiding Weapons, Aiding Terrorists; Annan: War Not Inevitable," *CNN.com*	February 6, 2003, (morning)

Appendix B

Synoptic Views of Discourse

⌘

The term "discourse" has taken on two related, but somewhat different meanings. First, for Foucault (1972), discourse is a way of representing knowledge, a conventional way of thinking that governs what can be said about a given subject at some historical moment (Hall 1997, 44). However, we may also understand discourse as "social action and interaction, people interacting together in real social situations" (Fairclough 1995, 18). When I refer to "discourse," I typically have this latter sense of the term in mind. Such "situated discourse" involves human participants who negotiate the meaning of signs in context. These signs include language, visuals, and other types of symbols that people produce in order to communicate (Hodge & Kress 1988). When a group of symbols is used to perform some job in some context, we refer to this semiotic configuration as a *text* (Halliday 1989, 10).[1] Of course, textual meaning cannot be divorced from context. In fact, there is a dialectical relationship between context and discourse, whereby context shapes discourse and discourse, in turn, shapes context.[2]

Most scholars who investigate situated discourse—regardless of their specific field—would probably agree on these basic points—that text and context are dialectically related, and that the meaning of a text is always negotiated between dialogic partners in real social situations. Thus, researchers with different backgrounds and interests view discourse similarly. In the next section, I identify four such similar views of discourse: a rhetorical view, a systemic-functional view, an intertextual view, and a critical view. I refer to these views as *synoptic* because they all share basic assumptions about discourse. On the other hand, each view affords different questions about discourse and enables researchers to glean unique insights about texts. Thus, synthesizing these different views can help us fill in some of the gaps that any one view of discourse would inevitably leave open. Below I discuss each perspective, noting how each enhances my study.

A Rhetorical View of Discourse

As Perelman and Olbrechts-Tyteca (1969) note, rhetorical study entails identifying and analyzing the discursive techniques by which rhetors induce or increase "adherence of minds" (14). That is, rhetoric is concerned with the discourse employed to induce or increase *persuasion*—which we may define as agreement or commitment to certain premises. The rhetorical view assumes that discourse is motivated semiotic activity, that is, symbolic activity including but not limited to language (Kennedy 2007). This symbolic activity is always adapted to an audience and aimed at securing agreement or inducing action.

A major focus of rhetorical scholarship is the study of argumentation—for example, the relationship between premises and conclusions, as in the Aristotelian (2007) enthymeme; or between claims, data, and warrants, as in Toulmin's (1958) model. However, rhetors not only persuade audiences by means of explicit argumentation, they also (more subtly) "design" audiences, positioning them to accept certain attitudes by appealing to their ideological convictions and moral beliefs (Thieme 2010).

This notion of *positioning* an audience is critical to my study, and is worthy of elaboration. I start from the premise that every speech act positions some putative addressee, implying a "desired response" (Halliday & Matthiessen 2004, 108). For example, when you offer information, you prefer that your addressee will acknowledge (not contradict) that information (108). When you order goods and services, you desire that your addressee will carry out (not refuse) your order (108). As Martin and White (2005) suggest, we position audiences to respond in ways that conform to our expectations (93).[3] In other words, we position audiences to fulfill the "desired response."

To position an audience is not the same as to persuade an audience. When you position an audience, you *signal* to its members how you prefer them to respond to your utterance. When you persuade an audience, *they actually accept* your utterance and its embedded beliefs, assumptions, and proposals. When an audience has been persuaded, minds have changed—either its members believe something that they did not believe before, or they believe something more strongly than they did before. Thus, following Austin (1962), we might say that persuasion amounts to a perlocutionary effect—the response the speech act actually achieves, while positioning amounts to an illocutionary intention—what the speech act is aiming to achieve. Positioning an audience can certainly lead to persuasion, but it doesn't have to. After all, audiences can recognize that someone is trying to persuade them—recognize how someone *expects* them to respond—yet still "refuse their adherence" to that person's assertion (Perelman & Olbrechts-Tyteca 1969, 65). Of course, when audiences fail to produce a "desired response," they may incur a social cost. For example, expressing disagreement can cause embarrassment, and interlocutors generally seek to avoid, or at least, mitigate such "face-threatening acts" (Brown & Levinson 1978). In this study, I am principally interested in how audiences are positioned—that is, the ways that rhetors *imply* certain audience responses and actions. I make no claims as to whether audiences accept how they are positioned, whether they are in fact persuaded.[4]

Without resorting to argumentation, rhetors can position audiences in many ways. Many scholars note, for instance, that the very use of language is rhetorical. As Burke (1966) explains, language is never neutral—it is not a "reflection of reality" but a "selection of reality"—and "a deflection of reality" (45). That is, language is not a transparent vehicle for communicating truth, but a means for construing and filtering experience—a way of directing audiences "to *look at* some things and *overlook* others" (Herrick 2005, 226). Linguistic descriptions may "covertly"[5] position audiences, as rhetors define reality in ways that advance certain values and beliefs, "without having to defend such values and beliefs explicitly" (Schiappa 2003, 131). Often, rhetoric functions not through "claims supported by reasons," but through representations of reality that are "proclaimed as if they were indisputable facts" (Zarefsky 1998, 5).

Of course, representations of reality are often inflected with value-based discourse. As Perelman and Olbrechts-Tyteca (1969) explain, "One appeals to values in order to induce the hearer to make certain choices rather than others, and, most of all, to justify those choices so that they may be accepted and approved by others" (75). That is, by referring to values, rhetors can represent certain actions as justifiable and can, thus, create a "disposition toward action" (74). So, while "factual" descriptions position audiences to *believe* that some state of affairs is true or real, value-based descriptions position audiences to *act* in accordance with community standards.

In sum, the rhetorical view posits that discourse is not only directed at an audience, but is aimed at *persuading* an audience. More precisely, discourse—whether it is explicitly argumentative or not—is aimed at positioning audiences to accept certain propositions and/or perform certain actions. Rhetorical analysis, then, involves examining and explaining the discursive strategies rhetors employ to influence audiences in particular contexts. While the rhetorical view provides many valuable analytic approaches,[6] other disciplines offer methodologies that may be better equipped to account for micro-discursive and multi-semiotic phenomena. With this in mind, I now turn to the other views of discourse, which, I argue, supply useful methodological frameworks that can enhance rhetorical analysis.

A Systemic-Functional and Multimodal View of Discourse

Systemic-functional (SF) approaches to both linguistic and multimodal discourse analysis can provide the kind of methodological rigor that many rhetoricians are seeking (Eisenhart & Johnstone 2008).[7] Moreover, as Fahnestock (2011) points out, Halliday's approach to linguistic analysis "offer[s] rhetorical scholars an enriched view of the persuasive potential of ordinary language" (10). Systemic-functional linguistics, or SFL, conceives of language as a network of meaning potential—that is, as a social semiotic *resource* for making meaning (Halliday 1978; Halliday & Matthiessen 2004). What this implies is that meanings—for example, the meanings of words—are not fixed by some static, rule-bound system. Instead, meanings are *made* in contextualized use. People are free to draw from the meaning potential of language—to represent reality in ways that correspond to their perception of context and to their rhetorical objectives.

As in rhetorical scholarship, SFL views text and context as reciprocally interdependent. In fact, an important theoretical insight in Halliday's (1978) model is that context is realized *in* and *through* language. In other words, language is both the realization of the context and a force that realizes or enacts the context.[8] As Andrus (2011) explains, context does not "determine" a given text; instead, context is "constituted in interaction, in real time, and is thus open to revision and re-representation by the individuals orienting toward and using discourse" (118). SFL posits that language realizes various aspects of context by simultaneously performing three essential *metafunctions*—ideational, interpersonal, and textual. The ideational metafunction is primarily concerned with construing physical reality. The interpersonal metafunction enacts social relationships and social roles. And the textual metafunction organizes various discursive elements into a coherent whole.

SFL provides a systematic method of textual analysis that helps to ground our inquiry into stylistic choice (Zdenek & Johnstone 2008). With its micro-analytic focus on lexis[9] and grammar, SFL uncovers the "constitutive rhetoric" (Charland 1987) whereby rhetors *construe* reality and *interact with* putative audiences. That is, SFL directs analysts to see how rhetors (1) position audiences to accept certain "claims to reality" and (2) align audiences into communities of value that dispose them to act in certain ways.[10]

For instance, an SFL transitivity analysis (Halliday & Matthiessen 2004, 179–97) provides a systematic method for examining linguistic representations of reality. Such an analysis reveals how rhetors choose to construe various actions, circumstances, and the participants involved in them. It can show how rhetors strategically name (or fail to name) actors and assign (or fail to assign) responsibility for various events. To take a familiar example, we can imagine a politician choosing between the following three options: (1) "We made mistakes," (2) "Mistakes were made," or (3) "Mistakes occurred" (see table B.1).[11]

Table B.1. SFL Transitivity Analysis

We	made	mistakes
Actor	**Process: material**	**Goal**
Mistakes	were made	
Goal	**Process: material**	
Mistakes	occurred	
Actor	**Process: material**	

A transitivity analysis accounts for the lexicogrammatical differences between these three constructions and helps us determine why rhetors may choose one versus another.

While transitivity focuses on the ideational metafunction, Martin and White's (2005) appraisal framework accounts for the interpersonal dimension of language.[12] Specifically, appraisal reveals how rhetors blend linguistic resources of tense, polarity, modality, and evaluation to establish rhetor-audience relationships and position audiences to be aligned with or opposed to certain communities of value. As Martin and White (2005) comment, "Appraisal analysis provokes a rehabilitation of the study of rhetoric within linguistic theory" (260).

Again, to take a mundane example, we may note a rhetorical difference between (1) Iraq possesses deadly weapons, and (2) Iraq may possess weapons (see table B.2).

In the first option, a negative evaluation (*deadly*) positions the audience to be both emotionally disturbed by the weapons and ideologically

Table B.2. Appraisal Analysis

Iraq	possesses	deadly	weapons
	Positive polarity; monoglossic—bare assertion	**(a) Negative judgment: propriety; (b) Negative affect: disquiet**	
Iraq	may possess	weapons	
	Positive polarity; dialogically expansive: entertain—modalized assertion		

opposed to the principal actor responsible for possessing them (Iraq). Furthermore, the assertion is a monoglossic "fact": it does not recognize or invite alternative viewpoints. Thus, the audience is positioned to take it for granted that Iraq possesses these weapons and that these weapons represent a deadly threat. Meanwhile, the second option contains no overtly evaluative lexis—and, therefore, no explicit indications that the putative audience should align itself against Iraq. The second option also contains a modal auxiliary (*may*), signaling that the rhetor recognizes and entertains dialogic alternatives. In other words, the rhetor positions the audience to understand that this is not a "fact," and other viewpoints (e.g., *Iraq may not have weapons*) are possible. An appraisal analysis, then, provides rhetoricians with a systematic approach for examining how rhetors create different degrees of "facticity" in their texts (Latour & Woolgar 1986, 80), opening and closing space for audiences to imagine alternative viewpoints. In addition, it provides a framework for analyzing the evaluative discourse that can induce audience action (Perelman & Olbrechts-Tyteca 1969, 74–75).

SFL also helps us understand the textual metafunction, how rhetors organize information and create meaningful coherence throughout an unfolding text. There are many ways to study the textual metafunction, but in this book I focus primarily on reference and lexical cohesion. *Reference* includes those grammatical devices that "point to" other items—either in the same text or in the outside environment (Halliday & Matthiessen 2004, 553). Meanwhile, *lexical cohesion* involves the semantic relationships (e.g., synonymy, antonymy, etc.) that link together various "content words" in a text (Hasan 1989, 79–82).

We can observe reference and lexical cohesion in the following text: "Eagles are beautiful (1). They soar in the sky (2). But chickens are ugly (3). They cluck on the ground (4)." Reference is displayed by the pronouns in clauses 2 and 4. In clause 2, *they* functions as an anaphoric reference—"pointing backwards" to the word *eagles* in clause 1. In clause 4, *they* reappears, now referring to a different lexical item: *chickens*. In each case, the pronoun and its antecedent are *co-referential*: they refer to the same thing. Such co-referentiality helps us track the identities of different participants across clauses (or between verbal and visual symbols).

Next, lexical cohesion helps us see the semantic links between different content words in a text. In the sample text, *eagles* and *chickens* are *co-hyponyms*: they are members of the same superordinate class—birds.

The words *beautiful* and *ugly* are *antonyms*: they have opposing experiential meanings. The words *sky* and *ground* are *converses* (Martin & Rose 2007, 86): they represent inversely related locations. Finally, the text also exhibits *collocation*: there are several words that co-occur so frequently in language use that we associate them with one another. For example, the words *eagles* and *soar* appear together so often that we recognize them as collocates; the same is true for the words *chickens* and *cluck*.

These lexical ties, dispersed across an entire text, help generate a coherent picture of a text's characters and their relationships to one another. Ultimately, meaningful links can also be discerned across several intertexts. Thus, for example, if we encountered the following utterance in a different text—*Eagles are stunning birds of flight*—we could say that it is intertextually linked to the sample above on the basis of shared ideational patterns (i.e., both suggest an eagles-fly thematic) and shared evaluations (i.e., both suggest a positive appreciation: eagles-beautiful). As I discuss below, such thematic formations are important to this study.

SF scholars maintain that all semiotic resources are capable of performing ideational, interpersonal, and textual metafunctions.[13] In fact, they have developed rich analytic tools for examining symbolic resources other than language, such as visual images (O'Toole 1994; Kress & Van Leeuwen 1996). Furthermore, they have sought to understand *multimodality*, how various symbolic resources combine and co-contextualize one another.[14] For example, Baldry and Thibault (2005) use a detailed table to account for nuances of visual, kinesic, and sound data in video texts. As illustrated in table B.3, I adapted Baldry and Thibault's (2005) methodology to study NBC news broadcasts.

Most SF scholars have not explicitly discussed how their approaches to multimodal text analysis relate to rhetorical theory.[15] However, it is clear that, as in the case of primarily linguistic texts, verbal-visual texts can position audiences to accept certain representations of reality and perform certain actions—without resorting to explicit argumentation. For example, a rhetor may select a given "visual transitivity frame" (Baldry & Thibault 2005, 122) that positions audiences to accept one representation of events rather than another. Likewise, a rhetor can employ visual evaluations (e.g., Maier 2009) that position audiences to align themselves with (or against) given social communities. The systemic-functional view of discourse, then, provides rhetorical scholars

Table B.3. Illustration of Multimodal Transcription for Video News Text

Time	Frame	Visual Image	Kinesic Action	Soundtrack	Interpretation
1.		CP: stationary + zooming in HP: direct VP: median D: MCS VC: tv screen, suit, papers in hand ⇒ studio report VS: Brokaw CR: blue CO: naturalistic VF: Brokaw: median, viewer Wording: IN DEPTH—in several places on screens behind Brokaw	[Brokaw stands]	[silence]	**Phase 1a** EXP • Actor; action: Brokaw's spoken discourse + images + wording enact joint thematics: *Colin Powell to give speech for war*; *Saddam Hussein/ Iraq is the enemy*; the *war is imminent in Iraq*

(continued)

Table B.3. *(continued)*

Time	Frame	Visual Image	Kinesic Action	Soundtrack	Interpretation
2.		As above	[Brokaw speaks] Image appears on screen in background	{RG: Brokaw} NBC news	• "Showdown with Iraq" ⇒ promotional discourse = CONFLICT • "Target Iraq" ⇒ military discourse ⇒ WAR • Countdown to a speech ⇒ promotional • Actor/ Pr/Goal/ Location: [speech] could move the world closer to war
3.		Brokaw: As above For Saddam: CP: stationary HP: direct/oblique VP: median D: CS VC: Saddam: microphone, suit, desk papers—some kind of address VF: Saddam: median, off screen Wording: IN DEPTH, bold white, caps, median size and salience, Q3-4 in backgrounded screen	As above; wording appears; Saddam speaks on television screen	in depth tonight	INT • "In depth" positions viewer to understand this as far-reaching, reporting ⇒ special • "Countdown" and "showdown" are both promotional; they position the viewer as spectator of a conflict that is exciting and entertaining.

with systematic methods for examining "micro-rhetoric" (Hopper 2007) across semiotic modes.

An Intertextual View of Discourse

Bakhtin (1981) was perhaps the first to note that discourse "*cannot fail to be oriented* toward the 'already uttered,' the 'already known,' the 'common opinion'" (279). Indeed, texts always refer to prior texts, and draw upon what has come before to make new meanings (Porter 1986, 34). Intertextuality—a term coined by Kristeva (1980)—is the notion that, in a given text, components of other texts are always present (Fairclough 2003, 39). Rhetoricians often study intertextuality within the framework of genre criticism, examining how texts perform the same social action in typified situations.[16] But, as a macro-level approach, genre criticism is perhaps less appropriate for studying the small intertextual relations that obtain between only a few texts—texts that may not be of the same generic type.

Of course, many rhetorical critics have sought to understand intertextuality outside of the genre paradigm.[17] But there are productive ways of theorizing and studying intertextual phenomena, which rhetoricians, by and large, have not embraced. For instance, Thibault (1991) has developed critical intertextual analysis (CIA), an approach that seeks to identify the "patterned meaning relations" out of which texts are assembled (125). As Lemke (1995a) observes, rhetorical events don't need to allude to or imitate one another to be relevant intertexts. They need only relate to one another on the basis of overarching meanings or thematic formations. Several scholars have examined how these thematic formations are retained across texts—even if the given texts never reference one another or use the same words.[18] I draw on this work in my study, showing for example how overarching meanings from Powell's speech reappear in subsequent news reports, even as specific wordings change.

It is also productive to think of intertextuality in terms of *recontextualization*, the process of extracting elements from one discursive context—decontextualizing them—and relocating them in another (Bauman & Briggs 1990). As Linell (1998) observes, however, recontextualization involves more than simply relocating discourse. Recontextualization also entails the *transformation* of prior discourse—as rhetors alter the content of past utterances and inflect "old" speech with new meanings. Of course, as rhetors alter and evaluate prior discourses, they also position audiences to be more or less aligned with those discourses and the communities that espouse them.

A number of scholars have investigated the kinds of small transformations that are observable when aspects of one text are recontextualized in another.[19] Drawing on this scholarship, I attempt to uncover how journalists transform Powell's discourse as they recontextualize it in their news reports. However, this study is unique in that it attempts, at a micro-discursive level, (1) to account for intertextual transformations across *multimodal* texts, and (2) to suggest how these transformations implicate and *re*position putative audiences (see chapter 4). In addition, this study attempts to account for prospective intertextuality, the way texts anticipate future texts. Specifically, I investigate how news reports *precontextualize* Powell's speech, introducing and predicting elements of Powell's address before he delivered it (chapter 3). In sum, the intertextual view demands that analysts look at texts in relation to one another, and helps to account for the discursive strategies rhetors employ as they draw upon and transform prior texts—and shape future ones.

A Critical View of Discourse

Over a decade ago, Jasinski (2001) speculated that critical discourse analysis (CDA) "might prove instructive in trying to link text and ideological context, close reading, and critical rhetoric" (96). Since then, several rhetoricians have employed CDA concepts and reading strategies.[20] CDA is not a methodology,[21] but an *approach* to studying discourse that seeks to challenge the unjust exercise of power. A major tenet of CDA is that research should begin with "prevailing social problems" (Van Dijk 1986, 4, quoted in Wodak 2001, 1)—and should try, to the degree that it is possible, to critically intervene in these problems.

Because CDA researchers make their political commitments explicit, they are sometimes accused of imposing ideological readings on texts. CDA practitioners reject this claim on two main grounds. First, just because CDA scholars have political interests, it does not follow that their analyses are invalid. As Carvalho (2008) puts it, "ideological commitment . . . does not equal analytic distortion" (162).[22] Second, CDA practitioners stress that, despite claims to objectivity, no research paradigm is actually free from politics. As Hodges and Nilep (2007) explain, "Critical scholarship does not pretend to operate from an Archimedean point outside the social world it studies. Critical scholarship recognizes that such a view from nowhere does not exist, and that analysts are also participants in the world under study" (4). Thus, CDA scholars maintain that the best course of action is to make one's political leanings transparent.

With this in mind, CDA scholars seek "to expose existing wrongs in society in an effort to shape a better world" (Hodges & Nilep 2007, 4). In particular, CDA posits that scholars should work to expose and confront discursive manifestations of illegitimate power relations, including the ways that dominant groups use language and other semiotic resources to enact unjust social arrangements (Van Dijk 1993, 249–50). Of course, CDA is not the only discipline concerned with social problems. However, it is unique in its attempt to systematically uncover how social problems are enacted and sustained through the often microscopic workings of discourse. That is, CDA uses sophisticated linguistic and semiotic analyses to detect instances of discursive manipulation that would otherwise go unnoticed.

In this study, I begin with what I take to be a serious social problem—namely, unjust and illegitimate war. I focus, in particular, on the war in Iraq, which I regard as unjust and illegitimate not only because the U.S. public was misled into the war on the basis of willfully distorted intelligence (Bamford 2004), but also because the war needlessly killed thousands of U.S. troops (U.S. Department of Defense 2011) and tens of thousands of Iraqi civilians (Kelland 2011)—not to mention the millions more who were injured or displaced by the violence. Given this assessment of the Iraq War, a major focus of this study is the degree to which journalists who covered Colin Powell's 2003 speech contributed discursively to the justification for violence. In lay terms, I want to know whether and to what degree journalists "helped" Colin Powell as he tried to legitimate military action in Iraq.

Several scholars have argued that major news media outlets are often dominated by a kind of "elite discourse"—a discourse that generally serves the interests of the politically and economically powerful (Fairclough 1995; Herman & Chomsky 1988; Van Dijk 1993; 1998; 2009). Van Dijk (1993; 1998) defines elites as those people with special power resources—including privileged access to, and control of, channels of mass communication. Thus, elites include politicians and other government officials, and, of course, members of the media (who act as gatekeepers). Because these elites have unique access to mass-media channels, Van Dijk (1993) reasons, they have unsurpassed power to influence public opinion. Indeed, power abuse occurs when elites attempt to manufacture consensus for unjust social practices (Herman & Chomsky 1988)—for example, when political leaders convince people that participation in an unnecessary war is actually in their own best interest. The target of Van Dijk's criticism, then, is discursive power *abuse*—the unethical and hegemonic (Gramsci 1971) persuasion of the public.

In some CDA accounts, elite actors seem to work in concert to mislead the public and sustain unequal power structures. But it is possible to take a more nuanced view of discourse and elite domination. Fairclough (1989; 1995; 2003), for instance, recognizes the role of resistance in the face of dominance. While he generally accepts the notion of hegemony, he also emphasizes that power relations are relations of struggle. Those who hold power must work constantly to reaffirm it, while those who do not are always capable of resisting or perhaps seizing power for themselves. In fact, Fairclough argues that every text contains traces of this social struggle. In every text, various "voices"—some aligned, some opposed—are articulated together. Fairclough (1995; 2003) is also much more sensitive to the often discrepant and varying discourses of the dominant class. While he (1995) does not deny that there is a degree of complicity between news media and government, he is quick to point out that there is also a great deal of complexity, even direct conflict, in their relationship. Again, traces of this conflict can be observed in texts.

I do not assume that news media merely reiterate the discourse of political leaders, pandering to the agenda of the state. This is surely an oversimplification. However, I also do not assume that news media, as "vanguards of the public," carefully interrogate political rhetoric, challenging unjust and inaccurate claims. This is surely a myth. Instead, I propose that insofar as journalists promote and *legitimate* (Berger & Luckmann 1966; Fairclough 2003; Habermas 1976, Van Dijk 1998; Van Leeuwen 2007) the call-to-arms discourse of politicians, they behave irresponsibly and against the public interest. Like Fairclough (1995), I believe that public audiences may always resist how they are discursively positioned to think and act. Still, I am persuaded by Van Dijk's

(1993, 1998) argument that journalists' privileged access to mass media gives them enormous power to influence public attitudes.

The critical view, then, supplies a theory of discursively enacted power abuse. This view compels us to treat "elite" rhetorical performances as something more than linguistic artistry tailored to a specific audience and occasion. It asks that we also view elite discourse as a potentially unjust exercise of power, a way of manipulating others to achieve illegitimate goals (Van Dijk 2006). Ultimately, I adopt a critical view because I believe that a project focusing on mainstream journalism demands a critical perspective. In a mediated democracy such as ours, it is imperative that we interrogate the degree to which the press serves the interests of government, particularly when government commits itself to the ugly business of war.

Appendix C

Intertextual Precedents for Powell's Arguments

⌘

As shown in table C.1, many of Powell's arguments and much of his evidence had already been presented by George W. Bush in earlier speeches. Here I limit the comparison to two prior speeches by Bush—his 2002 Cincinnati address and his 2003 State of the Union. These represent the most thorough articulations of the administration's case against Iraq—prior to Powell's speech anyway. It is worth noting, of course, that elements of Powell's argument were also previewed by other administration officials in public statements over many months. As the table also indicates, Powell unveiled plenty of new evidence for his presentation. However, this new evidence basically supplemented the major arguments of his speech, arguments that were already circulating from the White House:

- According to Resolution 1441, Iraq is required to actively and verifiably disarm or face serious consequences.
- Iraq has not disarmed: it has biological and chemical weapons and is seeking nuclear weapons.
- Iraq is hiding its WMDs from inspectors and undermining their work.
- Iraq could pass WMDs to terrorists since it is known to support top-level al-Qaeda figures.
- Iraq could use WMDs for its own reasons: it has already displayed aggression toward regional neighbors and killed its own citizens.
- Iraq must be confronted immediately—for the safety of the world and for the sake of the U.N.'s legitimacy.

Table C.1. Comparison of Key Prewar Speeches

Argument/ Evidence	Bush's Cincinnati Speech (October 7, 2002)	Bush's State of the Union (January 28, 2003)	Powell's U.N. Speech (February 5, 2003)
Twelve years of Iraqi deception	[In the 1990s], the U.N. inspections program was met with systematic deception. The Iraqi regime bugged hotel rooms and offices of inspectors to find where they were going next. They forged documents, destroyed evidence, and developed mobile weapons facilities to keep a step ahead of inspectors.	Twelve years ago, Saddam Hussein faced the prospect of being the last casualty in a war he had started and lost. To spare himself, he agreed to disarm of all weapons of mass destruction. For the next 12 years, he systematically violated that agreement. He pursued chemical, biological, and nuclear weapons even while inspectors were in his country.	Iraq had already been found guilty of material breach of its obligations stretching back over 16 previous resolutions and 12 years. Resolution 1441 was not dealing with an innocent party, but a regime this council has repeatedly convicted over the years.

(*continued*)

Table C.1. *(continued)*

Argument/ Evidence	Bush's Cincinnati Speech (October 7, 2002)	Bush's State of the Union (January 28, 2003)	Powell's U.N. Speech (February 5, 2003)
Resolution 1441 was final chance for Iraq to disarm.		Almost three months ago, the United Nations Security Council gave Saddam Hussein his final chance to disarm. He has shown instead utter contempt for the United Nations and for the opinion of the world.	Resolution 1441 gave Iraq one last chance, one last chance to come into compliance or to face serious consequences. No council member present in voting on that day had any allusions about the nature and intent of the resolution or what serious consequences meant if Iraq did not comply. . . . We wrote 1441 to give Iraq one last chance. Iraq is not so far taking that one last chance.
Iraq has made no active effort to disarm in breach of 1441.		It is up to Iraq to show exactly where it is hiding its banned weapons, lay those weapons out for the world to see, and destroy them as directed. Nothing like this has happened.	This council placed the burden on Iraq to comply and disarm. . . . The facts on Iraq's behavior demonstrate that Saddam Hussein and his regime have made no effort—no effort—to disarm as required by the international community.

(continued)

Table C.1. *(continued)*

Argument/ Evidence	Bush's Cincinnati Speech (October 7, 2002)	Bush's State of the Union (January 28, 2003)	Powell's U.N. Speech (February 5, 2003)
Iraq is still producing weapons in violation of 1441 (and earlier resolutions).	[Iraq] possesses and produces chemical and biological weapons. It is seeking nuclear weapons.	Nothing to date has restrained [Saddam Hussein] from his pursuit of these [chemical, biological, and nuclear] weapons.	Indeed, the facts and Iraq's behavior show that Saddam Hussein and his regime are concealing their efforts to produce more weapons of mass destruction.
Iraq is deceiving inspectors, concealing weapons.		The dictator of Iraq is not disarming. To the contrary, he is deceiving. From intelligence sources, we know, for instance, that thousands of Iraqi security personnel are at work hiding documents and materials from the U.N. inspectors, sanitizing inspection sites and monitoring the inspectors themselves.	Everything we have seen and heard indicates that, instead of cooperating actively with the inspectors to ensure the success of their mission, Saddam Hussein and his regime are busy doing all they possibly can to ensure that inspectors succeed in finding absolutely nothing. . . . We know that Saddam Hussein has what is called, quote, "a higher committee for monitoring the inspections teams." [The committee's] job is not to cooperate, it is to deceive; not to disarm, but to undermine the inspectors; not to support them, but to frustrate them and to make sure they learn nothing.

(continued)

Table C.1. *(continued)*

Argument/ Evidence	Bush's Cincinnati Speech (October 7, 2002)	Bush's State of the Union (January 28, 2003)	Powell's U.N. Speech (February 5, 2003)
Intercepted communication shows deception.			This message would have verified to the inspectors that . . . they were trying to clean up the area to leave no evidence behind of the presence of weapons of mass destruction.
Iraq ordered removal of prohibited weapons from palaces.			We know that Saddam's son, Qusay, ordered the removal of all prohibited weapons from Saddam's numerous palace complexes.
Iraq has hidden prohibited materials in homes and cars.			We know that Iraqi government officials, members of the ruling Baath Party. and scientists have hidden prohibited items in their homes. Other key files from military and scientific establishments have been placed in cars that are being driven around the countryside by Iraqi intelligence agents to avoid detection.

(continued)

Table C.1. *(continued)*

Argument/ Evidence	Bush's Cincinnati Speech (October 7, 2002)	Bush's State of the Union (January 28, 2003)	Powell's U.N. Speech (February 5, 2003)
Iraq is moving rocket launchers to avoid inspection.			Numerous human sources tell us that the Iraqis are moving . . . weapons of mass destruction to keep them from being found by inspectors. . . . We know from sources that a missile brigade outside Baghdad was disbursing rocket launchers and warheads containing biological warfare agents to various locations, distributing them to various locations in western Iraq.
Satellite photos show weapons being moved.			We also have satellite photos that indicate that banned materials have recently been moved from a number of Iraqi weapons of mass destruction facilities.
Satellite photos show active chemical weapons facilities			Look at the image on the left. On the left is a close-up of one of the four chemical bunkers. The two arrows indicate the presence of sure signs that the bunkers are storing chemical munitions.

(continued)

Table C.1. *(continued)*

Argument/ Evidence	Bush's Cincinnati Speech (October 7, 2002)	Bush's State of the Union (January 28, 2003)	Powell's U.N. Speech (February 5, 2003)
Iraq is blocking U-2 surveillance		Iraq is blocking U-2 surveillance flights requested by the United Nations.	Iraq also has refused to permit any U-2 reconnaissance flights that would give the inspectors a better sense of what's being moved before, during and after inspectors. . . . The regime only allows interviews with inspectors in the presence of an Iraqi official, a minder.
Iraq is impersonating and coaching scientists on what to say to inspectors.		Iraqi intelligence officers are posing as the scientists inspectors are supposed to interview. Real scientists have been coached by Iraqi officials on what to say.	In mid-December weapons experts at one facility were replaced by Iraqi intelligence agents who were to deceive inspectors about the work that was being done there. . . Iraqi experts were ordered to report to the headquarters of the special security organization to receive counterintelligence training The training focused on evasion methods, interrogation resistance techniques, and how to mislead inspectors.

(continued)

Table C.1. *(continued)*

Argument/ Evidence	Bush's Cincinnati Speech (October 7, 2002)	Bush's State of the Union (January 28, 2003)	Powell's U.N. Speech (February 5, 2003)
Saddam has orders to kill scientists who cooperate with inspectors.		Intelligence sources indicate that Saddam Hussein has ordered that scientists who cooperate with U.N. inspectors in disarming Iraq will be killed, along with their families.	Saddam Hussein had all Iraqi scientists warned of the serious consequences that they and their families would face if they revealed any sensitive information to the inspectors . . . divulging information is punishable by death.
Iraq has mobile biological weapons labs.		From three Iraqi defectors we know that Iraq, in the late 1990s, had several mobile biological weapons labs. These are designed to produce germ warfare agents and can be moved from place to a place to evade inspectors.	One of the most worrisome things that emerges from the thick intelligence file we have on Iraq's biological weapons is the existence of mobile production facilities used to make biological agents. Let me take you inside that intelligence file and share with you what we know from eye witness accounts.
Iraq has developed systems to deliver biological agents.			The Iraqi regime has also developed ways to disburse lethal biological agents, widely and discriminately into the water supply, into the air.

(continued)

Table C.1. *(continued)*

Argument/ Evidence	Bush's Cincinnati Speech (October 7, 2002)	Bush's State of the Union (January 28, 2003)	Powell's U.N. Speech (February 5, 2003)
Iraq has not accounted for anthrax.	In 1995, after several years of deceit by the Iraqi regime, the head of Iraq's military industries defected. It was then that the regime was forced to admit that it had produced more than 30,000 liters of anthrax and other deadly biological agents. The inspectors, however, concluded that Iraq had likely produced two to four times that amount. This is a massive stockpile of biological weapons that has never been accounted for, and is capable of killing millions.	The United Nations concluded in 1999 that Saddam Hussein had biological weapons materials sufficient to produce over 25,000 liters of anthrax; enough doses to kill several million people. He hasn't accounted for that material. He has given no evidence that he has destroyed it.	Iraq declared 8,500 liters of anthrax, but UNSCOM estimates that Saddam Hussein could have produced 25,000 liters. If concentrated into this dry form, this amount would be enough to fill tens upon tens upon tens of thousands of teaspoons. And Saddam Hussein has not verifiably accounted for even one teaspoonful of this deadly material.

(continued)

Table C.1. *(continued)*

Argument/ Evidence	Bush's Cincinnati Speech (October 7, 2002)	Bush's State of the Union (January 28, 2003)	Powell's U.N. Speech (February 5, 2003)
Iraq has not accounted for botulinum toxin.		The United Nations concluded that Saddam Hussein had materials sufficient to produce more than 38,000 liters of botulinum toxin; enough to subject millions of people to death by respiratory failure. He hasn't accounted for that material. He's given no evidence that he has destroyed it.	We know from Iraq's past admissions that it has successfully weaponized not only anthrax, but also other biological agents, including botulinum toxin, aflatoxin, and ricin. . . . The Iraqis have never accounted for all of the biological weapons they admitted they had and we know they had.

(continued)

Table C.1. *(continued)*

Argument/ Evidence	Bush's Cincinnati Speech (October 7, 2002)	Bush's State of the Union (January 28, 2003)	Powell's U.N. Speech (February 5, 2003)
Iraq has not accounted for mustard gas and other chemical weapons.	We know that the regime has produced thousands of tons of chemical agents, including mustard gas, sarin nerve gas, and VX nerve gas. Saddam Hussein also has experience in using chemical weapons. He has ordered chemical attacks on Iran, and on more than forty villages in his own country. These actions killed or injured at least 20,000 people, more than six times the number of people who died in the attacks of September 11.	Our intelligence officials estimate that Saddam Hussein had the materials to produce as much as 500 tons of sarin, mustard, and VX nerve agent. . . . He's not accounted for these materials. He has given no evidence that he has destroyed them. U.S. intelligence indicates that Saddam Hussein had upwards of 30,000 munitions capable of delivering chemical agents. . . . Saddam Hussein has not accounted for the remaining 29,984 of these prohibited munitions. He has given no evidence that he has destroyed them	Saddam Hussein has never accounted for vast amounts of chemical weaponry: 550 artillery shells with mustard gas, 30,000 empty munitions and enough precursors to increase his stockpile to as much as 500 tons of chemical agents. . . . These quantities of chemical weapons are now unaccounted for. Dr. Blix has quipped that, quote, "Mustard gas is not marmalade. You are supposed to know what you did with it."
Intercepted communication confirms existence of nerve agents.			We know that they [have horrible nerve agents]. And this kind of conversation confirms it.

(continued)

Table C.1. *(continued)*

Argument/ Evidence	Bush's Cincinnati Speech (October 7, 2002)	Bush's State of the Union (January 28, 2003)	Powell's U.N. Speech (February 5, 2003)
Iraq has long-range ballistic missiles.	Iraq possesses ballistic missiles with a likely range of hundreds of miles—far enough to strike Saudi Arabia, Israel, Turkey, and other nations—in a region where more than 135,000 American civilians and service members live and work.		Sources inside Iraq indicate that Saddam Hussein retains a covert force of up to a few dozen Scud variant ballistic missiles. These are missiles with a range of 650 to 900 kilometers.
Iraq is developing new ballistic missiles programs.			What I want you to know today is that Iraq has programs that are intended to produce ballistic missiles that fly of 1,000 kilometers. One program is pursuing a liquid fuel missile that would be able to fly more than 1,200 kilometers. And you can see from this map, as well as I can, who will be in danger of these missiles.

(continued)

Table C.1. *(continued)*

Argument/ Evidence	Bush's Cincinnati Speech (October 7, 2002)	Bush's State of the Union (January 28, 2003)	Powell's U.N. Speech (February 5, 2003)
Iraq has UAVs that can be used to deploy biological or chemical weapons.	We've also discovered through intelligence that Iraq has a growing fleet of manned and unmanned aerial vehicles that could be used to disperse chemical and biological weapons across broad areas. We are concerned that Iraq is exploring ways of using UAVs for missions targeting the United States.		UAVs outfitted with spray tanks constitute an ideal method for launching a terrorist attack using biological weapons. Iraq admitted to producing four spray tanks. But to this day, it has provided no credible evidence that they were destroyed, evidence that was required by the international community. . . . Iraq is now concentrating . . . on developing and testing smaller UAVs. . . . Iraq could use these small UAVs which have a wingspan of only a few meters to deliver biological agents to its neighbors or if transported, to other countries, including the United States.

(continued)

Table C.1. *(continued)*

Argument/ Evidence	Bush's Cincinnati Speech (October 7, 2002)	Bush's State of the Union (January 28, 2003)	Powell's U.N. Speech (February 5, 2003)
Iraq has historically lied about nuclear weapons.	Before the Gulf War, the best intelligence indicated that Iraq was eight to ten years away from developing a nuclear weapon; after the war, international inspectors learned that the regime had been much closer. The regime in Iraq would likely have possessed a nuclear weapon no later than 1993. The inspectors discovered that Iraq had an advanced nuclear weapons development program, had a design for a workable nuclear weapon, and was pursuing several different methods of enriching uranium for a bomb. Before being barred from Iraq in 1998, the International Atomic Energy Agency dismantled extensive nuclear weapons-related facilities, including three uranium-enrichment sites. That same year, information from a high-ranking Iraqi nuclear engineer who had defected revealed that despite his public promises, Saddam Hussein had ordered his nuclear program to continue. The evidence indicates that Iraq is reconstituting its nuclear weapons program.		[In 1991] Saddam Hussein had a massive clandestine nuclear weapons program that covered several different techniques to enrich uranium, including electromagnetic isotope separation, gas centrifuge, and gas diffusion. . . . If Saddam had not been stopped, Iraq could have produced a nuclear bomb by 1993, years earlier than most worst-case assessments that had been made before the war. In 1995, as a result of another defector, we find out that, after his invasion of Kuwait, Saddam Hussein had initiated a crash program to build a crude nuclear weapon in violation of Iraq's U.N. obligations. Since 1998, his efforts to reconstitute his nuclear program have been focused on acquiring . . . sufficient fissile material to produce a nuclear explosion. . . . Saddam Hussein is determined to get his hands on a nuclear bomb.

(continued)

Table C.1. *(continued)*

Argument/ Evidence	Bush's Cincinnati Speech (October 7, 2002)	Bush's State of the Union (January 28, 2003)	Powell's U.N. Speech (February 5, 2003)
Iraq has a stable of nuclear scientists.	Saddam Hussein has held numerous meetings with Iraqi nuclear scientists, a group he calls his "nuclear mujahedeen"—his nuclear holy warriors.		He has a cadre of nuclear scientists with the expertise, and he has a bomb design.
Iraq has aluminum tubes that can be used to enrich uranium.	Iraq has attempted to purchase high-strength aluminum tubes and other equipment needed for gas centrifuges, which are used to enrich uranium for nuclear weapons.	The International Atomic Energy Agency confirmed in the 1990s that Saddam Hussein had an advanced nuclear weapons development program, had a design for a nuclear weapon, and was working on five different methods of enriching uranium for a bomb. Our intelligence sources tell us that he has attempted to purchase high-strength aluminum tubes suitable for nuclear weapons production.	[Saddam] has made repeated covert attempts to acquire high-specification aluminum tubes. . . . Most U.S. experts think they are intended to serve as rotors in centrifuges used to enrich uranium.
Iraq is trying to procure magnets and balancing machines for nuclear weapons.			We also have intelligence from multiple sources that Iraq is attempting to acquire magnets and high-speed balancing machines; both items can be used in a gas centrifuge program to enrich uranium.

(continued)

Table C.1. *(continued)*

Argument/ Evidence	Bush's Cincinnati Speech (October 7, 2002)	Bush's State of the Union (January 28, 2003)	Powell's U.N. Speech (February 5, 2003)
Iraq has sponsored terrorists in the Middle East, including members of al-Qaeda.	Over the years, Iraq has provided safe haven to terrorists such as Abu Nidal, whose terror organization carried out more than ninety terrorist attacks in twenty countries that killed or injured nearly 900 people, including twelve Americans. Iraq has also provided safe haven to Abu Abbas, who was responsible for seizing the *Achille Lauro* and killing an American passenger. And we know that Iraq is continuing to finance terror, and gives assistance to groups that use terrorism to undermine Middle East peace.	Evidence from intelligence sources, secret communications, and statements by people now in custody reveal that Saddam Hussein aids and protects terrorists, including members of al-Qaeda.	Iraq and terrorism go back decades. Baghdad trains Palestine Liberation Front members in small arms and explosives. Saddam uses the Arab Liberation Front to funnel money to the families of Palestinian suicide bombers in order to prolong the Intifada. And it's no secret that Saddam's own intelligence service was involved in dozens of attacks or attempted assassinations in the 1990s.
Iraq has made contacts with al-Qaeda for decades.	We know that Iraq and al-Qaeda have had high-level contacts that go back a decade.		This understanding builds on decades long experience with respect to ties between Iraq and al-Qaeda. . . . Early al-Qaeda ties were forged by secret, high-level intelligence service contacts with al-Qaeda, secret Iraqi intelligence high-level contacts with al-Qaeda.

(continued)

Table C.1. *(continued)*

Argument/ Evidence	Bush's Cincinnati Speech (October 7, 2002)	Bush's State of the Union (January 28, 2003)	Powell's U.N. Speech (February 5, 2003)
Iraq harbors and provides assistance to a senior al-Qaeda leader, al-Zarqawi, who prepares chemical and biological attacks.	Some al-Qaeda leaders who fled Afghanistan went to Iraq. These include one very senior al-Qaeda leader who received medical treatment in Baghdad this year, and who has been associated with planning for chemical and biological attacks.		Iraq today harbors a deadly terrorist network headed by Abu Musab al-Zarqawi, an associate and collaborator of Osama bin Laden and his al-Qaeda lieutenants. Zarqawi's network helped establish another poison and explosive training center camp. And this camp is located in northeastern Iraq. You see a picture of this camp. Zarqawi's activities are not confined to this small corner of north east Iraq. He traveled to Baghdad in May 2002 for medical treatment, staying in the capital of Iraq for two months while he recuperated to fight another day.
Iraq has provided al-Qaeda with weapons training.	We have learned that Iraq has trained al-Qaeda members in bomb making, poisons, and deadly gases		As with the story of Zarqawi and his network, I can trace the story of a senior terrorist operative telling how Iraq provided training in these weapons to al-Qaeda.

(continued)

Table C.1. *(continued)*

Argument/ Evidence	Bush's Cincinnati Speech (October 7, 2002)	Bush's State of the Union (January 28, 2003)	Powell's U.N. Speech (February 5, 2003)
Saddam could decide to supply WMDs to terrorists.	Iraq could decide on any given day to provide a biological or chemical weapon to a terrorist group or individual terrorists. Alliances with terrorists could allow the Iraqi regime to attack America without leaving any fingerprints.	Secretly, and without fingerprints, [Saddam] could provide one of his hidden weapons to terrorists, or help them develop their own.	Ambition and hatred are enough to bring Iraq and al-Qaida together, enough so al-Qaeda could learn how to build more sophisticated bombs and learn how to forge documents, and enough so that al-Qaeda could turn to Iraq for help in acquiring expertise on weapons of mass destruction.
Saddam's WMDs will help him fulfill his ambitions for regional domination.	Iraq's weapons of mass destruction are controlled by a murderous tyrant, who has already used chemical weapons to kill thousands of people. This same tyrant has tried to dominate the Middle East, has invaded and brutally occupied a small neighbor, has struck other nations without warning, and holds an unrelenting hostility towards the United States.	With nuclear arms or a full arsenal of chemical and biological weapons, Saddam Hussein could resume his ambitions of conquest in the Middle East and create deadly havoc in that region.	For more than twenty years, by word and by deed Saddam Hussein has pursued his ambition to dominate Iraq and the broader Middle East using the only means he knows, intimidation, coercion, and annihilation of all those who might stand in his way. For Saddam Hussein, possession of the world's most deadly weapons is the ultimate trump card, the one he must hold to fulfill his ambition.

(continued)

Table C.1. *(continued)*

Argument/ Evidence	Bush's Cincinnati Speech (October 7, 2002)	Bush's State of the Union (January 28, 2003)	Powell's U.N. Speech (February 5, 2003)
Iraq has tortured and killed its own citizens.	On Saddam Hussein's orders, opponents have been decapitated, wives and mothers of political opponents have been systematically raped as a method of intimidation, and political prisoners have been forced to watch their own children being tortured.	The dictator who is assembling the world's most dangerous weapons has already used them on whole villages, leaving thousands of his own citizens dead, blind, or disfigured. Iraqi refugees tell us how forced confessions are obtained: by torturing children while their parents are made to watch. International human rights groups have cataloged other methods used in the torture chambers of Iraq: electric shock, burning with hot irons, dripping acid on the skin, mutilation with electric drills, cutting out tongues, and rape.	Saddam Hussein's use of mustard and nerve gas against the Kurds in 1988 was one of the twentieth century's most horrible atrocities; 5,000 men, women, and children died. His campaign against the Kurds from 1987 to 1989 included mass summary executions, disappearances, arbitrary jailing, ethnic cleansing, and the destruction of some 2,000 villages. He has also conducted ethnic cleansing against the Shi'a Iraqis and the Marsh Arabs whose culture has flourished for more than a millennium. Saddam Hussein's police state ruthlessly eliminates anyone who dares to dissent. Iraq has more forced disappearance cases than any other country, tens of thousands of people reported missing in the past decade.

(continued)

Table C.1. *(continued)*

Argument/ Evidence	Bush's Cincinnati Speech (October 7, 2002)	Bush's State of the Union (January 28, 2003)	Powell's U.N. Speech (February 5, 2003)
If the U.N. fails to act, it will be irrelevant.	The United Nations would betray the purpose of its founding, and prove irrelevant to the problems of our time.		Iraq has now placed itself in danger of the serious consequences called for in U.N. Resolution 1441. And this body places itself in danger of irrelevance if it allows Iraq to continue to defy its will without responding effectively and immediately.
We should not wait for Saddam to grow stronger.	If we know Saddam Hussein has dangerous weapons today—and we do–does it make any sense for the world to wait to confront him as he grows even stronger and develops even more dangerous weapons?		Given Saddam Hussein's history of aggression, given what we know of his grandiose plans, given what we know of his terrorist associations and given his determination to exact revenge on those who oppose him, should we take the risk that he will not some day use these weapons at a time and the place and in the manner of his choosing at a time when the world is in a much weaker position to respond?

(continued)

Table C.1. *(continued)*

Argument/ Evidence	Bush's Cincinnati Speech (October 7, 2002)	Bush's State of the Union (January 28, 2003)	Powell's U.N. Speech (February 5, 2003)
The United States cannot accept the threat from Saddam Hussein	Today in Iraq, we see a threat whose outlines are far more clearly defined—and whose consequences could be far more deadly. Saddam Hussein's actions have put us on notice—and there is no refuge from our responsibilities.	Before September the 11, many in the world believed that Saddam Hussein could be contained. But chemical agents, lethal viruses, and shadowy terrorist networks are not easily contained. . . . Trusting in the sanity and restraint of Saddam Hussein is not a strategy, and it is not an option. . . . America will not accept a serious and mounting threat to our country and our friends and our allies.	The United States will not and cannot run that risk to the American people. Leaving Saddam Hussein in possession of weapons of mass destruction for a few more months or years is not an option, not in a post–September 11 world.

Appendix D

Attitudinal Discourse in Linguistic and Multimodal Texts

⌘

The three main regions of attitude are affect, judgment, and appreciation. Table D.1 shows how these regions are broken down into subcategories.

In this research, I distinguished between *inscribed* and *invoked* attitudes. In the first case, explicitly attitudinal lexis is employed. In the latter case, "The selection of ideational meanings is enough to invoke evaluation, even in the absence of attitudinal lexis that tells us directly how to feel" (62). As Martin and White (2005) explain, explicit inscriptions of attitude "act as *sign-posts* . . . telling us how to read the ideational selections that surround them" (64, my emphasis). In other words, an inscription of attitude can tell us how to discern invoked attitudes elsewhere in a text even when, strictly speaking, there is no evaluative lexis to speak of. Take, for instance, the following lines from Powell's address:

Table D.1. Subcategories of Affect, Judgment, and Appreciation

Attitude Categories		Domain	Positive Examples	Negative Examples
Affect	Un/happiness	Affairs of the heart	Happy	Sad
	In/security	Ecosocial well-being	Anxious	Confident
	Dis/ satisfaction	Pursuit of goals	Fascinated	Bored
Judgment	Normality	How special?	Normal	Odd
	Capacity	How capable?	Competent	Incompetent
	Tenacity	How dependable?	Careful	Reckless
	Veracity	How honest?	Honest	Deceptive
	Propriety	How far beyond reproach?	Law-abiding	Corrupt
Appreciation	Reaction: impact	Did it grab me?	Engaging	Tedious
	Reaction: quality	Did I like it?	Beautiful	Ugly
	Composition: balance	Did it hang together?	Logical	Contradictory
	Composition: complexity	Was it hard to follow?	Detailed	Simplistic
	Valuation	Was it worthwhile?	Convincing	Unconvincing

Source: Adapted from Martin and White (2005).

1. Saddam Hussein's use of mustard and nerve gas against the Kurds in 1988 was one of the 20th century's most **horrible atrocities**.
2. 5,000 men, women and children died. (UN/2.5/CP)

Out of context, the second clause might be taken as non-attitudinal. However, the bolded inscription "horrible atrocities" in the first clause works as a signpost that directs the reader to interpret the second clause as evaluative (and not merely factual). We immediately understand that the 5,000 people described in clause 2 did not merely die; they were *killed horribly and atrociously*. Thus, even without any explicit evaluation, clause 2 undoubtedly reinforces a negative judgment of Saddam Hussein.

Coding attitudinal lexis is not always straightforward. As Martin and White (2005) explain, "The realisation of an attitude tends to splash across a phase of discourse, irrespective of grammatical boundaries" (10). Thus, while a single word is *prototypically* the coding unit for inscriptions of attitude, they may also be realized in phrases. This can lead to coding ambiguities. Take, for example, the following sentence: "The design was **deceptively simple**." As Read, Hope, and Carroll (2007) suggest, one might be tempted to code the bolded phrase as two separate attitudes: an instance of negative judgment (*deceptively*) followed by an instance of positive appreciation (*simple*). However, a better alternative would be to code the entire phrase as one instance of positive appreciation. Because of the potential for uncertainty, I enlisted the help of a second, independent coder familiar with Martin and White's scheme. Based on a 15 percent sample of the linguistic data, we achieved an inter-rater agreement of .885. Coding differences were discussed and reconciled. I also consulted the other rater to discuss data that did not appear in this 15 percent sample, if I felt the coding was particularly ambiguous.

Coding *invoked* attitudes was trickier. These attitudes can span a word, a phrase, or an entire clause—and they are not explicitly suggested by the presence of core evaluative lexis (e.g., good/bad). As Martin and White (2005) suggest, such implicit evaluations can introduce an "undesirable element of subjectivity into the analysis," but ignoring them is even more problematic since it "amounts to a suggestion that ideational meaning is selected without regard to the attitudes it engenders" (62). I once again enlisted the help of a second coder. This time my colleague and I took a collaborative coding approach. The idea here is to "reach agreement on each code through collaborative discussion rather than independent corroboration" (Smagorinsky 2008, 401). This is a more painstaking approach to inter-rater agreement, but a thoughtful exchange about each segment of data is particularly constructive when trying to tease out linguistically variable implications of attitude.

Visual Attitudes

As a number of scholars have remarked, visuals also have an evaluative function. For instance, Kress and Van Leeuwen (1996) have shown how visuals can suggest different relationships of *involvement*, *detachment*, and *power* between viewers and represented participants. Martin (2002) has discussed how interpersonal attitudes can be enacted in print texts with verbal-visual components. And Maier (2009) has extended this framework to account for attitudinal meaning in dynamic films. Based in part on this work, I introduce my own approach to studying visual attitude (see table D.2). The scheme adopts Martin and White's (2005) general categories of affect, judgment, and appreciation. Affect concerns the emotional impact of an image. Judgment concerns the social acceptability of depicted visual actions performed by human agents. And appreciation concerns the value of non-human aspects of the depicted world—including semiotic artifacts and natural phenomena.

Following Baldry and Thibault (2005), I also distinguish between the "depicted world of the text," and the "visual kinaesthesis in the viewer" (191). The depicted world includes what is actually represented in a visual image. Meanwhile, the visual kinaesthesis of the viewer specifies the viewer's virtual bodily position with regard to the depicted world. If, for instance, a camera pans left, this creates the illusion of the viewer turning his or her head left—and thus specifies a kind of virtual body position for the viewer (who may in reality be looking straight ahead at a screen). Either the depicted world *or* visual kinaesthetic information (provided by camera angle and movement) can be resources for expressing attitudes.

The basic coding unit for visual attitudes is the visual salience, the figure with the most "informational prominence" in a pictorial image or video shot (see Baldry and Thibault 2005, 199, 228–30). To ensure reliability, I again enlisted the services of an independent coder. Based on a sample of 15 percent of the visual data, our inter-rater agreement was .941. Coding differences were discussed and reconciled.

Importantly, none of the resources that I have identified in table D.2 *automatically* indicates a category of visual attitude. Visual attitudes must always be interpreted in light of context variables—including the wider socio-historical situation in which a text unfolds, as well as the local co-textual environment. In fact, we cannot consider visual attitude as separate or distinct from linguistic attitude. As Maier (2009) insists, "No single semiotic mode is supposed to carry the whole or only evaluative information" (172). Thus, the analyst can rely on verbal inscriptions of attitude to help discern the attitudinal implication of visual images. And the analyst can draw upon explicitly evaluative visuals to help discern the attitudinal implication of co-deployed linguistic representations.

Table D.2. Visual Attitudes

Attitude Type		Resources from Depicted World	Kinaesthetic Resource	Example	Source
Affect	Personal relationship	Gaze and/or body angle of depicted is directed at viewer.	Viewer is virtually close to the depicted image.		CNN 2.5
	Impersonal relationship	Gaze and/or body angle of depicted is directed away from viewer.	Viewer is virtually far away from the depicted image.		NBC SR 2.5
	Affinity	Facial expression of depicted is warm, inviting, or otherwise friendly.			NBC 2.4
	Antipathy	Facial expression of depicted is cold, dead, angry, or otherwise off-putting.			NBC 2.4

(continued)

Table D.2. *(continued)*

Attitude Type		Resources from Depicted World	Kinaesthetic Resource	Example	Source
	Security	Depicted is performing some action that connotes feelings of security, safety, protection (e.g. grand-mother baking cookies for a child).		No instances	
	Insecurity	Depicted is performing some action that connotes feelings of insecurity, danger, vulnerability (e.g., terrorists training at a camp).	Camera tricks (e.g., spinning an image), irregular camera movements (e.g., shaking), or disorienting transitions from shot to shot		NBC 2.4
JUDGMENT	Propriety	Depicted is performing an action that is striking for its praiseworthiness—according to audience standards (e.g., a doctor administering medicine to sick children).		No instances	

(continued)

Table D.2. *(continued)*

Attitude Type		Resources from Depicted World	Kinaesthetic Resource	Example	Source
	Impropriety	Depicted is performing an action that is considered socially and perhaps ethically improper to the audience.			NBC 2.4
APPRECIATION	Remarkable	Nonhuman item serves as visual focus of depicted world (e.g., a sunrise).	Close-up shot or zoom may further suggest the importance of that which is depicted.		NBC 2.5
	Unremarkable	Nonhuman item serves as background of depicted world.	Standard camera movements and angles suggest nothing remarkable (i.e., not worth "zooming in for a better look").	Unremarkable and therefore uncoded	

APPENDIX E

Attitudes about Powell and Iraq

⌘

This appendix reports findings about textual attitudes, providing additional details for each news outlet examined in this study. Table E.1 shows how journalists in each news narrative expressed attitudes about Powell and Iraq. Table E.2 shows how non-authorial voices in each news narrative expressed attitudes about Powell and Iraq.

Table E.1. Detailed Results for Journalists' Attitudes about Powell and Iraq

	Appraised			
Appraiser	Powell/Powell's presentation		Iraq/Saddam/Iraqi rebuttals	
	Neg.	Pos.	Neg.	Pos.
NBC (2.4)	0	2	7	1
NBC (2.5)	0	23	19	1
NBC (SR 2.5)	0	23	6	0
NYT (2.5)	0	2	2	0
NYT (2.6)	2	13	1	0
CNN.com (2.5)	0	6	2	0
CNN.com (2.6)	0	2	1	0
Total for news voices	**2**	**71**	**38**	**2**

Table E.2. Detailed Results for Attitudes of Non-Authorial Voices in News Narratives

	Appraised			
Appraiser*	Powell/ Powell's Presentation		Iraq/ Saddam / Iraqi Rebuttals	
	Neg.	Pos.	Neg.	Pos.
Non-Authorial Voices in NBC (2.4)				
U.S. voices	0	4	4	0
U.N. voices	0	0	1	0
Iraqi voices	1	0	0	2
International voices				

(*continued*)

Table E.2. *(continued)*

Appraiser*	Powell/ Powell's Presentation		Iraq/ Saddam / Iraqi Rebuttals	
	Neg.	Pos.	Neg.	Pos.
Totals	1	4	5	2
Non-Authorial Voices in NBC news (2.5)				
U.S. voices	0	7	31	0
U.N. voices	0	0	0	0
Iraqi voices	10	0	0	3
International voices	1	1	1	0
Totals	11	8	32	3
Non-Authorial Voices in NBC news (SR 2.5)				
U.S. voices	0	3	17	0
U.N. voices				
Iraqi voices				
International voices				
Totals	0	3	17	0
Non-Authorial Voices in NYT (2.5)				
U.S. voices	0	2	15	0
U.N. voices	1	1	3	1
Iraqi voices	0	0	0	3
International voices	0	0	1	0
Totals	1	3	19	4
Non-Authorial Voices in NYT (2.6)				
U.S. voices	2	0	38	0
U.N. voices	0	2	3	0

(continued)

Table E.2. *(continued)*

Appraiser*	Powell/ Powell's Presentation		Iraq/ Saddam / Iraqi Rebuttals	
	Neg.	Pos.	Neg.	Pos.
Iraqi voices				
International voices				
Totals	2	2	41	0
Non-Authorial Voices in CNN.com (2.5)				
U.S. voices	0	6	8	0
U.N. voices				
Iraqi voices	0	0	0	1
International voices				
Totals	0	6	8	1
Non-Authorial Voices in CNN.com (2.6)				
U.S. voices	0	0	17	0
U.N. voices	0	3	2	1
Iraqi voices	6	0	0	1
International voices				
Totals	6	3	19	2
Total for Non-Authorial Voices	**21**	**29**	**141**	**12**

*Powell's voice is included among U.S. voices.

Appendix F

Conventions of Precontextualization in Mainstream Journalism

⌘

Precontextualization may take a number of forms. First, journalists can rely upon "advance copies" to report what a political leader will say later on. In this case, the journalist technically recontextualizes the "advance copy" in order to precontextualize the politician's future discourse. Second, journalists can rely upon "insider sources" and their strategic leaks. In this case, they once again recontextualize the words of anonymous "officials" in order to precontextualize the future speech of the central political figure. Third, journalists may independently speculate about what a political leader will say. In this case, they rely on their own knowledge and intuition to predict or hypothesize about the future address.

Depending on the strategy of precontextualization employed, reporters have more or less freedom to frame future discourse, to imbue it with their own evaluative and ideological accents. Likewise, depending on the form of precontextualization, reporters are more or less likely to report future discourse accurately. At one extreme, when reporters quote from an "advance copy" of a speech, they are effectively tethered to the text and have less space to put their own "spin" on the future semiotic event. As long as these "pre-quotations" don't differ significantly from the future utterance, we may call them accurate. At the other extreme, when reporters speculate about an upcoming address, they have significant freedom to construe future discourse according to their own beliefs and values. Such speculative "pre-reports" are also more susceptible to inaccuracy. In table F.1, I outline various conventions of precontextualization in corporate media environments.

Table F.1. Conventions of Precontextualization in Mainstream Journalism

Convention	Description	Example	Reporter Freedom	Report "Accuracy"
Precontextualization based on "advance copy"	Relying on an advance copy, the reporter quotes or indirectly reports what a speaker will say in a future address.	No instances in this corpus, since no advance copy was provided to the press	If reporters *quote* the advance copy, there is little space for reinterpretation. If they *indirectly report* the advance copy, there is more space for reinterpretation.	If the speech does not differ from the advance copy, the quotation will be accurate. Inaccuracy is more likely when reporters paraphrase advance copies.

(continued)

Table F.1. *(continued)*

Convention	Description	Example	Reporter Freedom	Report "Accuracy"
Precontextualization based on "strategic leaks"	Reporter quotes or indirectly reports the words of a political insider who projects what some other speaker will say or do in a future address.	Secretary of State Colin L. Powell will show the United Nations evidence . . . that Iraq has worked to conceal illegal arms . . . , *American officials said today*. (NYT/2.5/JPSW)	If reporters *quote* the insider's words, they have little space for reinterpretation. If they *indirectly report* an insider's assertion, they have freedom to filter this speech through their own ideological prism.	Even when reporters quote government officials verbatim, they still rely on hearsay accounts of what will be said, and increase the likelihood that their report will be inaccurate. When they paraphrase leaks, there is even more space for inaccuracy, since they are not only relying on hearsay accounts, but also infusing these accounts with their own values.
Precontextualization based on speculation	Reporter independently projects what a speaker will say or do in a future address without consulting or referencing any "official source."	[Powell] may attempt to suggest that there has been a link between Iraq and terrorist groups. (NBC SR/2.5/RB).	Reporters have significant freedom to imagine what a speaker will say and construe this speech "in their own words."	Inaccuracy is quite possible, but reporters can mitigate this by modalizing claims, or by keeping predictions general or obvious.

Appendix G

The Engagement System, Temporality, and Presence

⌘

The Engagement framework consists of two main categories: monogloss assertions that recognize no alternative viewpoints and heterogloss assertions that do recognize alternative viewpoints. Heterogloss assertions are further divided into (1) expansive resources that are more "open" to different voices and value positions and (2) contractive resources that tend to "close off" the expression of other viewpoints. In table G.1, I outline specific possibilities in each category.

As Martin and White (2005) suggest, "resources [of engagement] act to 'write the reader into the text,'" portraying speakers as "taking for granted that the addressee shares with them a particular viewpoint, or as anticipating a given proposition will be problematic (or unproblematic), or as assuming that the reader may need to be won over to a particular viewpoint, and so on" (95). Engagement, then, is related to constitutive rhetoric (Charland 1987)—indeed it is a key means by which rhetors constitute and enact relationships with their "imagined" audiences.

As in the case of attitude, coding engagement resources can present challenges. Coding units can vary—spanning single words or entire phrases—and there is room for ambiguity (see Read, Hope, & Carroll 2007). Once again, I enlisted the help of a second, independent coder familiar with Martin and White's (2005) scheme. Based on a 15 percent sample of the linguistic data, we achieved an inter-rater agreement of .812. Coding differences were discussed and reconciled.

Table G.1. The Engagement System

Engagement Categories		Types	Subtypes	Typical Realizations	Example
MONOGLOSS	*Undialogized*	Bare assertion			Iraq has WMDs.
		Presupposition			*Iraq's WMDs* could threaten the United States (presupposes WMDs exist).
HETEROGLOSS	*Dialogic expansion*	Entertain	Modality	Perhaps, probably, possibly, maybe, it's possible, may, must, should, and so on.	Iraq *may* have WMDs.
			Evidentiality	It seems, apparently, evidently, and so on.	Iraq *seems to* have WMDs.

(continued)

Table G.1. *(continued)*

Engagement Categories		Types	Subtypes	Typical Realizations	Example
		Attribute	Acknowledge	X said, X believes, According to X, and so on.	*Bush says* Iraq has WMDs.
			Distance	X claims, it is rumored that, and so on.	*Bushclaims* Iraq has WMDs.
	Dialogic contraction	Disclaim	Deny/ negate	not + verb, non- X, no X, and so on.	Iraq *doesn't* have WMDs.
			Counter	Although, even though, still, but, however, yet, and so on.	War may not happen, *even though* Iraq has WMDs.
		Proclaim	Endorse	X demonstrates, X shows, X proves, and so on.	Powell *showed* that Iraq has WMDs.
			Concur	Naturally, of course, obviously, admittedly, and so on.	*Obviously*, Iraq has WMDs.
			Pronounce	I contend, there is no doubt that, the facts are, and so on.	*The fact is* that Iraq has WMDs.

Source: Adapted from Martin and White (2005).

Analysis of Temporality and Presence

To study precontextualization, I had to examine representations of the future in relation to representations of the present and past. To begin, I examined linguistic resources of *tense and temporality* to determine whether a given representation was located in the past, present, or future. I developed the scheme for temporality outlined in table G.2. I have included examples from various news narratives in my corpus.[1]

Importantly, I also accounted for what might be called *invoked futures*—whereby the future is called to mind even when the simple future tense is not used. Note, for example, the present-tense utterance in table G.2: "And an update on U.S. troops in the Gulf. There are now 113,000 within striking distance of Iraq." Even though this is a present-tense assertion, the circumstantial element (*within striking distance of Iraq*) seems to invoke future military violence. Indeed, it almost seems as though U.S. troops are preparing to strike Iraq at any moment. Such utterances were double-coded in terms of temporality as both *present* and *invoked future*, since they appeared to describe present events and project future ones.

Finally, I analyzed how representations of the past, present, and future were endowed with *rhetorical presence* (Perelman & Olbrechts-Tyteca 1969). In table G.3, I offer some guidelines for dimensionalizing this important rhetorical concept. Of course, by drawing a distinction between visual and linguistic presence in table G.3, I do not mean to suggest that presence may take only one or the other form. As I have emphasized throughout, presence and other rhetorical strategies are multimodal, and were analyzed as such.

Table G.2. Dimensions of Temporality

Temporal Dimension	Example
Distal past	[Adlai E. Stevenson's] presentation coincided with the most dangerous moment of the cold war, when the United States confronted the Soviet Union over the placement of missiles in Cuba. (NYT/2.6/SW)
Proximal past	Today, Hans Blix said Iraq must do more to cooperate. (NBC/2.4/AM)

(continued)

Table G.2. *(continued)*

Temporal Dimension	Example
Present	And an update on U.S. troops in the Gulf. There are now 113,000 within striking distance of Iraq. (NBC/2.5/TB)
Proximal future	Here in the Security Council tomorrow, France will be the hardest sell. (NBC/2.4/AM)
Distal future	If [the Security Council] does not address this now in a truly consequential way, *we will all face a very great danger in the future*. (NBC/2.5/RB)

Table G.3. Dimensions of Presence

Type	Description	Typical Realizations
Linguistic presence	Motivated selection of elements and "verbal magic" are used to make certain events seem more salient and captivating. (Perelman & Olbrechts-Tyteca 1969, 169)	Nominalization, metaphor, vivid description, vocal emphasis, repetition, lexical proliferation, spatiotemporal proximization (Cap 2006)
Visual presence	Visual resources make a represented event spatially proximate, salient, or emotionally evocative.	Emotionally evocative images (typically photographic, rather than abstract charts and graphs), camera movements (e.g., zoom), close distance, direct gaze, facial expression, body movement
Intra- and intertextual presence	Jointly enacted verbal-visual thematic formations recur (within and/or across texts) and thus become more salient for the audience.	N/A

Appendix H

Coding Categories for Audience Repositioning

⌘

"Repositioning" is a term I employ to describe how the illocutionary effect of an assertion changes when it is recontextualized. Recall that every assertion "positions" some putative audience, implying a "desired response" (Halliday & Matthiessen 2004, 108). When an "original" assertion is recontextualized and transformed in a new context, the desired response changes and the audience hearing the re-represented utterance is positioned differently. I identified four such broad ways in which audiences were repositioned by the various news narratives:

- *Enhancement*. News discourse positions audiences to regard Powell's claims as more salient, more certain, or more warranted than they otherwise would have. Journalists (1) endow Powell's claims with enhanced presence, (2) close down dialogic space for alternative viewpoints (by failing to attribute claims to Powell, or by deleting elements of Powell's speech that would tend to reduce the certainty of his claims), or (3) add "supporting evidence" not present in Powell's speech.

- *Legitimation*. News discourse positions audiences to regard Powell and his argument as legitimate: authoritative, justified, reasonable, and so on. Journalists add evaluations (both visual and verbal), endorsements, or other forms of legitimation discourse (rationalization, moralized analogy, etc.) that essentially *comment on* Powell or his speech in positive ways, enacting a positive ethos for Powell (see chapter 2).[1]
- *"Impartial" Re-representation*. News discourse recontextualizes Powell's speech in ways that are basically "faithful" and "disinterested" with regard to the original discourse. Journalists attribute claims to Powell and do not comment on, qualify, or enhance Powell's discourse in any overt way. Audiences are positioned to regard Powell's claims more or less as they were during Powell's speech. However, since the journalists select these claims for re-representation, they are still, to a certain degree, endowed with rhetorical presence.
- *Qualification*. News discourse positions audiences to view Powell's argument as less certain or less substantive than they would have if they had viewed the original speech. Journalists open up dialogic space to question Powell's claims by adding modalizations, evidentials, or distancing attributions that qualify the certainty of Powell's assertions. Qualification also occurs when news discourse deletes elements from Powell's multimodal discourse (e.g., pronouncements) such that Powell's argument is "depleted" in the journalistic context.

It is worth noting that coding was non-exclusive. That is, more than one code could be assigned to a given recontextualization. In fact, it was common for audiences to be repositioned in multiple and divergent ways as Powell's discourse was recontextualized. Thus, the overall count (number of instances) for each core category does not necessarily reflect the complex ways that rhetorical audiences were repositioned from moment to moment in the news texts. With this in mind, observe table H.1, which identifies core categories (and their subtypes), and observe the frequency with which each category occurred in the different news narratives.

Since units of analysis were variable, I requested the help of a second analyst to verify reliability of the coding scheme. My colleague and I took a collaborative coding approach (Smagorinsky 2008, 401). Specifically, after conducting my initial analysis, I trained the second analyst in my coding apparatus and sat down with her to discuss every single code that I had applied. In each case, we came to a consensus about whether a given code was appropriate, occasionally refining the coding scheme itself to make it more precise.

Table H.1. Coding Categories for Audience Repositioning by Journalists

Core Categories (#)	Core Definition	Subtypes (#)	Subtype Description	Example
ENHANCEMENT NBC: 47 NYT: 26 CNN: 16 **Total: 89**	Recontextualization adds elements to Powell's argument that position audience to view Powell's argument as stronger, more present, more warranted.	Enhanced presence NBC: 34 NYT: 20 CNN: 11	Added verbal-visual resources, more forceful (Martin & White 2005) relexicalizations, or deletion of key circumstances render Powell's argumentative points more salient, proximal, or striking to the audience.	Piece by piece the new case laid out today linking Iraq to Osama bin Laden's al-Qaeda network. (NBC/2.5/TB)  (Images of terrorists in training and Osama bin Laden add visual presence to the "terror threat" described in Powell's presentation.)

(continued)

Table H.1. *(continued)*

Core Categories (#)	Core Definition	Subtypes (#)	Subtype Description	Example
		Dialogic contraction NBC: 8 NYT: 6 CNN: 5	Powell's claims are rendered less open to debate because of failure to attribute to Powell (bare assertions), deletion of modals and evidentials that originally qualified Powell's argument, or addition of counters, pronouncements, and denials.	[In the voice intercept] two top officers are heard plotting to deceive top nuclear inspector Mohamed ElBaradei. (NBC/2.5/AM) (This is Powell's interpretation of the voice intercept, but it is represented as a self-evident fact.)
		Supporting evidence NBC: 5 NYT: 0 CNN: 0	Visual or verbal elements not originally present in Powell's speech are added in news discourse in ways that seem to lend support to claims attributed to Powell.	[Powell claimed] that members of Zarqawi's network have been arrested recently in London and Paris. (NBC/2.5/JM) 

(continued)

Table H.1. *(continued)*

Core Categories (#)	Core Definition	Subtypes (#)	Subtype Description	Example
Legitimation NBC: 27 NYT: 16 CNN: 2 **Total: 45**	Recontextualization evaluates Powell and his discourse positively, positioning audiences to view Powell/ presentation as legitimate.	Positive evaluation NBC: 19 NYT: 13 CNN: 2	Journalistic text adds positive evaluation (affect, judgment, and appreciation) or endorsement of Powell and/or his speech.	It was a **masterful** performance. (NBC/2.5/TB)
		Us/them signals NBC: 7 NYT: 1 CNN: 1	Added visual discourse signals an Us/Them conflict between America (us) and Iraq (them) and reminds viewer that Powell is "with Us."	[Powell] spelled out with visual aids and a prosecutor's rhetoric the administration's case against Saddam Hussein. (NBC/2.5/TB) 
		Good reason NBC: 1 NYT: 2 CNN: 0	A "good" rationale is provided for Powell's speech or other rhetorical act.	**As evidence Iraq was cheating the inspectors all along,** Powell played a conversation taped the day before they returned to Iraq last November. (NBC/2.5/AM)

(continued)

Table H.1. *(continued)*

Core Categories (#)	Core Definition	Subtypes (#)	Subtype Description	Example
"Impartial" re-representation NBC: 11 NYT: 18 CNN: 8 **Total: 37**	Journalists re-represent Powell's speech (through recordings, quotations, or reports) in ways that are generally faithful to the original discourse, but which nevertheless add presence to certain moments in Powell's discourse.	"Objective" report NBC: 6 NYT: 18 CNN: 8	Powell's speech is relexicalized in news; a "neutral" reporting verb is chosen, and the relevant additions and deletions do not strengthen or reduce the "force" of Powell's original claim.	Powell: [Resolution 1441] was designed to be an early test. They failed that test. (UN/2.5/CP) NBC: Powell said Iraq has failed the test. (NBC/2.5/AM)
		"Objective" recording NBC: 5 NYT: 0 CNN: 0	Powell's speech is replayed in journalistic context without any obvious editing or editorializing.	This body places itself in danger of irrelevance. (NBC/2.5/CP) 

(continued)

Table H.1. *(continued)*

Core Categories (#)	Core Definition	Subtypes (#)	Subtype Description	Example
QUALIFICATION NBC: 18 NYT: 5 CNN: 2 **Total: 24**	Recontextualization qualifies Powell's utterances, positioning audiences to view Powell's argument as less certain or warranted.	Teleological uncertainty NBC: 6 NYT: 2 CNN: 0	Journalist asks open question or employs other resources that raise doubt as to whether Powell accomplished his argumentative goals.	Colin Powell **tried to persuade** the world that Saddam Hussein will never let U.N. inspectors find his hidden weapons. (NBC/2.5/AM)
		Depletion NBC: 5 NYT: 1 CNN: 1	Journalists delete pronouncements or compelling evidence from Powell's case and, thus, reduce the strength of Powell's argument.	Powell: **We know, we know** from sources that a missile brigade outside Baghdad was dispersing rocket launchers and warheads. (UN/2.5/CP) NBC 2.5: Powell said . . . a missile brigade outside Baghdad was dispersing rocket launchers and warheads. (NBC/2.5/AM.CP)

(continued)

Table H.1. *(continued)*

Core Categories (#)	Core Definition	Subtypes (#)	Subtype Description	Example
		Modalization NBC: 4 NYT: 2 CNN: 1	Added modal resources and evidentials qualify the epistemic certainty of Powell's claims, or added counter-expectancy tends to diminish the "expected" strength of Powell's case.	There was plenty of new detailed information about Iraq's **alleged** ties to terrorists. (NBC/2.5/JM)
		Distancing attribution NBC: 3 NYT: 0 CNN: 0	Use of distancing reporting verb (especially *claims*) dissociates journalist from Powell's claim and leaves viewer maximal space to consider dialogic alternatives.	Powell **claimed** that members of Zarqawi's network have been arrested recently in London and Paris. (NBC/2.5/JM)

Note: Examples are drawn from the NBC broadcast on February 5, but frequencies are reported for all three news outlets.

Appendix I

A Four-Phased Analytic Approach

⌘

In this book, I have adopted a four-phased analytic approach. The first three phases include detailed verbal-visual discourse analysis and provide a foundation for the fourth phase, a rigorous intertextual study. Below I discuss what each analytic phase enables us to see. For convenience, I have also charted descriptions of the phases in tables (I.1–I.4).

Phase 1 of the analysis is designed to uncover the lexical and grammatical choices that rhetors make as they construe reality and evaluate human actions (see table I.1). The investigation begins with a transitivity analysis that focuses attention on how rhetors encode happenings in the world, the people involved in them, and the surrounding circumstances. In short, transitivity analysis allows us to see the strategies that rhetors employ as they define the world for their audiences. Next, an attitude analysis investigates how rhetors reference shared values both to identify with audiences and to induce action. Finally, a study of legitimation devices shows us how rhetors position audiences to regard social actions as natural, rational, or necessary. In sum, phase 1 helps us to see how rhetors define reality, advance value positions, and promote their moral and political interests.

Phase 2 entails examining how rhetors use language to enact relationships with their putative audiences (see table I.2). This phase begins with a survey of utterance types and the responses they imply. This initial survey helps the analyst see whether rhetors (1) offer services that they expect their audiences will accept (*let me give you a closer look*, UN/2.5/CP); (2) demand that their audiences perform some action (*look at the image on the left*, UN/2.5/CP); (3) state information that they expect their audiences will acknowledge (*on the left is a close-up of one of the four chemical bunkers*, UN/2.5/CP); or (4) pose questions that they expect their audiences will answer or consider (*Where did Iraq take all of this equipment?* UN/2.5/CP).

The survey of statement types is followed with a more robust examination of the engagement resources by which rhetors seek to negotiate claims with their imagined addressees. This analysis focuses attention on the linguistic resources rhetors use to assume audience agreement (*of course, this is a critical moment for the administration*); close down debate on a given topic (*Iraq is not telling the truth*); open up space for epistemic possibilities (*Iraq could equip UAVs with spray devices*); distance themselves from others' assertions (*Iraq claims it has no weapons*); endorse speakers and arguments (*Powell spelled out the administration's case*); or counter audience expectations (*Saddam Hussein is already doing damage control*). Meanwhile, a graduation analysis shows how rhetors control the intensity of their vocabulary, maximizing their commitment to given attitudes (*it's a very compelling case*) or endowing representations of the world with added rhetorical presence (*showdown with Iraq*). In general, phase 2 allows us to see the micro-linguistic devices rhetors employ to *position* audiences, conveying how they expect audiences to respond to their utterances and signaling their tolerance for alternative viewpoints.

Phase 3 focuses on the interaction of different semiotic elements in multimodal texts (see table I.3). Video texts are transcribed and analyzed using Baldry and Thibault's (2005) method of tabulating visual, kinesic, and sound data on a phase-to-phase basis. Meanwhile, static multimodal texts are studied using Kress and Van Leeuwen's (1996)

Table I.1. Examining the Rhetoric of Representation and Evaluation

Procedure	Description	Purpose
Transitivity analysis	• Focused SFL transitivity analysis of all verbal data (Halliday & Matthiessen 2004) with additional focus on representations of social actors and actions (Van Leeuwen 2008) • Identification of nominalizations and passivizations	• Reveals how rhetors position audiences to accept as true particular representations of reality • Considers why rhetors choose to construe events one way rather than another
Attitude analysis	• Analysis of verbal inscriptions (and tokens) of attitude (Martin & White 2005) • Analysis covers affect (emotional language), judgment (evaluation of human behavior), and appreciation (evaluation of semiotic or natural events).	• Highlights micro-features of language that align audiences into communities of value, and dispose them toward action (Perelman & Olbrechts-Tyteca 1969) • Shows how rhetors assess certain social actions favorably and others unfavorably, i.e., one way that rhetors (de)legitimate social activity • Indicates how rhetors construe their own ethos, and the ethos of others • Suggests how rhetors appeal to pathos, i.e., position audiences to adopt an emotional response to some representation of the world
Legitimation analysis	• Examination of discourse used to explain and justify institutional activities • Analysis covers authorizations, moral evaluations, rationalizations and mythopoesis (Van Leeuwen 2007) • Investigation of "Us and Them" (de)legitimation devices (Van Dijk 1998) • Analysis of temporal legitimation (Cap 2006; Dunmire 2008; Oddo 2011)	• Reveals how rhetors justify social actions—not only through evaluative discourse, but through other discursive strategies—e.g., credentials flashed on screen during a field reporter's story legitimate (i.e., authorize) that journalist's assertions

Table I.2. Investigating the Rhetor-Audience Relationship

Procedure	Description	Purpose
Engagement analysis	• Analysis of speech functions and desired responses (Halliday & Matthiessen 2004, 108) • Following Martin and White's (2005) framework: • Identification of unmodalized monoglossic assertions and presuppositions • Analysis of dialogically expansive resources which open up space for alternative viewpoints • Analysis of dialogically contractive resources that seek to suppress the expression of alternative viewpoints	• Indicates the signals rhetors employ to tell their putative audiences how they expect them to respond to the current assertion (Martin & White 2005, 93) • Shows how rhetors position audiences to respond to their utterances—in some cases, utterances are represented as uncertain or contentious; in other cases, they are represented as maximally warrantable, or even incontrovertible
Graduation analysis	• Following Martin and White's (2005) framework: • Analysis of force, including intensified lexis (e.g., "fell" vs. "plummeted") • Analysis of focus, including the sharpening and softening of attitudes (e.g., "scary" vs. "a little scary")	• Suggests how rhetors may "up-scale" or "down-scale" the intensity of their evaluations or the degree of their commitment to an assertion (Martin & White 2005, 135–36) • Shows how rhetors endow certain lexical items with presence or anti-presence (Perelman &Olbrechts-Tyteca 1969) • Highlights how rhetors acknowledge alternative viewpoints—e.g., saying that something is "a little scary" opens space for an alternative assessment

framework for "reading images" in conjunction with Baldry and Thibault's (2005) approach to cluster analysis.[1] Both approaches allow the analyst to systematically study various semiotic modes—both individually and in combination.

Finally, *phase 4* draws on the first three phases to account for intertextual phenomena (see table I.4). The first step of this phase is to

Table I.3. Accounting for Intersemiosis

Procedure	Description	Purpose
Multimodal transcription and analysis of video texts	• Following Baldry and Thibault (2005), systemic-functional multimodal analysis of *videos* • Multimodal transcription of visual frames, visual images, kinesic actions, and the soundtrack (including transcription of spoken discourse) • Account of intersemiosis (Blair 2004; Hagan 2007; Royce 2002; 2007; Van Leeuwen 2005) • Metafunctional coding of each multimodal "phase" in video texts	• Accounts for the meaningful interplay of verbal-visual resources • Suggests how readers/viewers are positioned to accept representations of reality, and aligned into communities of value based on the configuration of multimodal textual elements
Multimodal transcription and analysis of print and internet texts	• Initial cluster analysis of print and digital pages (Baldry & Thibault 2005) • Transcription of visual transitivity and attitudinal stance (Baldry & Thibault 2005; Kress & Van Leeuwen 1996; Machin 2007) • Account of intersemiosis (Blair 2004; Hagan 2007; Royce 2002; 2007; Van Leeuwen 2005) • Overall metafunctional coding of visual-verbal data	• Accounts for the meaningful interplay of verbal-visual resources • Suggests how readers/viewers are positioned to accept representations of reality, and aligned into communities of value based on the configuration of multimodal textual elements

identify the polyphonic mix of voices present in a given rhetorical performance. This helps us perceive what kinds of voices are "allowed" to participate in a text, and whether these voices are representative of a fully diverse society (or, conversely, a single dominant group). Next, we can look across discursive events to examine how particular "utterances"[2] are extracted from an "original" text and recontextualized in a new rhetorical environment. Using a table, we can place the original utterance alongside its recontextualized counterpart, and systematically chart verbal and visual micro-transformations. This allows us to discern how rhetors change the meaning of prior texts—and position audiences to regard those prior texts as more or less persuasive.

Phase 4 also includes a study of "implicit intertextuality"—how texts draw upon prior discursive events (and anticipate future ones) *without* explicitly referencing them. Using Thibault's (1991) method of critical intertextual analysis, we can identify overarching thematic formations that are rearticulated across several texts. In other words, we can see how generic "talking points" get repeated by different speakers who essentially say the "same thing" using different words (and other semiotic resources). By discerning thematic formations, we can see intertextual continuity: how dominant meanings recurrently emerge to link different speakers, texts, and contexts (e.g., "IRAQ LIES"). Of course, we can also observe thematic formations which oppose the dominant ones ("IRAQ IS TRUTHFUL") and index an intertextual struggle. So examining thematic formations also permits us to see how certain transitive chains of authority are enacted (corroboration and contradiction) and suggests how different voices vie for supremacy in the intertextual field of discourse.

Table I.4. Tracing Voices, Continuities, and Transformations across Texts

Procedure	Description	Purpose
Voice analysis	• Catalog of explicit voices "speaking" in each text—including authorial voices and external sources (Fairclough 2003) • Coding of all speakers by title and relevant "role" (politician, journalist, government official, etc.)	• Catalog of various voices indicates whether discourse is open to a plurality of ideological positions or dominated by "elite" speakers

(continued)

Table I.4. *(continued)*

Procedure	Description	Purpose
Comparison of recontextualized speech with speech in its original context	• Identification of explicit recontextualizations—recordings, reports, or quotations • Identification and analysis of antecedent source material from which recontextualizations are drawn (phases 1–3) • Comparative multimodal tabulation—i.e., chart juxtaposing recontextualization and original source material (Oddo 2013) • Identification of micro-transformations based on systemic-functional heuristic categories (Oddo 2013) • Coding of transformations as suggested by data (Glaser & Strauss 1967; Strauss 1987; Haas & Witte 1998) • Analytic coding of audience repositioning	• Charts the semantic and rhetorical transformation of an original speech event as aspects of it are recontextualized • Indicates how rhetorical audiences are repositioned and realigned as a consequence of recontextualization
Analysis of *implicit* intertextuality	• Identification of multimodal representations that do not overtly reference original speech as the "source" • Identification of overarching thematic formations in a text (Thibault 1991; Dunmire 2009; Oddo, forthcoming) • Identification of similar (and contrary) thematic formations in original speech event • Analysis of indirect rearticulation (and rebuttal) of prior speech	• Illustrates whether "talking points" are rearticulated in various discursive contexts • Speaks to the overall rhetorical presence of generic meanings across rhetorical events (Perelman &Olbrechts-Tyteca 1969).

Notes

⌘

Notational Scheme

1. Two different speakers will occasionally appear in a single excerpt of a televised newscast. In such cases, I separate the initials of each speaker by a period (.). Thus, AM.CP means that Andrea Mitchell speaks in the first part of the excerpt, and Colin Powell speaks in the latter part of the excerpt. In such excerpts, it should be obvious when one speaker stops talking and another begins.

Introduction. The Rhetorical Life of Colin Powell's U.N. Speech

1. I introduce the idea of precontextualization in chapter 3. This term is meant to draw attention to the anticipatory nature of intertextuality—how journalists introduce and predict elements of future political discourse.

2. Conceivably, if Powell's case failed, it could have provoked both civilian and military leaders to withdraw from the war effort. As Zinn (2007) reminds us, echoing Albert Einstein, "Where men and women will refuse to fight, governments will be helpless to wage war" (190).
3. Typically, Bush would send speeches concerning intelligence to the CIA before delivering them in public. The other members of his administration, however, were less careful. For instance, the first major speech about Iraq by an administration official was *not* evaluated by the CIA. In his address before the Veterans of Foreign Wars, Dick Cheney (2002) expressed "no doubt" about Iraq's weapons of mass destruction, including its continued development of a nuclear weapons program. According to Jami Miscik, a CIA official who heard the speech, "Our reaction was, 'Where is he getting that stuff from? Does he have a source of information that we don't know about?'" (quoted in Suskind 2006, 167–69). Powell, too, was known to make allegations about Iraq without first checking them with intelligence analysts. As DeYoung (2007) reports, before preparing his U.N. speech, Powell had "only a cursory knowledge of the intelligence underlying" the Bush administration's case, and his "language on Iraq had become almost as loose as Cheney's" (441). More than once, Powell repeated unsubstantiated allegations about Iraq assisting al-Qaeda terrorists and importing uranium to build nuclear weapons.
4. The rhetoric of political fundamentalism is perhaps best characterized by Bush's (2001) famous ultimatum presented to potential allies following the 9/11 attacks: "Either you are with us, or you are with the terrorists." Needless to say, many nations did not embrace such polarizing binary discourse (Domke 2004, 30).
5. This argument was first suggested by Bush in a 2002 speech to the U.N. It was repeated frequently by many members of the administration—including Powell in his 2003 address.
6. The U.N.'s reputation was likely to be damaged *internationally*—regardless of whether Powell convinced the Security Council to adopt a new resolution. If Powell's case was unpersuasive to the Council, but the United States still pursued war, then the U.N. could be seen as an ineffective institution, one that failed to prevent an unnecessary and illegitimate conflict. If Powell's case persuaded the Security Council and the U.N. supported the war, it could be seen as a submissive accessory to aggressive U.S. foreign policy. See Thakur (2004) for an interesting comment.
7. Most Europeans viewed Saddam Hussein as a danger to world peace, but most other countries were not convinced of this. Even among those that distrusted him, there was very little support for military action (Goot 2004, 249).
8. Europeans were more likely to support a U.N.-authorized war. However, most citizens around the world reported that they would not support war in Iraq under any circumstances. See Goot (2004) for details.

9. I place "preemptive" in scare quotes because as Keller and Mitchell (2006b) point out, the term was being misused by the Bush administration—at least according to the U.S. Department of Defense *Dictionary of Military Terms*. Preemptive violence confronts *imminent* danger; i.e. it preempts a strike that is about to take place. What the Bush administration was calling for was more appropriately called preventive violence, i.e., a strike at a *potential* enemy who might be capable of an attack in the future (4, 10–11). The rhetorical (mis)use of the term "preemptive" surely helped the administration secure support for the war. See Dunmire (2009; 2011) for a relevant intertextual analysis of the "Bush Doctrine."
10. As noted, members of the administration could always claim that war was legitimate without U.N. approval. But they viewed this as a more risky option.
11. The NBC news broadcasts were accessed from the Vanderbilt Television News Archive. The two articles from the *New York Times* were obtained from microfilm archives. Finally, the two Internet news reports from CNN.com were accessed using the *Internet Archive: Wayback Machine* (http://www.archive.org/web/web.php), a virtual library of now-expired digital content on the Web.
12. Though alternative sources of information have proliferated in recent years, they still "reach only small, factional audiences, and do not speak with [a] singular, agenda-reinforcing voice" (Bennett, Lawrence, & Livingston 2007, 58). Meanwhile, the "uniformity of content" that characterizes the mainstream press makes it the "default reality option—a highly visible and focused version of events in the midst of a sea of chaotically competing alternative accounts" (56). In addition, the mainstream press still enjoys the status of "official" news, whereas alternative media are more often dismissed as "subjective" journalism (57).
13. Generally speaking, elite news providers heavily influence less elite media entities (Reese & Danielian 1989). Thus, it is quite possible that news reports from these three elite sources are very similar to the reports elsewhere in the mainstream press, though additional research would obviously be needed to confirm this hypothesis. It is also worth noting that intermedia agenda setting occurs between the elite news providers themselves. Elite newspapers like the *Times* are likely to influence news content on television networks like NBC (Golan 2006) and high-profile news websites like CNN.com (Paterson 2005).
14. Just before the Iraq War and in the first few days of the conflict, television was the most popular method of obtaining news in America, followed by newspapers. Still, most Internet users did obtain news online, usually from websites associated with television networks, like CNN.com. Roughly 20 percent of online users reported that the Internet helped shape their views about the war. See Raine, Fox, & Fallows (2003) for details.
15. As Boorstin (1961) pointed out long ago, news consumers may ignore editorial content, but they are likely to notice and accept the "facts" of news reports (20).
16. I am including in the category of "histories of the prewar period" not only scholarship by academics in universities, but also book-length chronicles written by

journalists. While the journalistic chronicles may be "non-academic," they often serve as primary source material for scholarly histories of the war. Academic histories consulted for this study include T. H. Anderson (2011), Gardner (2010), Hybel & Kaufman (2006), O'Sullivan (2009), Rutherford (2004), and Warshaw (2009). (I also consulted Keller & Mitchell [2006a], which includes contributions from military affairs specialists, political scientists, and communication scholars.) Journalistic chronicles include DeYoung (2007), Hoyle (2008), Isikoff & Corn (2006), Unger (2007), and Woodward (2004).

17. For example, Cheney's August 2002 speech to the Veterans of Foreign Wars, Bush's September 2002 address to the United Nations General Assembly, Bush's October 2002 speech in Cincinnati, Bush's 2003 State of the Union address, and Powell's U.N. presentation.
18. This basic story is reiterated in more or less the same words by DeYoung (2007), Hoyle (2008), Unger (2007), Isikoff & Corn (2006), and Woodward (2004). I will detail some of this information in chapter 1.
19. As Rutherford (2004) indicates, editorial comments also helped to discredit the U.N. For example, he points to a political cartoon that depicts Powell sitting with a frustrated expression on his face, as he addresses a U.N. Security Council composed of "clowns and fools" (23).
20. In fact, most rhetorical analyses of call-to-arms discourse deal primarily with political speeches (Campbell & Jamieson 2008; Hatzenbuehler & Ivie 1983; Ivie 1980; 2005; Medhurst et al. 1997)—and not the news reports that cover them.
21. Bitzer (1998) proclaimed that journalists may be the most important rhetoricians in the political arena. And since his influential essay, a number of rhetorical scholars have turned their attention to the persuasive properties of news reports. See K. V. Anderson (2011), Anderson & Stewart (2005), Baym (2003), Bormann (1982), Brummett (1999), Ceccarelli (2011), Cisneros (2008), Combs & Mansfield (1976), Condit & Selzer (1985), Daniel (2002), Dauber (2001), Demo (2007), Gronbeck (1997), Hariman & Lucaites (2002; 2007), Harold & DeLuca (2005), Houck (2005), Jamieson (1984; 1988), Jamieson & Waldman (2003), Kuypers (2002), LaRacey (2008), Marlier (1989), Medhurst (2009), Ott & Aoki (2002), Wilkie (1981), and Zelizer (2010). (Scholars from other academic disciplines [e.g. Edelman 1985] have also drawn on rhetorical theory in their analyses of journalism.) Most rhetorical scholars who study journalism analyze media coverage of criminal trials, public scandals, or political campaigns. However, few rhetorical scholars have closely examined *prewar journalism*. In fact, Kuypers (2006) may be the only rhetorical analyst to contribute a book-length study focusing on news coverage of George W. Bush's justifications for war.
22. A similar trend is evident in the excellent edited collection *Hitting First* (Keller & Mitchell 2006a). The editors include three chapters about "public discourse justifying the use of preventive force" in Iraq (Goodnight, Payne, Rockmore). While these chapters do much to illuminate the discourse produced by the Bush

administration, they pay scant attention to the press reports that (re)mediated this discourse.

23. Finn (2010), too, who studies the visual representations in Powell's address, comes to a remarkably similar conclusion: the visual evidence was weak and unpersuasive, and, thus, "people need to be more critically aware" of their own (and presumably others') representational choices (46).
24. I am principally interested in American journalism, as opposed to international news coverage. See Nikolaev and Hakanen (2006) for a robust picture of the international debate over the war as it was represented by news media outlets across the globe. See Allan and Zelizer (2004) for a discussion of the strengths and limitations of international war reporting since 1990, including commentary on issues such as censorship, embedded reporting, and propaganda.
25. While Kuypers's (2006) project bears some similarity to my own, there are some important methodological differences between our studies. First, Kuypers's analysis includes newspaper editorials and "soft news" outlets where one would expect subjective, opinionated journalism. By contrast, this study is exclusively interested in "hard news" stories that supposedly report only the "facts." Second, Kuypers focuses on a wide range of media sources, including those with presumably little public influence (e.g., ABC's *World News Now*). Meanwhile, this study focuses on a few major news outlets with enormous public audiences. Third, Kuypers almost exclusively examines print-linguistic aspects of his data, even in heavily visual television news programs. This study, on the other hand, aims to account for the dynamic between verbal reports and visual images.
26. See Calabrese (2005), Gasher (2003), Harmon & Muenchen (2009), Hayes & Guardino (2010), Kumar (2006), Livingston & Robinson (2006), Lule (2004), and Ravi (2005).
27. Hodges (2011) also shows that these same phrases were resisted by journalists and other sources in the news. However, his data indicate that resistance to Bush's discourse was much more likely *after* the war began.
28. See also Entman and Page (1994) for a discussion of press autonomy during wartime.
29. See Lakoff and Johnson (1980) for a discussion of how metaphors highlight and hide different aspects of reality.
30. And if we follow the metaphor, they repeat those claims in a form that is weaker than the original: scientifically speaking, an echo is not as strong as the original sound.
31. To be clear, scholars who use the "echo" metaphor certainly recognize that journalists do more than merely repeat government claims (Bennett 2012, 42–43; Domke 2004, 184). My point is that when we use words like "record," "repeat," and "echo" to describe the discourse of the press, we draw attention away from the significant rhetorical labor that journalists do to reframe political utterances.

32. Since frames "call attention to some aspects of reality, while obscuring other elements" (Entman 1993, 55), some rhetoricians have related them to Kenneth Burke's (1966) notion of "terministic screens" (Ott & Aoki 2002).
33. Since the Bush administration's discourse dominated the press during the run-up to war in Iraq, a "prowar" frame was fully developed in the media, while an "antiwar" counterframe was either underdeveloped or excluded altogether. Entman (2004) has suggested that citizens benefit most from news stories that exhibit "frame parity," the existence of two fully developed competing narratives about an issue (47–48). However, frame parity is exceedingly rare in mainstream news (Entman 2004; Bennett, Lawrence, & Livingston 2007).
34. See studies by Iyengar (1991), Kahneman & Taversky (1984), Kinder & Sanders (1996), Pan & Kosicki (1993) Sniderman, Brody, & Tetlock (1991), and Zaller (1992).
35. In addition, whereas other titles often focus on journalism *during* the Iraq War, I examine a particularly important day of *pre*war coverage—i.e., the news that informed public decision-making about war at a time when bloodshed was, presumably, still avoidable.
36. Kuypers (2006) has shown the value of "comparative frame analysis," which contrasts the frames of an original speech with frames found in subsequent press reports about that speech. In chapter 4, I take a similar approach, though I draw much more on discourse analytic concepts as I analyze Powell's presentation in relation to subsequent recontextualizations in the press.

Chapter One. The Campaign for War in Iraq: Contextualizing Powell's Speech in Political and Media Discourse

1. I place "regime change" in scare quotes to highlight that these are not my words. As a nominalization (see subsequent chapters), the phrase "regime change" obscures the actual process of replacing one regime with another. In fact, in choosing this phrase, the Bush administration condensed *several* complicated processes (troops fight war to take down Saddam Hussein's government; the United States instates an interim government; Iraqis elect a new "legitimate" government) into a specific thing. This micro-rhetorical strategy arguably allowed the Bush team to make "regime change" seem rather straightforward, when, in reality, it would be a thorny, multifaceted struggle.
2. The decision had apparently been made without any serious internal discussion about the merits or consequences of an invasion (DeYoung 2007, 429).

3. Bush and Blair did worry about how the public might respond to a war that had not been explicitly authorized by the U.N. If necessary, Bush reasoned, they could trigger a new war resolution by provoking a confrontation with Iraq. He suggested painting a U.S. reconnaissance aircraft in U.N. colors and then flying it over Iraq with fighter cover. "If Saddam fired on them, he would be in breach," Bush argued (Van Natta 2006). In the meantime, Bush and Blair agreed that their "diplomatic strategy had to be arranged around the military planning" (Van Natta 2006).
4. Of course, Bush had other ways of "winning over" members of the Security Council. Around this time, the National Security Agency (NSA) hatched an illegal operation to spy on "swing voters" in the U.N. to ensure that their reactions to Powell's address would be "favorable to U.S. goals" (Mitchell & Mitchell 2008, 7–8).
5. In fact, Tony Blair was much more interested than Bush in getting a second U.N. resolution. The UK public was especially opposed to war unauthorized by the U.N. Moreover, Blair had been warned that launching a war without a second resolution would be illegal (Bremer 2009).
6. While the intent is to create a consensus picture of the intelligence community, the CIA's judgments tended to override the judgments of other agencies (Friedman 2013).
7. The production and reception of the 2002 NIE is perhaps worthy of a book-length study. Interestingly, Bush never requested the document. Already bent on going to war, the hawks in the administration did not want to allow any "venting of whatever opposition there was to . . . conventional wisdom on weapons of mass destruction" (Goodman 2006). To his credit, Senator Bob Graham, head of the Intelligence Committee, demanded that the CIA produce the NIE in fall 2002 so that Congress might make an informed decision about the need for war. In response, Tenet assembled a team that would produce a document favorable to the administration's goals (Goodman 2006). Indeed, former deputy executive director of the CIA John Brennan (2006) explains that analysts working on the NIE understood they were supposed to create an "intelligence base that would justify going forward with war." The document was written in just a few weeks, and was assembled so that dissenting opinions and uncertainties about the WMD case were relegated to endnotes. Still, the dissents were voluminous—totaling about ten to fifteen pages (McLaughlin 2006). John McLaughlin, former deputy director of the CIA, estimates that only about six members of Congress actually read the whole document. The rest were content to skim the executive summary, which projected more certainty about Iraq's banned weapons.
8. In fact, the intelligence on the alleged mobile biological weapons labs came from a single source, known as "Curveball." Only one American intelligence official actually met with Curveball, and this official concluded that he was unreliable and possibly an alcoholic (Isikoff & Corn 2006, 131).

9. The NIE conceded that the intelligence community had "little specific information" on Iraq's chemical weapons (Isikoff & Corn 2006, 135). Indeed, the basic conclusion was that the chemical weapons Iraq once possessed were now unaccounted for. This did not necessarily mean that these weapons still existed.
10. As noted later, the audiotapes could *confirm* Iraqi compliance with inspections, depending on one's interpretation.
11. The satellite photos depicted sites that had already been inspected by the U.N. Powell claimed that these sites manufactured chemical and biological weapons. But such claims could not be verified by satellite image—and they were disproven just days after his address when inspectors looked at them again and found nothing (Leung 2009)
12. Both the Energy Department and the State Department strongly refuted the view that Iraq's aluminum tubes could be used in nuclear weapons. The air force rejected the notion that Iraq had unmanned aerial vehicles that could attack the United States with biological weapons (McLaughlin 2006).
13. In fact, officials in Iraq eventually uncovered documents in which Saddam Hussein cautioned his supporters against "getting too close to Islamic jihadists" (Risen 2004). Moreover, al-Qaeda operatives ultimately told the CIA that Osama bin Laden had explicitly rejected working with Saddam Hussein (Risen 2004). It's probably true, as Powell claimed, that a terrorist named Abu Musab al-Zarqawi operated in Iraq. But it is doubtful that Zarqawi was actually working with bin Laden and al-Qaeda (Hoyle 2008, 332). Moreover, Zarqawi operated in a territory that was not controlled by Saddam Hussein and Zarqawi never collaborated with the Iraqi government (Isikoff & Corn 2006, 187, 335). Other testimony about Iraq's ties to terrorists was not reliable as it had come from a detainee who continually changed his story under conditions of torture (Isikoff & Corn 2006, 119–24).
14. See Hoyle (2008) for a good summary of the planning and delivery of Powell's speech.
15. Unlike Bush, Powell had the advantage of presenting photographs and videos that the public had never before seen. The apparent novelty of these exhibits helped them gain currency in later press reports.
16. Straw denies that the meeting ever took place.
17. In fact, most of the human sources were defectors from the Iraqi National Congress (INC), a highly politicized exile group headed by Ahmad Chalabi. Chalabi had ambitions to take over Iraq and had been lobbying for Saddam Hussein's overthrow for years. Thus, he and the INC were highly unreliable. Indeed, most of the "informants" introduced to the CIA were "charlatans, asylum seekers, and hustlers simply saying what Chalabi and the INC wanted (or told) them to say in exchange for the group's assistance in getting them to Europe or America" (Isikoff & Corn 2006, 53).

18. As Klumpp (2005) put it, Powell's presentation was a "multimedia tour de force" (6).
19. Information on congressional reactions was taken from Firestone (2003).
20. American journalists surely bear much responsibility for the positive response among the U.S. public, a point I return to in the next section and throughout this book.
21. All of these statements are quoted in "In Their Words" (2003).
22. The comments from these international editorials were drawn from three English-language summaries of world opinion about Powell's address: Marr et al. (2003), Thomas (2003), and "Where's the Proof" (2003).
23. The *Guardian* advised that "America and Britain must not jump the gun" and go to war. The liberal tabloid *The Daily Mirror* was more blunt, asking derisively, "Where's the *proof*, Colin?"
24. In the Middle East reactions were even more negative. The *Jordan Times* declared that Powell's speech "did not amount to convincing evidence of Iraqi noncompliance, or that Iraq presents any real or imminent danger to any party." *Al Riyadh* of Saudi Arabia accused America of wanting to "control oil resources" in order to sustain its "hegemony" in the Middle East. And the independent Tunisian paper *As-Shourouq* declared that it "felt sorry for the United States," which was putting on a "circus" in lieu of convincing evidence and exposing its disrespect for the U.N. process.
25. As O'Sullivan (2009) reminds us, Powell had once suggested that "even junior officers should resign if they felt strongly about administration policies" (178). But curiously Powell did not resign—or threaten to do so—even as he saw the bogus intelligence files on Iraq and observed the myopic planning of the Bush administration. Powell's silence is all the more curious when we consider his famous critiques of Vietnam-era groupthink and his public disputes with President Clinton over policies he opposed. Powell had once criticized political leaders for deluding themselves into believing the Vietnam War was necessary (172). But he was unable or unwilling to prevent a similar kind of groupthink from overtaking the Bush administration. And, in 1993, as chairman of the Joint Chiefs, Powell had openly challenged Clinton about the prospect of gays in the military, leading the president to believe that he might resign in protest (179). But Powell raised no such public challenges to Bush over the far more serious matter of war in Iraq. O'Sullivan also notes that, before Powell, several secretaries of state had resigned or threatened to resign over matters of principle (179). In contrast, writes O'Sullivan, Powell will be remembered as a "servant of power" (196).
26. See, for example, Bennett (2012), Bennett, Lawrence, & Livingston (2007), Bennett & Livingston (2003), Domke (2004), Glasgow University Media Group (1976; 1985), Haridakis, Hugenberg, & Wearden (2009), Herman & Chomsky (1988), and Van Dijk (1993).

27. Bennett's (1990) indexing model is rivaled by two other models of the relationship between government and the media: the hegemony model and the cascade model. The hegemony model (Herman & Chomsky 1988) posits that mainstream journalism almost always amounts to pro-government propaganda. Reporters rarely present alternative viewpoints, because they are tethered to government officials who, regardless of their party, agree on core principles (e.g., capitalism). The cascade model (Entman 2004) maintains that information flows (or cascades) can move in multiple directions—whether downward from the government to the press to the public, or upward from the public to the government. The press, then, can challenge the government (Althaus 2003; Althaus et al. 1996), though this is relatively rare. Bennett and colleagues (2007) show how an expanded indexing theory can account for both propagandistic reporting and those moments when the press challenges government.
28. For example, after spending several minutes reviewing (and endorsing) Colin Powell's presentation, NBC news devoted roughly 20 seconds to responses from U.N. delegates—near the end of its first report about Colin Powell's speech and just before a second report that reaffirmed the authority of Powell's assertions. Meanwhile, the *Times* printed more complete responses from France, Russia, and China—but did so on page A21, below the fold.
29. See Kernell (1997) on the utility of "going public" with a political message.
30. This was all part of WHIG's marketing strategy. The administration relied on "allies" in the press (e.g., Judith Miller) to publicize its leaks, and further spread its message by blitzing Sunday talk shows (T. H. Anderson 2011, 105).
31. To find a truly different opinion of Powell's speech, one really had to go "off the beaten path." The editorial from the *World Socialist Web Site* (2003) is fascinating for its probing critique of Powell's address ("Powell's U.N. Speech"). In retrospect, this editorial shines in comparison to the fawning coverage in mainstream editorials.
32. While Powell (2012) says he regrets delivering his U.N. speech, he maintains that the war in Iraq was justified.

Chapter Two. The Chief Prosecutor and the Iraqi Regime: Intertextual Ethos and Transitive Chains of Authority

1. According to Powell's former chief of staff Larry Wilkerson, Vice President Cheney told Powell before the speech that he could "afford to lose some poll points" (quoted in Isikoff & Corn 2006, 174).

2. Ethos is a fraught concept with a very long intellectual history. See Amossy (2001) for a discussion of possible different components of ethos: reputation, institutional position, social role, and discursive performance. See Baumlin and Baumlin (1994) and Hyde (2004b) for recent edited collections about the concept. See Benoit (1990), Halloran (1982), Sattler (1947), and Sullivan (1993) for discussions of ethos in classical rhetoric. See Miller (2001) and Warnick (2007) for discussions of ethos in computer simulations and online environments. See Anderson (2007) for an attempt to dissociate ethos from identity. See Crismore and Farnsworth (1989) for an early attempt to study ethos using discourse-analytic methods. See Yoos (1979) for an attempt to bridge ethos with Kantian ethics.
3. In the *Rhetoric*, Aristotle tends to downplay the significance of prior reputation, since it falls outside the scope of artistic proof. He declares that ethos "should result from the speech"—and "not from a previous opinion" about the speaker (*On Rhetoric* 1.2.4).
4. See also Miller (1974).
5. See Allen (2000) for an excellent introduction to Bakhtin's theory (14–30).
6. Like Aristotle, Perelman and Olbrechts-Tyteca (1969) define oratorical ethos as "the impression that a speaker, by means of his words, gives of himself" (319). As Leff (2009) points out, Perelman and Olbrechts-Tyteca also borrow from Isocrates in their conceptualization of ethos (306–7).
7. Of course, signaling value positions is by no means the only way of projecting ethos. As Garver (1994) insists, authorial ethos is mainly a by-product of arguing well. Moreover, explicit self-evaluation may backfire since "it is often not good to talk about oneself" (Amossy 2001, 8). Still, in the context of contemporary mass media, journalists often promote themselves using evaluative discourse. And, when it comes to enacting ethos for other people, rhetors inevitably employ evaluative vocabulary.
8. I recognize that "value positions" are quite different from Aristotelian "values." For Aristotle, values were akin to teleological goals that one inhabited through virtuous living. "Value positions," on the other hand, are more like discursive signals that one employs to reference a community norm. Still, understanding these discursive signals gives us clues as to how rhetors seek communion with their audiences (Perelman & Olbrechts-Tyteca 1969, 51).
9. As the parenthetical examples indicate, resources in each region of attitude can be either positive or negative.
10. Categories of appreciation and judgment map onto Perelman and Olbrechts-Tyteca's act-person dyad. Specifically, resources of appreciation can be used to express attitudes about semiotic *acts*—such as arguments, speeches, and presentations. Meanwhile, resources of judgment may be used to comment directly on the character and credibility of another *person* in a text.
11. Powell's victory in Iraq was hyped as the end of the "Vietnam Syndrome" and a restoration of U.S. military supremacy (Applebome 1991).

12. Only Jesus Christ and Martin Luther King were mentioned more often (Taylor 2001).
13. As Cheng (2012) observes, a major task for Powell at the U.N. was to reconstitute his ethos as a "hawk," i.e., to prove that the evidence had now convinced him that war was necessary. Cheng highlights the discursive mechanisms by which Powell displayed his "conversion" during his address. But, as I suggest below, Powell was certainly not the only agent to reconstitute his ethos. For many months before he spoke at the U.N.—and in the days following—the international press featured numerous stories declaring Powell's transformation from war doubter to war advocate. His performance at the U.N. was probably less important in the constitution of his new ethos than the performances of journalists around the world.
14. In the days following the 9/11 attacks, he had reportedly opposed retaliation against Iraq (Tyler & Sciolino 2001). And later he had persuaded the president to relax his demands for a unilateral "preemptive strike," convincing Bush to instead pursue a program of international weapons inspections (Strobel 2002).
15. To cull the following examples, I conducted a series of searches using LexisNexis. Looking at all English-language news stories before Powell's address, I searched for narratives that included the words *Colin Powell* in the headline and lead. I then looked within these articles for certain key words: *reputation*, *moral*, *dove*, *hero*, *My Lai*, *Iran Contra*, *gay + military + ban*. Initially, I searched for the first four terms (*reputation-hero*), which I derived from historical accounts of Powell's reputation before his U.N. address (e.g., Isikoff & Corn 2006). Based on this initial search, I then looked for the latter three terms (*My Lai*, etc.). Essentially, I had uncovered a few articles that mentioned these terms negatively in relation to Powell and I wanted to see if there were any similar stories. After discarding irrelevant and repeated articles, I was left with 151 items. I read these articles informally, without coding every instance of attitudinal lexis. But even a conventional reading shows that the vast majority of the articles portrayed Powell in strongly positive terms, even the ones that mentioned potentially damaging events (e.g., the Iran-Contra affair). It is beyond the scope of this study to provide a full account of these stories, but I have tried to choose examples that are characteristic of the field.
16. The 1995 stories are chock full of positive judgments of Powell: candid, cautious, honest, decent, intelligent, respected, etc. As Howard Kurtz (1995) observed at the time: "Even by the standards of modern media excess, there has never been anything quite like the way the press is embracing, extolling, and flat-out promoting this retired general."
17. As this last headline indicates, Powell's race was a frequent topic of discussion in the mid-1990s. Much like Barack Obama in 2008, Powell was considered by many to be a figure who could transcend race and perhaps heal racial tensions. Talk of Powell's race seems to have subsided by the time of his U.N. speech, and how Powell's role as an African American affected his credibility is an open

question. I follow Anderson (2007) in understanding race as an aspect of identity (rather than ethos), since race is a trans-situational aspect of the self, rather than a discursive accomplishment that suits the rhetorical situation (97–98). Of course, Powell's racial identity could have indirect "ethos effects," since people draw inferences about a person's character based on his or her identity (100).

18. When asked during the first Gulf War about the number of Iraqi civilians being killed, Powell famously said, "It's not a number I'm terribly interested in" (quoted in Zinn 2002, 86). This is evidence of moral disengagement, not moral authority (Bandura 1998).

19. And, indeed, if we were to look at Powell's address, we would find that he employs a number of interesting argumentative strategies to enact his own authority. For instance, Powell uses a rhetorical strategy of *dubitatio*—or feigned doubt about his authority to speak—portraying himself as a plainspoken non-specialist as a way of identifying with his audience. A good example of this occurs when Powell comments on Iraq's aluminum tubes, which, he alleged, were being used to enrich uranium for nuclear weapons: "I am no expert on centrifuge tubes, but just as an old army trooper, I can tell you a couple of things." Powell's self-effacing comments ("no expert" and "just an old army trooper") position his audience to regard him as a straight-talking man whose knowledge is founded in a kind of "blue-collar" experience. In feigning doubt about his expertise, Powell represents himself as a more trustworthy speaker. Interestingly, he then goes on to provide what may only be considered expert knowledge about how the "anodized coating" on the tubes exceeds typical manufacturing specifications. See Cheng (2012) for a more robust examination of how Powell constituted his ethos during his presentation.

20. NBC, for example, included the following headline along the bottom of the screen: "Powell: The Case Against Iraq." The use of the definite article ("the") indicates the uniqueness of Powell's "case," and implies that other "cases" made by the Bush administration are less relevant. During the speech, NBC would also reprint Powell's claims on the bottom of the screen, sometimes in ways that enhanced their veracity. For example, the following was repeatedly projected: "First hand evidence of mobile biological weapons labs." This caption to Powell's discourse baldly asserts that such firsthand evidence actually exists, and thus adds to the credibility of Powell's earlier claim.

21. I also included in this category invited consultants who were *not* explicitly given an NBC title. I did this because these consultants were similar to the other consultants (who had NBC credentials) in that they were invited to speak live on camera about current events. Moreover, as I point out below, these non-affiliated consultants were *always* assigned some kind of credibility by a journalist. This suggested that their authority was on par with that of the news-affiliated consultants.

22. On its face, "senior" is merely a descriptor of longevity. However, in the context of professional journalism, the title of "senior correspondent" is not automatically

reserved for the correspondent with the longest duration of employment. According to Paul Warren, a veteran publisher in the news industry, the title is only conferred upon journalists with significant experience and a distinguished record of quality reporting (personal communication, January 15, 2013). Thus, we sometimes find boastful press releases aimed at publicizing the "exciting news" that some journalist has been named "Senior Correspondent" (e.g., McNair 2011).

23. According to my coding scheme for visual attitudes, I interpreted this instance as a positive visual appreciation. The virtual radar device indicates something about the global importance of the (non-human) news stories that Brokaw is discussing.

24. In fact, at the top of the page inside the *Times* a brief headline for the story reads: "Threats And Responses: The Powell Indictment."

25. In Martin and White's (2005) scheme this kind of positive reporting clause is not technically an attitude, but a resource of engagement called *endorsement* (126). Here, I have coded endorsements as positive attitudes, i.e., as *appreciations* of artistic performances (56). For my purposes, the difference between endorsing Powell's speech (Powell *laid out* his case) and appreciating Powell's speech (Powell presented a *well-organized* case) is less important than the fact that both express something positive about Powell's ethos.

26. In fact, the journalists and invited analysts in other news stories also occasionally chose reporting verbs that subtly endorsed Powell, the Sayer: *spelled out* (NBC/2.5), *laid out* (NBC/2.5/SR), and *laid down the fact* (NBC/2.5/SR). Such endorsements were never employed to describe the Iraqi response to Powell's case. In other words, the Iraqis always *claimed*, *said*, or *asserted*. They never *laid out* or *spelled out* their rebuttal.

27. This observation is based on collocational research. As described in appendix B, verbal collocates are words that co-occur so frequently in language use that we associate them with one another. "Regime" is strongly correlated with words signifying repression and violent crime. In fact, lexicographer Michael Rundell (2012) recently analyzed corpus data to compare collocates of "regime" with collocates of "dictatorship." As Rundell (2012) explains: "Both [words] are modified, with more or less equal frequency, by the adjectives *repressive, corrupt, tyrannical,* and *brutal*, while *authoritarian* and *oppressive* are even more likely to collocate with *regime* than with *dictatorship*. It's a similar story with the verbs. When these nouns are in the subject position, both occur frequently with neutral words like *rule* or *govern*. But, if the linguistic evidence is anything to go by, regimes have an even stronger tendency than dictatorships to *persecute, murder, oppress, imprison* and *torture* people." In short, "regime" has strongly negative resonances, resonances that inevitably carry over to modifiers like "Iraqi."

28. In addition to these negative judgments of "Iraq," there are also a number of negative judgments about Iraq's (then) leader, Saddam Hussein. I will treat these in greater detail in the next chapter.

29. As discussed in chapter 1, a thematic formation is an overarching generic meaning realized by more specific wordings within and across texts (Thibault 1991). Baldry and Thibault (2005) explain that thematic formations can be construed on the basis of jointly constructed verbal and visual semiotic resources.
30. The lowercase *t* in a given bracketed code represents that the given instantiation is an invoked token of attitude, as opposed to an explicit inscription. Meanwhile, (+ / –) indicates whether the attitude being advanced is positive or negative. I will occasionally use this convention again below.
31. In fact, in news narratives that came after Powell's presentation, there were more attributions to Powell than to any other external voice.
32. These other U.S. voices consistently outnumbered the Iraqi voices represented in the news reports.
33. For instance, if a reporter said, "Powell *points out*" or "Powell *shows*" or "Powell *demonstrates*," it would suggest an authorial endorsement of Powell's assertion.
34. See Martin and White (2005, 112–17).
35. Following Perelman and Olbrechts-Tyteca (1969), these transitive chains of authority may be classified as quasi-logical arguments of transitivity, which make it possible to infer a relationship between two variables based on argumentative implication (227–30).
36. The historical debate about the "true character" of Christopher Columbus—a debate partly inspired by the work of historian Howard Zinn (2003)—shows how a person's ethos may be constituted intertextually long after that person expires.
37. Assassinating Saddam Hussein was not the stated goal of the Bush administration, which centered its arguments on disarming Iraq of alleged WMDs. Nevertheless, American audiences likely understood from prewar discourse that the U.S. wished to kill the Iraqi leader. The American press accounted for some of this prewar discourse. As illustrated in the next chapter, journalists sometimes construed Saddam Hussein as a key target of potential U.S. violence, and reporters often assumed that U.S. troops would "strike Saddam" personally (e.g., Roberts 2002). For their part, members of the Bush administration were coy about their intentions regarding Saddam Hussein, but their public comments often hinted at the possibility of ending his life. In the summer of 2002, for example, Bush vowed to "use all tools at [his] disposal" to enact "regime change" (Bush 2002d), and he officially authorized the CIA to kill Saddam Hussein if necessary in order to oust him from power (Teather 2002). Later that fall, press secretary Ari Fleischer actually invited Iraqi dissidents to assassinate Saddam Hussein, and the National Security Council further clarified that laws barring assassination only applied to the U.S. government, not to the Iraqi people (Roth 2002). As one former CIA agent declared on CNN: "We intend to get rid of Saddam. We intend to kill him. Whether we call it an assassination or a coup d'etat or a simple invasion, he's going to end up dead" (Baer 2002). Bush seems to have shared this view—and he expressed it candidly when out of the public eye. As first reported in May 2002,

the president announced his intentions most clearly to Condoleezza Rice and a group of U.S. senators: "F—k Saddam. We're taking him out" (Eisenberg 2002). It should come as no surprise, then, that the very first U.S. attack in the war was a so-called decapitation strike aimed at killing the Iraqi leader (King et al. 2003). (Saddam Hussein and his henchmen escaped this strike and others like it, but Iraqi civilians were not so lucky [Glaister 2004]). Ultimately, of course, Saddam Hussein was executed by the Iraqi Special Tribunal, after he was found guilty of crimes against humanity. The journalists in this study could not have foreseen this event, but their discourse surely helped bolster the view that Saddam was a "bad" man who deserved whatever violence might be coming to him.

Chapter Three. Undercutting Saddam's Denials: Precontextualization and Audience Alignment

1. See Dunmire (2010) for an excellent review of "futurology" studies.
2. Grusin (2010) does not restrict his discussion to media coverage before the Iraq War. To illustrate the role of premediation in contemporary journalism, he also explores the news coverage premediating Hurricane Gustav, the 2008 economic "meltdown," and the so-called Twitter Revolution in Iran. A number of other scholars have also discussed future-oriented reporting. Jamieson and Waldman (2003), for instance, argue that the press frequently plays the role of "soothsayer," as "reporters have been called upon to predict political events in the near and distant future" (74). Similar conclusions have been reached by Jaworski, Fitzgerald, and Morris (2003) and Dunmire (2011). More generally, Geert Hofstede (2001) has discussed the uncertainty avoidance factor in American culture: the widespread tendency to avoid the unknown by being prepared for it. Typically, Americans tend to accept the unknown more easily than other counties. However, polling research shows that, after the 9/11 attacks, Americans understandably felt the need for more stability and clarity (Adams 2005). This research supports Grusin's claim that the desire to premediate the future likely increased following the attacks of September 11, 2001.
3. Following Cap (2006; 2008; 2010), this legitimation technique may be understood as a kind of *temporal proximization*, whereby temporally remote events are represented as capable of influencing speaker and addressee in the present.
4. As Dunmire notes, the distinction between "proximal" and "distal" futures was first identified by Fleischman (1982).
5. As Baldry and Thibault (2005) explain, the term *visual collocation* refers to the cluster of secondary items—such as dress, location, body, and occupation—depicted in an image and which together "function to specify either the role of the participant or the activity which he or she is performing" (198).

6. In fact, a number of psychological studies (e.g., Schienle et al. 2006) have suggested that images of mutilation elicit emotions of fear, disgust, and arousal, and generally have a greater capacity to capture attention. See also Hill's (2004) discussion of visual rhetoric, which relates Perelman's concept of presence with psychological research on "vivid information."
7. Since we cannot photograph the future, we understand that the depicted event has already happened.
8. Indeed, the headline is not a question open to debate (what happens if we leave Afghanistan?), but an assertion that presents an awful future that is guaranteed—*unless* U.S. troops stay in Afghanistan. Importantly, the viewer is subsumed in the "we" of the if-clause. That is, the viewer is part of the "we" who are already in Afghanistan, and is thus construed as capable of preventing the horrible mutilation of young girls in that country.
9. See Blair (2004) for a discussion of verbal-visual arguments.
10. Dialogic contraction suppresses alternative viewpoints, but, unlike monoglossic assertions, it at least recognizes that these alternative viewpoints exist.
11. In addition to the engagement framework, I also rely heavily on multimodal video analysis (Baldry & Thibault 2005), rhetorical analysis of presence and temporality (Perelman & Olbrechts-Tyteca 1969; Toulmin 1958), and critical intertextual analysis of *thematic formations*, i.e., overarching generic meanings that are realized by more specific wordings within and across texts (Thibault 1991).
12. Like all corporate-owned news agencies, NBC News competed with other commercial news providers (ABC, CBS) for market share, and, so, it had an interest in breaking the Powell story in advance. At the time, NBC was owned by the General Electric Company, a giant weapons manufacturer and energy supplier that secured billions of dollars during the Iraq War—both in contracts with the Pentagon and post-invasion "reconstruction" projects (Solomon 2005; Webb 2008). Thus, NBC News was a subsidiary of a corporation with a vested interest in war, though we may only speculate as to whether corporate executives pressured editors to produce stories that favored an invasion of Iraq.
13. Powell's address was first mentioned on NBC's *Nightly News* on January 28, 2003—eight days before Powell spoke at the U.N. Over the next week, NBC pre-reported Powell's speech six more times. (February 1—the day of the *Columbia* disaster—was the only day that did not include some report about Powell's upcoming address). This string of news stories included a detailed preview of the speech on February 3 as well as a "countdown" to Powell's speech on February 4 that is the subject of this chapter. In any case, the sheer number of anticipatory reports suggests the degree to which Powell's speech had been precontextualized in news narratives before its delivery.
14. I make this claim having consulted dozens of news reports that previewed Powell's address. In all the reports surveyed, the journalists *never* refer to an "advance copy" and *never* pre-quote Powell. When they preview Powell's presentation, they

consistently cite anonymous officials or hedge about the types of evidence Powell might include. These indicators suggest that, while the Bush team leaked *information about* Powell's speech, the administration did not supply journalists with Powell's *text*.

15. Almost every evening, NBC provides an "In Depth" segment during the course of its nightly news broadcast. According to the NBC News website, this segment features "a longer-form piece examining the top news story of the day" ("About" 2009). Thus, while the "In Depth" segment recurs, it is still positively distinguished from the other news segments on a given day as a "deep examination" of the "top" story. In Martin and White's (2005) terms "in depth" represents a positive appreciation of the news report's complexity. In contrast to a "superficial" report, Brokaw implies, this one will be thorough and well researched.
16. "War" is typically encoded as a noun, rather than a verb. Thus, though we sometimes speak of one nation "warring with" another, we more typically speak of "a war" between nations. Here I choose to refer to "war" as a nominalization in order to highlight the fact that Brokaw selected a noun (war) when he could have selected a verb (e.g., to attack). The significance of this nominalization is that it obscures the flesh-and-blood actors responsible for the action. Imagine, for instance, if instead of predicting that Powell's speech "could move the world closer to war," Brokaw had suggested that it "could move the world closer to the day when the United States will attack Iraq."
17. In this case, we can imagine the following lexical scale of intensity: *difference of opinion* (low), *confrontation* (median), *showdown* (high). By selecting a word that is maximally intense, Brokaw enhances his investment in the value position, and closes down space for alternative positions.
18. Here the lexical scale of intensity might be conceived in the following way: *time before* (low), *run-up* (median), *countdown* (high).
19. See Lule (2004) for an excellent study of predominant metaphors in NBC's prewar coverage.
20. Specifically, the lexical relationship between "Saddam Hussein" and "Iraq" is one of *meronymy* (see Halliday & Matthiessen 2004, 574–75).
21. As Bennett (2012) observes, personalization and dramatization are characteristic of contemporary news framing. Thus, there should be no surprise that a potential war is reduced to an exciting showdown between two people. For other discussions of personalization, dramatization, and news spectacle, see Cappella & Jamieson (1997), Edelman (1988), Gans (1979), Gitlin (1980), Graber (1989), Iyengar (1991), Johnson-Cartee (2005), Martín Rojo (1995), and Paletz & Entman (1981).
22. Of course, the word "hunt" never appears in Resolution 1441, a document that describes the job of U.N. weapons inspectors in far less dramatic terms: monitoring, inspecting, and verifying.

23. Hypertextuality is, of course, a unique feature of Internet texts, and is a key part of the intertextual experience for any website visitor. Unfortunately, tracing every link on CNN.com is beyond the scope of this study. However, the "Showdown" link is worth exploring because it is displayed so saliently and is clearly featured as the macro-theme for the entire news story about Colin Powell.
24. The apparent protagonist/antagonist binary is consistent with the "actant model" of narrative (Greimas 1971; Greimas & Porter 1977). According to this model, various actants, or generic character types, perform classic functions in every narrative. Typically, a subject (protagonist) is the focus of the narrative as she or he tries to secure or deliver some valuable object. Meanwhile, an antisubject (antagonist) opposes the subject and tries to thwart his or her efforts. In this case, Colin Powell is the subject trying to deliver a valuable message to the U.N. about the dangers of Iraq. Meanwhile, Saddam Hussein is the antisubject who tries to frustrate the successful delivery of this message by deceiving inspectors and lying about his hidden weapons. Following Van Dijk (1998), the protagonist/antagonist pairing can be mapped onto an implicit "Us/Them" binary. In other words, the viewer is positioned to regard Powell as the protagonist who is one of Us, while Saddam Hussein, as antagonist, is one of Them. Arguably, this ideological alignment is built into the generic structure of the narrative.
25. The reporter responsible for the video content, John King, is mentioned but is not construed as responsible for the first sentence of the caption. Thus, the expectation that Powell's speech will produce conclusive proof seems to be widespread.
26. Of course, there is good reason to doubt Powell's insistence that he "wasn't talking about war." He suggested in his speech that continuing inspections would not work since Iraq would simply continue to hide weapons and deceive the inspectors. And he certainly seemed to imply at various points that war was necessary. Nonetheless, the fact that Powell never explicitly called for war should not be overlooked. In fact, it could be argued that journalists' precontextualization of Powell's speech primed viewers to see it as a call-to-arms address and not as a diplomatic appeal to strengthen inspections.
27. A number of prominent figures have suggested that, when it invaded Iraq, the United States initiated an aggressive war against a sovereign nation. For example, the International Commission of Jurists declared on the eve of the war that the United States and its allies were "poised to launch an outright illegal invasion, which amounts to a war of aggression" (Hibbitts 2003). Later, U.N. secretary-general Kofi Annan agreed that the war was "illegal" and a direct violation of the U.N. Charter (MacAskill & Borger 2004). Even within the United States, scholars and legal experts repeatedly criticized the government for, as one renowned attorney put it, "death-dealing aggression" (Clark 2004). Of course, the U.S. government claimed that the war was not an aggressive action, but a "preemptive" intervention—one that was legally justified based on Iraq's violation of previous U.N. resolutions.

28. The fact that these men are inspectors is specified both verbally by Mitchell and visually by their blue U.N. caps and white "hazardous material" suits.
29. Of course, Mitchell leaves some space to wonder whether his efforts to make this point will succeed. After all, Powell will *try* to make the point; he might not succeed at making the point. My concern here, however, is that NBC prepositioned audiences to accept this point by making it seem persuasive.
30. As far as I can tell, this particular image did not appear in Powell's address. However, Powell did use other, similar satellite images in making his argument. In this case, Mitchell's report merely prepares viewers to regard these images as important.
31. Traditionally speaking, priming occurs when journalists make some issues more salient than others, and thereby influence "the standards by which governments, presidents, policies, and candidates for public office are judged" (Iyengar & Kinder 1987, 63). In this book, I use the term more informally, referring to the process of making some future scenario salient, and thereby preparing audiences to attend to it later on. In fact, priming has been variously defined, and it is not always clear how it is different from framing and agenda setting. For different analyses and discussions of priming, see Entman (2007), Gross & D'Ambrosio (2004), Iyengar & Simon (1993), Kim, Scheufele, & Shanahan (2002), Price, Tewksbury, & Powers (1997), and Scheufele (2000).
32. On the other hand, the "facelessness" of these unidentified speakers makes them difficult to challenge (see below).
33. It's also worth noting that the word "even" in the "then" clause enacts a counter-expectancy in which the viewer's presumed expectation—that Russia cannot be won over by Powell's case—is countered by the claim that even Russia can be won over.
34. And even if the viewer could not identify him visually, Mitchell's speech (i.e., her utterance of the word "Saddam") enacts an identity for the man in the video.
35. Interestingly, the *New York Times* (Fisher 2003) also carried an image of this marcher in a story about the military rally. The caption reads: "Suicide bombers in hooded white uniforms hung with sticks of explosives marched . . . yesterday in Mosul, Iraq." There is a lexical tie between "suicide bomber" and "terrorist" because the first term is very likely to be collocated with the second. In any case, even without this helpful caption, a viewer would nevertheless regard this hooded man as threatening and terrorist-like given his dress. In fact, he appears to be a cross between several different "villains" familiar to an American audience: a stereotypical Muslim terrorist (as in frame 136), a KKK member, and a storm trooper from the movie *Star Wars*.

Chapter Four. America's Best Intelligence: Recontextualization and Rhetorical Transformation

1. In paratactic structures, two "equal" clauses are placed side by side. In other words, the meaning of one clause does not depend on the other. Conversely, in hypotactic arrangements, one clause is subordinate to or dependent upon another.
2. This is not to say that quoting does not also transform original discourse. For instance, Calsamiglia & López Ferrero (2003) point out that journalists often employ direct quotation to recontextualize others' speech based on the assumption that quoting is more objective and neutral. However, their study makes clear that even when journalists directly quote other speakers, presumably to "remain faithful" to what was originally said, they still (inadvertently) reshape the meaning of prior discourse. As Bakhtin (1981) and Volosinov (1973) make clear, recontextualized words are always "refracted" and "reaccented" by the new speaker.
3. See Matoesian (2000) for a study that examines how an audio recording enters into intertextual relationships with other texts in a courtroom setting.
4. Different scholars have used different terms to refer to these taken-for-granted assumptions. Fairclough (2003) prefers the term *assumption*, as noted below. Others prefer the term *presupposition* (Martin & White 2005; Porter 1986). And still others prefer the term *presumption* (Perelman & Olbrechts-Tyteca 1969).
5. For an alternative catalog of "levels of intertextuality" see Bazerman (2004).
6. See, for instance, Bakhtin (1981; 1986), Bazerman (1993; 2004), Buttny & Williams (2000), Calsamiglia & López Ferrero (2003), Dunmire (2009), Fairclough (1995; 2003), Hodges (2008a), Lemke (1983; 1985; 1995a; 1995b), Oddo (2011), Selzer (1993), Thibault (1991), and Volosinov (1973). However, as Bauman and Briggs (1990) suggest, several scholars have been interested in "intersemiotic translation" (76). See for instance: Bucholtz (2000), Fine (1984), Hymes (1981), Iedema (2003), and Kress (2003).
7. Baldry and Thibault (2005) examine how texts are linked through *multimodal thematic formations*—overarching meanings construed "on the basis of joint verbal-visual resources which work in partnership" (50). Meanwhile, Van Leeuwen's (2005; 2008) work suggests how elements from one social context are transformed when they are recontextualized in another. Specifically, Van Leeuwen (2005) studies how discourse transforms real social actions into textual representations. According to Van Leeuwen (2005), when social reality is represented in discourse, four basic types of transformation occur: exclusion, rearrangement, addition, and substitution. Van Leeuwen's categories are similar to the categories of transformation I identify below. However, my project is different in that I am studying purely textual transformations, rather than the transformation of social reality into discourse.

8. Comparisons were based on transitivity analysis (Halliday & Matthiessen 2004), Appraisal analysis (Martin & White 2005), critical intertextual analysis (Thibault 1991), and multimodal text analysis (Baldry & Thibault 2005).
9. Audience repositioning was coded using a grounded theory approach (Glaser & Strauss 1967; Strauss 1987).
10. I borrow this term from McCarthy (1988).
11. *Implicit rearticulation* occurs when a speaker makes an assertion or an assumption that is semantically similar to assertions or assumptions made by a prior speaker, without attributing the assertion to that prior speaker. *Implicit rebuttal* occurs when a speaker makes an assertion that is semantically antonymous or contrary to a prior speaker's assertion. In a sense, the speaker implicitly recontextualizes a thematic formation from the prior speaker's text, only to negate it. As shown in table 4.4, only the *New York Times* included speakers who implicitly rebutted Powell's arguments more frequently than they rearticulated his claims. But, as suggested in chapter 2, these rebuttals were presented far less frequently and less prominently than Powell's assertions.
12. It also indexes that Powell's rhetoric was forensic—i.e., concerned with determining the nature and cause of past events (as is often done in judicial proceedings).
13. Keep in mind, that Powell never explicitly said that the United States desired war with Iraq, though this was surely implied (Zarefsky 2007).
14. After all, "cases" are built by prosecutors in a court of law.
15. In Martin and White's (2005) terms, "chilling" is a negative appreciation that describes the reaction triggered by a semiotic artifact (i.e., the "example" from Powell's presentation). Of course, "chilling" also strongly implies an emotional response of fear.
16. This quotation was drawn from a content box on CNN's website—next to the main article about Powell's talk. The content box purports to list the "key points" from Powell's presentation.
17. In other parts of its report, CNN does a better job of attributing this interpretation to Powell, as noted below.
18. As Woodward (2004) reports, Powell embellished his translation of this recording: "*Clean out all of the areas*, the scrap areas, the abandoned areas. *Make sure nothing is there*." The italicized portions were added by Powell, but they never appeared in the official translation of the recording that was displayed on the "big screen" at the U.N. Powell's verbal distortion of the recording would seem to be newsworthy, but none of the outlets in this study mentioned it.
19. Mitchell seems to assume that the anthrax spray is something viewers can see with their own eyes in the video. She might have questioned how one can determine with any certainty that something is "simulated anthrax" by looking at a grainy reconnaissance video. She might have also considered why one should be alarmed about "simulated anthrax" (whatever that is) in the first place.

20. Interestingly, before Powell delivered his presentation, the State Department's Bureau of Intelligence and Research warned him that the claim that Iraq's UAVs were well suited for this purpose was "weak" (Schwarz 2008). Obviously, this warning did not prevent Powell from including the questionable charge in his presentation.
21. In fact, the UAVs had never been designed to spray WMDs. About a year after Powell's speech the *Washington Post* reported: "Since Powell's speech . . . investigations by U.S. weapons inspectors have determined that the UAVs, or drones, were not designed to spread deadly toxins, but to fly unarmed reconnaissance missions" (Kessler & Pincus 2004).
22. As she utters this remark, a young Iraqi soldier is displayed holding a rifle in the visual track. Perhaps this soldier is supposed to be representative of the two Iraqi officers in Powell's voice intercept.
23. In fact, as before, Powell never explicitly says that the officers are plotting to deceive ElBaradei—though it is implied in his argument. So, not only did Mitchell fail to attribute this claim to Powell, she also made his claim explicit when it was only implicit in his address.
24. The clip from Powell's performance is once again enhanced with digital images of the U.S. and Iraqi flags waving in the background.
25. See Bamford (2008) for a discussion of intelligence officials' admissions about the ambiguity of the NSA intercepts included in Powell's presentation (143–45).
26. In fact, at the conclusion of her report, Mitchell says that "U.S. officials believe that the opponents to military action were reading from scripts prepared before Powell's presentation." This assertion, sourced to unnamed (and, thus, unchallengeable) officials, only strengthens the idea that Powell's opponents were simply unwilling to listen to his convincing evidence.
27. I tend to view this proposition as a part of Powell's claim, but there is some space for confusion. Powell certainly never says "and the threat continues today," though this is implied throughout his discussion of the "ties" between Iraq and al-Qaeda.
28. According to Hoyle (2008): "In January 2003, the Jordanian terrorist Abu Musab al-Zarqawi was not an associate or collaborator of bin Laden or al-Qaeda, as Powell claimed. A troubled long-distance alliance was not negotiated by al Qaeda's leadership and al-Zarqawi until 2005, long after the Iraqi insurgency began" (332).
29. For a discussion of the ideological implications of nominalization, see Fairclough (1992b; 2003), Fowler (1991), Dunmire (2005), Thompson (2004), and Trew (1979).
30. This congruent version is not meant to be the "correct" version, but a hypothetical reconstruction that allows us to more easily discern the effects of nominalization.
31. It is worth noting that whether construed as a verb or a noun the word "link" always seems to suggest a strong connection between two entities. As a noun,

"link" connotes a tangible object, an "ironclad" connection such as the links in a chain. But even when we say a person linked two objects in an argumentative context, we may still suggest that this person created a seemingly "physical" connection. Thus, even if we de-nominalize Miklaszewski's assertion *and* remove the superlative modifier (*strongest*) from the equation, we are still left with a construction that represents Powell as having productively "tied" Iraq to al-Zarqawi. Compare the following:

A. Powell most strongly linked Iraq with this man/terrorist (congruent version)

B. Powell linked Iraq with this man/terrorist (de-nominalized version without superlative)

In both A and B, Powell seems to have accomplished his rhetorical goal: linking Iraq to a terrorist. We can reduce this sense, only if we choose a slightly weaker synonym for "link" (C), or add a conative verb that qualifies the degree of Powell's success (D):

C. Powell *correlated* Iraq with this man/terrorist (de-nominalized version with "weaker" synonymous verb).

D. Powell *attempted to* link Iraq with this man/terrorist (de-nominalized version with added conative).

32. See Baldry and Thibault (2005) for a discussion of how gaze, facial expression, and color may enact interpersonal relationships between viewer and image. See Olson (2009) for a discussion of the "rhetorical re-circulation" of an image in colonial America.
33. Notably, we find an attribution to Powell at the end of a long sentence (*Secretary of State Colin Powell said*), This "trailing attribution" positions readers to initially accept as fact the idea that Iraq has consorted with al-Qaeda for years via a "shadowy go-between." Only after absorbing this information does the reader learn that it is actually Powell's assertion (Fahnestock 2011).
34. As it turns out, the "agent" from Saddam's government was actually a spy whom Saddam had placed in Ansar al-Islam to get information about the group. As Bergen (2011) explains, just because Saddam infiltrated the group with a spy does not mean that Saddam had control over the group. In fact, the senior CIA officer on the case found no connection between the activities of the training camp in northern Iraq and Saddam Hussein's government in Baghdad (144–45).
35. Powell also asserted that Zarqawi had traveled "freely" in and out of Baghdad, and that he had set up a base of operations there. Based on this, he claimed that Saddam had knowledge of Zarqawi's presence in Iraq. But, again, Powell did not

say that Zarqawi was colluding with Saddam's government or functioning as a "go-between."

36. Miklaszewski might also have questioned whether an ambiguous, black-and-white photograph taken from outer space can demonstrably *show* a terrorist training camp producing deadly toxins.
37. This is another example of what Huckin (2002) refers to as "manipulative silence."
38. Of course, Miklaszewski also adds the video image of Osama bin Laden. This image undoubtedly endows bin Laden with added visual presence, and enhances his role as the terrorist leader with an allegedly direct link to Iraq.
39. Moreover, Miklaszewski foregrounds the "terrorist link" in the thematic portion of the clause, and backgrounds the attribution (*from a senior al-Qaeda leader*) and evidential (*apparently*) in the new portion of the clause. Here, I am using the words "thematic" and "new" in the Hallidayan sense. Accordingly, the thematic portion of any clause comes at the beginning and serves as a "point of departure" that is "given" in the message. The remainder of the clause, called the new, typically presents fresh information (see Martin & Rose 2007, 87–218). Thus, Miklaszewski heightens the sense that *the most direct terrorist link* is a taken-for-granted point of departure, a given.
40. Of course, it's difficult to see how an alleged relationship between unnamed "al-Qaeda associates" and unnamed people somewhere in the nation of Iraq could be called a "direct terrorist link." More on this below.
41. Isikoff & Corn (2006) report that the al-Qaeda detainee referred to in Powell's presentation was actually a man named Ibn al-Shaykh al-Libi. What Powell did not report (and appears not to have known) is that a number of intelligence officials doubted the credibility of al-Libi's testimony (122). Moreover, several members of the FBI were convinced that al-Libi had invented this story while being tortured in the CIA's extraordinary rendition program (122). Indeed, according to Isikoff & Corn (2006), al-Libi recanted his entire testimony, explaining that he had made up the tale only because his interrogators had been "killing" him (124). What this means in terms of my project is that the visual shot of the "ricin" document could *not* have been related to this detainee's fictional story about pursuing weapons from Iraq—and NBC knew it. In other words, NBC displayed this misleading visual—apparently for effect—knowing that it was unrelated to the detainee's (and Powell's) testimony.

Chapter Five. Political Discourse, the Press, and the Public Good

1. See Hodges (2011) for an excellent intertextual analysis that examines, in part, how the Bush administration's "war on terror" narrative was consumed and interpreted by different public audiences.
2. See Ishizaki and Kaufer (2012) for a discussion of DocuScope, a computational tool for conducting corpus-based rhetorical analysis. See Stubbs (1996) for a discourse-analytic approach to corpus analysis.
3. Donald Rumsfeld (2011) has also publicly questioned Powell's claims that he was misled by the CIA. As Rumsfeld puts it in his recent memoir: "Powell had spent decades in uniform and had become the most senior military officer in our country, and at every level he had spent long hours dealing with intelligence. As President Reagan's national security adviser, he routinely had been exposed to reporting and analysis from the intelligence community. As secretary of state, his department's own intelligence agency reported to him. There was no one else in the administration who had even a fraction of his experience in intelligence matters, including CIA Director Tenet. Powell was not duped or misled by anybody" (449).
4. It is not true that President Bush relied exclusively on the NIE in making his judgments about the need for war. First, both Bush and Cheney delivered speeches about the dangers of Iraq's WMDs long before the NIE had been produced (Payne 2006). In other words, the public campaign for war began even before the intelligence on Iraq had been assessed. Moreover, as former intelligence analyst Vincent Cannistraro (2006) explains, the president also received daily intelligence briefings that included critical information not found in the NIE. In fact, the president was probably well aware of the dissenting opinions about Iraq's WMDs. On the other hand, Vice President Cheney allegedly chastened intelligence staffers who supplied the president with dissenting opinions during the daily briefings (Cannistraro 2006).
5. A so-called white paper was released publicly in fall 2002, but this document was rather different from the NIE. Indeed, the white paper omitted the dissents, caveats, and uncertainties that had been included in the classified NIE (Isikoff & Corn 2006, 138–40).
6. See Boykoff & Boykoff (2004).
7. As Johnson (1984) explains, ethos has been associated with the self since ancient times, whether it is defined as an artistic construction of the self adapted to a particular occasion (Aristotle, Cicero, etc.) or as the intrinsic moral self of a given speaker (Plato, Quintilian, Augustine).
8. A number of scholars have suggested that ethos is not necessarily a projection of the self, but a projection of the collective community. Wei (2002), for example, explicitly argues for the notion of "collective ethos," claiming that modern

corporations don't attempt to construct images of themselves as much as they attempt to tap into shared cultural codes. Medhurst (2004) argues that the candidates in the 2000 U.S. presidential election projected the ethos of American democracy as indicated by their repeated references to religious values that bind Americans together. Blair and Michel (2004) also suggest the notion of a collective national identity, as evinced in the production and reception of the Mount Rushmore monument. Meanwhile, Amossy (2001) explicitly argues that any one person's ethos may be co-constructed by others. Specifically, she posits that one's prior reputation is largely assembled by others speakers—through rumor and media narratives.

9. As (Van Dijk 2008; 2009) makes clear, these "relevant aspects" of the communicative situation do not directly influence language use. Instead, the way participants mentally define a situation (their context model) controls their discourse production. In other words Van Dijk, like Vatz (1973), argues that the rhetorical situation is not located in external reality, but defined by rhetors as they interpret and describe the world.
10. See also Patterson & Donsbagh (1996).
11. See *Communication Studies* 50, no 1 (1999), for a tribute to Samuel Becker. See especially Vande Berg (1999) for a discussion of Becker's influence in critical media studies. See Biesecker (2010) for a response to Becker (1971) that seeks to integrate his approach to communication with a Lacan-inspired theory of "evental rhetoric."
12. According to Blommaert (2005), a centering institution is one that effectively regulates communication, compelling speakers to create recognizably "normative" meanings in order to be heard. Here I am adapting Blommaert's definition somewhat, focusing on the active role that these institutions play in altering "original" discourse.
13. Pun intended.
14. Wrote McClellan (2008): "The collapse of the administration's rationales for war, which became apparent months after our invasion, should have never come as such a surprise. The public should have been made much more aware, before the fact, of the uncertainties, doubts, and caveats that underlay the intelligence about the regime of Saddam Hussein. The administration did little to convey those nuances to the people; the press should have picked up the slack but largely failed to do so because their focus was elsewhere—on covering the march to war, instead of the necessity of war" (156–57). While I largely agree with McClellan's assessment, I must say that it takes a lot of audacity for an administration official like McClellan to repeatedly advance administration propaganda during the run-up to war, and then, years later, criticize the press for not "catching" the administration's exaggerated claims.

Appendix B. Synoptic Views of Discourse

1. Researchers establish the boundaries of texts through "entextualization processes" (Silverstein & Urban 1996, 4). As Johnstone (2008) explains, "Texts . . . do not exist independently of discourse analysts' choices about how to 'entextualize': how to select and delimit chunks out of the flow of talk or writing, make these chunks into texts, and treat them analytically" (20).
2. A number of scholars have debated how to theorize social context, and how best to account for it (Biesecker 1989; Bitzer 1968; Consigny 1974; Edbaur 2005; Fairclough 2003; Halliday & Matthiessen 2004; Vatz 1973; Van Dijk 2008; 2009; Witte 1992). But all generally agree on the basic point that social interaction and context are interrelated.
3. For a social-psychological view on "positioning theory," see van Langenhove and Harré (1999).
4. On the other hand, because the rhetors under study are journalists who presumably enjoy a certain air of credibility and authority, I shall assume that there is a degree of social pressure exerted on public audiences to regard journalistic reports as accurate and valid.
5. Indeed, Fairclough (2003) argues that such "hortatory reports" have a "covert prescriptive intent, aimed at getting people to act in certain ways on the basis of representations of what is" (96).
6. Burgchardt (2010) and Foss (2009) survey several approaches to rhetorical criticism. Some well-known methods include dramatistic analysis (Burke 1954; 1969), neo-classical criticism (e.g., Leff & Mohrmann 1974), metaphor analysis (e.g., Ivie 1987), contextual analysis (Bitzer 1968), argument analysis (Toulmin 1958), ideographic criticism (McGee 1980), narrative criticism (Fisher 1984), and genre criticism (e.g., Campbell & Jamieson 1978).
7. Johnstone and Eisenhart (2008) provide a wealth of rhetorical studies that employ discourse-analytic methods. Among those that draw on SFL are Cramer (2008), Dunmire (2008), Eisenhart (2008), Ritivoi (2008), and Zdenek (2008).
8. See also Auer & Di Luzio (1992), Drew & Heritage (1992), Johnstone (2008), and Thibault (1991).
9. "Lexis" is basically synonymous with "vocabulary." Many linguists make a distinction between lexical items that have referential meaning (e.g., *dog*) and grammatical items that do not (e.g., *very*). Some blur this distinction. Halliday, for instance, conceives of grammar and vocabulary not as discrete categories, but as two poles of a single continuum known as the "lexicogrammar" (Halliday & Matthiessen 2004, 24).
10. While systemic-functional linguistics is an important method of discourse analysis, it is by no means the only or even the most popular approach. For general introductions to DA, see Barton & Stygall (2002), Johnstone (2008), Gee (2005), and Schiffrin, Tannen, and Hamilton (2001). See Van Leeuwen (2008) for an approach

to critical discourse analysis that draws upon and extends the SFL framework. See Fairclough (2003; 2010) for an approach to critical discourse analysis that draws upon a diverse range of linguistic and critical social theories. See Van Dijk (2008; 2009) for a sociocognitive approach to critical discourse analysis. See Wodak (2011) for an explanation and application of the discourse-historical approach. See Richardson (2012) for approaches to journalism discourse and Montgomery (2007) for an approach to the discourse of broadcast journalism. For criticisms of systemic-functional linguistics, see Blommaert (2005) and Van Dijk (2008).

11. I am indebted to Barbara Johnstone for suggesting this example.
12. Martin & White's (2005) discussion of appraisal fits within a wider body of discourse scholarship on stance and evaluation. For other relevant studies, see Biber & Finegan (1989), Hunston & Thompson (2000), Englebretson (2007), and Jaffe (2009).
13. This is not to say that all semiotic resources are equally capable of making the same meaning (Kress & Van Leeuwen 1996).
14. See Baldry & Thibault (2005), Iedema (2003), Kress (2003; 2005), Kress & Van Leeuwen (1996; 2001), Lemke (2002), O'Halloran (1999; 2004; 2008), O'Toole (1994), and Royce (2002).
15. Of course, several scholars have turned their attention to analyzing images from a rhetorical perspective (Foss 1994; Olson, Finnegan, & Hope 2008; Hariman & Lucaites 2007; Hill & Helmers 2004). Generally speaking, these scholars have yet to embrace the micro-analytic tools provided by SF researchers.
16. See Bazerman (1988), Berkenkotter & Huckin (1993), Campbell & Jamieson (1978; 2008), Devitt (1991), Jamieson (1975), and Miller (1984).
17. As rhetoricians have increasingly studied intertextuality, many have embraced Mikhail Bakhtin as part of the "rhetorical tradition" and have used his conceptual categories to guide criticism (Bazerman 1993; Bialostosky 2004; Bizzell & Herzberg 2001; D'Angelo 2009; Farmer 1998; Murphy 1997; Selzer 1993). Jasinski (1997a) for instance, has examined heteroglossia and polyphony in the *Federalist Papers*, and has recommended (1997b) that scholars trace the "performative traditions" that enable, constrain, and permeate rhetorical performances. Employing close reading strategies, Leff (1992; 2001) and Murphy (2001) have similarly sought to show how prior texts, voices, controversies, and traditions simultaneously constrain and facilitate rhetorical invention
18. See Dunmire (2009; 2011), Oddo (2011; 2014), Thibault (1991), and Lemke (1983; 1985; 1995a; 1995b).
19. For example, Trew (1979) investigates how a story of police violence incrementally changes across different press reports. Fahnestock (1986) examines how scientific research is modified as it is accommodated in popular magazines. And Hodges (2008a) studies how a military general's discourse is politicized as it is re-represented by White House officials.

20. Ritivoi (2008), for instance, finds that, compared to ideographic criticism (McGee 1980), critical discourse analysis offers a more nuanced approach to studying ideological rhetoric. Other rhetoricians have also found CDA to be a powerful mechanism for studying political and judicial discourse (Andrus 2011; Huckin 1997, 2002; Huckin, Andrus, & Clary-Lemon 2012; Dunmire 2009; Oddo 2011).
21. Much CDA scholarship relies, at least partially, on Hallidayan systemic-functional methodologies. Moreover, CDA studies have employed rhetorical and argumentation analysis (Fairclough & Fairclough 2012; Reisigl & Wodak 2001; Van Leeuwen & Wodak 1999) and intertextual analysis (Fairclough 1992a; Thibault 1991). Finally, it is worth noting that Kress and Van Leeuwen (1996; 2001), who essentially invented multimodal text analysis, are also critical discourse analysts. Thus, CDA is very much compatible with the rhetorical, systemic-functional, intertextual, and multimodal project that I am undertaking.
22. In fact, Van Dijk (2001) claims, CDA scholarship must be "better" than other approaches—more empirically grounded—if it is to be accepted by the mainstream research community (353).

Appendix G. The Engagement System, Temporality, and Presence

1. For the sake of simplicity, I have left out the visual data that accompanied these spoken reports; obviously, the visuals were taken into account during the analysis.

Appendix H. Coding Categories for Audience Repositioning

1. If you are wondering why there is no "delegitimation" category, it is because the journalists never *explicitly* commented on Powell or his discourse in negative ways. On a few occasions, journalists suggested that Powell may not have persuaded his audience. However, I deemed these suggestions to be far too mild to be considered delegitimizing. Instead I noted them as qualifications of Powell's argument. Specifically, I coded them as instances of "teleological uncertainty," that is, uncertainty as to whether Powell accomplished his argumentative goals.

Appendix I. A Four-Phased Analytic Approach

1. According to Baldry and Thibault (2005), a cluster is a recognizable group of verbal and/or visual items that form a semantic whole as a consequence of spatial proximity and lexical cohesion (31). An example might be an image and its caption in a newspaper. Texts are comprised of multiple clusters, which have both an internal coherence and a meaningful relationship to one another.
2. I place "utterances" in quotation marks because I do not want to suggest that I mean only spoken words. For my purposes, an original utterance can just as easily be a multimodal configuration.

Bibliography

⌘

"About *NBC Nightly News*." 2009, March 2. *MSNBC.com*. Retrieved April 18, 2013: http://www.msnbc.msn.com/id/3689499/ns/nbcnightlynews/t/about-nbc-nightly-news/#.UAchafWPvQs.

Adams, M. 2005. *American Backlash: The Untold Story of Social Change in the United States*. New York: Penguin.

Allan, S., and B. Zelizer. 2004. *Reporting War: Journalism in Wartime*. New York: Routledge.

Allen, G. 2000. *Intertextuality*. London: Routledge.

"Al Qaeda, Iraq Partners in Terror—Powell." 2003, February 6. *CNN.com*. Retrieved May 6, 2013: http://web.archive.org/web/20030416135755/http://www.cnn.com/2003/US/02/05/sprj.irq.alqaeda.links/.

Althaus, S. L. 2003. "When News Norms Collide, Follow the Lead: New Evidence for Press Independence." *Political Communication* 20(4): 381–414.

Althaus, S. L., J. A. Edy, R. M. Entman, and P. Phalen. 1996. "Revising the Indexing Hypothesis: Officials, Media, and the Lybia Crisis." *Political Communication* 13: 407–21.

Althaus, S. L., and D. M. Largio. 2004. "When Osama Became Saddam: Origins and Consequences of the Change in America's Public Enemy #1." *Political Science and Politics* 37: 795–99.

Altheide, D. 2002. *Creating Gear: News and the Construction of Crisis.* Hawthorne, NY: Aldine de Gruyter.

Amossy, R. 2001. "Ethos at the Crossroads of Disciplines: Rhetoric, Pragmatics, and Sociology." *Poetics Today* 22(1): 1–23.

Anderson, D. 2007. *Identity's Strategy: Rhetorical Selves in Conversion.* Columbia: University of South Carolina Press.

Anderson, K. V. 2011. "'Rhymes with Blunt': Pornification and U.S. Political Culture." *Rhetoric & Public Affairs* 14(2): 327–68.

Anderson, K. V., and J. Stewart. 2005. "Politics and the Single Woman: The 'Sex and the City Voter' in Campaign 2004." *Rhetoric & Public Affairs* 8(4): 595–616.

Anderson, T. H. 2011. *Bush's Wars.* New York: Oxford University Press.

Andrus, J. 2011. "Beyond Texts in Context: Recontextualization and the Coproduction of Texts and Contexts in the Legal Discourse, Excited Utterance Exception to Hearsay." *Discourse & Society* 22: 115–36.

Applebome, P. 1991, March 4. "After the War: National Mood; War Heals Wounds at Home, but Not All." *New York Times*, A1.

Aristotle. 2007. *On Rhetoric: A Theory of Civic Discourse.* Trans. G. A. Kennedy. New York: Oxford University Press.

Auer, P., and A. Di Luzio, eds. 1992. *The Contextualization of Language.* Amsterdam: John Benjamins.

Austin, J. L. 1962. *How to Do Things with Words.* Oxford: Oxford University Press.

Bacevich, A. 2010. *Washington Rules: America's Path to Permanent War.* New York: Metropolitan Books.

Baer, R. 2002, November 16. "Iraq: Five Questions." *CNN presents.* [Television Broadcast]. [Transcript]. Atlanta: Cable News Network. Available: Lexis Nexis.

Bagdikian, B. 2004. *The New Media Monopoly.* Boston: Beacon.

Bakhtin, M. M. 1981. *The Dialogic Imagination: Four Essays.* Ed. M. Holquist. Trans. C. Emerson and M. Holquist. Austin: University of Texas Press.

———. 1984. *Problems of Dostoevsky's Poetics.* Ed. and trans. C. Emerson. Minneapolis: University of Minnesota Press.

———. 1986. *Speech Genres and Other Late Essays.* Ed. C. Emerson and M. Holquist. Trans. V. W. McGee. Austin: University of Texas Press.

Baldry, A. P., and P. J. Thibault. 2005. *Multimodal Transcription and Text Analysis: A Multimedia Toolkit and Coursebook with Associated On-line Course.* London: Equinox.

Bamford, J. 2004. *A Pretext for War: 9/11, Iraq, and the Abuse of America's Intelligence Agencies.* New York: Doubleday.

———. 2008. *The Shadow Factory: The Ultra-secret NSA from 9/11 to the Eavesdropping on America.* New York: Anchor Books.

Bandura, A. 1998. "Mechanisms of Moral Disengagement." In *Origins of Terrorism: Psychologies, Ideologies, Theologies, States of Mind,* ed. W. Reich, 161–91. Washington, DC: Woodrow Wilson Center Press.

Barabak, M. Z. 2003, February 9. "Showdown with Iraq: The Times Poll." *Los Angeles Times,* A1.

Barthes, R. 1977. *Image—Music—Text.* Trans. Stephen Heath. New York: Hill and Wang.

Barton, E., and G. Stygall, eds. 2002. *Discourse Studies in Composition.* Cresskill, NJ: Hampton Press.

Bauman, R., and C. L. Briggs. 1990. "Poetics and Performance as Critical Perspectives on Language and Social Life." *Annual Review of Anthropology* 19: 59–88.

Baumlin, J. S., and T. F. Baumlin, eds. 1994. *Ethos: New Essays in Rhetorical and Critical Theory.* Dallas: Southern Methodist University Press.

Baym, G. 2003. "Strategies of Illumination: U.S. Network News, Watergate, and the Clinton Affair." *Rhetoric & Public Affairs* 6(4): 633–56.

Bazerman, C. 1988. *Shaping Written Knowledge: The Genre and Activity of the Experimental Article in Science.* Madison: University of Wisconsin Press.

———. 1993. "Intertextual Self-Fashioning: Gould and Lewontin's Representations of the Literature." In *Understanding Scientific Prose,* ed. Jack Selzer, 20–41. Madison: University of Wisconsin Press.

———. 2004. "Intertextuality: How Texts Rely on Other Texts." In *What Writing Does and How It Does It: An Introduction to Analysis of Text and Textual Practice,* ed. C. Bazerman and P. Prior, 83–96. Mahwah, NJ: Lawrence Erlbaum.

Becker, S. L. 1971. "Rhetorical Studies for a Contemporary World." In *The Prospect of Rhetoric,* ed. L. F. Bitzer and E. Black, 21–43. Englewood Cliffs, NJ: Prentice Hall.

Bennett, W. L. 1990. "Toward a Theory of Press-State Relations." *Journal of Communication* 40(2): 103–25.

———. 1994. "The News about Foreign Policy." In *Taken by Storm: The Media, Public Opinion, and U.S. Foreign Policy in the Gulf War,* ed. W. L. Bennett and D. L. Paletz, 12–40. Chicago: University of Chicago Press.

———, 1996. "An Introduction to Journalism Norms and Representations of Politics." *Political Communication* 13: 373–84.

———. 2012. *News: The Politics of Illusion*. 9th ed. New York: Longman.

Bennett, W. L., R. G. Lawrence, and S. Livingston. 2007. *When the Press Fails: Political Power and the News Media from Iraq to Katrina*. Chicago: University of Chicago Press.

Bennett, W. L., and S. Livingston. 2003. "A Semi-independent Press: Government Control and Journalistic Autonomy in the Political Construction of News." *Political Communication* 20(4): 359–62.

Bennett, W. L., and J. B. Manheim. 1993. "Taking the Public by Storm: Information, Cueing, and the Democratic Press in the Gulf Conflict." *Political Communication* 10: 331–52.

Benoit, W. 1990. "Isocrates and Aristotle on Rhetoric." *Rhetoric Society Quarterly* 20(3): 251–59.

Benson, T. W. 2004. Series Editor's "Preface." In *The Ethos of Rhetoric*, ed. M. J. Hyde, ix–x. Columbia: University of South Carolina Press.

Bergen, P. L. 2011. *The Longest War: The Enduring Conflict between America and al-Qaeda*. New York: Free Press.

Berger, P., and T. Luckmann. 1966. *The Social Construction of Reality*. Harmondsworth: Penguin.

Berkenkotter, C., and T. Huckin. 1993. "Rethinking Genre from a Sociocognitive Perspective." *Written Communication* 10: 475–509.

Bialostosky, D. 2004. "Aristotle's *Rhetoric* and Bakhtin's Discourse Theory." In *A Companion to Rhetoric and Rhetorical Criticism*, ed. W. Jost and W. Olmstead, 393–408. Malden, MA: Blackwell.

Biber, D., and E. Finegan. 1989. "Styles of Stance in English: Lexical and Grammatical Marking of Evidentiality and Affect." *Text* 9: 93–124.

Biesecker, B. A. 1989. "Rethinking the Rhetorical Situation from within the Thematic of *Différance*." *Philosophy and Rhetoric* 22: 110–30.

———. 2010. "Prospects of Rhetoric for the Twenty-First Century: Speculations on Evental Rhetoric Ending with a Note on Barack Obama and a Benediction by Jacques Lacan." In *Reengaging the Prospects of Rhetoric: Current Conversations and Contemporary Challenges*, ed. M. J. Porrovechhio, 16–36. New York: Routledge.

Bitzer, L. F. 1968. "The Rhetorical Situation." *Philosophy & Rhetoric* 1: 1–14.

———. 1998. "Political Rhetoric." In *Landmark Essays on Contemporary Rhetoric*, ed. T. B. Farrell, 1–22. Mahwah, NJ: Hermagoras Press.

Bizzell, P., and B. Herzberg. 2001. *The Rhetorical Tradition: Readings from Classical Times to the Present*. 2nd ed. Boston: Bedford / St. Martin's.

Blair, C., and N. Michel. 2004. "The Rushmore Effect: Ethos and National Collective Identity." In *The* Ethos *of Rhetoric*, ed. M. J. Hyde, 156–96. Columbia: University of South Carolina Press.

Blair, J. A. 2004. "The Rhetoric of Visual Arguments." In *Defining Visual Rhetorics*, ed. C. A. Hill and M. Helmers, 41–61. Mahwah, NJ: Lawrence Erlbaum.

Blitzer, W., and H. Kurtz. 2001, September 22. "Dan Rather Speaks Out." *CNN Tonight*.

Blix, H. 2010. "Feb. 5, 2003: Colin Powell Speaks at U.N." *Newsweek*. (Special Online Issue: *20/10: The Decade in Rewind*). Retrieved April 18, 2013 from http://2010.newsweek.com/top-10/most-important-dates/colin-powell-speaks-to-un.html.

Blommaert, J. 2005. *Discourse: A Critical Introduction*. New York: Cambridge University Press.

Boorstin, D. J. 1961. *The Image: A Guide to Pseudo-events in America*. New York: Vintage Books.

Bormann, E. G. 1982. "A Fantasy Theme Analysis of the Television Coverage of the Hostage Release and the Reagan Inaugural." *Quarterly Journal of Speech* 68: 133–45.

Boykoff, M. T., and J. M. Boykoff. 2004. "Balance as Bias: Global Warming and the U.S. Prestige Press." *Global Environmental Change* 14(2): 125–36.

Brancaccio, D. (interviewer) and L. Wilkerson (interviewee). 2006, February 3. *PBS Now*. [Interview Transcript]. Retrieved April 16, 2013 from http://www.pbs.org/now/politics/wilkerson.html.

Bremer, J. 2009, November 30. "Secret Letter Shows Blair 'Knew Iraq War Was Illegal.'" *The Week*. Retrieved April 4, 2003, from http://www.theweek.co.uk/politics/18195/secret-letter-shows-blair-%E2%80%98knew-iraq-war-was-illegal%E2%80%99.

Brennan, J. 2006. Interview. *Frontline*. PBS. Retrieved April 18, 2013, from http://www.pbs.org/wgbh/pages/frontline/darkside/interviews/brennan.html.

"Briefing by Secretary Colin Powell, Egyptian Foreign Minister Amre Moussa." 2001, February 21. Retrieved February 6, 2013, from *Information Clearing House*, http://www.informationclearinghouse.info/article4810.htm.

Brown, P., and S. C. Levinson. 1978. *Politeness: Some Universals in Language Usage*. Cambridge: Cambridge University Press.

Brummett, B. 1999. "Burke's Representative Anecdote as a Method in Media Criticism." In *Contemporary Rhetorical Theory: A Reader*, ed. J. L. Lucaites, C. M. Condit, and S. Caudill, 479–93. New York: Guilford.

Bucholtz, M. 2000. "The Politics of Transcription." *Journal of Pragmatics* 32: 1439–65.

Bumiller, E. 2011, January 20. "'Band of Brothers' Mark Gulf War Anniversary." *New York Times*, A16.

Burgchardt, C., ed. 2010. *Readings in Rhetorical Criticism*. 4th ed. State College, PA: Strata Publishing.

Burke, K. 1954. *Permanence and Change*. 3rd ed. Berkeley: University of California Press.

———. 1966. *Language as Symbolic Action*. Berkeley: University of California Press.

———. 1969. *A Grammar of Motives*. Berkeley: University of California Press.

Burkeman, O., E. MacAskill, and J. Henley. 2002, November 7. "Threat of War: How Fixer Powell Struck the Deal: The Resolution Secretary of State Clipped Wings of Hawks and Doves." *The Guardian*, 4.

Bush, G. W. 2001, September 20. "Address before a Joint Session of the Congress on the United States Response to the Terrorist Attacks of September 11." Retrieved January 23, 2013, from http://www.presidency.ucsb.edu/ws/?pid=64731.

———. 2002a, January 29. "President Delivers State of the Union Address." Available: http://georgewbush-whitehouse.archives.gov/news/releases/2002/01/20020129-11.html.

———. 2002b, September 12. "President's Remarks at the United Nations General Assembly." Available: http://georgewbush-whitehouse.archives.gov/news/releases/2002/09/20020912-1.html.

———. 2002c, October 7. "President Bush Outlines Iraqi Threat." Available: http://georgewbush-whitehouse.archives.gov/news/releases/2002/10/20021007-8.html.

———. 2002d, July 8. "The President's News Conference." Available: http://www.presidency.ucsb.edu/ws/index.php?pid=64951.

———. 2003, January 28. "Address before a Joint Session of the Congress on the State of the Union." Retrieved April 11, 2013, from http://www.presidency.ucsb.edu/ws/index.php?pid=29645.

Buttny, R., and P. L. Williams. 2000. "Demanding Respect: The Uses of Reported Speech in Discursive Constructions of Interracial Contact." *Discourse & Society* 11: 109–33.

Calabrese, A. 2005. "Casus Belli: U.S. Media and the Justification of the Iraq War." *Television & New Media* 6(2): 153–75.

Calabrese, A., and B. Burke. 1992. "American Identities: Nationalism, the Media and the Public Sphere." *Journal of Communication Inquiry* 16(2): 52–73.

Calsamiglia H., and C. López Ferrero. 2003. "Role and Position of Scientific Voices: Reported Speech in the Media." *Discourse Studies* 5(2): 147–73.

Campbell, K. K., and K. H. Jamieson. 1978. *Form and Genre: Shaping Rhetorical Action*. Falls Church, VA: Speech Communication Association.

———. 2008. *Presidents Creating the Presidency: Deeds Done in Words*. Chicago: University of Chicago Press.

Cannistraro, V. 2006. Interview with *Frontline*. *PBS.org*. Retrieved April 18, 2013, from http://www.pbs.org/wgbh/pages/frontline/darkside/themes/nie.html.

Cap, P. 2006. *Legitimisation in Political Discourse: A Cross-disciplinary Perspective on the Modern US War Rhetoric*. Newcastle, UK: Cambridge Scholars Press.

———. 2008. "Toward the Proximization Model of the Analysis of Legitimization in Political Discourse." *Journal of Pragmatics* 40: 17–41.

———. 2010. "Axiological Aspects of Proximization." *Journal of Pragmatics* 42: 392–407.

Cappella, J. N., and K. H. Jamieson. 1997. *Spiral of Cynicism: The Press and the Public Good*. New York: Oxford University Press.

Capus, S. (Executive Producer). 2003a, February 4. *NBC Nightly News with Tom Brokaw*. New York. Retrieved on February 1, 2010, from *Vanderbilt Television News Archive*.

———. (Executive Producer). 2003b, February 5. *NBC Nightly News with Tom Brokaw*. New York. Retrieved on February 1, 2010, from *Vanderbilt Television News Archive*.

———. (Executive Producer). 2003c, February 5. *NBC Special Report: The Case against Iraq*. New York. Retrieved on February 1, 2010, from *Vanderbilt Television News Archive*.

Carvalho, A. 2008. "Media(ted) Discourse and Society: Rethinking the Framework of Critical Discourse Analysis." *Journalism Studies* 9(2): 161–76.

Ceccarelli, L. 2011. "Manufactured Scientific Controversy: Science, Rhetoric, and Public Debate." *Rhetoric & Public Affairs* 14(2): 195–228.

Charland, M. 1987. "Constitutive Rhetoric: The Case of the Peuple Québécois." *Quarterly Journal of Speech* 73(2): 133–50.

Cheney, R. 2002, August 26. "Vice President Cheney's Speech to the Veterans of Foreign Wars." *Project for the New American Century*. Available: http://www.newamericancentury.org/iraq-082602.htm.

Cheng, M. S. 2012. "Colin Powell's Speech to the UN: A Discourse Analytic Study of Reconstituted Ethos." *Rhetoric Society Quarterly* 42(5): 424–49.

Chilton, P. 1987. "Metaphor, Euphemism, and the Militarization of Language." *Current Research on Peace and Violence* 10: 7–19.

Chivers, C. J. 2003, February 6. "Kurds Puzzled by Report of Terror Camp." *New York Times*, A22.

Cisneros, J. D. 2008. "Contaminated Communities: The Metaphor of 'Immigrant as Pollutant' in Media Representations of Immigration." *Rhetoric & Public Affairs* 11(4): 569–601.

Clark, R. 2004, January 29. "Letter from Mr. Ramsey Clark to the Secretary-General of the United Nations." *I.P.O. Information Service*. Retrieved January 30, 2013, from http://i-p-o.org/ipo-nr-iraq-clark-29jan04.htm.

CNN/*USA Today*/Gallup. 2003, February 5. "Colin Powell's U.N. Speech Impact." In *The Gallup Poll: Public Opinion 2003*, 51–52. Lanham, MD: Rowman & Littlefield.

Colistra, R. 2012. "Shaping and Cutting the Media Agenda: Television Reporters' Perceptions of Agenda- and Frame-Building and Agenda-Cutting Influences." *Journalism & Communication Monographs* 14(2): 85–146.

Combs, J. E., and M. W. Mansfield, eds. 1976. *Drama in Life: The Uses of Communication in Society*. New York: Hastings House.

Condit, C. M., and J. A. Selzer. 1985. "The Rhetoric of Objectivity in the Newspaper Coverage of a Murder Trial." *Critical Studies in Mass Communication* 2: 197–216.

Consigny, S. 1974. "Rhetoric and Its Situations." *Philosophy and Rhetoric* 7: 175–86.

Cook, T. 1998. *Governing with the News: The News Media as a Political Institution*. Chicago: University of Chicago Press.

Cramer, P. A. 2008. "Controversy as a Media Event Category." In *Rhetoric in Detail: Analyses of Rhetorical Text and Talk*, ed. B. Johnstone and C. Eisenhart, 279–305. Amsterdam: John Benjamins.

Crismore, A., and R. Farnsworth. 1989. "Mr. Darwin and His Readers: Exploring Interpersonal Metadiscourse as a Dimension of Ethos." *Rhetoric Review* 8(1): 91–112.

D'Alessio, D., and M. Allen. 2000. "Media Bias in Presidential Elections: A Meta-analysis." *Journal of Communication* 50(4): 133–56.

D'Angelo, F. 2009. "The Rhetoric of Intertextuality." *Rhetoric Review* 29(1): 31–47.

Daniel, S. L. 2002. "Integrating Rhetoric and Journalism to Realize Publics." *Rhetoric & Public Affairs* 5(3): 507–24.

Dauber, C. E. 2001. "The 'Shot Seen Round the World': The Impact of the Images of Mogadishu on American Military Operations." *Rhetoric & Public Affairs* 4(4): 653–87.

Demo, A. T. 2007. "The Afterimage: Immigration Policy after Elián." *Rhetoric & Public Affairs* 10(1): 27–49.

Dennis, E. E. 1997. "How 'Liberal' Are the Liberal Media, Anyway? The Continuing Conflict of Professionalism and Partisanship." *Press/Politics* 2: 115–19.

Devitt, A. J. 1991. "Intertextuality in Tax Accounting: Generic, Referential, and Functional." In *Textual Dynamics of the Professions: Historical and Contemporary Studies of Writing in Professional Communities*, ed. C. Bazerman and J. Paradis, 336–57. Madison: University of Wisconsin Press.

DeYoung, K. 2007. *Soldier: The Life of Colin Powell*. New York: Vintage Books.

Domke, D. S. 2004. *God Willing? Political Fundamentalism in the White House, The "War on Terror," and the Echoing Press.* London: Pluto Press.

Donaldson, S. 1989, August 11. *ABC World News Tonight*.

Drew, P., and J. Heritage. 1992. "Analyzing Talk at Work: An Introduction." In *Talk at Work: Interaction in Institutional Settings*, ed. P. Drew and J. Heritage, 3–61. New York: Cambridge University Press.

Dunmire, P. 1997. "Naturalizing the Future in Factual Discourse: A Critical Linguistic Analysis of a Projected Event." *Written Communication* 14: 221–63.

———. 2005. "Preempting the Future: Rhetoric and Ideology of the Future in Political Discourse." *Discourse & Society* 16(4): 481–513.

———. 2008. "The Rhetoric of Temporality: The Future as Linguistic Construct and Rhetorical Resource." In *Rhetoric in Detail: Analyses of Rhetorical Text and Talk*, ed. B. Johnstone and C. Eisenhar, 81–112. Amsterdam: John Benjamins.

———. 2009. "'9/11 Changed Everything': An Intertextual Analysis of the Bush Doctrine." *Discourse & Society* 20(2): 195–222.

———. 2010. "Knowing and Controlling the Future: A Review of *Futurology*." *Prose Studies* 32(3): 240–63.

———. 2011. *Projecting the Future through Political Discourse: The Case of the Bush Doctrine*. Amsterdam: John Benjamins.

Edbauer, J. 2005. "Unframing Models of Public Distribution: From Rhetorical Situation to Rhetorical Ecologies." *Rhetoric Society Quarterly* 35: 5–24.

Edelman, M. 1977. *Language and Politics*. New York: Academic Press.

———. 1985. *The Symbolic Uses of Politics.* Urbana: University of Illinois Press.

———. 1988. *Constructing the Political Spectacle*. Chicago: University of Chicago Press.

Eisenberg, D. 2002, May 6. "We're Taking Him Out." *CNN.com*. Available: http://archives.cnn.com/2002/ALLPOLITICS/05/06/time.out/.

Eisenhart, C. 2008. "Reporting Waco: The Constitutive Work of Bureaucratic Style." In *Rhetoric in Detail: Analyses of Rhetorical Text and Talk*, ed. B. Johnstone and C. Eisenhart, 57–79. Amsterdam: John Benjamins.

Eisenhart, C., and B. Johnstone. 2008. "Discourse Analysis and Rhetorical Studies." In *Rhetoric in Detail: Analyses of Rhetorical Text and Talk*, B. Johnstone and C. Eisenhart, 3–21. Amsterdam: John Benjamins.

Ellis, R. 2003, February 25. "The Surrender of MSNBC." *allyourtv.com*. Retrieved March 1, 2014, from: https://www.commondreams.org/views03/0226-11.htm.

Engel, M. 2002, May 17. "US Media Cowed by Patriotic Fever, Says CBS Star: Network News Veteran Admits National Mood Caused Him to Shrink from Tough Questions on War in Afghanistan." *The Guardian*. Available: http://www.guardian.co.uk/media/2002/may/17/terrorismandthemedia.broadcasting.

Englebretson, R., ed. 2007. *Stancetaking in Discourse*. Amsterdam: John Benjamins.

Entman, R. M. 1993. "Framing: Toward a Clarification of a Fractured Paradigm." *Journal of Communication* 43(4): 51–58.

———. 2003. "Cascading Activation: Contesting the White House's Frame after 9/11." *Political Communication* 20(4): 415–32.

———. 2004. *Projections of Power: Framing News, Public Opinion, and U.S. Foreign Policy*. Chicago: University of Chicago Press.

———. 2007. "Framing Bias: Media in the Distribution of Power." *Journal of Communication* 57: 163–73.

Entman, R. M., and B. Page. 1994. "The News before the Storm: Limits to Media Autonomy in Covering the Iraq War Debate." In *Taken by Storm: The Media, Public Opinion, and U.S. Foreign Policy in the Gulf War*, ed. W. L. Bennett and D. L. Paletz, 82–101. Chicago: University of Chicago Press.

Erickson, K. V. 1989. "Presidential Leaks: Rhetoric and Mediated Political Knowledge." *Communication Monographs* 56(3): 199–214.

"Ex-Aide: Powell Misled Americans." 2003, October 15. *CBS News*. Retrieved April 13, 2013, from http://www.commondreams.org/headlines03/1015-01.htm.

Fahnestock, J. 1986. "Accommodating Science: The Rhetorical Life of Scientific Facts." *Written Communication* 3(3): 275–96.

———. 2011. *Rhetorical Style: The Uses of Language in Persuasion*. New York: Oxford University Press.

Fairclough, I., and N. Fairclough. 2012. *Political Discourse Analysis: A Method for Advanced Students*. London: Routledge.

Fairclough, N. 1989. *Language and Power*. London: Longman.

———. 1992a. "Discourse and Text: Linguistic and Intertextual Analysis within Discourse Analysis." *Discourse and Society* 3: 193–217.

———. 1992b. *Discourse and Social Change*. Cambridge: Polity Press.

———. 1995. *Media Discourse*. New York: Arnold.

———. 2003. *Analyzing Discourse: Textual Analysis for Social Research*. London: Routledge.

———. 2004. "Critical Discourse Analysis in Researching Language in the New Capitalism: Overdetermination, Transdisciplinary and Textual Analysis." In *Systemic Functional Linguistics and Critical Discourse Analysis: Studies in Social Change*, eds. L. Young and C. Harrison, 123–38. London: Continuum.

———. 2010. *Critical Discourse Analysis: The Critical Study of Language*. 2nd ed. Harlow: Pearson Education.

Fairness and Accuracy in Reporting. 2003, March 18. "In Iraq Crisis, Networks Are Megaphones for Official Views." Available: http://www.fair.org/reports/iraq-sources.html.

Farmer, F., ed. 1998. *Landmark Essays on Bakhtin, Rhetoric, and Writing*. Mahwah, NJ: Lawrence Erlbaum.

Fine, E. C. 1984. *The Folklore Text: From Performance to Print*. Bloomington: Indiana University Press.

Finn, J. 2010. "Powell's Point: 'Denial and Deception' at the U.N." *Visual Communication* 9(1): 25–49.

Firestone, D. 2003, February 6. "Powell Gets Good Reviews, but Few Stands Are Changed." *New York Times*, A22.

Fisher, I. 2003, February 5. "A Diverse Band of Volunteers Sends a Warning to America." *New York Times*.

Fisher, W. 1984. "Narration as a Human Communication Paradigm: The Case of Public Moral Argument." *Communication Monographs* 51: 1–22.

Fleischman, S. 1982. *The Future in Thought and Language*. Cambridge: Cambridge University Press.

Foss, S. K. 1994. "A Rhetorical Schema for the Evaluation of Visual Imagery." *Communication Studies* 45: 213–24.

———. 2009. *Rhetorical Criticism: Exploration and Practice*. 4th ed. Long Grove, IL: Waveland Press.

Foucault, M. 1972. *The Archaeology of Knowledge*. London: Tavistock.

Fowler, R. 1991. *Language in the News*. London: Routledge.

Friedman, B. 2013, February 26. "Powell's Chief of Staff: Iraq Intel Was 'Outright Lies,' but Powell Didn't 'Knowingly Lie' at UN." Retrieved April 18, 2003, from http://truth-out.org/news/item/14799-powells-chief-of-staff-iraq-intel-was-outright-lies-but-powell-didnt-knowingly-lie-at-un.

Gaiter, D. J., and G. F. Seib. 1995, November 7. "Moral Authority: Many Voters Believe Powell Could Bridge the Nation's Racial Divide." *Wall Street Journal*, A1.

Gans, H. 1979. *Deciding What's News*. New York: Vintage Books.

Gardner, L. 2010. "The Ministry of Fear: Selling the Gulf Wars." In *Selling War in a Media Age: The Presidency and Public Opinion in the American Century*, ed. K. Osgood and A. K. Frank, 224–49. Gainesville: University Press of Florida.

Garver, E. 1994. *Aristotle's* Rhetoric: *An Art of Character*. Chicago: University of Chicago Press.

Gasher, M. 2003. "News Reportage in the War in Iraq." In *Bring [ap]Em On: Media and Politics in the Iraq War*, ed. L Artz and Y. R. Kamalipour, 209–24. New York: Rowman and Littlefield.

Gee, J. P. 2005. *An Introduction to Discourse Analysis: Theory and Method*. London: Routledge.

Geisler, C. 2004. *Analyzing Streams of Language: Twelve Steps to Systematic Coding of Text, Talk, and Other Verbal Data*. New York: Pearson Longman.

Gershkoff, A., and S. Kushner. 2005. "Shaping Public Opinion: The 9/11 Connection in the Bush Administration's Rhetoric." *Perspectives on Politics* 3(3): 525–37.

Gilbert, N. 1977. "Referencing as Persuasion." *Social Studies of Science* 7: 113–22.

Gillespie, M. 2001, March 27. "Powell Leads List of Popular Public Speakers." Retrieved January 15, 2013, from http://www.gallup.com/poll/1864/powell-leads-list-popular-public-speakers.aspx.

Gitlin, T. 1980. *The Whole World Is Watching: News Media in the Making and Unmaking of the New Left*. Berkley: University of California Press.

Glaister, D. 2004, June 14. "High Profile Air Strikes 'Killed Only Civilians.'" *The Guardian*. Available: http://www.guardian.co.uk/world/2004/jun/14/iraq.usa.

Glaser, B., and A. Strauss. 1967. *The Discovery of Grounded Theory: Strategies for Qualitative Research*. Chicago: Aldine.

Glasgow University Media Group. 1976. *Bad News*. London: Routledge.

———. 1985. *War and Peace News*. Philadelphia: Open University Press.

Golan, G. 2006. "Inter-media Agenda Setting and Global News Coverage: Assessing the Influence of the *New York Times* on Three Network Television Evening News Programs." *Journalism Studies* 7(2): 323–33.

Goffman, E. 1974. *Frame Analysis*. New York: Harper and Row.

Goodman, M. 2006. Interview with *Frontline*. *PBS.org*. Retrieved April 18, 2013, from http://www.pbs.org/wgbh/pages/frontline/darkside/themes/nie.html.

Goodnight, T. 2006. "Strategic Doctrine, Public Debate, and the Terror War." In *Hitting First: Preventive Force in U.S. Security Strategy*, ed. W. W. Keller and G. R. Mitchell, 93–114. Pittsburgh: University of Pittsburgh Press.

Goot, M. 2004. "Introduction: World Opinion Surveys and the War in Iraq." *International Journal of Public Opinion Research* 16(3): 239–68.

Gordon, M. R., and J. Miller. 2002, September 8. "U.S. Says Hussein Intensified Quest for A-bomb Parts." *New York Times*. Available: http://www.nytimes.com/2002/09/08/world/threats-responses-iraqis-us-says-hussein-intensifies-quest-for-bomb-parts.html.

Graber, D. 1989. *Mass Media and American Politics*. 3rd ed. Washington, DC: Congressional Quarterly Press.

Gramsci, A. 1971. *Selections from the Prison Notebooks*. London: Lawrence and Wishart.

"Greatest American Military General of All Time? Public Says Eisenhower, Patton, and MacArthur." 2000, December 8. Retrieved January 15, 2013, from http://www.gallup.com/poll/2236/greatest-american-military-general-all-time-public-says-patton.aspx.

Greimas, A. J. 1971. "Narrative Grammar: Units and Levels." *MLN* 86: 793–806.

Greimas, A. J., and C. Porter. 1977. "Elements of a Narrative Grammar." *Diacritics* 7: 23–40.

Gronbeck, B. E. 1997. "Tradition and Technology in Local Newscasts: The Social Psychology of Form." *Sociological Quarterly* 38(2): 361–74.

Gross, K., and L. D'Ambrosio. 2004. "Framing Emotional Response." *Political Psychology* 25(1): 1–29.

Gross, A. G., and R. D. Dearin. 2003. *Chaim Perelman*. Albany: State University of New York Press.

Grusin, R. 2010. *Premediation: Affect and Mediality after 9/11*. New York: Palgrave Macmillan.

Haas, C., and S. P. Witte. 1998, April. "Using the Grounded Theory Approach to Manage Tensions between Data and Claim in Studies of Situated Literacy." Paper presented at the American Educational Research Association Annual Meeting, San Diego, CA.

Habermas, J. 1976. *Legitimation Crisis*. Trans. Thomas McCarthy. London: Heinemann.

Hagan, S. 2007. "Visual/Verbal Collaboration in Print: Complementary Differences, Necessary Ties, and an Untapped Rhetorical Opportunity." *Written Communication* 24(1): 49–83.

Hall, S. 1982. "The Rediscovery of Ideology: Return of the Repressed in Media Studies." In *Culture, Society and the Media*, ed. M. Gurevitch, T. Bennett, J. Curran, and J. Woolacott, 56–90. London: Methuen.

———. 1997. "The Work of Representation." In *Representation: Cultural Representations and Signifying Practices*, ed. S. Hall, 13–74. London: Sage Publications.

Halliday, M. A. K. 1978. *Language as Social Semiotic*. Baltimore: University Park Press.

———. 1985. *An Introduction to Functional Grammar*. London: Edward Arnold.

———. 1989. "Part A." In *Language, Context, and Text: Aspects of Language in a Social Semiotic Perspective*, by M. A. K. Halliday and R. Hasan, 2nd ed., 1–49. Oxford: Oxford University Press.

Halliday, M. A. K., and C. Matthiessen. 2004. *An Introduction to Functional Grammar*. London: Hodder Education.

Hallin, D. 1986. *The Uncensored War: The Media and Vietnam*. Berkeley: University of California Press.

———. 1987. "Hegemony: The American News Media from Vietnam to El Salvador, a Study in Ideological Change and Limits." In *Political Communication Research*, ed. D. Paletz, 3–25. Norwood, NJ: Ablex.

———. 1994. "The Media, the War in Vietnam, and Political Support: A Critique of the Thesis of an Oppositional Media." In *We Keep America on Top of the World: Television Journalism and the Public Sphere*, ed. D. C. Hallin, 40–57. New York: Routledge.

Hallin, D. C., R. K. Manoff, and J. K. Weddle. 1993. "Sourcing Patterns of National Security Reporters." *Journalism Quarterly* 70: 753–66.

Halloran, M. 1982. "Aristotle's Concept of Ethos, or If Not His Somebody Else's." *Rhetoric Review* 1: 58–63.

Hanley, C. 2003, August 11. "Powell's Case for Iraq War Falls Apart 6 Months Later." Associated Press. Available: http://www.commondreams.org/headlines03/0811-09.htm.

Haridakis, P., B. S. Hugenberg, and S. T. Wearden, eds. 2009. *War and the Media: Essays on News Reporting, Propaganda, and Popular Culture*. Jefferson, NC: McFarland.

Hariman, R., and J. L. Lucaites. 2002. "Performing Civic Identity: The Iconic Photograph of the Flag Raising at Iwo Jima." *Quarterly Journal of Speech* 88: 363–92.

———. 2007. *No Caption Needed: Iconic Photographs, Public Culture, and Liberal Democracy*. Chicago: University of Chicago Press.

Harmon, M., and R. Muenchen. 2009. "Semantic Framing in the Build-up to the Iraq War: Fox v. CNN and Other U.S. Broadcast News Programs." *ETC: A General Review of Semantics* 66(1): 12–26.

Harold, C., and K. M. DeLuca. 2005. "Behold the Corpse: Violent Images and the Case of Emmett Till." *Rhetoric & Public Affairs* 8(2): 263–86.

Hart, R. P. 1987. *The Sound of Leadership: Presidential Communication in the Modern Era*. Chicago: University of Chicago Press.

Hatzenbuehler, R. L., and R. L. Ivie. 1983. *Congress Declares War: Rhetoric, Leadership, and Partisanship in the Early Republic*. Kent, OH: Kent State University Press.

Hasan, R. 1989. "Part B." In *Language, Context, and Text: Aspects of Language in a Social Semiotic Perspective*, by M. A. K. Halliday and Ruqaiya Hasan, 2nd ed., 51–118. Oxford: Oxford University Press.

Hayes, D., and M. Guardino. 2010. "Whose Views Made the News? Media Coverage and the March to War in Iraq." *Political Communication* 27(1): 59–87.

Herman, E. S., and N. Chomsky. 1988. *Manufacturing Consent: The Political Economy of the Mass Media*. New York: Pantheon.

Herndl, C., B. Fennell, and C. Miller. 1991. "Understanding Failures in Organizational Discourse: The Accident at Three Mile Island and the Shuttle Challenger Disaster." In *Textual Dynamics of the Professions*, ed. C. Bazerman and J. Paradis, 279–330. Madison: University of Wisconsin Press.

Herrick, J. A. 2005. *The History and Theory of Rhetoric: An Introduction*. 3rd ed. Boston: Pearson Education.

Hibbitts, B. 2003, March 18. "International Commission of Jurists Dismayed at Move towards Iraq War." *Jurist*. Retrieved January 30, 2013, from http://jurist.org/paperchase/2003/03/international-commission-of-jurists.php.

Hill, C. A. 2004. "The Psychology of Rhetorical Images." In *Defining Visual Rhetorics*, ed. C. A. Hill and M. Helmers, 25–40. Mahwah, NJ: Lawrence Erlbaum.

Hill, C. A., and M. Helmers, eds. 2004. *Defining Visual Rhetorics*. Mahwah, NJ: Lawrence Erlbaum.

Hitchens, C. 2000, December 27. "The Case against Powell." *Globe and Mail* (Canada), A21.

Hodge, R., and G. Kress. 1988. *Social Semiotics*. Ithaca, NY: Cornell University Press.

Hodges, A. 2008a. "The Politics of Recontextualization: Discursive Competition over Claims of Iranian Involvement in Iraq." *Discourse & Society* 19(4): 483–505.

———. 2008b. "The Dialogic Emergence of 'Truth' in Politics: Reproduction and Subversion of the 'War on Terror' Discourse." *Colorado Research in Linguistics* 21: 1–12.

———. 2011. *The "War on Terror" Narrative: Discourse and Intertextuality in the Construction and Contestation of Sociopolitical Reality*. New York: Oxford University Press.

Hodges, A., and C. Nilep. 2007. "Introduction." In *Discourse, War and Terrorism*, ed. A. Hodges and C. Nilep, 1–17. Philadelphia: John Benjamins.

Hofstede, G. 2001. *Culture's Consequences: Comparing Values, Behaviors, Institutions and Organizations across Nations.* 2nd ed. London: Sage.

Hopper, P. 2007. "Linguistics and Micro-rhetoric: A Twenty-First Century Encounter." *Journal of English Linguistics* 35(3): 236–52.

Houck, D. W. 2005. "Killing Emmett." *Rhetoric & Public Affairs* 8(2): 225–62.

Hoyle, R. 2008. *Going to War: How Misinformation, Disinformation, and Arrogance Led America into Iraq*. New York: Thomas Dunne Books.

Huber, J. 2003. "Sleepwalking Democrats and American Public Support for Bush's Attack on Iraq." *Constellations* 10(3): 392–407.

Huckin, T. 1997. "Critical Discourse Analysis." In *Functional Approaches to Written Text*, ed. T. Miller, 78–92. Washington, DC: US Information Agency.

———. 2002. "Textual Silence and the Discourse of Homelessness." *Discourse & Society* 13(3): 347–72.

Huckin, T., J. Andrus, and J. Clary-Lemon. 2012. "Critical Discourse Analysis and Rhetoric and Composition." *College Composition and Communication* 64(1): 107–29.

Hunston, S., and G. Thompson, eds. 2000. *Evaluation in Text: Authorial Stance and the Construction of Discourse*. New York: Oxford University Press.

Hutcheson, J., D. Domke, M. A. Billeaudeaux, and P. Garland. 2004. "U.S. National Identity, Political Elites, and a Patriotic Press Following September 11." *Political Communication* 21: 27–51.

Hybel, A., and J. Kaufman. 2006. *The Bush Administrations and Saddam Hussein: Deciding on Conflict*. New York: Palgrave Macmillan.

Hyde, M. J. 2004a. "Introduction: Rhetorically We Dwell." In *The* Ethos *of Rhetoric*, ed. M. J. Hyde, xii–xxviii. Columbia: University of South Carolina Press.

———, ed. 2004b. *The* Ethos *of Rhetoric*. Columbia: University of South Carolina Press.

Hyland, K. 2004. "A Convincing Argument: Corpus Analysis and Academic Persuasion." In *Discourse in the Professions: Perspectives from Corpus*

Linguistics, ed. U. Connor and T. A. Upton, 87–112. Amsterdam: John Benjamins.

Hymes, D. H. 1981. *"In Vain I Tried to Tell You": Essays in Native American Ethnopoetics*. Philadelphia: University of Pennsylvania Press.

Iedema, R. 2003. "Multimodality, Resemiotization: Extending the Analysis of Discourse as Multi-semiotic Practice." *Visual Communication* 2(1): 29–57.

Iedema, R., S. Feez, and P. R. R. White. 1994. "Appraisal and Journalistic Discourse." Excerpted from *Media Literacy*. Sydney, Disadvantaged Schools Program, NSW Department of School Education. Available: http://www.grammatics.com/appraisal/MediaLit-Appraise.pdf.

"In Their Words: The Security Council." 2003, February 6. *New York Times*. A21.

"Iraq's Response: 'Incorrect Allegations.'" 2003, February 6. *New York Times*. A21.

"Irrefutable." (Editorial). 2003, February 6. *Washington Post*. Available: http://www.washingtonpost.com/ac2/wp-dyn/A32515-2003Feb5?language=printer.

Ishizaki, S., and D. Kaufer. 2012. "Computer-Aided Rhetorical Analysis." In *Applied Natural Language Processing: Identification, Investigation, and Resolution*, ed. P. M. McCarthy and C. Boonthum-Denecke, 276–96. Hershey, PA: Information Science Reference.

Isikoff, M., and D. Corn. 2006. *Hubris*. New York: Crown.

Isocrates. 1929. *Antidosis*. Trans. G. Norlin. London: Loeb Classical Library.

Ivie, R. L. 1980. "Images of Savagery in American Justifications for War." *Communication Monographs* 47: 279–94.

———. 1987. "Metaphor and the Rhetorical Invention of Cold War Idealists." *Communication Monographs* 54(2): 165–82.

———. 2005. *Democracy and America's War on Terror*. Tuscaloosa: University of Alabama Press.

Iyengar, S. 1991. *Is Anyone Responsible?* Chicago: University of Chicago Press.

Iyengar, S., and D. R. Kinder. 1987. *News That Matters*. Chicago: University of Chicago Press.

Iyengar, S., and A. Simon. 1993. "News Coverage of the Gulf Crisis and Public Opinion: A Study of Agenda-Setting, Priming, and Framing." *Communication Research* 20: 365–83.

Jaffe, A., ed. 2009. *Stance: Sociolinguistic Perspectives*. New York: Oxford University Press.

Jamieson, K. H. 1975. "Antecedent Genre as Rhetorical Constraint." *Quarterly Journal of Speech* 61: 406–15.

———. 1984. *Packaging the Presidency: A History and Criticism of Presidential Advertising*. New York: Oxford University Press.

———. 1988. *Eloquence in an Electronic Age*. New York: Oxford University Press.

———. 2007. "Justifying the War in Iraq: What the Bush Administration's Uses of Evidence Reveal." *Rhetoric & Public Affairs* 10(2): 249–74.

Jamieson, K. H., and P. Waldman. 2003. *The Press Effect: Politicians, Journalists and the Stories That Shape the Political World*. New York: Oxford University Press.

Jasinski, J. 1997a. "Heteroglossia, Polyphony, and the *Federalist Papers*." *Rhetoric Society Quarterly* 27(1): 23–46.

———. 1997b. "Instrumentalism, Contextualism, and Interpretation in Rhetorical Criticism." In *Rhetorical Hermeneutics: Invention and Interpretation in the Age of Science*, ed. A. Gross and W. M. Keith, 195–224. Albany: State University of New York Press.

———. 2001. *Sourcebook on Rhetoric: Key Concepts in Contemporary Rhetorical Studies*. Thousand Oaks, CA: Sage.

Jaworski, A., and R. Fitzgerald. 2008. "'This Poll Hasn't Happened Yet': Temporal Play in Election Predictions." *Discourse and Communication* 2(1): 5–27.

Jaworski, A., R. Fitzgerald, and D. Morris. 2003. "Certainty and Speculation in News Reporting of the Future: The Execution of Timothy McVeigh." *Discourse Studies* 5(1): 33–49.

John, S. L., D. Domke, K. Coe, and E. S. Graham. 2007. "Going Public, Crisis after Crisis: The Bush Administration and the Press from September 11 to Saddam." *Rhetoric & Public Affairs* 10(2): 195–220.

Johnson, N. 1984. "Ethos and the Aims of Rhetoric." In *Essays on Classical Rhetoric and Modern Discourse*, ed. R. J. Connnors, L. Ede, and A. Lunsford, 98–114. Carbondale: Southern Illinois University Press.

Johnson-Cartee, K. S. 2005. *News Narratives and News Framing: Constructing Political Reality*. Lanham, MD: Rowman and Littlefield.

Johnstone, B. 2008. *Discourse Analysis*. 2nd ed. Malden, MA: Blackwell.

Johnstone, B., and C. Eisenhart, eds. 2008. *Rhetoric in Detail: Discourse Analyses of Rhetorical Talk and Text*. Philadelphia: John Benjamins.

Kahneman, D., and A. Taversky. 1984. "Choices, Values and Frames." *American Psychologist* 39: 341–50.

Kaufer, D. S., and B. Butler. 2000. *Designing Interactive Worlds with Words: Principles of Writing as Representational Composition*. Mahwah, NJ: Lawrence Erlbaum.

Kaufer, D. S., and K. M. Carley. 1993. *Communication at a Distance: The Influence of Print on Sociocultural Organization and Change*. Hillsdale, NJ: Lawrence Erlbaum.

Kaufer, D. S., S. Ishizaki., B. Butler, and J. Collins. 2004. *The Power of Words: Unveiling the Speaker and Writer's Hidden Craft*. Mahwah, NJ: Lawrence Erlbaum.

Kaufer, D. S., S. J. Parry-Giles, and B. Beigman Kelbanov. 2012. "The 'Image Bite,' Political Language, and the Public/Private Divide: NBC News Coverage of Hillary Clinton from Scorned Wife to Senate Candidate." *Journal of Language and Politics* 11(3): 336–56.

Kelland, K. 2011, February 16. "Civilian Death Study Rates 'Dirty War' in Iraq." Reuters. Retrieved from: http://www.reuters.com.

Keller, W. W., and G. R. Mitchell, eds. 2006a. *Hitting First: Preventive Force in U.S. Security Strategy*. Pittsburgh: University of Pittsburgh Press.

———. 2006b. "Preemption, Prevention, Prevarication." In *Hitting First: Preventive Force in U.S. Security Strategy*, ed. W. W. Keller and G. R. Mitchell, 3–26. Pittsburgh: University of Pittsburgh Press.

———. 2006c. "Preventive Force: Untangling the Discourse. In *Hitting First: Preventive Force in U.S. Security Strategy*, ed. W. W. Keller and G. R. Mitchell, 239–63. Pittsburgh: University of Pittsburgh Press.

Kellner, D. 2001. *Grand Theft 2000: Media Spectacle and a Stolen Election*. Lanham, MD: Rowman and Littlefield.

Kellner, D., and J. Share. 2005. "Toward Critical Media Literacy: Core Concepts, Debates, Organizations, and Policy." *Discourse: Studies in the Cultural Politics of Education* 26(3): 369–86.

Kelly, M. L. 2010, June 28. "Byrd's Legacy: 18,000 Votes Later, He Loved His Job." *npr.org*. Available: http://www.npr.org/templates/story/story.php?storyId=128159605.

Kennedy, G. 2007. *Aristotle: On Rhetoric—a Theory of Civic Discourse*. New York: Oxford University Press.

Kernell, S. 1997. *Going Public: New Strategies of Presidential Leadership*. 3rd ed. Washington, DC: Congressional Quarterly.

Kessler, G., and W. Pincus. 2004, February 1. "A Flawed Argument in the Case for War." *Washington Post*, A1.

Key, I. 2000, December 18. "The Unstoppable Rise of Colin Powell, the All-American Hero; Has This Little Boy Become the Most Powerful Man in the World?" *The Express*, 8.

Kibby, L. 2001, September 27. "Leader: America's Military Hero Is Fighting His Toughest Battle—for Moderation; Colin Powell: A Dove among Hawks in the War Cabinet." *The Express*, 11.

Kim, S. H., D. A. Scheufele, and J. Shanahan. 2002. "Think about It This Way: Attribute Agenda-Setting Function of the Press and the Public's Evaluation of a Local Issue." *Journalism & Mass Communication Quarterly* 79(1): 7–25.

Kinder, D. R., and L. M. Sanders. 1996. *Divided by Color: Racial Politics and Democratic Ideals*. Chicago: University of Chicago Press.

King, J., and D. Ensor. 2003, February 6. "Powell: Iraq Hiding Weapons, Aiding Terrorists; Annan: War Not Inevitable." *CNN.com*. Available: http://cgi.cnn.com/2003/US/02/05/sprj.irq.powell.un/index.html.

King, J., D. Ensor, J. McIntyre, and C. Plante. 2003, March 20. "'Decapitation Strike' Was Aimed at Saddam." *CNN.com*. Available: http://articles.cnn.com/2003-03-20/world/sprj.irq.target.saddam_1_saddam-hussein-targets-of-military-importance-strike?_s=PM:WORLD.

Klaehn, J. 2002. "A Critical Assessment of Herman and Chomsky's 'Propaganda Model.'" *European Journal of Communication* 17(2): 147–82.

Klein, J. 1994. "Can Colin Powell Save America?" *Newsweek* 124(15): 20.

Klumpp, J. F. 2005. "Facts, Truth, and Iraq: A Call to Stewardship of Democratic Argument." *Engaging Argument: Selected Papers from the 2005 NCA/AFA Summer Conference on Argumentation*. 1–17.

Kress, G. R. 1993. "Against Arbitrariness: The Social Production of the Sign as a Foundational Issue in Critical Discourse Analysis." *Discourse & Society* 4(2): 169–91.

———. 2003. *Literacy in the New Media Age*. London: Routledge.

———. 2005. "Gains and Losses: New Forms of Texts, Knowledge, and Learning." *Computers and Composition* 22: 5–22.

———. 2010. *Multimodality: A Social Semiotic Approach to Contemporary Communication*. New York: Routledge.

Kress, G. R., and T. Van Leeuwen. 1996. *Reading Images: The Grammar of Visual Design*. London: Routledge.

———. 2001. *Multimodal Discourse: The Modes and Media of Contemporary Communication*. London: Arnold.

Kristeva, J. 1980. *Desire in Language: A Semiotic Approach to Literature and Art*. New York: Columbia University Press.

Kumar, D. 2006. "Media, War, and Propaganda: Strategies of Information Management during the 2003 Iraq War." *Communication and Critical/Cultural Studies* 3(1): 48–69.

Kumar, M. J. 2007. *Managing the President's Message: The White House Communications Operation*. Baltimore: John Hopkins University Press.

Kurtz, H. 1995, September 13. "Pressing for Powell: A General Trend; News Media Embrace Would-be Candidate in a Gush of Boosterism." *Washington Post*, A01.

Kuypers, J. A. 2002. *Press Bias and Politics: How the Media Frame Controversial Issues*. Westport, CT: Praeger.

———. 2006. *Bush's War: Media Bias and Justifications for War in a Terrorist Age*. Lanham, MD: Rowman and Littlefield.

Lakoff, G., and M. Johnson. 1980. *Metaphors We Live By*. Chicago: University of Chicago Press.

Lane, C. 1995, April 17. "The Legend of Colin Powell." *New Republic*, 20.

LaRacey, M. 2008. "The Presidential Newspaper as an Engine of Early American Political Development: The Case of Thomas Jefferson and the Election of 1800." *Rhetoric & Public Affairs* 11(1): 7–46.

Latour, B. 1987. *Science in Action: How to Follow Scientists and Engineers through Society*. Cambridge: Harvard University Press.

Latour, B., and S. Woolgar. 1986. *Laboratory Life: The Construction of Scientific Facts*. Princeton, NJ: Princeton University Press.

Lawrence, R. G. 2000. "Game-Framing the Issues: Tracing the Strategy Frame in Public Policy News." *Political Communication* 17(2): 93–114.

Layne, C. 1991. "Why the Gulf War Was Not in the National Interest." *Atlantic Monthly* 268(1): 55; 65–81.

Leff, M. 1992. "Things Made by Words: Reflections on Textual Criticism." *Quarterly Journal of Speech* 78: 223–31.

———. 2001. "Lincoln at Cooper Union: Neo-classical Criticism Revisited." *Western Journal of Communication* 65: 232–48.

———. 2009. "Perelman, Ad Hominem Argument, and Rhetorical Ethos." *Argumentation* 23: 301–11.

Leff, M., and G. P. Mohrmann. 1974. "Lincoln at Cooper Union: A Rhetorical Analysis of the Text. *Quarterly Journal of Speech* 60: 346–58.

Lemke, J. L. 1983. "Thematic Analysis: Systems, Structures, and Strategies." *Recherches Semiotiques/Semiotic Inquiry* 3(2): 159–87.

———. 1985. "Ideology, Intertextuality, and the Notion of Register." In *Systemic Perspectives on Discourse,* ed. J.D. Benson and W.S. Greaves, 275–94. Norwood, NJ: Ablex.

———. 1991. "Text Production and Dynamic Text Semantics." In *Functional and Systemic Linguistics: Approaches and Uses*, ed. E. Ventola, 23–38. Berlin: Mouton de Gruyter.

———. 1995a. "Intertextuality and Text Semantics." In *Discourse in Society: Systemic Functional Perspectives*, ed. Peter H. Fries and Michael Gregory, 85–114. Norwood, NJ: Ablex.

———. 1995b. *Textual Politics: Discourse and Social Dynamics*. London: Taylor & Francis.

———. 2002. "Travels in Hypermodality." *Visual Communication* 1: 299–325.

Leung, R. 2009, February 11. "The Man Who Knew." *cbsnews.com*. Retrieved April 11, 2013 from http://www.cbsnews.com/2100-500164_162-577975.

Lewis, R. L. 2001. *Effective Non-profit Management*. Gaithersburg, MD: Aspen.

Linell, P. 1998. "Discourse across Boundaries: On Recontextualizations and the Blending of Voices in Professional Discourse." *Text* 18(2): 143–57.

Livingston, S., and L. Robinson. 2006. "Strange Bedfellows: The Emergence of the Al Qaeda-Baathist News Frame Prior to the 2003 Invasion of Iraq." In *Leading to the 2003 Iraq War: The Global Media Debate*, ed. A.G. Nikolaev and E.A. Hakanen, 21–37. New York: Palgrave.

Lopez-Escobar, E., P. J. Llamas, M. McCombs, and F. R. Lennon. 1998. "Two Levels of Agenda Setting among Advertising and News in the 1995 Spanish General Elections." *Political Communication* 15(2): 225–38.

Luke, C. 1994. "Feminist Pedagogy and Critical Media Literacy." *Journal of Communication Inquiry* 18(2): 30–47.

———. 1997. *Technological Literacy*. Melbourne, Australia: National Languages & Literacy Institute.

Lule, J. 2004. "War and Its Metaphors: News Language and the Prelude to War in Iraq, 2003." *Journalism Studies* 5(2): 179–90.

MacAskill, E., and J. Borger. 2004, September 15. "Iraq War Was Illegal and Breached UN Charter, Says Annan." *The Guardian*. Retrieved January 30, 2013, from http://www.guardian.co.uk/world/2004/sep/16/iraq.iraq.

MacDonald, S. P. 2002. "Prose Styles, Genres, and Levels of Analysis." *Style* 36(4): 618–39.

MacRoberts, M. H., and B. R. MacRoberts. 1986. "Quantitative Measures of Communication in Science: A Study of the Formal Level." *Social Studies of Science* 16: 151–72.

Machin, D. 2007. *Introduction to Multimodal Analysis*. New York: Oxford University Press.

Maier, C. D. 2009. "Visual Evaluation in Film Trailers." *Visual Communication* 8(2): 159–80.

Maingueneau, D. 1999. "Ethos, Scenographie, Incorporation." In *Images de soi dans le discours. La construction de l'ethos*, ed. R. Amossy, 75–100. Lausanne: Delachaux et Niestle.

Manheim, J. 1991. *All of the People, All the Time: Strategic Communication and American Politics*. Armonk, NY: M. E. Sharpe.

Marlier, J. 1989. "Fifteen Minutes of Glory: A Burkean Analysis of Press Coverage of Oliver North's Testimony." *Political Communication and Persuasion* 6: 269–88.

Marr, I., G. Hamer Burke, S. Thibeault, and S. Wangsness, eds. 2003, February 6. "Powell Makes 'Persuasive' Case but Doesn't Sway the 'Unconvinced.'"

Retrieved February 11, 2013, from http://rejjy.freeshell.org/Foreign_Media_Reaction/2003/wwwh30260.html.

Martin, J. R. 2002. "Fair Trade: Negotiating Meaning in Multimodal Texts." In *The Semiotics of Writing: Transdisciplinary Perspectives on the Technology of Writing*, ed. P. Coppock 311–38. Turnhout, Belgium: Brepols.

Martin, J. R., and D. Rose. 2007. *Working with Discourse: Meaning beyond the Clause*. 2nd ed. London: Continuum.

Martin, J. R., and P. R. R. White. 2005. *The Language of Evaluation: Appraisal in English*. New York: Palgrave Macmillan.

Martín Rojo, L. 1995. "Division and Rejection: From the Personification of the Gulf Conflict to the Demonization of Saddam Hussein." *Discourse & Society* 6(1):49–80.

Matoesian, G. 2000. "Intertextual Authority in Reported Speech: Production Media in the Kennedy Smith Rape Trial." *Journal of Pragmatics* 32: 879–914.

McCarthy, C. 1995, October 3. "Powell's 'Journey' Pays No Heed to the Toll." *Washington Post*, C10.

McCarthy, M. 1988. "Some Vocabulary Patterns in Conversation." In *Vocabulary and Language Teaching*, ed. R. Carter and M. McCarthy, 181–200. London: Longman.

McClellan, S. 2008. *What Happened: Inside the Bush White House and Washington's Culture of Deception*. Philadelphia: Public Affairs.

McClintock, P. 2003, December 2. "NBC Leads Evening Newscasts in Viewers: Peacock Struts News Stuff; ABC Ties in Demo." *Variety*. Available: http://www.variety.com/article/VR1117896490?categoryid=14&s=h&p=0&cs=1.

McCombs, M. E. 2004. *Setting the Agenda: The Mass Media and Public Opinion*. Malden, MA: Blackwell.

McCombs, M. E., and D. L Shaw. 1972. "The Agenda-Setting Function of Mass Media." *Public Opinion Quarterly* 36: 176–87.

McFadden, R. D. 2003, February 16. "From New York to Melbourne, Cries for Peace." *New York Times*, A20.

McGee, M. C. 1980. "The 'Ideograph': A Link between Rhetoric and Ideology." *Quarterly Journal of Speech* 66: 1–16.

———. 1990. "Text, Context, and the Fragmentation of Contemporary Culture." *Western Journal of Speech Communication* 56: 91–111.

McKerrow, R. E. 1989. "Critical Rhetoric: Theory and Praxis." *Communication Monographs* 51: 91–111.

McLaughlin, J. 2006. "Interview with *Frontline*." *PBS.org*. Retrieved April 18, 2013, from http://www.pbs.org/wgbh/pages/frontline/darkside/interviews/mclaughlin.html.

McNair, S. 2011, October 17. "John Roberts Named Senior Correspondent for CBS News." *cbspressexpress.com*. Available: http://www.cbspressexpress.com/cbs-news/releases/view?id=29505.

Medhurst, M. J. 2004. "Religious Rhetoric and the Ethos of Democracy: A Case Study of the 2000 Presidential Campaign." In *The* Ethos *of Rhetoric*, ed. M. J. Hyde, 114–35. Columbia: University of South Carolina Press.

———. 2009. "Mitt Romney, 'Faith in America,' and the Dance of Religion and Politics in American Culture." *Rhetoric & Public Affairs* 12(2): 195–221.

Medhurst, M. J., R. L. Ivie, P. Wander, and R. L. Scott. 1997. *Cold War Rhetoric: Strategy, Metaphor, and Ideology.* 2nd ed. East Lansing: Michigan State University Press.

Mermin, J. 1997. "Television News and American Intervention in Somalia: The Myth of a Media-Driven Foreign Policy." *Political Science Quarterly* 112: 385–403.

———. 1999. *Debating War and Peace: Media Coverage of U.S. Intervention in the Post-Vietnam Era*. Princeton, NJ: Princeton University Press.

Miller, A. B. 1974. "Aristotle on Habit (*nθos*) and Character (*eθos*): Implications for the Rhetoric." *Speech Monographs* 41: 309–16.

Miller, C. R. 1984. "Genre as Social Action." *Quarterly Journal of Speech* 70: 151–67.

———. 2001. "Writing in a Culture of Simulation: *Ethos* Online." In *The Semiotics of Writing: Transdisciplinary Perspectives on the Technology of Writing*, ed. P. Coppock, 253–79. Turnhout, Belgium: Brepols.

Miller, J., and J. Preston. 2003, January 30. "Blix Says He Saw Nothing to Prompt a War." *New York Times*. Available: http://www.nytimes.com/2003/01/31/international/middleeast/31BLIX.html.

Mitchell, G. 2008, June 2. "Tom Brokaw Defends War Coverage: The 'Coverup' Continues." *Huffington Post*. Available: http://www.huffingtonpost.com/greg-mitchell/tom-brokaw-defends-war-co_b_104636.html.

Mitchell, M., and T. Mitchell. 2008. *The Spy Who Tried to Stop a War: Katherine Gun and the Secret Plot to Sanction the Iraq Invasion*. Sausalito, CA: PoliPoint Press.

Montgomery, M. 2007. *The Discourse of Broadcast News: A Linguistic Approach*. London: Routledge.

Moore, D. W. 2002, November 26. "Public: If Iraq Fails Inspections, Second U.N. Resolution Needed for War: Finding Weapons of Mass Destruction Not Enough Justification for War." Gallup News Service. Available:

http://www.gallup.com/poll/7303/public-iraq-fails-inspections-second-un-resolution-needed-war.aspx.

———. 2003, February 4. "Powell's U.N. Appearance Important to Public: Secretary of State Enjoys More Credibility on Iraq than Bush." Gallup News Service. Available: http://www.gallup.com/poll/7720/powells-un-appearance-important-public.aspx.

Moss, D. 1991, March 8. "Powell: Joint Chiefs Chair 'a Born Leader.'" *USA Today*, 4E.

Murphy, J. M. 1997. "Inventing Authority: Bill Clinton, Martin Luther King, Jr., and the Orchestration of Rhetorical Traditions." *Quarterly Journal of Speech* 83(1): 71–89.

———. 2001. "Mikhail Bakhtin and the Rhetorical Tradition." *Quarterly Journal of Speech* 87(3): 259–77.

New York Times Company. 2011. *New York Times* circulation data. Available: http://www.nytco.com/investors/financials/nyt-circulation.html.

Nikolaev, A. G., and E. A. Hakanen, eds. 2006. *Leading to the 2003 Iraq War: The Global Media Debate*. New York: Palgrave Macmillan.

Niven, D. 2002. *Tilt? The Search for Media Bias*. New York: Praeger.

O'Brien, T. 1990. *The Things They Carried*. New York: Random House.

Oddo, J. 2011. "War Legitimation Discourse: Representing 'Us' and 'Them' in Four U.S. Presidential Addresses." *Discourse & Society* 22(3): 287–314.

———. 2013. "Discourse-Based Methods across Texts and Semiotic Modes: Three Tools for Micro-rhetorical Analysis." *Written Communication* 30(3): 236–75. [Special issue on methodology]

———. 2014. "Variation and Continuity in Intertextual Rhetoric: From the 'War on Terror' to the 'Struggle against Violent Extremism.'" *Journal of Language and Politics* 13(3).

O'Halloran, K. L. 1999. "Interdependence, Interaction and Metaphor in Multisemiotic Texts." *Social Semiotics* 9(3): 317–54.

———. 2004. "Visual Semiosis in Film." In *Multimodal Discourse Analysis: Systemic Functional Perspectives*, ed. K. O'Halloran, 84–130. London: Continuum.

———. 2008. "Systemic Functional-Multimodal Discourse Analysis (SF-MDA): Constructing Ideational Meaning Using Language and Visual Imagery." *Visual Communication* 7(4): 443–75.

Olson, L. C. 2009. "Pictorial Representations of British America Resisting Rape: Rhetorical Re-circulation of a Print Series Portraying the Boston Port Bill of 1774." *Rhetoric & Public Affairs* 12(1): 1–35.

Olson, L. C., C. A. Finnegan, and D. S. Hope, eds. 2008. *Visual Rhetoric: A Reader in Communication and American Culture*. Newbury Park, CA: Sage.

O'Sullivan, C. D. 2009. *Colin Powell: American Power and Intervention from Vietnam to Iraq*. Lanham, MD: Rowman & Littlefield.

O'Toole, M. 1994. *The Language of Displayed Art*. London: Leicester University Press.

Ott, B. L., and E. Aoki. 2002. "The Politics of Negotiating Public Tragedy: Media Framing of the Matthew Shepard Murder." *Rhetoric & Public Affairs* 5(3): 483–505.

Ott, B. L., and C. Walter. 2000. "Intertextuality: Interpretive Practice and Textual Strategy." *Critical Studies in Media Communication* 17(4): 429–46.

Paletz, D. L., and R. M. Entman. 1981. *Media Power Politics*. New York: Free Press.

Pamuk, O. 2004. *Snow*. New York: Knopf.

Pan, Z., and G. M. Kosicki. 1993. "Framing Analysis: An Approach to News Discourse." *Political Communication* 10: 55–75.

Parry-Giles, S. J. 2000. "Mediating Hillary Rodham Clinton: Television News Practices and Image-Making in the Postmodern Age." *Critical Studies in Media Communication* 17(2): 205–26.

Paterson, C. 2005. "News Agency Dominance in International News on the Internet." In *Converging Media Diverging Politics: A Political Economy of News in the United States and Canada*, ed. D. Skinner, J. Compton, and M. Gasher, 145–64. Lexington: Rowman and Littlefield.

Patterson, T. E. 1993. *Out of Order: How the Decline of Political Parties and the Growing Power of the News Media Undermine the American Way of Electing Presidents*. New York: Knopf.

Patterson, T. E., and W. Donsbagh. 1996. "News Decisions: Journalists as Partisan Actors." *Political Communication* 13(4): 455–68.

Payne, R. 2006. "Deliberate before Striking First." In *Hitting First: Preventive Force in U.S. Security Strategy*, ed. W. W. Keller and G. R. Mitchell, 115–36. Pittsburgh: University of Pittsburgh Press.

Pellegrini, F. 2000, December 16. "Powell, Bush Has a Leadoff Hit." *Time Magazine*. Retrieved January 15, 2013, from http://www.time.com/time/nation/article/0,8599,92102,00.html.

Perelman, C., and L. Olbrechts-Tyteca. 1969. *The New Rhetoric: A Treatise on Argumentation*. Trans. J. Wilkinson and P. Weaver. Notre Dame, IN: University of Notre Dame Press.

Pew Research Center. 2001, November 21. "Terror Coverage Boost News Media's Images." Retrieved January 30, 2013, from http://www.people-press.org/2001/11/28/terror-coverage-boost-news-medias-images/.

———. 2003, March 18. "America's Image Further Erodes, Europeans Want Weaker Ties." Retrieved January 30, 2013, from http://www.people-press.org/2003/03/18/americas-image-further-erodes-europeans-want-weaker-ties/.

Plesch, D., and R. Norton-Taylor. 2003, June 1. "Transcripts Raise Alarm across NATO." *The Guardian*. Retrieved April 18, 2013, from http://www.guardian.co.uk/politics/2003/jun/02/uk.iraq.

"Poll Ranks NBC's Brokaw Most Trusted News Anchor." 2003, April 2. Available: http://www.usatoday.com/money/media/2003-04-02-trusted-anchors_x.htm.

Porter, J. E. 1986. "Intertextuality and the Discourse Community." *Rhetoric Review* 5: 34–47.

Powell, C. 2003, 5 February. "U.S. Secretary of State Colin Powell Addresses the U.N. Security Council." Available: http://georgewbush-whitehouse.archives.gov/news/releases/2003/02/20030205-1.html.

———. 2012. *It Worked for Me: In Life and Leadership*. New York: HarperCollins.

"Powell Lays Out Convincing Evidence of Iraq's Defiance." (Editorial). 2003, February 5. *USA Today*. Available: http://www.mafhoum.com/press4/131P75.htm.

"Powell Takes Iraq Case to U.N." 2003, February 5. *BBC News*. Retrieved May 2, 2013, from http://news.bbc.co.uk/2/hi/middle_east/2727489.stm.

"Powell to Make Case against Iraq: Secretary of State to Give Crucial Address to Security Council." 2003, February 5. *CNN.com*. Available: http://articles.cnn.com/2003-02-05/us/sprj.irq.powell.un.scene_1_state-colin-powell-weapons-inspectors-presentation?_s=PM:US.

"Powell's Smoking Gun." (Editorial). 2003, February 6. *Wall Street Journal*. Available: http://www.ph.ucla.edu/epi/bioter/powellsmokinggun.html.

"Powell's U.N. Speech Triggers Countdown to War in Iraq." (Editorial). 2003, February 6. *World Socialist Web Site*. Available: http://www3.wsws.org/articles/2003/feb2003/powe-f06.shtml.

Powlick, P. J. 1995. "The Sources of Public Opinion for American Foreign Policy Officials." *International Studies Quarterly* 39: 427–51.

Preston, J., and S. R. Weisman. 2003, February 5. "Powell to Charge Iraq Is Shifting Its Illegal Arms to Foil Inspectors." *New York Times*, A1. Available: http://query.nytimes.com/gst/fullpage.html?res=9D07E3DA1F38F936A35751C0A9659C8B63&pagewanted=all.

Price, V., D. Tewksbury, and E. Powers. 1997. "Switching Trains of Thought: The Impact of News Frames on Readers' Cognitive Responses." *Communication Research* 24: 481–506.

Project for Excellence in Journalism. 2004. *The State of the News Media 2004: An Annual Report on American Journalism*. Available: http://www.stateofthemedia.org/2004/narrative_networktv_audience.asp?cat=3&media=4.

Raine, L., S. Fox, and D. Fallows. 2003. "The Internet and the Iraq War: How Online Americans Have Used the Internet to Learn War News, Understand Events, and Promote Their Views." *Pew Internet and American Life Project*, 1–11.

Ravi, N. 2005. "Looking beyond Flawed Journalism: How National Interests, Patriotism, and Cultural Values Shaped the Coverage of the Iraq War." *Harvard International Journal of Press/Politics* 10(1): 45–62.

Read J., D. Hope, and J. Carroll. 2007. "Annotating Expressions of Appraisal in English." In *Proceedings of the Linguistic Annotation Workshop at ACL '07*, 93–100. Prague.

Reese, S. D., and L. H. Danielian. 1989. "Intermedia Influence and the Drug Issue: Converging on Cocaine." In *Communication Campaigns about Drugs: Government, Media, Public*, ed. P. J. Shoemaker, 29–46. Hillsdale, NJ: Lawrence Erlbaum.

Reese, S. D., A. Grant, and L. H. Danielian. 1994. "The Structure of News Sources on Television: A Network Analysis of *CBS News, Nightline, MacNeil/Lehrer*, and *This Week with David Brinkley*." *Journal of Communication* 44(2): 84–107.

Reisigl, M., and R. Wodak. 2001. *Discourse and Discrimination: Rhetorics of Racism and Anti-Semitism*. New York: Routledge.

Rennie, D. 2003, February 10. "Powell Boosts Support in U.S." *Daily Telegraph* (London). Retrieved April 18, 2013, from http://www.telegraph.co.uk/news/worldnews/northamerica/usa/1421636/Powell-boosts-support-in-US.html.

Reynolds, N. 1993. "Ethos as Location: New Sites for Understanding Discursive Authority." *Rhetoric Review* 11(2): 325–38.

Richardson, J., ed. 2012. *Language and Journalism*. New York: Routledge.

Risen, J. 2004, January 14. "Hussein Warned Iraqis to Beware Outside Fighters, Document Says." *New York Times*, A1.

Ritivoi, A. 2008. "Talking the (Political) Talk: Cold War Refugees and Their Political Legitimation through Style." In *Rhetoric in Detail: Discourse Analyses of Rhetorical Talk and Text*, ed. B. Johnstone and C. Eisenhart, 33–56. Philadelphia: John Benjamins.

Rivenburgh, N. K. 2000. "Social Identity and News Portrayals of Citizens Involved in International Affairs." *Media Psychology* 2(3): 3–29.

Roberts, J. 2002, 8 October. *CBS Evening News with Dan Rather*. Retrieved on January 12, 2013, from *Vanderbilt Television News Archive*.

Roberts, M., and M. McCombs. 1994. "Agenda Setting and Political Advertising: Origins of the News Media." *Political Communication* 11(3): 249–62.

Robinson, W. 2000. "Sentence Focus, Cohesion, and the Active and Passive Voices." *Teaching English in the Two-Year College* 27(4): 440–45.

Rockmore, T. 2006. "On Justifying the First Blow." In *Hitting First: Preventive Force in U.S. Security Strategy*, ed. W. W. Keller and G. R. Mitchell, 137–50. Pittsburgh: University of Pittsburgh Press.

Roth, B. 2002, October 2. "Bush Rejects Senate's Iraq Plan; Spokesman Says Assassination, Exile Economical Means to End." *Houston Chronicle*, A20.

Royce, T. 2002. "Multimodality in the TESOL Classroom: Exploring Visual-Verbal Synergy." *TESOL Quarterly* 36(2): 191–205.

———. 2007. "Inter-semiotic Complementarity: A Framework for Multimodal Discourse Analysis." In *New Directions in the Analysis of Multimodal Discourse*, ed. T. D. Royce and W. L. Bowcher, 63–109. Mahwah, NJ: Lawrence Erlbaum.

Rumsfeld, D. 2011. *Known and Unknown: A Memoir*. New York: Sentinel.

Rundell, M. 2012, January 6. "Which Is Worse—Regime or Dictatorship? *macmillandictionaryblog.com*. Available: http://www.macmillandictionaryblog.com/which-is-worse-regime-or-dictatorship.

Rutherford, P. 2004. *Weapons of Mass Persuasion: Marketing the War against Iraq*. Toronto: University of Toronto Press.

Safire, W. 1994, September 22. "Haiti Deal Makes Clinton, Powell Look Bad." *Chicago Tribune*. Retrieved January 16, 2013, from http://articles.chicagotribune.com/1994-09-22/news/9409220134_1_foreign-policy-jimmy-carter-gen-colin-powell.

———. (Editorial). 2002, January 31. "'To Fight Freedom's Fight.'" *New York Times*. Available: http://www.nytimes.com/2002/01/31/opinion/to-fight-freedom-s-fight.html?ref=georgewbush.

Sattler, W. M. 1947. "Conceptions of Ethos in Ancient Rhetoric." *Speech Monographs* 14: 55–65.

Schaefer, T. M. 1997. "Persuading the Persuaders: Presidential Speeches and Editorial Opinion." *Political Communication* 14(1): 97–111.

Scheufele, D. A. 2000. "Agenda-Setting, Priming, and Framing Revisited: Another Look at Cognitive Effects of Political Communication." *Mass Communication & Society* 3: 297–316.

Schiappa, E. 2003. *Defining Reality: Definitions and the Politics of Meaning*. Carbondale: Southern Illinois University Press.

Schienle, A., A. Schäfer, A. Hermann, B. Walter, R. Stark, and D. Vaitl. 2006. "fMRI Responses to Pictures of Mutilation and Contamination." *Neuroscience Letters* 393: 174–78.

Schiffrin, D., D. Tannen, and H. E. Hamilton, eds. 2001. *Handbook of Discourse Analysis*. Malden, MA: Blackwell.

Schmitt, E. 1999, April 4. "The World; the Powell Doctrine Is Looking Pretty Good Again." *New York Times*. Retrieved from http://www.nytimes.com/1999/04/04/weekinreview/ the-world-the-powell-doctrine-is-looking-pretty-good-again.html.

Schneider, B. 2003, January 31. "Powell: Reluctant Warrior Has a Change of Heart." *CNN.com*. Retrieved January 15, 2013, from http://www.cnn.com/2003/ALLPOLITICS/01/31/ip.pol.opinion.powell/.

Schwarz, J. 2008, February 5. "The U.N. Deception: What Exactly Colin Powell Knew Five Years Ago, and What He Told the World." *Mother Jones*. Available: http://motherjones.com/mojo/2008/02/un-deception-what-exactly-colin-powell-knew-five-years-ago-and-what-he-told-world.

Selzer, J. 1993. "Intertextuality and the Writing Process." In *Writing in the Workplace*, ed. R. Spilka, 171–80. Carbondale: Southern Illinois University Press.

———. 2004. "Rhetorical Analysis: Understanding How Texts Persuade Readers." In *What Writing Does and How It Does It: An Introduction to Analyzing Texts and Textual Practices*, ed. C. Bazerman, 279–307. Mahwah, NJ: Lawrence Erlbaum.

Sigal, L. V. 1973. *Reporters and Officials*. Lexington, MA: D.C. Heath.

Silverstein, M., and G. Urban. 1996. "The Natural History of Discourse." In *Natural Histories of Discourse*, ed. M. Silverstein and G. Urban, 1–17. Chicago: University of Chicago Press.

Simons, H. W. 2007. "Introduction." *Rhetoric & Public Affairs* 10(2): 177–82.

Slavin, B. 2002, December 3. "Colin Powell's Patient Diplomacy 'Paying Off.'" *USA Today*, 8A.

Smagorinsky, P. 2008. "The Method Section as Conceptual Epicenter in Constructing Social Science Research Reports." *Written Communication* 25(3): 389–411.

Sniderman, P. M., R. Brody, and P. Tetlock. 1991. *Reasoning and Choice: Explorations in Political Psychology*. New York: Cambridge University Press.

Solomon, N. 2005. "The Military-Industrial-Media Complex: Why War Is Covered from the Warriors' Perspective." Fairness and Accuracy in Reporting. Retrieved May 3, 2013, from: http://www.fair.org/index.php?page=2627.

Society of Professional Journalists. 1996. "Code of Ethics." *spj.org*. Available: http://www.spj.org/ethicscode.asp.

Sparrow, B. 1999. *Uncertain Guardians: The News Media as a Political Institution*. Baltimore: Johns Hopkins University Press.

Stewart, C. O. 2008. "How Media Controversy Can Influence a Scientific Publication: The Case of Robert L. Spitzer's 'Reparative Therapy' Study." In *Rhetoric in Detail: Discourse Analyses of Rhetorical Talk and Text*, ed. B. Johnstone and C. Eisenhart, 255–78. Philadelphia: John Benjamins.

Strauss, A. 1987. *Qualitative Analysis for Social Scientists*. New York: Cambridge University Press.

Strobel, W. P. 2002, November 10. "U.N. Iraq Vote a Victory for Powell; the Secretary of State Fought Hard to Win Support for It, Both at Home and on the Security Council." *Philadelphia Inquirer*, A02.

Stubbs, M. 1996. *Text and Corpus Analysis*. Cambridge: Cambridge University Press.

Sullivan, D. S. 1993. "The Ethos of Epideictic Encounter." *Philosophy & Rhetoric* 26(2): 113–33.

Suskind, R. 2006. *The One Percent Doctrine: Deep Inside America's Pursuit of Its Enemies since 9/11*. New York: Simon and Schuster.

Swales, J. 1990. *Genre Analysis: English in Academic and Research Settings*. Cambridge: Cambridge University Press.

Swearingen, C. J. 1994. "*Ethos*: Imitation, Impersonation, and Voice." In Ethos: *New Essays in Rhetorical and Critical Theory*, ed. J. S. Baumlin and T. F. Baumlin, 15–148. Dallas: Southern Methodist University Press.

Taylor, H. 2001, August 15. "America's Heroes." Retrieved January 15, 2013, from http://www.harrisinteractive.com/vault/Harris-Interactive-Poll-Research-AMERICAS-HEROES-2001-08.pdf.

Teather, D. 2002, June 16. "Bush Gives CIA Green Light to Kill Saddam." *The Guardian*. Available: http://www.guardian.co.uk/world/2002/jun/17/iraq.usa.

Thakur, R. 2004. "How the Iraq War Harmed the UN. *United Nations University Newsletter*. Retrieved February 4, 2013, from http://archive.unu.edu/update/archive/issue30_2.htm.

"The Case against Iraq." (Editorial). 2003, February 6. *New York Times*. Available: http://query.nytimes.com/gst/fullpage.html?res=9906E3DE173BF935A35751C0A9659C8B63.

"The *Times* and Iraq." (Editor's Note). 2004, May 26. *New York Times*. Available: http://www.nytimes.com/2004/05/26/international/middleeast/26FTE_NOTE.html.

Thibault, P. J. 1991. *Social Semiotics as Praxis*. Minneapolis: University of Minneapolis Press.

Thieme, K. 2010. "Constitutive Rhetoric as an Aspect of Audience Design: The Public Texts of Canadian Suffragists." *Written Communication* 27: 36–56.

Thomas, J. 2003, February 6. "Rating the Powell Show." *Slate*. Retrieved February 11, 2013, from http://www.slate.com/articles/news_and_politics/international_papers/2003/02/rating_the_powell_show.html.

Thompson, G. 2004. *Introducing Functional Grammar*. London: Hodder Education.

Tibbetts, J. 2002, September 2. "Powell Cautions against U.S. Attack on Iraq." *Calgary Herald*, A8.

Toulmin, S. E. 1958. *The Uses of Argument*. Cambridge: Cambridge University Press.

Trew, T. 1979. "Theory and Ideology at Work." In *Language and Control,* ed. R. Fowler, B. Hodge, G. Kress, and T. Trew, 94–116. Boston: Routledge and Kegan Paul.

Trotta, L. 1995, August 8. "D'Amato Decries Powell for Backing Military's Gay Ban." *Washington Times*, A4.

Tyler, P. E. 2003, February 6. "Intelligence Break Led U.S. to Tie Envoy Killing to Iraq Qaeda Cell." *New York Times*. A1, A16.

Tyler, P. E., and E. Sciolino. 2001, September 20. "A Nation Challenged: Washington; Bush's Advisers Split on Scope of Retaliation." *New York Times*, A1.

Unger, C. 2007. *The Fall of the House of Bush*. New York: Scribner.

United Nations Security Council. 2002, November 8. Resolution 1441. Available: http://daccess-dds-ny.un.org/doc/UNDOC/GEN/N02/682/26/PDF/N0268226.pdf?OpenElement.

U.S. Department of Defense. 2011. "Operation Iraqi Freedom (OIF) US Casualty Status." Retrieved from: http://www.defense.gov/news/casualty.pdf.

Vande Berg, L. R. 1999. "The Critical Sense: Three Decades of Critical Media Studies in the Wake of Samuel L. Becker's 'Rhetorical Studies for the Contemporary World.'" *Communication Studies* 50(1): 72–81.

Van Dijk, T. A. 1986. *Racism in the Press*. London: Arnold.

———. 1988. *News Analysis: Case Studies of International and National News in the Press*. Hillsdale, NJ: Lawrence Erlbaum.

———. 1993. *Elite Discourse and Racism*. Newbury Park, CA: Sage.

———. 1998. *Ideology: A Multidisciplinary Approach*. London: Sage.

———. 2001. "Critical Discourse Analysis." In *Handbook of Discourse Analysis*, ed. D. Tannen, D. Schiffrin, and H. Hamilton, 357–71. Oxford: Blackwell.

———. 2006. "Discourse and Manipulation." *Discourse & Society* 17(2): 359–83.

———. 2008. *Discourse and Context: A Sociocognitive Approach*. Cambridge: Cambridge University Press.

———. 2009. *Society and Discourse: How Social Context Influences Text and Talk*. Cambridge: Cambridge University Press.

van Langenhove, L., and R. Harré. 1999. "Introducing Positioning Theory." In *Positioning Theory: Moral Contexts of Intentional Action*, ed. R. Harré & L. van Langenhove, 14–31. Oxford: Blackwell.

Van Leeuwen, T. 2005. *Introducing Social Semiotics*. London: Routledge.

———. 2007. "Legitimation in Discourse and Communication." *Discourse & Communication* 1(1): 91–112.

———. 2008. *Discourse and Practice: New Tools for Critical Discourse Analysis*. New York: Oxford University Press.

Van Leeuwen, T., and R. Wodak. 1999. "Legitimizing Immigration Control: A Discourse-Historical Analysis." *Discourse Studies* 1(1): 83–118.

Van Natta, D. 2006, March 27. "Bush Was Set on Path to War, British Memo Says." *New York Times*. Available: http://www.nytimes.com/2006/03/27/international/europe/ 27memo.html?_ r=1& pagewanted=print.

Vatz, R. E. 1973. "The Myth of the Rhetorical Situation." *Philosophy and Rhetoric* 6: 154–61.

Volosinov, V. N. 1973. *Marxism and the Philosophy of Language*. Trans. Ladislav Matejka and I. R. Titunik. Cambridge: Harvard University Press.

Walters, B. 1995, September 15. "Who Is Colin Powell?" *20/20*, American Broadcasting Corporation.

Wardell, J. 2003, January 31. "Polls Show Divide in Europe over Iraq." Associated Press News Archive. Retrieved February 4, 2013, from http://www.apnewsarchive.com/2003/Polls-Show-Divide-in-Europe-Over-Iraq/id-a7fd6397fa07c331573d696f646a8e55?SearchText=http%3A//www.apnewsarchive.com/2003/Polls-Show-Divide-in-Europe-Over-;Display_.

Warnick, B. 2007. *Rhetoric Online: Persuasion and Politics on the World Wide Web*. New York: Peter Lang.

Warshaw, S. A. 2009. *The Co-presidency of Bush and Cheney*. Stanford, CA: Stanford University Press.

Watson, R. 2002, October 17. "Powell: A Dove in the City of Hawks." *The Times* (London), 19.

Waxman, H. A. 2004. "Iraq on the Record: The Bush Administration's Public Statements on Iraq." The United States House of Representatives Committee on Government Reform, Minority Staff, Special Investigations Division.

Webb, S. 2008, September 28. "Iraq Signs Billion-Dollar Power Deals with GE, Siemens." Reuters. Retrieved May 2, 2013, from http://www.reuters.com/article/2008/09/28/us-iraq-ge-siemens-idUSTRE48Q30Y20080928.

Wei, Y. K. 2002. "Corporate Image as Collective Ethos: A Poststructuralist Approach." *Corporate Communications* 17(4): 269–76.

Weisman, S. R. 2003, February 6. "Powell, in U.N. Speech, Presents Case to Show Iraq Has Not Disarmed." *New York Times*, A1. Available: http://www.nytimes.com/2003/02/06/world/threats-responses-security-council-powell-un-speech-presents-case-show-iraq-has.html.

———. 2005, September 9. "Powell Calls His U.N. Speech a Lasting Blot on His Record." *New York Times*. Available: http://www.nytimes.com/2005/09/09/politics/09powell.html.

Weiss, D. 2009. "'New Mexico's Always been Patriotic and Loyal to the Country': Uncritical Journalistic Patriotism in Wartime." In *War and the Media: Essays on News Reporting, Propaganda, and Popular Culture*, ed. P. M. Haridakis, B. S. Hugenberg, and S. T. Wearden, 183–204. Jefferson, NC: McFarland.

"Where's the Proof, Colin?" 2003, February 5. *Newsweek*. Retrieved February 11, 2013, from http://www.thedailybeast.com/newsweek/2003/02/05/where-s-the-proof-colin.html.

Wilkerson, L. 2013, February 6. "Interview with A. Maté & A. Goodman." *Democracy Now!* Retrieved April 18, 2003, from http://www.democracynow.org/2013/2/6/decade_after_iraq_wmd_speech_at?autostart=true.

Wilkie, C. 1981. "The Scapegoating of Bruno Richard Hauptmann: The Rhetorical Process in Prejudicial Publicity." *Central States Speech Journal* 32: 100–110.

Witte, S. 1992. "Text, Context, Intertext: Toward a Constructivist Semiotic of Writing." *Written Communication* 9: 237–308.

Wodak, R. 2001. "What CDA Is About—a Summary of Its History, Important Concepts and Its Developments." In *Methods of Critical Discourse Analysis*, ed. R. Wodak and M. Meyer, 1–13. London: Sage.

———. 2011. *The Discourse of Politics in Action: Politics as Usual*. 2nd ed. New York: Palgrave Macmillan.

Woods, K. M., M. E. Pease, W. Stout, J. Murray, and G. Lacey. 2006. *The Iraqi Perspectives Report: Saddam's Senior Leadership on Operation Iraqi Freedom from the Official U.S. Joint Forces Command Report*. Annapolis: Naval Institute Press.

Woodward, B. 2004. *Plan of Attack*. New York: Simon and Schuster.

Yellin, J. 2008, May 28. "Interview Transcript." *Anderson Cooper 360 Degrees*. Available: http://transcripts.cnn.com/TRANSCRIPTS/0805/28/acd.01.html.

Yoos, G. E. 1979. "A Revision of the Concept of Ethical Appeal." *Philosophy & Rhetoric* 12(1): 41–58.

Young, R. E., A. L. Becker, and K. L. Pike. 1970. *Rhetoric: Discovery and Change*. New York: Harcourt, Brace, and World.

Zaller, J. 1992. *The Nature and Origins of Mass Opinion*. New York: Cambridge University Press.

Zaller, J., and D. Chiu. 1996. "Government's Little Helper: U.S. Press Coverage of Foreign Policy Crises, 1945–1991." *Political Communication* 13: 385–405.

Zarefsky, D. 1998. "Definitions." In *Argument in a Time of Change: Definitions, Frameworks, and Critiques*, ed. J. F. Klumpp, 1–11. Annandale: National Communication Association.

———. 2007. "Making the Case for War: Colin Powell at the United Nations." *Rhetoric & Public Affairs* 10(2): 275–302.

Zdenek, S. 2008. "Muted Voices: Cochlear Implants, News Discourse, and the Public Fascination with Curing Deafness." In *Rhetoric in Detail: Analyses of Rhetorical Text and Talk*, ed. B. Johnstone and C. Eisenhart, 147–71. Amsterdam: John Benjamins.

Zdenek, S., and B. Johnstone. 2008. "Studying Style and Legitimation: Critical Linguistics and Critical Discourse Analysis." In *Rhetoric in Detail: Analyses of Rhetorical Text and Talk*, ed. B. Johnstone and C. Eisenhart, 25–31. Amsterdam: John Benjamins.

Zelizer, B. 2010. *About to Die: How News Images Move the Public*. New York: Oxford University Press.

Zinn, H. 2002. *Terrorism and War*. New York: Seven Stories Press.

———. 2003. *A People's History of the United States: 1492–Present*. New York: HarperCollins.

———. 2007. *A Power Governments Cannot Suppress*. San Francisco: City Lights Books.

Index

⌘

B

C

D

E

F

G

H

I

L

M

S

V

W